THE PROGRESSIVE UNDERGROUND

Vol 3

KEV ROWLAND

Edited by Jonathan Downes
Typeset by Jonathan Downes. Kev Rowland
Cover by Martin Springett
This edition - layout by SPiderKaT for CFZ Communications
Using Microsoft Word 2000, Microsoft Publisher 2000, Adobe Photoshop CS.

First published by Gonzo Multimedia 2020

c/o Brooks City,
6th Floor New Baltic House,
65 Fenchurch Street,
London EC3M 4BE
Fax: +44 (0)191 5121104
Tel: +44 (0) 191 5849144
International Numbers:
Germany: Freephone 08000 825 699
USA: Freephone 18666 747 289

ISBN: 978-1-908728-90-6

Dedicated to my incredible wife Sara: without her support, Feedback would never have kept going for all the years it did. It is also dedicated to my amazing daughters Nicola, Elizabeth, Hannah and Amanda, who grew up thinking that having a dad stuck at a computer all the time, while playing strange and often unusual music very loudly, was the normal thing to do.

Also to Jon Downes for believing in me and challenging me to do this, to Martin Springett for being a wonderful friend and providing incredible artwork and designs, and to Corinna Downes for all the support she provided in this process.

Foreword

I met Kevin long before the era of the Internet. We used to write letters to each other, exchanging the latest news from the world of progressive rock. From time to time, we would send each other cassettes with the music of British and Polish bands. However, what I did most, was read the fanzine Feedback that was edited by Kevin, and even today, I still have all the issues in my archives. Back then, when I was reading Kev's reviews, I was surprised to learn that there were so many artists scattered around the globe, playing valuable music. I was also impressed that Kev could write about it in such a fascinating way. I admit that the work that he did for Feedback was an inspiration for me when I was founding the website www.mlwz.pl for my radio show.

Kev and I used to meet often in the 90s. Any time I was in London or nearby, he would always take me to his house in Dorking where I met his charming wife Sara and their fantastic daughters. We would also go to gigs together. I remember the group Sphere played in his local pub sometime in the mid-90s, and some twenty years later I met the keyboard player Neil Durant during the Polish show of IQ, and surprisingly he remembered that first meeting of ours.

Thanks to these visits, shows, countless letters and Feedback magazines, but also thanks to the CDs and tapes sent from Poland we were discovering many new bands and a lot of great music together. We had a lot of fun; those were great days.

Today, although Kevin lives in New Zealand, practically nothing has changed. Well, maybe we do not see each other so often, but Kev's passion for discovering new music and sharing his impressions and opinions with the readers has always impressed me very much, both now and 25 years ago. The proof of this incredible hobby is this book, which I devoured in one night. I know that I will be coming back to this book often and I think that so will other readers.

Artur Chachlowski, www.mlwz.pl

I first met Kev in 1991 when my band Legend had released our debut album. This was greeted by the majority of the music scene with complete derision. Progressive rock was at that time considered at best a total irrelevance, at worst an abomination in the face of god! But in the wilderness there were a handful of supporting voices, first and foremost being Kev Rowland. He gave a young and impressionable Legend hope, which was precious beyond measure!

He proved that there were people out there who still loved Progressive Rock in its myriad forms. Indeed over the years Kev has served the Progressive Rock community in countless ways, helping bands to network with other bands and with the various underground publications and societies that were out there and interested. He has tirelessly promoted the genre, with his insightful reviews and measured criticism, designed to nurture rather than condemn, all with a boundless enthusiasm and wit, fuelled only by the love of the music and his encyclopaedic knowledge of the genre.

Kev has always been generous with his time, devoting many hours to putting together Feedback Magazine and attending gigs, writing in depth reviews, talking to artists and fans alike. And all of this to help bring the Prog Community into its rightful place in the pantheon of music genres. He is driven purely by the love of the music and the creativity with no thought of personal gain and I am proud to call him, and indeed, his wonderful family, my friends.

Stephen Paine, Legend

Introduction

Here is the third and final volume of my three-book series, documenting the progressive rock scene of 1991-2006, through all the progressive reviews and interviews I wrote during that period. I may no longer agree with the sentiments in some cases, but here they are as they originally appeared, warts and all. It doesn't profess to cover every important band and release during that period, but instead is a reflection of material I either purchased or was sent to review. If you already have the other volumes in the series then you already know the story below, and if not why not? Where else can you find reviews like these? Record Collector said of Volume 1, "A book that will be quickly referred to as a bible".

This series of books is an attempt to shine a light on an unfamiliar period of progressive rock to many, with the aim of not only providing a historical record but also hopefully piquing the interest of readers to discover some of these bands. Some are long gone by now, while others are still out there, but hopefully these books will assist in providing some small form of recognition to them. So much music, so little time, but if you search for it there are some gems to be heard, and hopefully these volumes can be a guide.

Read on, I hope you enjoy it.

At the end of the Sixties, musicians realised that they were no longer constrained by having to fit into defined musical forms and the three-minute single. Instead, the only limits were their musical ability and imagination: this led to an explosion of music as styles as diverse as jazz, blues and classical crashed headlong into electric and eclectic instrumentation. Progressive rock was born, and not only was it embraced by fans worldwide but also by critics (at least for a while) and bands as diverse as Jethro Tull, Genesis, Pink Floyd, King Crimson, ELP and Gentle Giant among many others found huge success and sales. However, 1976 was year zero for prog, with punk supposedly sweeping away the 'dinosaurs' of music.

As far as many critics (and it must be said many fans as well), this was the end for the prog scene, although some bands from the Seventies still found huge success in both albums and ticket sales. The only prog band recognised as such to gain major success within the UK was Marillion, but once Fish had parted ways, they also suffered the same fate. One wonders if anyone had been brave enough to tarnish Radiohead with the 'progressive' label if they would have had success.

After leaving university in 1984 I was in London, and thought if I joined Mensa, I might be able to make new friends. Although I had little in common with many of the 35,000 members, I discovered there were sub-clubs called Special Interest Groups, and in 1988 saw an advert asking if there was anyone interested in rock music, which led to RockSIG. I wanted to be involved, so inundated the secretary with pieces. The first newsletter came out in October 1988 and at 28 pages was respectable enough but inside #5 (April 1990) the secretary announced her resignation. I had enjoyed writing and thought I would give it a shot. After all, it couldn't be much hassle, right? I produced #6 in Nov 1990 - it came in at 60 pages and I soon realised this length could not last. I was right. It got bigger!

In 1991 I was lent me some music by Galahad and Twelfth Night, and some copies of a fanzine called 'Blindsight'. I loved the music and wrote to Galahad to buy their CD and cassette and was soon corresponding with Stu Nicholson. Shortly thereafter, a demo arrived from Big Big Train. I knew nothing of the band, but they had sent me music. What would happen if I contacted the bands whose addresses were in Blindsight to see if they wanted me to write about what they were doing? I could never have imagined what would happen.

A reader poll in #11 gave our newsletter a name and over the years 'Feedback' grew until it reached a peak with #50, which gave postal workers hernias in August 1998 and was some 284 pages long! I became very involved with some bands, trying to get gigs for both Freewill (and running their newsletter) and Credo, and writing the blurb for a Galahad compilation. In 2006, some sixteen years, 80+ issues and more than 11,000 pages of print later I stepped down, as we moved to New Zealand.

The support of my amazing wife and family over those sixteen years must be recognised, as I could not have done it without them. Sara became used to our bedroom being awash with CDs, photos, press releases etc., and by the end I was on my fifth computer, having started running the mag using an electronic typewriter with 1K of memory!!

As Feedback was produced officially as a "newsletter" for a closed group, it did mean that those who were members were treated in my writing more as friends than public, and that they all knew something about the scene either through direct involvement or from reading what I had written previously. This book captures a time gone by, and one that now we have ready access to information can never exist again, but back then it was very special indeed.

Album Reviews

T

VOICES

For 'T' read Thomas Thielen, the former Scythe guitarist who released his debut solo album, "Naïve", back in 2001. He has now returned with his second, where he plays all the instruments himself as well as providing the vocals. This does not sound like a solo album, but much more like a group work, and one soon quickly moves away from the feel that this is the work of just one man to confronting the bleakness and darkness of this album. He is bringing in musical themes and influences such as modern Marillion, IQ, Radiohead, Peter Gabriel and Geoff Mann but this is a depressing album, honest it is. That is not to say that there is no levity within it, but this is certainly not something to play when you feel that the world is about to end. The photos on the front and rear of the booklet add to the feeling that here is a Roger Waters look at life, tempered by Tom Watts (although the vocals are much better), and that T has been to a dark place and now he wants us to visit with him. As to whether I have enjoyed listening to this then that is a hard thing to say. I am glad that I have heard it, and there are times when I feel that it will be just the right thing to listen to, but for general listening pleasure then I normally move to something a little more light-hearted.

This is not one for those who enjoy their prog at the lighter end of the scale, but if you want to investigate someone looking at the bleaker side of life then this is very well constructed and performed.

#89, Sep 2006

TALE
RIVERMAN VOL. 1
I was intrigued when I had a letter asking me if I would be interested in reviewing the debut CD by a South African group, Tale. On closer investigation, I discovered that Tale are just one man, Rob Granville, with assorted other musicians. 'Riverman Vol. 1' is the first in what is expected to be a long series of albums, each with the same book-type cover so that they build into a set (although as this took more than two years to record I doubt if it is going to be a very long series). There is no doubt where Rob's influences have come from, as they seem to start with 'Dark Side Of The Moon' and go as far as 'Wish You Were Here'. That may be a little unfair, but on repeated listening it is only the vocals and additional acoustic guitar that shows that it is not Floyd themselves. I am the last person to say that a band should sound totally original, but it is a little off-putting at times, especially with the sax solo which sounds as if it is on the wrong album.

So, an album full of melodies and emotion. I am sure that many Floyd listeners will welcome it with open arms, but at the same time it may well stop many from enjoying it. It will be interesting to see if there is any more in the series, and how Rob's music progresses.
#26, Dec 1994

TALISMA
CORPUS
This is the third album from the Canadian instrumental trio, and with an emphasis firmly on all three being lead musicians this is quite an album. One of the most important aspects to their sound is the bass playing of Donald Fleurent who plays a multitude of different basses, often within the same song at the same time (clever chap), so this gives them a very clear tonal colour. But this is not a band that is led by the bass by any means, as there is plenty of extremely solid drumming and very rock-solid guitar. Add a few synths here and there for some extra variation, combined with a band that are out to rock, as opposed to just impress and the result is an album that does just that. Yes, there are obviously heavy elements of prog and to a lesser degree plenty of jazz, but this is a rock album.

Each song is quite different to the last, and as none of them stretch over four minutes (and some are less than two) this means that the listener does not get frustrated. There is also an extremely interesting bass take on Bach's "Gavotte En Rondeau" (who mentioned Manowar?). Overall an album that has plenty of depth but is also light and is enjoyable throughout. This is an instrumental album to which I will often return.
#78, Apr 2004

TANGERINE DREAM
GREAT WALL OF CHINA
Yet another 'Original Motion Picture Soundtrack' from those lovable Germans, this album is solely the work of Edgar and Jerome Froese. It is also one of the most listenable albums of theirs that I have heard, although I do have to confess to not searching out their music a great deal. 11 'songs', and if you like keyboard instrumental pieces then this is one that you should probably try to hear. If you are after guitars or music that cannot be construed as New Age, then look elsewhere. *#59, July 2000*

TEA FOR THE WICKED
OUT TO LUNCH
Tea For The Wicked released their debut CD earlier this year, but I have only just caught up with them. They are a four-piece from Essex comprising Arfa Roach (vocals, keyboards), Tony Hands (guitar), Jack Grigor (bass) and Steve Shaw (drums). They managed to get the money together to record the CD as they won the Harlow Battle of the Bands. So, they should be good, right? Wrong. They are bloody excellent! I was hooked right from the first track "Dream On", which has some wonderful Martin Barre-style guitarwork. Arfa has also been likened to Ian Anderson, but this is not Jethro Tull. Listen to "Jeanie's Song", which is an out and out belter, and discover why they are appealing to such a large audience. They are prog enough for the proghead, melodic enough for those who like a gentler style, but loud and heavy enough for the headbanger. They slide easily from one style to another and mix and mingle them well. Arfa also displays a gentle touch with a harmonica, which adds yet another element to lift them above the crowd. 'Out To Lunch' is a delight, and I am surprised that Tea For The Wicked have not got a higher profile. Listen to the political rant of "One Day The Sheep Will Turn Violent", or the refusal to bow down to old age in "Slow Down" and enjoy the use of words. This is a great album that I know will appeal to many who do not normally listen to this type of music.
#31, Oct 1995

TEA FOR THE WICKED
WICKED TEAPOT
Some of you may be aware that I sometimes write for that wonderful underground magazine 'Rock 'n' Reel', and one day I was reading the letters section of the latest issue and came across one from someone in Canada thanking RnR for introducing him to a brilliant band. That band was Tea For The Wicked, and the original review was by me about their debut album. I fell in love with it on first hearing, but things have been a little quiet over the last couple of years. You can imagine my surprise when the phone rang the other night and it was vocalist/keyboard player Arthur Roach ringing to

tell me that they had a new album out and would I be interested in reviewing it? Would I?! TFTW have become a harder edged outfit than previously, and while there are still enough (just) keyboards for those who want them to be a prog band, they have become more than ever a melodic rock band, with both feet firmly in the Seventies. These are songs with exceptionally strong lyrics, as opposed to volume-based noisemeisters. Some of them are reminiscent of Tull, while "Swampy" has nothing but classic Galahad stamped all over it. That is probably my favourite, as it belts along with a great hook in the chorus. For my sins, I have yet to catch this band live, but it is an oversight that I am going to do my best to remedy if possible. This is yet another slice of great rock from the Essex boys. *#46, Dec 1997*

TEMPEST
TURN OF THE WHEEL

Right, hands up all of you who like Jethro Tull, enjoy Fairport and The Levellers? Off you go to your local record emporium and do not come back until you have a copy of this in your greasy paws. Oh, not released until December 2nd? Well, I will let you off this once but make sure that you get down there at the crack of dawn (you want to be first in the queue don't you?) on Dec 2nd to get this wonderful album. Tempest were formed eight years ago in North Carolina by Norwegian Leif Sorbye (who ought to be renamed Ian Anderson) who contributes lead vocals, acoustic and electric mandolins and octave-mandolas, flute (of course), harmonica and bodhran. The other guys are Rob Wullenhjohn (guitars, vocals), Adolfo Lazo (drums) and Jay Mania (bass). Guests contribute violins while keyboards are added by Keith Emerson and Robert Berry (who also produced the album). 'Turn Of The Wheel' is the fifth album by the band and I am mortified that I have not heard any of the others. They mix folk, Celtic and traditional influences with rock in a way that probably only Fairport and Tull have fully mastered. They do come across as a very Tull-sounding band but as Leif is using Norwegian as opposed to English folk it does give the music a very different edge. The violin is extremely important in all that they do (I notice that although only four guys are credited as being in the band the photo shows five), so I presume that they are between players. They rock with the best of them, as well as jigging and reeling, and some of the traditional pieces are performed in Norwegian but who cares? This is an album that any proggers into folk in the slightest must simply kill to have. Wonderful. *#38, Nov 1996*

TERCIA
CARNIVAL

I received this demo CD from Fred Lievens, and know nothing about the band, apart from what I am hearing, which is very strange indeed. Female vocals and 'different' music make them sound as if they have been listening to Van De Graaf Generator, King Crimson, Legend, some Metallica, Anekdoten and early Genesis, then decided to play them all at once. The result is eight tracks of very intense prog that is difficult to listen to (and must be bloody impossible to play), yet at the same time is extremely exciting. If the casual music lover heard this, then they would probably run a mile. For those with a greater interest outside the chart then this has a lot to offer. I am not sure if Fred is selling these, or what is happening with the band, but based on this I am sure that they will soon have a deal. *#59, July 2000*

THESSERA
FOOLED EYES

This is the debut album from this Brazilian band that were formed in 2003, when they decided that they wanted to produce progressive metal that was influenced by styles as diverse as fusion, blues, Brazilian rhythms and classical music. The line-up is comprised of Marcelo Quina (vocals), Nando Costa (guitar), Raphael Lamim (guitar), Marcelo Mattos (bass), Rodolfo Amaro (keyboards) and Fernando Cerutti (drums) and it is of very little surprise to me to see that they have already performed with Angra – a band with whom they have some similarities. Of course, if you are a prog band you may as well go the whole hog and the debut album is a concept telling the story of young artist Andrew Hesser and what happens to him before and after his engagement party. It certainly does not sound like a debut and comes across with the power and passion of Fates Warning with the keyboards cutting across the guitars and the dramatic drums always driving the band on to greater heights. It is not the sort of music that I would have imagined coming out of South America as they keep their Brazilian roots in check a lot of the time and produce music that is very hard hitting and very North American/German in flavour. This is going to take a lot of the prog metal community by storm – debuts are not supposed to sound as strong and polished as this. It is not perfect, there is still room for improvement, but for a starting place it is a damn good place to be.
#89, Sep 2006

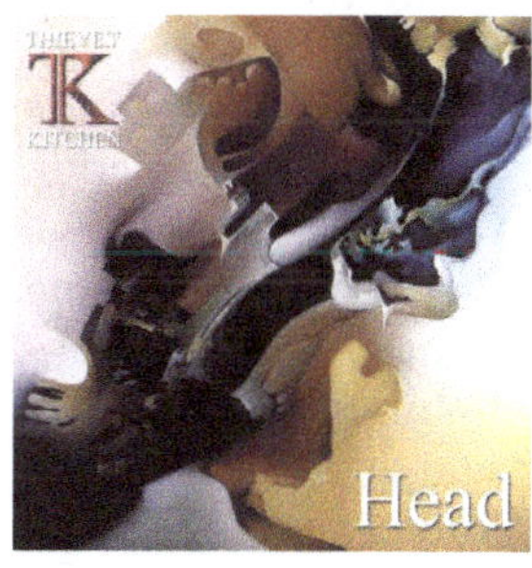

THIEVES' KITCHEN
HEAD

This is the debut album by UK proggers Thieves' Kitchen which is the band featuring ex-GLD drummer Mark Robotham. It is quite ambitious for a debut as the opener is sixteen minutes long, and the closing song is almost twenty minutes in length. They have tried to mix early Genesis with Coliseum II, with the keyboard and guitar melody lines often being played as one. Mark has also switched to playing electric drums, which gives the overall sound a slightly different feel. It is an album that contains good ideas, but they do not always appear to gel quite as well as they should have done. This may be because this debut has appeared relatively quickly after the band were formed, and they are still finding their musical feet as it were. I must admit to not liking the drum sound at all, but am aware that others may like that style, it's just that I'm not one of them: it sounds too artificial, too machine-like. I am sure that Thieves' Kitchen will find themselves a place within the progressive underground in the UK, which is not

nearly as vibrant as it was even five years ago, but I can't hear much here that would let them move beyond that. It is possible that this album is just too soon and maybe the next one will be better.
#57, Mar 2000

THIEVES' KITCHEN
ARGOT

I met Mark Robotham a few weeks ago and he told me how well this was selling, a fact also confirmed by Malcolm Parker at GFT. I was determined to give this a good hearing, so I waited until I was in the car for a long drive and put it on. There are only four songs, but the album is over an hour in length, and they have decided to print the lyrics, but each song in a different language! (My good mate Artur Chachlowski provided the translation for "Escape"). "John Doe Number One" kicks off the album, and at twenty minutes plus I settled in to be impressed. You can tell that there is a 'but' coming, can't you? It's not my fault. I wanted to like this album, I was determined to do so, but it cannot be my type of prog. I found that my attention kept wandering. Passages that should have gripped my attention just did not. I know that there are going to be some who feel that this is a wonderful album, bringing together bands as diverse as King Crimson, Gentle Giant and Genesis, but it just did not do anything for me.
#63, Jul 2001

THIEVES' KITCHEN
SHIBBOLETH

It is probably fair to say that over the years I have not been TK's biggest fan, so when this arrived in the post, I was in no rush to put it in the player. However, a long drive home one day gave me the opportunity to listen to this all the way through in one sitting. But even from the first delicate notes and drum introduction of "The Picture Slave" I felt that something quite dramatic had changed either in the music or in my appreciation of it. There is a feeling of sense of purpose – the band knows what they want to achieve and are going to get there, no matter what. This is complex prog with the entire band linking in at a very high level indeed. This hearkens back not to the heady days of neo-prog but further back to the time of bands like ELP where musical ability and a lack of knowledge or caring of boundaries made the prog scene so vibrant and exciting. There is more than a hint of jazz (particularly in some of the keyboards), and one is kept looking for the next stage. The one thing that the band now needs to consider is whether they need to become one of those very rare beasts, an instrumental prog outfit. It is not that Amy's vocals are poor, just that for most of this album there is no room for her, and even when she makes an appearance the vocals are not as high in the mix as they might be, but this does give the music a different edge to many. This album has certainly caused me to have a major rethink of TK, and I am sure that many more progheads will be turned onto the band by this superb album. With one track nearly twenty-four minutes in length there

is something here for everyone, with enough twists and turns to make this constantly interesting. This is an album that I have enjoyed, and which has made me look forward to the next one, which will get onto my player with far more alacrity.
#76, Oct 2003

DAVID THOMAS & RONNIE GUNN
THE GIANTS DANCE

Anybody recognise the above names? No? Well, it is obvious that you're not Genesis completists then. Ronnie and David were both members of The Spoken Word with fellow Charterhouse pupils Peter Gabriel and Anthony Phillips. This was the band that eventually merged with The Garden Wall to form Genesis: David was the vocalist with Ronnie on piano, with Peter at the time playing drums. They all kept in touch, with David even providing harmony vocals on "In The Wilderness" on 'From Genesis To Revelation'. David, Peter and Tony shared a flat for four years while David and Ronnie are still playing together. Some of the demos on the CD contain music from those early days, with the same piano featured on which songs such as "Firth of Fifth" and "Get 'Em Out By Friday" were written. Some of the songs are solo (by either), some are duets, while others are 'group' affairs. Anthony Phillips also helped in places so not surprisingly there is a very early Genesis feel to many of the songs. In fact, although many people may pick this up solely because of the Genesis connection, if they are fans of the Gabriel period of the band then there is a lot on here to enjoy.*#38, Nov 1996*

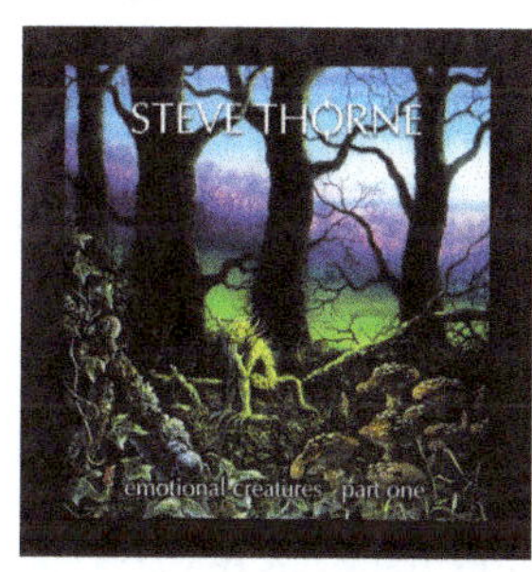

STEVE THORNE
EMOTIONAL CREATURES – PART ONE

Steve Thorne is not a name that I have come across before, but obviously within the prog field I am very much in the minority as appearing on this CD are all of Jadis, Paul Cook (IQ), Tony Levin (King Crimson), Nick D'Virgilio (Spock's Beard, Tears For Fears) and Geoff Downes (Asia). Steve plays many instruments himself and the rest add touches as opposed to giving him a full band format for every song. Given the background of those involved one might think that this will be an out and out progressive rampage but that is a long way from the truth. What we have here is very much a songs-based album, often with acoustic guitar as the starting point, while Steve often uses his vocals to put through some very strong messages. On "God Bless America" for example, he says that "England laps like a dog" and that "I'm so glad that we're friends, Cos I don't wanna die". It is hard to describe Steve's style, although Genesis would be a starting point, as would Peter Gabriel and even Michael Stipes. What is not in doubt is the quality in depth. A lot of work has gone into this not only in the songs but also in another excellent piece of production from Rob Aubrey and I notice that Tony Lythgoe who works on IQ's albums has been involved in the design of the excellent booklet. Mention should also be made of Danny Flynn for the great cover art, which is his interpretation of Squonk from the Genesis song of the same name. I digress – the only thing that is wrong with this album is that it is not available until April 26th so you must wait patiently for it. It is a wonderful record, with some real shade musically to contrast against the light and it is full of drama and passion. One to look out for – Steve has already written the follow-up. *#83, Mar 2005*

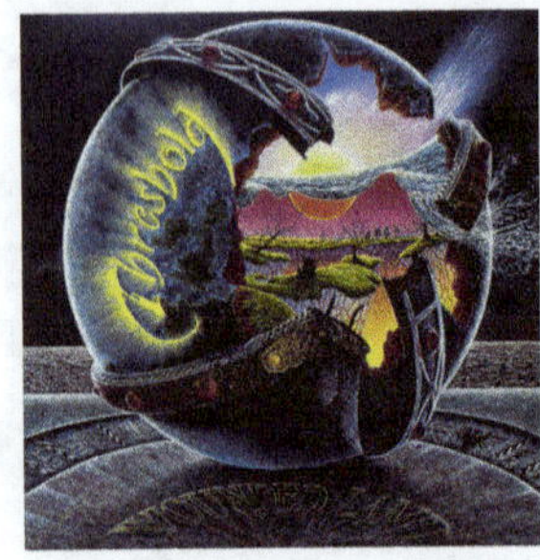

THRESHOLD
WOUNDED LAND

Threshold are originally a London-based band that came together in November 1988 when bassist Jon Jeary joined Karl Groom (guitar), Nick Midson (guitar) and Tony Grinham (drums) who had been working together for a while in different bands. They released several recordings and gigged throughout the UK, but the songs they were writing required a new singer, and Damian Wilson was added to the line-up in December 1991, as at this time, he was already recording demos with Karl. On the strength of the 'Days of Dearth' demo they signed a deal with IQ's GEP label in the summer of 1992. I must confess that I found this a little strange, seeing how Karl (with Clive Nolan) runs Thin Ice and has been involved with numerous recordings for the SI label. Jon was involved in the Casino sessions and Damian also records with Landmarq, both projects on the SI label. Anyway, the rest of 1992 was spent writing the album, along with other projects, and recording took place last December. It was during the recording of the album that it was felt that the services of a keyboard player were required who could enhance the style of music they were producing. Richard West had played with Karl and Jon in a previous band (as well as providing keyboards for the Shadowland tour), so was an obvious choice. On joining he went straight into the studio with the band to record 'Wounded Land'. While at the Jadis Whitchurch gig recently I met up with Karl in the chippie and over a bag of chips we discussed what he had been doing recently, and the subject of Threshold came up. He promptly produced the CD from his pocket and gave it to me. I was immediately taken by the cover which attempts to display what the album is about, namely man's destruction of the world we live in, Karl was very pleased and suitably modest about the CD. I went back into the hall where I met Clive Nolan who informed me that it was a seriously heavy album. I knew that Threshold were the heaviest band on the SI compilation, but I was not sure quite what to expect.

Whitchurch is quite a distance away from home, so I thought I would listen to the CD on the way home. Gently rising keyboards did not prepare me for the crashing guitarwork that was to follow. Crunching riffs that steam hammered their way into my already melted out brain meant that the CD was treated with some respect (and the volume turned down). There are those who would say that Threshold are treading a very fine line between HM and progressive, and there are also those who would say that Threshold trampled all over the line and created their own sound. To give you some idea of the effect, I think it is best to describe it as if Black Sabbath met Deep Purple in a dark alley and got mugged by Magnum, then this mish-mash was pulled firmly into the Nineties and given one of the best vocal talents in the business. Interested? You should be. The album has already had some rave reviews from some of the top rock magazines (as opposed to fanzines) on the continent, but we will wait and see if UK reviewers feel the same. Mind you, most of the rock magazines in this country have their heads so much up their collective asses that they can't see a good band let alone hear one. Eight tracks of mind-numbing intensity literally crunch their way into your brain. The keyboards manage to provide a lighter foil to the guitars, but this music is melodic yet at the same time heavy as lead. Call it what you will, but this is rock at it's very best. In #15, #16 and #17 I have raved over Damian's vocal ability, but it just cannot be said enough times: this bloke can sing like an angel and oozes class. Having seen him accompany himself on acoustic guitar I know what he is capable of, but here is the perfect answer to the crunching music. True, there is definite light and shade within the CD, and Damian copes with whatever the others demand of him.

Highlights? Well, to my ears "Sanity's End" (which just happens to be the longest track on the album at just over ten minutes) is the obvious high spot as it contains all the elements that make Threshold such a great band. Tony and Jon provide some amazing backbone with neither of them afraid to provide extra fills whenever they can; Karl and Nick crunch those riffs, while Richard lightens proceedings; then of course there is Damian. The song has a lighter section that makes it seem heavier when the songs kicks off again, then Damian hits notes higher than anyone should be able to. On a lyrical aspect, it deals with the problem of drug abuse connected with music: "Ravers, gyrators, heaving with sweat, have you tried any good ecstasy yet? If you do not wind up sleeping in gardens of stone, you'll be a new person if you ever get home". Eventually the song takes on new life and Richard provides some stunning keyboard runs, then trades solos with the two guitars as it just gets better and better. I'm exhausted at the end just listening to it: after playing it they must be totally drained. Although recorded at Thin Ice, Clive had nothing to do with this CD. Karl handled production on his own, and he has managed to capture real intensity and power. I have heard many 'mainstream' rock CDs that have not been produced as well as this. We have stunning songs brilliantly performed with excellent production and a stunning cover to boot. But will it sell? There is no real way that this can be called a prog album as it is far heavier than anything else I have heard, but it is on a prog label (the other four releases on GEP have been two IQ CDs, and one each by Niadem's Ghost and Jadis) so will Threshold be deemed to be a similar band? If reviewers are prepared to listen to this with open minds then I can see it doing very well, but I am afraid that this will probably not be the case. Threshold have plans for a tour of Europe later this year and should also be playing a few dates in the UK. The album is available through The Secret World.
#18, May 1993

THRESHOLD
PSYCHEDELICATESSEN
This was always going to be a difficult album for Threshold. After the success of 'Wounded Land' it was always going to be hard but having to replace a vocalist of the quality of Damian Wilson made it damn near impossible, so I am glad to report that replacement Glynn Morgan has done wonders. Also, drummer Tony Grinham had to leave due to personal reasons, so Karl's Shadowland cohort Nick Harradence stepped into the breach (although a permanent replacement has now been found). Threshold are based on rock solid bass and drums, heavy riffing guitars, keyboards for added lightness and

superb vocals. Combine that with great songs and you are onto a winner. Glynn's voice is slightly harsher at times, possibly more emotional, but fits in with the overall sound perfectly. The production seems more polished, and some of the songs more commercial than before ("Into The Light" has Def Leppard undertones). It is of no surprise to me that it is already selling extremely well in Europe (where it was released in October, the UK release is February). The winner for me must be "A Tension Of Souls" which is classic Threshold as the slow, extremely heavy, beginning gives way to solid riffs. At this stage, it is a standard heavy rock number, but this is being used as a device to provide contrast and it slowly builds, picks up speed and then vocals soar and harmonies abound as the song is transformed. This is good hard melodic rock that vies with bands such as Queensrÿche. Hard and certainly heavy, yet melodic at the same time, Threshold are defining the line and trampling all over it. In my original review, I described them as Black Sabbath meeting Deep Purple down in an alleyway and being mugged by Magnum. That still stands, but they are getting heavier and better all the time. *#27, Feb 1995*

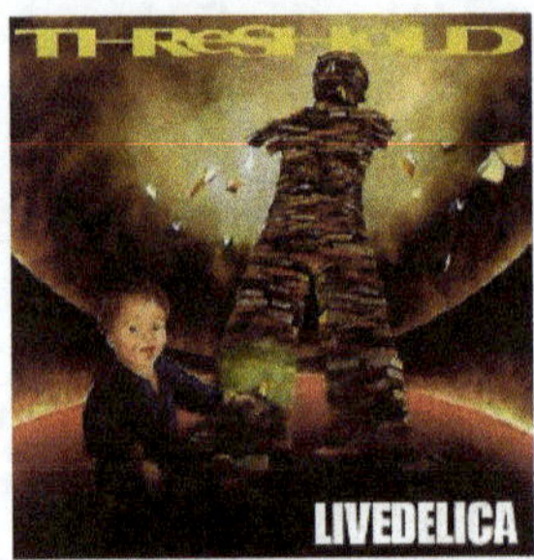

THRESHOLD
LIVEDELICA

All of you who read the reviews of Whitchurch in the last issue will realise just how much an impression Threshold made on those of us who were there. This mini CD (only forty minutes long) gives an idea of just what a potent force they are on stage. Recorded in Europe on their recent tour, it features three tracks from the debut 'Wounded Land' together with two from 'Psychedelicatessen'. Indeed, they have been kicking up quite a storm on foreign shores, even supporting Dream Theater. Threshold is literally stretching the musical barriers as they mix hard rock (boy is it heavy) with melody and the use of keyboards in a "prog" style. They seem to have to be viewed as a progressive band in its truest sense as they mix two genres in a way not usually seen these days. The use of a twin guitar attack with driving bass and drums is not uncommon; it is the quality of this combined with fluid rock keyboards and top-notch vocals that push it over the edge. Add to that wonderful songs, and there is the recipe for success. However, they ostracise many of the prog audience as they are so heavy and should find solace with the headbangers. Now, if only the main rock press would pick up on what is a fantastic band, they could go places. Right from the off, vocalist Glynn Morgan manages to make you forget that half of the set was recorded with another vocalist and considering just how highly Damian was rated by everybody that is no mean feat. The highlight of the album must be "Sanity's End", and at over eleven minutes in length it typifies all that is good about this outfit. They give it everything and shake and blast the hall to the ground. Mind you, the encore "Paradox" takes some beating. I defy anyone into guitar-oriented rock not to love this album. This is a British band that deserves and demands your respect and support. If you like Dream Theater then go out and discover a UK band doing what they are doing, but better.
#30, Aug 1995

THRESHOLD
EXTINCT INSTINCT

The third Threshold studio album sees not only the fourth different drummer in as many albums, but also the return of original vocalist Damian Wilson. Damian left to find his fortune in another band, leaving not only Threshold but Landmarq without a vocalist. Now he has re-joined both bands, basically putting two singers out of a job. I thought that Glynn Morgan was doing a good job with Threshold, but there is no denying that Damian is one of the top singers around. No matter how heavy and brain damaging the mayhem, his voice is still clear and powerful. It is three years since the last studio album, 'Psychedelicatessen', although 'Liveadelica' was released in the meantime and that is just too long to go without a good dose of Threshold. There are very few UK bands performing at this level, where hard technical progressive rock is the order of the day. This is not music for wimps, but at the same time there is reliance on melody and skill as opposed to sheer volume. Jon Jeary has locked into a groove with new drummer Mark Heaney, while Karl Groom and Nick Midson supply the fretwork power as always. Richard West is far more than a bit-part keyboard player, and his playing is an integral part of the whole sound. It may be a little unfair to review this so soon after arrival, as I have only played it twice, but it came after the deadline and I wanted it in this issue. Initial thoughts are that while not as immediate as 'Wounded Land', it is a grower with a great many good songs on it. Favourite as I write is probably "The Whispering", which goes through many styles of music, but always played with passion. If you have not heard Threshold before then now is the time to do so, and with Damian back on board you are going to be hearing a lot more about them in the future.

#40, Mar 1997

THRESHOLD
CLONE

Only having a promo, I am not too sure about the line-up, as Threshold release this their fifth album. What is obvious though is the change in vocalist. With Damian Wilson first leaving to join La Salle, and then returning when the project folded (a real shame as I have heard the unreleased album and it is truly superb) displacing the new singer, he has himself this time been replaced by ex-Sergeant Fury frontman Andrew 'Mac' McDermott. Whereas Threshold used to be seen very much as the UK's answer to Dream Theater, they have moved on and although there are a few prog influences this is now very much a melodic hard rock band. Although they have 'progressed', at the same time they have also looked towards their classic debut 'Wounded Land' and have brought in elements of that: during "Angels" I found myself being reminded of that album's classic number, "Sanity's End". Having seen these guys live, albeit a few years ago, I know that they are very much a metallic outfit in the concert environment and that part of their sound appears to have been captured here as never before. The riffs are crunched out, while at the same time the vocals and melodies sit happily over the top, bringing melody and harmony to proceedings. If you have heard Threshold in the past then you will know

what to expect, but this time it is better. There is no doubt that they have produced their best album since their debut, and after I have played it over the next few months, I may say that it is better than that. To those who have not heard of them then now is the time to discover one of the UK's best-kept secrets. It is no surprise to me at all that they are stars in Germany and Japan, it is a shame that we can't treat our own with the respect they deserve.
#51, Jan 1999

THRESHOLD
DECADENT

It was only when I was talking to Karl Groom during the recording sessions for the new Credo album that I discovered that this album had been released last year. Although Threshold is signed to GFT, they were given leave to release this remix/ rarities album on their own label. No "Sanity's End" (an all-time classic from the debut 'Wounded Land' which must be heard to be believed) but one of my other favourites, "Paradox", is on here. Hang on though; the version I know and love does not sound anything like this!! Where are all the guitars? Why so many keyboards? Why does it sound like a dance track? This is a fun album. Not many will have "Intervention" which had originally only featured on 'SI Compilation Too' (if you ever see a copy grab it, as there are many great songs included that still have to see the light of day elsewhere) but like all of the songs on here it has been heavily reworked, re-recorded or edited. They even close with a drum and bass number, but it is for power that Threshold is renowned. They are one of the few prog metal bands that can more than hold their own in exalted company, having toured with the likes of Dream Theater on the continent. While I may not recommend this to the new listener (go for the debut 'Wounded Land'), this is an album that those who have heard the band before will get a lot out of.

#58, May 2000

THRESHOLD
HYPOTHETICAL

They may be onto their fifth full studio release, but Threshold have yet to record more than one album with the same line-up. At least this time they have the same vocalist for two consecutive albums (a first) and have remained the same for three years. In prog-metal there is certainly no other UK act in the same league, and even American acts such as Enchant and Dream Theater have found it hard going when touring with them in Europe. While drummer and vocalist seats have been unsettled since the band's inception, the nucleus of guitarists Karl Groom and Nick Midson, with bassist Jon Jeary and keyboard player Richard West have been together since 1989. Karl is also an accomplished engineer, soundman and producer (being half of the Thin Ice team), and this helps in the band achieving an overall extremely heavy but also very polished sound. There are two longer songs on here, with "The Ravages Of Time" managing to go some

way in toppling "Sanity's End" from the debut album as my favourite all time Threshold song. The last time I saw these guys I got serious neck ache – if ever you thought that melodic rock could not stand up against 'normal' hard rock for power and passion then think again. Threshold are back in town.
#62, May 2001

THRESHOLD
CONCERT IN PARIS

This is a fan-club only release of the Paris concert last year and precedes the new studio album 'Critical Mass' which is currently going through final mix and should be available at the end of the summer. Threshold have long been the UK's premier prog metal outfit, and this collection shows why as while their debut 'Wounded Land' is viewed by many as a classic release, only one song from that album (the truly awesome "Paradox") is on this release. The rhythm section of Johanne James and Jon Jeary tie it all down which allows the twin guitars of Nick Midson and Karl Groom to lock horns with keyboardist Richard West, while rising above it all is vocalist Mac. This is metal with some prog roots, not the other way around. The keyboards play an important role, but this is a metal band that uses melody like a battering ram. The album starts life almost slowly, with the heavy riffing "Freaks", with Mac taking a small role in a lower vocal register. Soon the band start to open up, with the vocals much more centre stage, and the keyboard solo attempting to power through the twin riffs, but the music is much more than just power chords. There is lightness and shade, majesty and grandeur, but at the base of it all there is a rock band that wants to cure your dandruff and get inside your skull. This superb CD is available from their website and comes with a multimedia section that contains a screensaver, tour diary etc. that is quite interesting. If you have yet to discover the joys of Threshold but like your metal melodic and loud then now is the time.
#68, Jun 2002

THRESHOLD
CRITICAL MASS

It is nine years since Threshold released the awesome 'Wounded Land', and here they are back with their sixth studio album (which I think is the first time that they have released two studio albums with the same line-up, following on from 2001's 'Hypothetical'). While they have had some changes since their inception, the quartet of Karl Groom (guitar), Nick Midson (guitar), Jon Jeary (bass) and Richard West (keyboards) have been ever present. Add to that the vocal talents of Andrew 'Mac' McDermott and drummer Johanne James and you have the band that has been taking the banner of prog metal firmly to the forefront. Threshold have long been the UK's, and possibly Europe's, finest exponents of this intricate style of hard rock, and this album is sure to lift them to new heights. This is a band that is driven from the back, with Johanne hitting the drums very hard indeed, then add in the crunching riffs and bass lines that only come from playing together for so long, and the rock keyboards of Richard who is willing to provide walls of sound or lead roles as the song demands. With this album Mac has firmly come out of the shadow of Damian Wilson to stand firmly in the spotlight of his own making – while the band have moved on musically to produce by far their best album, he has more than been ready to meet the task and must now be one of the unsung rock vocalists in this country. It is melodic, it is gentle, it is heavy, it is hard, this is an album for all those who want music to be contemplative and thoughtful, intricate and clever, yet also with plenty of balls and aggression to match. This is their finest work to date and one that I heartily recommend. Play loud. Very loud. *#69, Aug 2002*

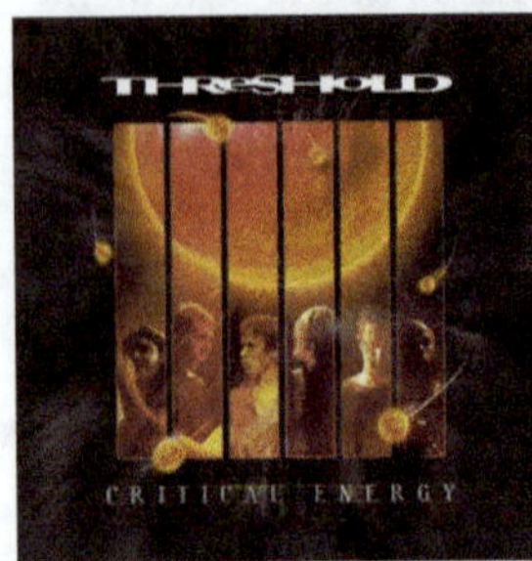

THRESHOLD
CRITICAL ENERGY

This is the companion double CD to the DVD of the same name (if you hurry you can buy both together as a special set) and captures the UK's premier prog metal band on the road. With new bassist Steve Anderson joining just in time for the tour, this captures the guys where they belong, very loud and in front of a crowd. Mac is one of the undiscovered, a good singer and front man who many outside of the prog scene will have never heard of, while the rest of the guys are certainly no slouches. Steve adds new touches while Johanne James is a powering drummer, driving the band ever forward. There are the twin guitars of Karl Groom and Nick Midson, who while knowing how to play widdly, are most at home providing power chords and riffing to allow keyboard player Richard West to either add touches of colour or to go totally over the top. Prog metal is a fusion of two types of music which many think do not belong together, but in the hands of a band that care about both then it can become an awesome format, and this is the case tonight. The band come on to an orchestral serenade, but suddenly the double bass drum pedals kick the band in, and it is all systems go. Every song shows why the band have such a strong reputation. Just when it can't get any heavier in come the keyboards and the song is taken into a new direction, maybe less heavy yet more intense. "Paradox" is a modern classic, driving and awesomely powerful while "Sanity's End" takes the genre to a new level. Prog metal just does not get any better than this. Get the DVD for home and the CD for the car where it can be turned up really LOUD!
#78, Apr 2004

THRESHOLD
SUBSURFACE

Given that the band have only recently released their wonderful live CD and DVD 'Critical Energy', I hadn't realised that a new studio album was going to follow so quickly. New bassist Steve Anderson is now firmly in the fold, and he seems very much at home as he links in with Johanne James. Nick Midson and Karl Groom are there to provide the metal riffs, while Richard West again either supports or rides melodic roughshod over the top of the maelstrom with some great keyboard lines. Add to that the great vocals of Mac and you have one of the finest bands in the UK scene. Chances are you will not read as much about them in the 'normal' press as others because they pursue a lone furrow in prog metal – this is music which can be brutally heavy yet maintain strange time signatures and melodic twists. "Mission Profile" opens proceedings – one of the more up-tempo numbers on the album, and one thing that kicks home from the opening note is the quality of the production: this is an album that can be played extremely loudly, that sounds polished but not sanitised.

For me the second song, "Ground Control", is one of the best for defining Threshold. It is riff-laden, yet also contains some strong keyboards, loads of harmony vocals, gentle and quiet sections which are then offset with passion and Mac shouting, "How can you face the future?" At times, there is almost a syncopated rhythm and always there is a definite feel that this is like nothing else around yet is also wonderfully powerful and melodic. This is music that may not be fashionable but sure as hell is strong stuff. Yes, they can bring in acoustic guitars when they want to, yes, they can bring in loads of influences, but these guys do not sound like anyone else. Simple ideas are used as well as the complex – at the end of "Stop Dead" Mac again sings the line "Well if you stop, dead" and the song does, totally. The first time it happened I stared at the player because it was so dramatic, not a good idea when you are bombing around the M25.... I ought to also mention the cover. The word on the TV says 'REFLECT' but look at the reflection and that states 'CONCEAL'. Again, a simple idea, but effective. Nine songs, all powerful, all giving strength and credence to the claim that Threshold should be much more well-known than they are. With a superb live set out earlier in the year, a headlining tour in Europe to come in the Autumn, and this indispensable album out on 2nd August maybe 2004 will be their year. On this evidence, it should be.
#80, Jul 2004

TIEMKO
ÇA TOURNE

Tiemko were a French band who released four albums at the end of the Eighties, beginning of the Nineties. This release is a compilation of previously unreleased material, much of which was improvised. The only problem with improvised material is that while it can be extremely intriguing and sometimes brilliant, there are also times when one cannot get onto the same wavelength as the musicians and the result is something that can be quite painful. This may not be as bad as the latter but certainly is not as innovative and wonderful as the former. The guys are all good musicians, and this has been well-produced, but it is not often that the listener gets a lot of enjoyment out of what is going on. They are strongly influenced by jazz but there are also moments when the music is quite heavy, with lots of over the top guitars and rock-like keyboards. Unusually for Musea this is an expanded release and it is possible to watch a video, an animation, and find out about the history of the band (although all the text is in French). Interesting, but no more than that.
#81, Dec 2004

TILES
TILES

The debut album from American act Tiles is making quite a stir among AOR/American rock fans. They have been likened to being a cross between Queen and Savatage, while vocalist Paul Rarick manages to come across as a hard rocking Dennis DeYoung. As you can imagine, there is a lot going on with a myriad of styles. During the instrumental "Dress Rehearsal", Chris Herin utilises some classic Alex Lifeson guitar sounds circa "2112" while "Trading Places" is like '80's Yes, especially "Changes". Songs are the order of the day, and Tiles prove that whatever style they are using; they never forget the importance of melody and structure. It is an album that will appeal to lovers of good rock that is hard, melodic and approachable yet is also demanding, changing and interesting. The abilities of the band shine in my favourite, "Token Pledge", as they belt through in their best technical rock approach. A song of many parts, the vocals soar above the guitar and bass interplay. This is not the last we have heard from Tiles, a name to look out for.

#34, Apr 1996

TILES
PRESENTS OF MIND

I reviewed Tiles' debut album some years ago, and now they are back with their third. As this has now been released on the German Inside Out label it is much easier to obtain than the others. They are being described as Detroit's leading progressive band but considering that Detroit's most well-known rock acts are probably Meatloaf, Ted Nugent and MC5 then maybe that tag is not too hard to obtain. Although the term 'progressive' could be put onto Tiles, it is much more in the sense of Rush than of say Genesis or King Crimson. Tiles are basically a hard rock band that are keen to experiment and move a little beyond the boundaries normally perceived by bands playing rock. In that sense, they could be said to be progressing, but as to adding anything new to the genre that maybe not. If a prog fan bought this, then I think they would be disappointed and go off and listen to Spock's Beard again instead. But if you are a technical rock fan who wants to hear a band prove that they can do more than play in four -four and know more than two chords then maybe this is for you. The harmonies are lush and inviting, and the music intricate, but at times there is the impression that Tiles are being just a little too clever for their own good. I came away with the impression that they are proud of their musical ability, possibly a little too proud, as some of the sections seemed to be more along the lines of "Hey look at me aren't I clever?" as opposed to any musical benefit. Songs such as "Facing Failure" show that when they get it right, they are very good indeed. This is one that needs to be heard prior to purchase but is worth investigating all the same.

#54, July 1999

TILES
WINDOW DRESSING
This is the fourth studio album from Tiles, and any band that starts with a song which is over seventeen minutes long is obviously full of confidence. That is the title cut, and it shows the many sides of Tiles as they mix melodic rock with loads of other forms to create a type of music which has obviously been heavily influenced by Rush. But although they have a guest keyboard player in Hugh Syme (who also provided the artwork) this is a four-piece rock band (they also have a guest violinist in Matthew Parmenter (Discipline), and a guest guitarist in Kim Mitchell – surely not the Kim Mitchell from Max Webster?), one that uses extra instruments to colour and flavour the proceedings, but not to take it over. The music is extremely melodic, and even crunchy when they require it, and the production of Terry Brown (Rush, IQ, Fates Warning etc.) has given the music an extra polish. It may not be pure progressive in the normal sense, but it has taken a hefty chunk of that genre and placed it with melodic rock to create an album that is very accessible on first listen yet also contains depths to enjoy and investigate. Yet another strong album from the Detroit based band.
#79, May 2004

TIMELINE
TIMELINE
This is the debut album by American outfit Timeline, and it has been receiving some excellent reviews within the prog genre. It was interesting to see that one person said how good the production was, as I honestly believe that this is the one thing that is letting this album down. In many ways, it reminds of me of the sort of music I was listening to in the early Nineties when I was being sent tapes by bands like Blyndsyde and although there are two guitarists this is not a prog metal album, but something that is very much prog rock. Eric Boles has a very interesting voice, with quite a range and seemingly a lot of power, and he comes across with a David Byron style, which does give the band a Heep flavour to add to the Rush and Saga that is already in the mix. The question is whether Timeline are a prog band at all as there are a lot of pomp influences, but whatever the genre this is an interesting album. Hopefully this will get them the major label support that they deserve, and I look forward to the next album with interest.
#85, Nov 2005

TIMELOCK
LOUISE BROOKS
Timelock are a Dutch band who came together in 1991. Singer Ruud Stoker (ex-The Last Detail), keyboard player Julian Driessen (ex-Ywis, ex-The Last Detail) combined forces with guitarist and keyboard player Ribus Hollenberg (ex-Ywis, ex-Q65), with the line-up being completed with the addition of Bert du Bruijne on bass (drums are programmed by Hollenberg). 'Louise Brooks' is loosely based on the life and times of the actress of the

same name and what is readily apparent that Timelock are, like Wings of Steel, a Dutch band heavily influenced by the other side of the Atlantic. However, here both feet are plunged firmly into AOR and devil take the hindmost. If you like that sort of rock, then here is an album that is worth getting. Ruud Stoker has a brilliant voice, great clarity and range, yet at the same time with loads of power. I would love to see this band live because I get the impression that he is a singer who can cut it. The rest of the band are not slouches either, with good tight harmonies, and powerful and accurate playing. Highlights? Well, in all honesty all the tracks are good, but mention should be made of the atmospheric ballad "Someday" which features some beautiful guest sax work: the vocals stand out. If I had to choose between these and Wings of Steel then I think Timelock would get the vote as this album is just so consistently good, and on top of that Ruud's vocals fit the music so perfectly.
#17, Mar 1993

TIMOTHY PURE
THE FABRIC OF BETRAYAL
I know absolutely nothing about this band except that they are a five-piece and are presumably American as this is an American release. I know nothing about the label either, as I was sent this from Poland. Inside the booklet it says that the album "is a collection of short stories comprising several different themes. The themes have been expanded upon and will be released in future as full-length works". I do not even know if this is a brand -new release, but whatever it is, it is bloody good. This is highly involved and delicate prog rock. It manages to avoid the AOR trap prevalent in many American prog and builds strands of music together like a spider's web to ensnare and captivate the listener. The lyrics too are of the very highest order, with many of them hinting of a darker side to life. At times, there are hints of Rush, sometimes Fish, sometimes Pendragon but while the music is very complex and complicated it is always accessible. I am going to do my best to find out more about this band and label before the next issue but if you are intrigued by yet another extremely good American act, following on from Spock's Beard, I urge you to get this album.
#39, Jan 1997

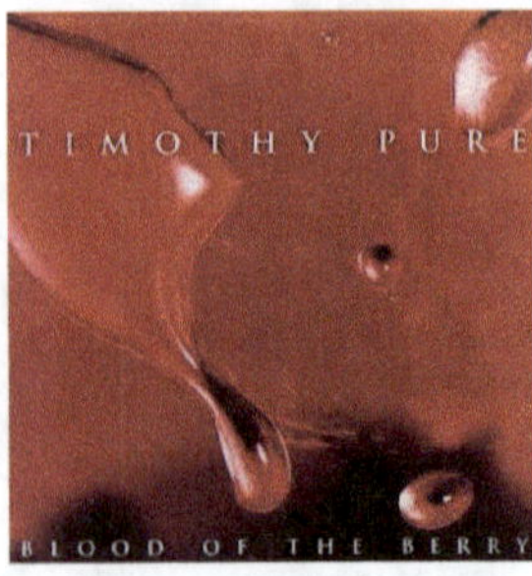

TIMOTHY PURE
BLOOD OF THE BERRY
Since the release of their debut, 'The Fabric of Betrayal', Timothy Pure have undergone some serious personnel changes. Keyboard player Matthew Still has now taken on lead vocals and with bassist Andre Neitzel are the only two remaining from the previous line-up. The new additions are Zod (guitars) and Chris Wallace (drums) while they have also used a guest female vocalist, Johnnie Hooper, on two songs. I was a big fan of the

debut and was a little wary as to what might have happened to the band musically, but I needn't have worried as while there have been some big changes, they have taken the band onto new levels. This is not a band that is as reliant on guitar as they used to be, but there is so much power and force that it is almost overpowering. This is keyboard and vocal driven prog at its very finest: controlled and always melodic, there is a vigour that many bands utilising a far heavier sound would not be able to compete with. This album sees the band move forwards and upwards from their very positive debut into an area where few have managed to be so convincing. It is very much a song-based album, and unusually for a prog band there are fourteen here on offer. America has managed to produce some very good progressive bands in the last few years, but with 'Blood Of The Berry' Timothy Pure have managed to show that while they do not sound like their compatriots, their music is more desirable and viable than most. A definite must purchase.

#44, Sept 1997

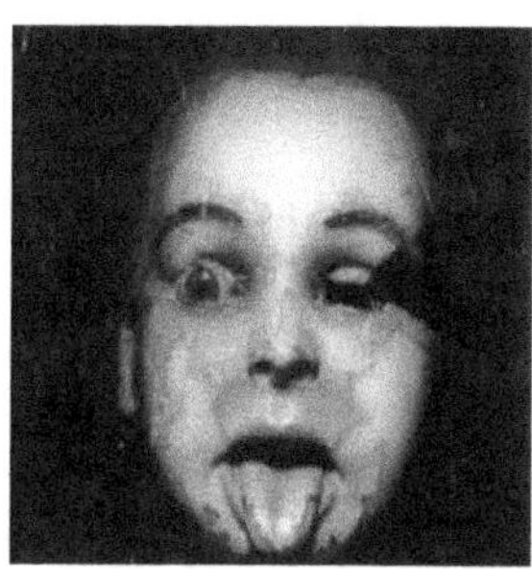

TIN SCRIBBLE
CHILDREN OF SATURN

Tin Scribble were formed out of the ashes of House of Usher, when bassist Mark Jardine and guitarist and singer Michael Allen Moore decided to pursue music that was more art rock and less traditional prog (if you know what I mean). The result is an album that is compelling, yet at times is very strange indeed and is almost unlistenable. This is not only due to the weird and unusual way that the music sometimes moves, but also the vocals. When I first played this, I felt that Michael was trying to sing out of his range and that the stylings he was utilising did not really suit. But this is an album that does repay repeated listening and I now instead think that I have a handle on what he is trying to do. The music has an almost Arabic feel to it, combined with an intensity and a darkness and the vocals are very much part of it. I remember reading an interview with Gene Simmons years ago saying that his rendition of "When You Wish Upon A Star" had to go flat and had to go sharp. That is the case here. Michael does not sound anything like Geoff Mann but there are times when what he is doing with his voice does remind me of him. The black and white album cover does portray the fact that this is not an ordinary album inside, and musically that is the case. This is something that is going to polarise the views of those within the prog scene and while I may not feel that this is indispensable it is certainly very interesting, and it is always good to see a band trying to move across boundaries. It is unusual, it is different, and for the more catholic listener.

#87, Apr 2006

TOP LEFT CORNER
MISTERY BOOK

I think these guys are Italian, and if they are then I must congratulate them on one of the best Italian prog albums it has been my pleasure to hear. Much more melodic rock than straight prog, they mix good tunes with some great guitarwork. On top of that Flavio

Mendo has a superb voice, full of emotion and depth yet at the same time capable of hitting the notes he wants to without straining. Right from the first song I knew that I was onto a winner. Quite often I listen to an album and it can be a struggle to get through it, but that was not the case here: each song is a joy, a new discovery waiting to be made. It is the simple touches that are effective, such as the use of a double bass drum pedal for added effect in a passage on "Wonder Why". This is an album that will appeal to the UK prog/rock market and I am surprised that I hadn't come across it before (this was released in 1994). It is undoubtedly one of the top releases on the Music Is Intelligence label.

#31, Oct 1995

ÁDÁM TÖRÖK & MINI
NOMAD OF THE WINDS

Ádám Török is well known in his native Hungary, playing not only progressive but also blues and jazz-fusion. In the mid Nineties, he was approached by Periferic to produce an album of instrumentals. It has taken five years, but now it is here. The initial comparison will be with Jethro Tull, not only for the extensive use of flute as the lead melodic instrument, but also because of the many differing styles that are obvious. There are other influences such as Colosseum, Camel and even Jadis, and there is also folk music of his homeland. The result is a very atmospheric album that relies on space and light. It is extremely melodic and accessible, while at the same time maintaining a certain aloofness, this is not common or garden prog. This is an album that will be enjoyed by many progheads if they can get to hear it.

#65, Dec 2001

TOUCHSTONE
CURIOUS ANGEL

It is always nice to hear new prog bands in the UK, and Touchstone were formed less than two years ago. This four track EP shows that the band have promise, and hopefully this will not be the last that we hear of them. Although they bring in Genesis and IQ references, this is a band that are looking outside of the normal prog scene as they bring in elements of far heavier bands while never veering into prog metal territory. Adam J Hodgson can provide the required widdly-widdly but seems to be happier either pushing through power chords or some great distorted solos where he proves that he can shred with the best of them. Rob Cottingham provides the keyboards and vocals, and on "See The Light" provides a great start to a piece that if it had a different guitar sound could have come from Jadis. This is a good example of their sound in that they switch from style to style within the song, not staying within one area. The only thing that I think lets this down at all is that at times the production of the vocals is not as good as it

could be, but if Clive or Karl was involved then this would soon be amended. These four tracks show great promise, with some great musicianship and interesting songs (although I am concerned that "Special" includes a direct lyrical lift from Lionel Ritchie's "Hello"). If you enjoy prog, why not give these guys a try?
#83, Mar 2005

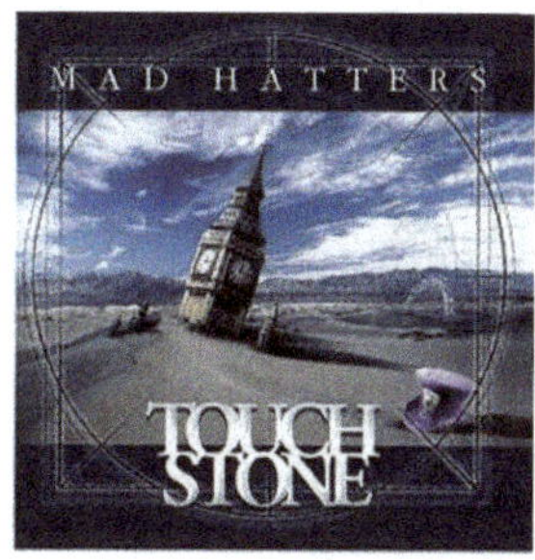

TOUCHSTONE
MAD HATTERS
This is the new EP from this Hertfordshire quintet, who comprise Rob Cottingham (vocals, keyboards), Liz Clayden (vocals), Adam Hodgson (guitars), Paul Moorghen (bass, backing vocals) and Simon Cook (drums). This is all about classic rock, prog rock, call it what you will, well performed and executed. Five songs, all showing different sides to the band but the most important part about this is that the music is so damn accessible and (whisper it) catchy. I mean, prog is supposed to be deadly serious and not for having a good time, Right? Wrong! This is boisterous bouncy music that can be serious and calm when it wants to be, but generally just does not. This is all about going back to a time when prog was all about having fun, which is something that these days not too many bands remember. The use of twin vocals works particularly well, with the two voices complimenting each other – also something that is unusual within the prog context. I can remember Mr So & So doing something like this towards the end of their career, but not many since with the male being dominant but the female being equally as important. Given that this is a self-release, one must admire the work that has gone into it. They recorded at John Mitchell's studio and used Rob Aubrey to mix it while the artwork of guitarist Adam Hodgson is superb. It all adds to a great package, which is most definitely worth it!
#89, Sep 2006

DEVIN TOWNSEND
PHYSICIST
From the superb, 'Infinity' Devin is back with a full band (he uses his cohorts from Strapping Young Lad) and has given us one of the most interesting albums I have heard for a while. It is an album of undisputed straight through the ears metal at tremendous pace, which must be played at speaker melting volume to get the full effect. But, if you can manage that (thank heavens for car CD players), you will be richly rewarded. Devin has set himself up as some mad Canadian hard rock Phil Spector, and although this album is often brutal in the extreme it is also one of the best produced. The music is a solid slab of sound that has been mixed and moulded to some strange blueprint only Devin has seen. The first four or five times I played this I was not sure, but by the time it had totally burned itself into my psyche I could just about see what Devin is striving for. This awesome album is not for the faint hearted.
#61, Feb 2001

DEVIN TOWNSEND
TERRIA

Devin is building a reputation for being one of the most uncompromising of artists, releasing music that is raw yet over-produced, simple but complex, easy to listen to but also bloody hard work! There is a little more lightness on this album than on 'Physicist', but not much. Devin is still trying to change production as we know it, pushing Phil Spector into new avenues. The times when he allows the music to shine through and his vocals to be unfettered is so unusual as to cause an interesting effect, obviously why he chooses to do so. This is much more than just music; it is how the songs are treated so they sound very different to anything else around. Remember, this is a man who first found fame with Steve Vai, then moved onto Front Line Assembly and The Wildhearts before forming his own band Strapping Young Lad. He is well used to volume, and how to use aggression but here it is behind a gossamer wall that only lets slip when he wills it. This is never easy to listen to and certainly will not appeal to the majority of either rockers or progheads, but they are the ones missing out. Masterful.

#64, Oct 2001

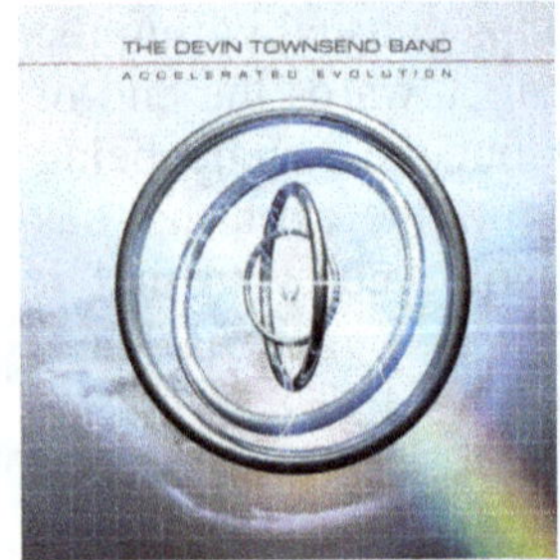

THE DEVIN TOWNSEND BAND
ACCCELERATED EVOLUTION

Strange, it seems only like last issue that I was reviewing the new album by Devin Townsend. Ah, but that was Strapping Young Lad, and now we have here The Devin Townsend Band which contains different musicians and is a totally different outfit and album, but it must be said that there are striking similarities. The main one of these is the Wall Of Sound approach to production which gives all of Devin's albums a distinctive and similar style, but while 'Accelerated Evolution' is obviously a Devin album, it is quite different to SYL. The latter is very much a heavy rock band, while TDTB although never far from the rock feel contains much more space in the music and manage to lose some of the intensity. "Deadhead" is almost dreamy in its style, with long held-down keyboard chords and the music and vocals swirling in the mix. But there are times on the album where the production is deliberately clear, and Devin's vocals are warm and untreated. That the man is a genius there is no doubt, and there seems to be no end to his abilities to take music and reinvent the style and format so that while appealing to many still sounds nothing like anyone else. He has announced a tour where both SYL and TDTB will be playing and that should be some show.

Yet again Devin has come up with a winner and for those who can't yet quite face the intensity of Strapping Young Lad or some of Devin's earlier albums then reach for this which probably has more immediacy of any of his so far. Of course, it still must be played loud….

#73, Apr 2003

TRACTOR
WORST ENEMIES

Tractor can trace their history back to 1966 when Jim Milne and Steve Clayton formed a band called The Way We Live. A few years down the line they sent some demos to record companies, not expecting Clive Selwood of Dandelion to arrive clutching a contract to sign them before anyone else. Their debut album 'A Candle For Judith' was released in 1971 but did not make the impact that was expected, and Dandelion boss John Peel suggested a name change to something earthier and Tractor was born. The second album (or first, depending on your viewpoint) was released at the end of 1972 and by January 1973 was No. 19 in Kid Jensen's chart on Radio Luxembourg (one place above Uriah Heep's 'Magicians' Birthday'). The complete history of the band from 1966 to the Nineties can be found in the informative booklet that accompanies this release. It is a collection of material from 1971 to 1991, and because of the time span is not the best introduction to the band, but is still an enjoyable album nonetheless.

The feeling for the most part is early Seventies prog, which is not surprising, but at times there are large elements of folk while at others it is quite heavy. However, "Argument For One" sounds like a class cut from late Seventies 10CC! Highlight is the closer, the 21 minute "Peterloo" that tells the story of the Manchester Reform Meeting of 1819 that was brutally ended by the military. Jim's vocals are very melodic and to the forefront of this song which features plenty of acoustic guitar and swirling keyboards. I hadn't heard a song about this event before, although I do remember being taught about it at school and lyrically this does it justice. Each section is musically quite differently, and it works well as a whole. Of course, if you are an old Tractor fan then this is an album that you must get, but it also interesting to lovers of prog as it expands into areas like folk, always with strong songs and vocals.
#44, Sept 1997

TRANCEPORT
TRANCEGLOBAL

This album does not have much immediate appeal but having listened to it a few times I can report that it is most definitely a 'grower'. It opens with "Future Foundation", which is almost hypnotic and certainly mesmerising. On listening to it on headphones I found it easy to blank myself off from the rest of the outside world and just stay deep inside the music. There is quite a lot of repeated melodies, but each of the nine tracks manage to maintain their own individuality. This is not something that would appeal to the hardened guitar freak, but for those who enjoy synthwork then this is one to look out for.
#20, Oct 1993

TRANSATLANTIC
SMPTE

The last supergroup of the 20th Century is here. Mike Portnoy (Dream Theater) thought it might be fun to work with Neal Morse (Spock's Beard), and a few e-mails later the line-up was completed by Roine Stolt (Flower Kings) and Pete Trewavas (Marillion). The impression coming strongly through the music is that Neal and Roine have been the two largest musical influences, although Neal plays much more Hammond Organ than would normally be found with the Beard. The opener manages to kick in at over thirty minutes in length, and there are two other tracks (one of which is a Procol Harum cover, "In Held (Twas) I"), which are over fifteen minutes long. They make the other two songs (both over five minutes long) seem very short in comparison. This is much more about traditional Seventies sounds, with a huge chunk of Steely Dan style sound being incorporated at times. Neal and Roine both sing lead vocals, while the others provide harmonies. The music is very intricate, very complex, very prog, but does not move into the prog metal style beloved by Mike and (at times) Neal. It is certainly the most progressive album to involve Pete for some years.... It is an album that any proghead will be queuing for when it hits the shops on April 10th. These guys prove that it does not need loads of volume. All it needs is a tune, some vocals, and some interplay (okay, so the tune is moving through different time signatures, and is extremely complicated and diverse while the vocal harmonies are spot on). "Mystery Train" is the one that sounds as if it could have been lifted straight from 'Day For Night' as the restrained verse leads into a very Spock's Beard style soaring chorus. This is just simply, a superb album.
#57, Mar 2000

TRANSATLANTIC
LIVE IN AMERICA

So, it is your sixth ever gig, on a tour supporting an album recorded when none of you were in the room at the same time. The only obvious thing to do is to record it, of course, then release it as a double CD with no 'cleaning up' at all. That it manages to work on any level is down to the skill of the players. All of them are in active bands, and the fact that they managed to bury the egos long enough to get on the road at all is something (although Pete Trewavas does point out that he usually plays in larger venues than this). They open with the thirty-minute-long "All Of The Above", which has Neal Morse stamped all over it. It is an adventurous piece that they manage to pull off, with Neal and Roine pulling the melody along while it is being driven hard by Pete and Mike Portnoy. They soon run out of tunes and "Mystery Train" segues into "Magical Mystery Tour" which itself becomes "Strawberry Fields Forever". The last song on the first CD is Neal Morse's "We All Need Some Light" (the only song written by just one of the band members). Having given some Beatles on the first CD it is to Genesis that they turn to on the second, with "Watcher Of The Skies" and "Firth Of Fifth" getting a blasting. Both Spock's Beard and Flower Kings have been playing Genesis songs in their set so perhaps this is not too much of a surprise. The closing

medley is the band having some fun as they play one song from each of their respective day jobs then put in another Beatles number for fun. Overall this is a good (but not great) live set. They need to write more material before the next tour, especially if they are going to record it again.
#62, May 2001

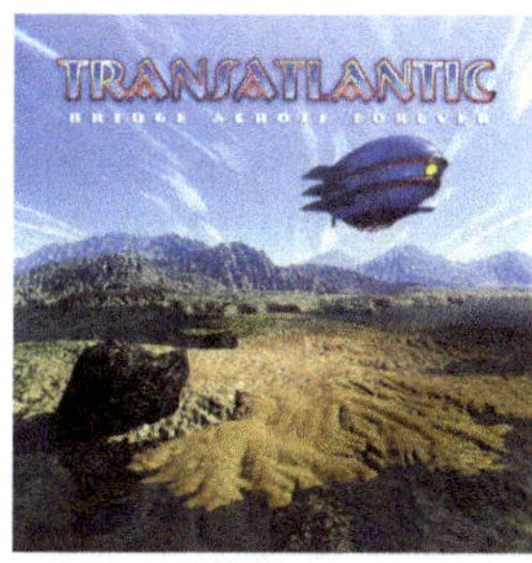

TRANSATLANTIC
BRIDGE ACROSS FOREVER
The Prog supergroup are back with their second studio offering. Only four tracks on this album, but as two of these are more than twenty-six minutes long and the other two are fourteen and five minutes long respectively then I think we can forgive them. The title cut is a solo ballad from Neal, with good piano, but he has almost put himself into the background on this album in the way that he has managed to keep his normal prog writing style under wraps. "Duel With The Devil" is one of the epics and it opens proceedings in a very Flower Kings, Pink Floyd fashion. The promo does not detail who wrote what, but I would be amazed not to see Roine's name on the credits. Broken into five sections it really does show the musical strength of this band. "Suite Charlotte Pike" starts, then stops with shouts of "Wassup!!" Take two starts almost immediately, and the band seem to be very much in a groove with a Beatle-esque slant on proceedings. After the title cut the other 26-minute epic "Stranger In Your Soul" closes the album, which contains not only some very traditional Genesis-style keyboards but also some great instrumental passages, and vocals from both Neal and Roine. With both being very much the leaders of their own bands, it is easy to overlook the rhythm section of Mike Portnoy and Pete Trewavas, but they are very much an integral part of the sound. This is an album that repays careful listening, with four top musos having a blast in the studio. Apparently, the full version will be available as a digipak with extra tracks (including "Shine On You Crazy Diamond") and some video footage.
#64, Oct 2001

TRANSATLANTIC
LIVE IN EUROPE
Take musicians from four of the top progressive rock bands around and there is a ready built supergroup. What makes this recording even more interesting now is because Neal not only left Spock's Beard when he decided to take a different course, he also left Transatlantic at the same time. In Morse, Mike Portnoy, Roine Stolt and Pete Trewavas there were four musicians and singers seemingly capable of turning their hands to anything they wanted and although the first live album was somewhat restricted by the band at the time not having much in the way of self-composed material, that was not a problem when it came to the 2001 tour which is captured here. There are six 'songs' on this double CD, with the extremely short "We All Need Some Light" only being six minutes in length. Yep, there are three songs on this album that are over thirty

minutes long! Now that is probably enough to get the progheads salivating, but how about incorporating side two of 'Abbey Road' into "Suite Charlotte Pike Medley"!? There are going to many who think that this album is self-indulgent and over-long, but the fan is just going to be happy that it has been made available. They bring together all the things that non-progheads think are the worst examples of this style of music, complex and complicated music that is overblown and pompous with harmony vocals and intelligent structuring of lyrics and their place in the piece. But to progheads this is a joy, with each song being better than the last, each one with sections (if not the whole thing) that has the listener shaking their head in wonderment and smiling. This is prog, and it's fun! Because all the guys had other 'main' bands this was only ever about making music that they wanted to, because they enjoyed it, and that enjoyment comes through on this album. It is also available as a double DVD or a double CD/double DVD limited edition. This is wonderful stuff.
#78, Apr 2004

TRANSIENCE
SLIDING

For what originally was going to be a solo project by Lands End keyboard player Fred Hunter, there is a lot of outside involvement. All the three other members of that band are integral to this one, so much so that Fred hasn't even written all the songs on the album. Lands End vocalist Jeff McFarland provides the focal point for much of the material, which is dreamy and contemplative. There are some wonderful parts on the album, and the fact that the musicians know each other so intimately is obvious. This is not music to rock you back on your heels, and it is important to be in the right frame of mind otherwise this will wash right over you. Very much a mood album, in the sense that one must be in the right mood to listen to it but get it just right then you will be richly rewarded. One to listen to prior to purchase
#59, July 2000

TRANSIENCE
PRIMORDIAL

This follow-up album to 1999's 'Sliding' has been delayed by Fred Hunter's illness, which he is extremely honest about in the booklet as he tells the story of the album. Happily, Fred appears to have recovered, and the line-up is completed by Mark Lavallee (drums), Jeff McFarland (vocals, guitars), Franceso Neto (guitar), and Steve Ades (sax) while Fred provided keyboards, bass and guitar. Of course, this band is a side project of Land's End, but they have a valid musical identity in their own right. This is music that is dreamy and reflective, sometimes lacking the edge, but it does not manage to drift totally into New Age. It works as background music as well as being listened to intently. There is always the danger of losing sense of everything that is going on around as this music can capture the listener, taking them into a different world.

The vocals are just enough to keep attention focussed, and the result is an album that while containing many softer passages a la Floyd, does not have as many dynamic shifts as other prog albums. An interesting exercise and hopefully it will not be as long until the next one.
#78, Apr 2004

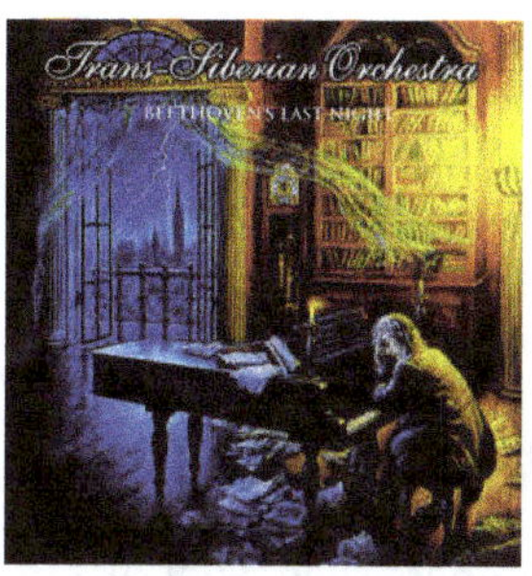

TRANS-SIBERIAN ORCHESTRA
BEETHOVEN'S LAST NIGHT

This is the third CD by an organisation (I think the word band probably does not fit this situation) that I have never heard of, who have managed to sell over 1.5 million albums to date. TSO are the brainchild of Savatage front man Jon Oliva, along with composer and producer Paul O'Neill and classical composer and conductor Robert Kinkel. They take classical ideas then fuse these with rock to bring out rock operas on a huge scale. The idea has been so popular that last year two versions of the band were on the road at the same time to satisfy demand. The rest of Savatage lay claim to most of the rock sections, while members of the New York Philharmonic are also in evidence. The story here is that of Beethoven's last night on earth when he is being tempted by the devil and the decisions he must take. There are twenty-two sections, and this is much more about being a full modern rock opera than just an album. It starts with a delicate rendition of the introduction of 'Moonlight Sonata' before becoming much more reminiscent of Savatage in flight. In many ways, this seems to be to be a logical progression from "Gutter Ballet", although here the orchestral passages and dynamics are much more in evidence. But as this is an opera does it work as a piece of music? Yes, dramatically so. As well as being original pieces, the fusing together of some of Beethoven's best loved pieces does give it both class and at the same time a sense of surprise, a wondering about what is going to happen next. This is an album that cannot be played in the background, but rather is one that should be listened to intently (with the booklet close to hand) to gain the most from. Yes, I liked this a lot, now all I must do is search out the earlier albums where they brought in Mendelssohn and Tchaikovsky.
#67, Apr 2002

TREEBEARD
HEAVY WOOD

Amazingly this has yet to be picked up by a label, so for now the band has released it on their own until a time when it is made more widely available. Because of this the CD is only available through their website or at gigs. Treebeard used to be called Acoustic Haze, something to do with the fact that Chris and Paul McMahon and Phil Chisnell (i.e. Haze) are in the band, along with Chris Jellis and Gordon Walker. Heavy wood is not only the name of the album but is also how they describe their music, and as they say in the booklet "is a trademark of Twice Bitten and is used entirely without permission or justification". Basically, they are an acoustic band, comprising many different types of stringed instruments plus percussion and violin. Four of the five guys take turns providing lead vocals while the album itself is a mix of songs and instrumentals, cover versions, rearranged traditional numbers and originals. This is not a folk album, although it does contain folk elements, and is an album that I have enjoyed immensely. In fact, the day I got it I played it three times back to back and as now found it hard to pick a favourite. It kicks off with "Wilderness Of Eden" from one of Chris and Paul's other bands, World Turtle, and here it takes on a new life with more depth and presence than the original. While there are a couple of World Turtle and a few Haze songs on the CD, it is also the songs that they have chosen to cover that come across with some impact. I defy anyone who listens to "It's The End Of The World As We Know It (And I Feel Fine)" to say that this is not superior in every way to the original REM song. I am not sure what a djembe is, but Paul Chisnell starts the song on it to great effect, and the mandolin and 12-string guitar combine with the harmony vocals and violin to take this song to great heights. Other favourites? Well I feel that I ought to mention "Nothing Ever Happens", oh and "The Hangman & The Papist", and the different version of "(Come Up And See Me) Make Me Smile" or the album closer "The Devil Went Down To Georgia". There are some nods to folk with some traditional numbers such as "Lark In The Morning" (made popular by Fairport) and the four-song medley that they have entitled "Percy In The Linen".

#70, Oct 2002

TRESPASS

IN HAZE OF TIME

Not only are Trespass one of those rare breeds within rock, a trio, but they are also a progressive outfit and come from that known hotbed of prog rock, Israel. As soon as you hear that it is a prog rock trio led by a keyboard player then it is inevitable that they are going to be compared with ELP, but according to the press release the main composer, Gil Stein, had not heard of ELP or The Nice or any other prog rock bands until he recorded the album. Now for me that is one step too far, as even though Israel may not be up to date in all things musical it is incomprehensible that he had not heard any prog music at all, especially given the name of the band. While the keyboard sounds being utilised are quite different, it is with ELP that this band has the most musical similarities. There is driving drumming and good strong bass, with just a little guitar but by the most important instrument are the keyboards. There are long instrumental sections but when there are vocals they are well sung and in English. The result is a debut album that is extremely listenable for the prog fan, while not breaking any new ground. It is well structured and not too self-indulgent, and Gil is a fine keyboard player while bassist Roy Bar-Tour and especially drummer Gabriel Weissman prove that they are no musical slouches either. Bearing in mind that Gil has never heard ELP how does he explain the honky tonk piano on "The Mad House Blues"? That aside, it is a fun album that does not take too much work to enjoy.

#70, Oct 2002

TRION
TORTOISE
Trion came about when Flamborough Head keyboard player Edo Spanninga wanted to test out some recording equipment. He brought in friends Eddie Mulder (guitars, bass etc., also Flamborough Head) and drummer Menno Boomsma (Odyssice) and Trion were born. The name came out of the fact that they were a trio, and that Edo was going to use the Mellotron exclusively throughout. This is an instrumental album, but vocals are not missed at all, as the music reaches back to the Seventies when prog was at its most popular. There are times when they sound a bit like Yes, or Genesis, but most of that is down to the main instrument being used. But although the Mellotron is an important instrument within the group, there is also plenty of room for some very fine guitar as well as flute and oboe. The drumming is just what one would expect, restrained yet bombastic, simple, but downright complex. This is music to drift into, to fall into a world that has long gone yet is still relevant today if there are people who want to enjoy it. The songs may drift into each other, but the first time I played this I sat there with a grin on my face as this is a joy from start to finish. As it is instrumental and not overbearing there is a danger that some people will only use this for background music but that will be their loss as this is mighty fine. An album that I enjoyed immensely, as will all other progheads who investigate it further.
#78, Apr 2004

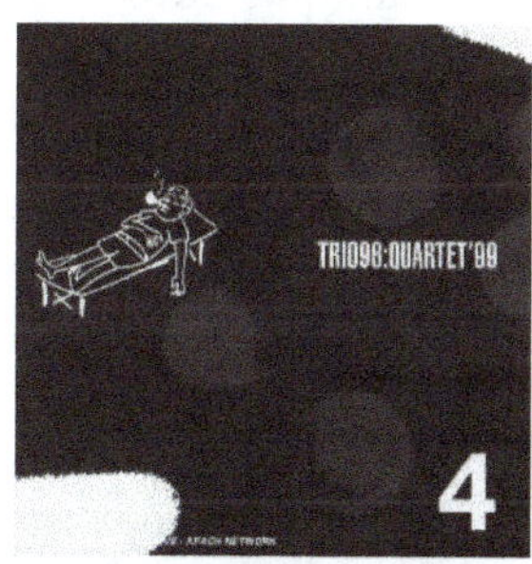

TRIO96
QUARTET '99

TRIO96
DUO '03
No information to be easily found on the web, so I will assume (yes, I do know what 'assume' stands for) that this Japanese band were originally a trio and were formed in 1996. By the time of the first of these albums, the band had increased to a quartet (you can see where I am going with this logic, can't you) of Ishikawa Kenji (guitar), Tanaka Yoshiro (drums), Yano Tamaki (tenor sax) and Eyrir Hiromasa (bass). Although they call themselves a quartet, and although there are some lead sax lines, this is mostly improvisational jazz with the main element being the guitar. Ishikawa is a fine guitarist (in fact they all appear to be strong musicians) and does go off on some wild tangents a la King Crimson.

By 2003 the band had shrunk to just guitar and drums, and this album was recorded live. As before, this is improvised music with heavy jazz elements but this time they have also taken a step back and there does appear to be slightly more structure to proceedings. This is particularly true of the opening track which has a far more prog-like gentle introduction. Without the other

instruments, they make more effort to fill the space and this they do well, but by only hearing this music on a CD instead of through live performance there is only so much that one can take. Improvisation is fine, but it does not normally transfer well to the recorded environment as the spontaneity can easily be lost.
#81, Dec 2004

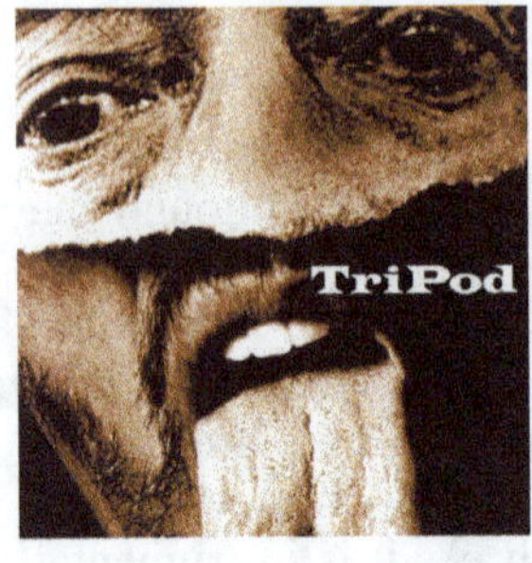

TRIPOD
TRIPOD

With a trio, I always thought that there was not a great deal that could be done with the band format, but I was wrong. Tripod comprises Steve Romano (percussion), Keith Gurland (alt & tenor sax, flute, clarinet, pedals, backing vocals) and Clint Bahr (lead vocals, 12 string bass and bass pedals). This certainly gives the band a different musical outlook on life, and one in which they work extremely hard to maintain interest without either keyboards or guitar to keep it going. When I was first reading about this, I was a little concerned that it was either going to be boring or unlistenable – I was wrong on both counts. If you do not mind trying some jazz that is out of the ordinary, then this is quite a find. Steve holds the backline together virtually on his own, as Clint is sometimes with him but often is to be found playing a counter melody so that Keith has something to pitch against. That Keith provides the main aural point is never in doubt. Clint has a voice that seems better suited to rock, and this provides a calming influence on proceedings. The overall effect is that of a band refusing to conform to any norms and produces music that is challenging yet is invigorating and exciting.
#76, Oct 2003

TRISTAN PARK
A PLACE INSIDE

Since the release of their debut 'At The End Of The Day' on their own label in 1993, Tristan Park have added another vocalist and signed to Cyclops who have just released the follow-up. Like their debut, this album mixes prog with North American AOR in a very pleasing manner. The songs are not over-long, with catchy riffs and hooks, but one of their major strengths is in the vocals. Every member of the band sings, and there are two 'lead' vocalists (although Chuck Dyac appears to be the main). Multi-layered harmonies abound and unlike many bands that rely on overdubbing to achieve the effect, I would have thought that in a live environment this must be a major part. As they are now with Cyclops this American outfit will have a much higher profile in Europe, which can only do them a lot of good as their previous effort was only available in specialist shops. This is an album that is well worth investigating and stands up well when compared with their debut.
#31, Oct 1995

TRISTAN PARK
LOOKING HOMEWARD

I have been a fan of Tristan Park since I heard their first album on Cyclops, and label boss Malcolm Parker and I have often debated their merits against those of Lands End – we have differing opinions as to which band is the better. I am glad to say that this album shows them growing ever stronger in the songwriting front, with the guitars still more to the fore than many prog bands. They never actually veer away from prog, but make sure that the 'rock' part of that equation is heard. The harmony vocals at the beginning of "Four Freedoms" take this song into a lighter element that belies the rockier passages that follow. This song is only three minutes long and is in total contrast to the thoughtful development of the preceding number, "An American Tragedy", which is more than sixteen minutes long. Tristan Park have produced easily their best album to date, one that will be fondly welcomed by all those into neo-prog. Recommended.

#50, Aug 1998

TR3NITY
THE COLD LIGHT OF DARKNESS

This album would be an ambitious undertaking for an established band, let alone a debut. This is the first album by Tr3nity, a four-piece from the UK, and they have started their career with a concept album that is dealing with the hard subject of child abuse and neglect, and the consequences of that. The character, Cathy, gets involved in the drug scene and has children of her own and promises to get herself sorted out but attempts suicide before finding a final solution. Lyrically this is a very strong album, although I did find that I got more out of the album by reading the story that was provided with it (perhaps some of that could have gone into the booklet?), which is available on their excellent website. The music combines elements of Pendragon with Pink Floyd and can be extremely dramatic and powerful indeed (such as at the end of "Into The Dark"), while the interplay between keyboards and guitar on "Which Way?" is impressive. The music can be very uplifting at times, which initially caused me to have an issue with the album as a whole. How can a subject as dark as this have music that is powerful and bright? But if this were a drone, a drudge to listen to, would anyone play it? The answer to that is no, and Tr3nity have managed to combine the dark storyline with music that is interesting and lyrics that are compelling. Chris Campbell's vocals are very clear, and fit the music well, which can be dramatic yet quiet, atmospheric yet in your face (listen to the epic "The Exposure Suite" and hear the 'Wish You Were Here' influences shine through).

This is an album that should be played a great deal, so that the layers of the onion can be peeled away. There are great depths and emotions that come with this work and based on this the band have a great future ahead of them.

#69, Aug 2002

TR3NITY
PRECIOUS SECONDS

Tr3nity are back with their second album, following on from their superb 'The Cold Light Of Darkness'. This is another concept but the subject matter this time is a bit cheerier than the last – to get the story go to their website for more details. Tr3nity have moved on: they are still one of the UK's undiscovered prog bands, but they are yet again fulfilling their objective, "music with a purpose". While their music still brings in elements of bands such as Camel and Pendragon, there is also more than a hint of Saga and even Styx in what they are doing. Five songs, each more than ten minutes long, with the closing "The Last Great Climb" managing to just break the twenty -minute barrier. There is so much space in this music that is possible to get inside it and have a rest on one of the held down keyboard chords, and just let the mind move with the swirling in and out. Two minutes into the last song and there is a change in tempo brought in by the introduction of piano which could have some straight from 'Wish You Were Here' - sounding nothing like Floyd but identical at the same moment.

When I played their debut album, I found that it took me a while to get into it, as I felt that the lyrics jarred slightly with the music, but it eventually won me over. No such problem this time as straight from the first playing I fell in love with it – I am sure that all progheads into good music will want to discover this British band.
#79, May 2004

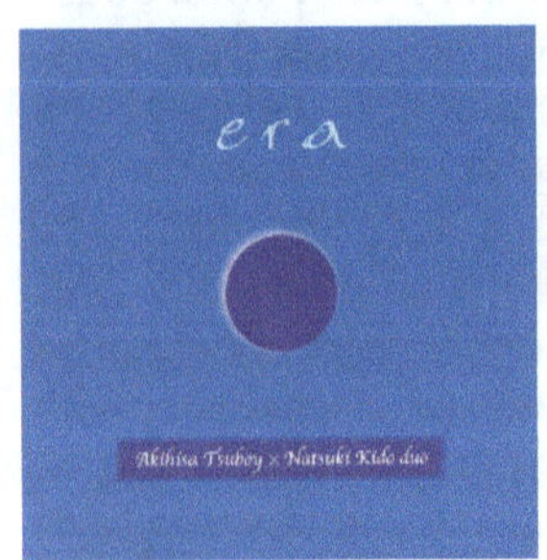

AKIHISA TSUBOY, NATSUKI KIDO DUO
ERA

The one problem with reviewing these Japanese albums that have been sent to me by Hiroshi is that it is very difficult to find out any information about the bands that I can understand. Although Poseidon do have translated pages, that is the only place to find out anything about the acts in English, which in this case is a real shame. This album was recorded live and features the partnership of Akihisa Tsuboy (violin, also in the band KBB) and Natsuki Kido on acoustic guitar. I first played it when driving down to Frome in the pouring rain and my feelings were lifted a great deal by being able to listen to this inspiring music. The songs can be soft and gentle, or can be driving and dynamic, often within the same piece of music. My favourite is the opener "Left Window" which just comes alive and the two musicians blast along on wings of passion, leaving themes only to return to them later. How can just two guys, with no overdubs, produce music of such majesty and passion? It is acoustic, and there are some folk themes, but this will appeal to a much wider audience than just folkers. But if you enjoy some of the Swarb-led pieces of Fairport of yore then this is something that you should endeavour to discover.
#72, Feb 2003

TSUKI NO UMI
SIVLE REDYC CHOWDER
This is the third album by Tsuki no Umi (which translates to Lunar Mare), released by Poseidon on their Vital Music imprint. An instrumental trio with more leanings to avant-garde jazz than to progressive rock, this is music that can be viewed as being quite challenging. There are times, okay make that most of the time, when the musicians appear to be working against each other instead of towards a common goal. The recording is not as good as it might be, and there are no overdubs, but this is an album where the listener had to be there instead of envisaging the experience. While they are clever at what they do, it wouldn't hurt to have stronger compositions. Difficult listening to say the least, but at least the three tracks come in at only thirty-one minutes long.
#81, Dec 2004

TSUNAMI
ANTHEM OF THE GREAT WAVE
Here is another band on the Music Is Intelligence label, which I am afraid I know nothing about. I think they are German, but of course I may well be wrong. Tsunami are a very guitar oriented prog band, with vocalist Alexander IV, as well as Marc de Dombayrre and Grodth Van Jaddon (who also plays keyboards) all contributing fretwork. What is a little surprising therefore, is that the guitars are not much more to the fore? Although the technical rock, a la classic Rush, is very enjoyable, I get the feeling that in concert the band are very much heavier than in the studio. This detracts somewhat to the very pleasant, although not earth-shattering, album. Opener "Spiderchess" is probably the best, with some soaring vocals and guitar breaks but the epic "Tsunami", which clocks in at just under twenty minutes, is worth mention with the extremely slow atmospheric build up. 'Anthem Of The Great Wave' is a good album, with some highlights, but these are few and far between.
#32, Dec 1995

LA TULIPE NOIRE
FADED LEAVES
Now this is something of a rarity, a new progressive rock album from Greece. It has been a long time since Aphrodite's Child and Vangelis hit the scene and this band is quite a different prospect. This is the third album from La Tulipe Noire (seems unusual to have a French name when they are Greek), and does seem to be a very mature work. They are a five-piece with a female vocalist in Irma, and this is thoughtful prog in many ways. Not only is the music structured and complex when it is required, it can also be simple and spacious. Irma has a very clear voice, and never strains so that she comes over almost as a female

version of Jon Anderson. There are some deep and meaningful lyrics, which deserve reading (thankfully the whole album is performed in English) and I am somewhat surprised not to have heard of this band before. It will not suit everyone, as while the songs are interesting and enjoyable, they do little in breaking new territory. They are probably more Floydian than many of the neo-prog bands around but there are still tinges of Marillion here and there. The result is a work that is very polished, and at times almost beautiful, and is certainly worth hearing even if it is not the most essential release of the year.
#70, Oct 2002

TWELFTH NIGHT
COLLECTOR'S ITEM

What an introduction this is to one of the UK's most under-rated progressive bands of the Eighties: if there is any justice in the world this band would have been mega huge. This is a compilation, taking in songs from albums together with some especially recorded items. It is impossible not to fall in love with this record, as even before starting the player you can see that you are onto a good thing as it is more than seventy-eight minutes long but only contains eight songs! There is a complete history of the band, as well as all the lyrics and recording details, meaning that the relative newcomer can sit back and enjoy the music without wondering what it is all about. There are songs here featuring both main singers employed by the band, namely Geoff Mann and Andy Sears, and I personally feel that Geoff added an extra element, both with his lyrics and vocals. Two relatively short songs mean that there is just room on this CD for two epics. "Sequences" is the one live song and tells the story of a solider at the front during the First World War. Geoff takes on many differing vocals parts, being at times the soldier, the sergeant major and the colonel. Musically it is also a song of many parts with loads of light and shade contrasting. I like Marillion, but "Forgotten Sons" just cannot compare with the depth of lyrics and musical ability contained herein. During the song, there is a quiet spell, broken by an officer's whistle and a voice shouting "Okay lads, over the top we go". Keyboards help us over the lip of the trench and then there is some frenetic guitarwork really giving the impression of all hell breaking loose and being under fire. Fantastic.

The other epic is "The Collector", clocking at more than nineteen minutes. It was a song written with Geoff that was first played in the summer of 1983, but with Geoff leaving in that November it was never recorded (although it had been played live). When the idea for the compilation came about, the original group reformed to put the record straight and went into the studio to get it down on tape. The song contains many themes and counter themes running throughout and is musically as well as lyrically incredibly complex. There is a long hallucinatory passage where the collector imagines seeing his old nanny at the foot his bed. The vocal style used on this passage contrast greatly with the choirboy style of the previous ones, which is totally different to that of the passage before. At no times can this be said to be a 'heavy' song, but more in the style of classic Genesis. The compilation closes with a re-recorded "Love Song". This was the closer to many a

Twelfth Night concert, the gentle acoustic guitar combined with sensitive keyboards and Geoff's melodic voice provides for a real coming together. It was originally recorded as being a brighter counterbalance to the gloomy lyrics on 'Fact and Fiction', where it appeared. As the song progresses there is a sense of oneness and you feel that you could wrap your arms around the person nearest and sing it out at the top of your voice. I can give this album no greater praise except to say that this it up there with 'Nothing Is Written' as my album of the year. Thankfully this should be available in all record stores, not just specialist outfits.
#11, Dec 1991

TWELFTH NIGHT
LIVE AND LET LIVE

In 1983 everything seemed to be going well for Twelfth Night, and then in September of that year vocalist Geoff Mann dropped the bombshell that he wanted to leave the band. So, the decision was made to play some final dates, and to record them for posterity. This took place at The Marquee on November 4th and 5th, and was watched by 735 people, with many more being turned away because the venue was full. Each show lasted two hours with the band playing five encores each night. It was not financially possible to have the sets fully recorded, but the engineers left the tape running during the encores on the second night and duly presented the band with an unexpected present. These songs were recorded directly onto two-track tape, so no later enhancements or alterations were possible. Originally, they were going to release the album on their own label, where it would have been TN007 (hence the idea of using a James Bond-style title), but Music For Nations stepped in to release it instead. The album was deleted in 1991 and has only now been made available on CD by SI Music who have endeavoured to present as good a package as possible, and much thought has gone into the presentation. There is a full history of the band, all the lyrics, loads of interesting facts, and a piece on Geoff to whom the album is dedicated. The sound has been cleaned up, and to make the CD even more complete they have added three songs not originally on the album. These are all encores from the second night and are "Creepshow", "East of Eden" and "Love Song".

The album kicks off with "The Ceiling Speaks", and it really does kick as both Clive and Andy riff those guitars (bass being provided by the keyboards for this song). Rightfully seen as a classic, it comes through with all the force and power of a rock band in full flow. You can feel the energy as Geoff dominates the stage: if anyone thinks that prog rock can be boring do not forget that first and foremost it is rock, and here is the band that should have been the biggest of them all. They were certainly the best! The sound has transferred well to CD and it plays just nicely at maximum volume. Next up is "The End of the Endless Majority", an instrumental written especially for the occasion. It shows off the slower more atmospheric side to the band, and leads well into the first of the three epics, "We Are Sane". This twelve-minute masterpiece describes the world where everyone plugs a little box into their head each day which tells them what to do and when to do it. "If the thought processes of an individual can be permanently limited to the point of strict conformity to an outside source of thought the said individual may no longer be considered as such". There is everything here that one could possibly want from a song, loads of emotion and many differing styles while always staying interesting. A great version of a great song. This leads into "Fact and Fiction", which is introduced by Geoff and Clive acting out parts of British and Russian leaders discussing nuclear war. "We are prepared to abandon war at any time as long as the other side does it first". The keyboard driven song is all about nuclear war and Geoff strides the stage spitting venom "And if the unthinkable should happen, and you hear the sirens call, well you can always find some shelter, behind a door against the wall, don't make me laugh!". This leads into the instrumental "The Poet Sniffs A Flower" which just envelops the listener and takes them into a magical world. A seventeen-minute masterpiece is next, namely "Sequences". I reviewed this back in #11 (this version also appears on 'Collector's Item') when I said it was fantastic, but really that does not do the song justice. Telling the story of soldiers in WWI, it is certainly one of the best examples of music and lyrics fitting together in perfection. When the lads get sent "over the top" the keyboards make you feel that it is happening, and when all hell breaks loose you are there dodging the bullets. Breath-taking, exhilarating and exhausting, all at the same time.

That is where the original album ends, but the CD continues with "Creepshow" which after "Sequences" seems quite a short song at only twelve minutes long. The difference in sound quality is not noticeable, which is surprising when these last three songs were only recorded on two-track. Geoff has no need to sing on this as the crowd provides all the vocals required, but he dominates throughout as the band go through all the intricacies of this complicated piece. Back to a far rockier number as "East of Eden" blasts out. The band are giving everything, and the extremely knackered crowd respond once again. The final song was the last song performed by Geoff on the last night he was in Twelfth Night. It is only fitting that this is "Love Song". When I got the CD, this was the first song I played, and I confess that I sat in front of the CD player with tears rolling down my face. There is so much emotion in this, one of the most beautiful songs ever written. Geoff sings his heart out for the very last time and the crowd are singing it with him and for him. Even now, having played it many times, it still brings a lump to my throat.

'Live and Let Live' is a fitting epitaph for Geoff: possibly Twelfth Night's finest gigs are captured here on CD. They were all in fine form those nights, giving Geoff a fitting farewell. Here is a live album that captures the emotion and pain for a band at the very peak of their career. If you do not buy any other live album this year, you must buy this one.
#19, Aug 1993

TWELFTH NIGHT
SMILING AT GRIEF
'Smiling At Grief' was recorded in two separate sessions back in 1981 (during the period between the two sessions keyboard player Rick Battersby left the band, although he would return after 'Fact and Fiction'). As 'Live At The Target' had been released only nine months earlier the recordings were initially only meant to demo new material, the first with a certain Mr. Geoff Mann. While in the studio they made the decision to record

the lengthy instrumental "Fur Helene Pt. 2" as it was no longer to feature in the live set, which meant that they had enough material for an album: a decision was made to release it only on cassette and to sell it at gigs. It has now been reissued on CD, remastered by drummer Brian Devoil, who has done much to keep the Twelfth Night name flying over recent years. It now has additional artwork (care of Geoff) and some previously unreleased songs, which makes this indispensable for TN fans. If you have never come across these guys before then you should be truly ashamed, as they released the best progressive rock album of the Eighties, 'Fact and Fiction', as well as one of the best live progressive albums of all time in 'Live and Let Live'. This album starts with "East of Eden", which was the song they performed on the David Essex Showcase in 1982. It is a typical TN song with strong lyrics and emotional vocals, driven by powering guitars and keyboards that were rarely at the forefront of what they were doing, but were extremely important, nonetheless. As with some of the other songs, the multi-talented Clive Mitten, not content with just providing bass and extra guitar, provided keyboards while guitarist Andy Revell and drummer Brian Devoil completed the line-up.

"This City" is a gentler song, carried along by the tortured vocals. Geoff was one of rock's top singers, with a style all his own that was instantly recognisable; it was no wonder that Andy Sears had such a hard job replacing him when he left. However, it is for track number four that Geoff will probably be most fondly remembered when people talk about this album. "Creepshow" is the song on which he was at his most menacing, almost frightening in his intensity. The music provides the perfect backdrop, as it is gentle and swaying while at the same time giving the impression that all is not quite right. Is it the bass solo that does it? Or that drum break? Gradually the menace increases, and the tempo picks up until Geoff screams the scream of a madman when it is far different to that of the earlier piece. It is Clive's bass playing that leads a lot of the melody, while Andy moves from background to menace with equal ease. On the superb live video available from Brian, Andy wonderfully handles this song, but he can't quite capture the intensity that can be found here. "Puppets" is a far more straight-ahead prog song, dominated by keyboards, and proves a welcome respite from what has gone before. "Fur Helene Pt. 2" showcases the band's instrumental abilities. There was magic between the five of them that lasted for far too short a period.

If you have not come across the guys before then I urge you to check out 'Collector's Item' (a superb introduction to the band with a good bio and photos), 'Live and Let Live' (the superb recordings of Geoff's final gigs) or 'Fact and Fiction' (the classic). When you have heard any of these then turn your attention to this wonderful re-release. Brian says that he has unearthed another twenty-five unissued songs, but it is up to us if they are ever released. I firmly believe that there is a market for progressive rock in the UK, and no one does it better than Twelfth Night.
#43, Aug 1997

TWELFTH NIGHT
COLLECTOR'S ITEM

There are plans to re-release much Twelfth Night material over the next few months, and Cyclops have started with this reissue of the 1991 compilation. The original release saw not only previously available TN masterpieces, but also the classic line-up recording the epic "The Collector" and a new version of "Love Song". To have these two songs alone made the collection a 'must have' for the hardened fan, so why go out ten years later and get the album again? Originally the compilation started with "Sequences" from the 'Live and Let Live' album. Rightfully viewed as one of their finest pieces, this most visual of songs dealt with a soldier's life in the First World War. Cyclops have already reissued that album and have dropped the song from this reissue. This has given them a lot of room, and they have replaced it with three other songs.

A Twelfth Night gig started with "The Ceiling Speaks", with both Clive Mitten and Andy Revell providing guitars – there was no room for bass. Like many TN fans I never thought that a studio recording had been made, but I was wrong!! It was one of four songs recorded in a session for MGM in 1983. This version does not capture the raw energy, but it comes pretty close. Next up is "Deep In The Heartland" from the same recordings. Historically this is interesting for the fan as it was reworked to become "Not On The Map" which in turn became "Blondon Fair" (which is also on this release). The other 'new' song is "Last Song", which appears on CD for the first time. What can be said about the other songs? How can anyone not listen to the power and majesty of "We Are Sane", one of the most epic of songs dealing with control of individual. "Art and Illusion" is the bubbly riposte to the previous more thoughtful number, with Andy Sears making his first appearance.

The album starts with Geoff's songs, then into Andy, but finishing with the new recordings featuring Geoff. Unlike Genesis, there is not such a huge musical shift between the two versions of the band, but many fans still favour the Mann. "The Collector" is one their longest studio recordings, at just over nineteen minutes, and to me epitomises all that was great about the band. Musically it hits many differing areas, and Geoff stretches himself both vocally and lyrically. It is one of the longest and most complex Christian songs ever released. And as the gig started with "The Ceiling Speaks", so it always ended with "Love Song". A song that is so full of passion that I can never fail to be moved emotionally when I hear it. Even before I received the reissue this was an album that I have been playing regularly since its' initial release.

The new tracks make it an even better collection and along with 'Live And Let Live' should be in every proghead's collection. Apparently, their great studio album 'Fact & Fiction' is going to be next, with many previously unreleased bonus songs. I can't wait.
#65, Dec 2001

TWELFTH NIGHT
FACT AND FICTION

How to review an album that I and many others view as one of the finest of its' kind? 'Fact and Fiction' remains to this day a supremely impressive album which captures a band at the pinnacle of their studio career. This is a reissue by Cyclops that manages to give us seven bonus songs on top of the original eight and restores the cover to its' original format (the MSI release had a negative cover, i.e. black on white instead of white on black). There is also a history of the recording process provided by Brian and overall this is a reissue that more than justifies purchase again even if you already own the MSI CD. But what is all the fuss about? Twelfth Night were the band that should have had the success of Marillion at least, and if Geoff hadn't decided to become a minister who knows what they might have achieved.

But back in the early Eighties the band had been reduced to a four-piece with the departure of keyboard player Rick Battersby, who later returned. This left the core line-up of Geoff Mann (vocals), Clive Mitten (bass, classical guitar, keyboards), Andy Revell (electric and acoustic guitars) and Brian Devoil (drums). The recording process took a year, during which time Marillion started to gain a lot of attention so the band decided to shift the attention away from some more commercial elements and dropped some numbers and rewrote others. The result was a progressive masterpiece.

The album starts with the second longest song, in "We Are Sane". Gentle held-down keyboards with Geoff singing falsetto and, in the background, there are the sounds of children playing and a radio being tuned. Gradually Geoff sings lower, the keyboards come down and the sense of menace starts to appear. Percussion starts not with Brian on drums but on typewriter as "Reports flop into the in trays". Even from very early in the album it becomes apparent that Twelfth Night just were not like any other prog band that was around at the time, or since. Prog bands often today are likened to Genesis, Marillion and IQ but rarely to TN. "We Are Sane" is about a Big Brother society where individuals are controlled by a small box they plug into their brains each day. The music swirls and changes, being beautiful and refreshing, or rocking and dramatic, as the need arises. There is a spoken word passage; all tricks utilised to make the song unusual and classic.

Following that is the more laid back "Human Being" which not only contains one of my favourite lyrics in any song ("If every time we tell a lie a little fairy dies; they must be building death camps in the garden") but also a powerful bass solo which is one of the best bass riffs ever. "This City" again starts slowly, with children in the background and in some ways is almost Floydian, except with far more menace and emotion from the Mann. It is stark and barren, with Geoff in total control. Next up is a small instrumental "World Without End" which acts as a gentle keyboard bridge into the title cut. It may only be four minutes long, but this keyboard dominated piece is one of their more powerful and thought provoking, all with no guitar! Given the current climate this song seems even more poignant "If the unthinkable should happen, and you hear the sirens call, Well you can always find some shelter behind a door against the wall, Don't make me laugh!!". This also gives way to an instrumental, "The Poet Sniffs A Flower" which features acoustic guitar and keyboards in gentle harmony until the drums kick in and they are off and racing, as they lead into the longest track on the album, the one with which Geoff will always be associated, "Creepshow". It starts gently enough, and we are invited into the creep show to see the exhibits (as in "Karn Evil 9", but here with an even more damning indictment on society). It is gentle, lulling and simple, or dramatic, rocking and complex. It can be a breaking voice, pure melody or a spoken statement of fact, whichever way you look at it this is one of the most important prog songs ever.

Given all the horrors and complexity that has gone on before, the only way to end the album was with a gentle number that gave the listener the chance to reflect. "Love Song" is pure and delicate, as Geoff sings about the power of love and what it can achieve. It is a song of restrained emotion here in the studio, which became an outpouring when performed in concert (listen to 'Live And Let Live' to get some idea). It builds and builds in tempo, on from the acoustic guitar to a more powerful prog rock number and to put it simply, out of all the many thousands of songs I have heard over the years, this is my number one.

Of course, that was where the original album ended but now there are the bonus numbers. "East Of Eden" was one of the band's most powerful stomping rock numbers (and was the song they performed on the David Essex Showcase!) and had originally been destined for the album but was instead released as a single along with "Eleanor Rigby". The band were not particularly noted for their cover versions, but this is a great take with the song taken from the Sixties into the Eighties and now imbued with the dramatic vocals of Geoff. "Constant (Fact and Fiction)" has nothing in common with "Fact and Fiction" and sounds like Geoff and Clive and a drum machine and is interesting, but was a work in progress, and was never developed any further. "Fistful Of Bubbles" shows the band experimenting with an almost reggae style in the chorus, and much more in the way of emotional guitar and is interesting but again was a work in progress. To the fan it is "Leader" that is by far the more interesting demo, as this is a song that had musically built out of a number called "Afghan Red" and would in turn become "Fact And Fiction". The verse is musically almost the same, with some of the final lyrics, and it is fascinating. "Dancing In The Dream" is a poptastic keyboard led song that is fun and is a song I have found myself singing. It reminds me of Men Without Hats and I wonder if a finished version of this had been released as a single what would have happened? The last song is a different version of "Human Being" which is only just over half the length of the finished article. Musically it is quite different and is more dynamic with in your face keyboards. The band seems to be bounding along on this much more rockified version.

So, there you have it, an album that should have been in every music lover's collection prior to this Cyclops reissue and definitely should be there now. Forget labels, this is music of the highest quality that deserves to be heard. An album that is now over twenty years old yet is relevant and powerful. Superb.
#73, Apr 2003

TWELFTH NIGHT
ART AND ILLUSION

So, having released one of the most important prog albums (ever!) and then managing to lose their vocalist, the next studio album was going to be very important for TN. They had said goodbye to Geoff with the double live album 'Live And Let Live' and they now had to introduce a new singer. Due to the current interest in the band they decided to release only a mini album on MFN and to save some of their longer, more progressive, works for another album that they planned to have out at the beginning of 1985. And so, it was that in August 1984 they recorded the five songs that were to feature on the album to be released in the October. This was their only album to make the national charts (hitting the heights of 83!) and gained acclaim for their punchy outlook. "Counterpoint" opens the album with gentle riffing and long held-down keyboards chords as the bass starts to drive the song along. This song lives on the strong rhythm section and soaring vocals which prove right from the off that even though Geoff was unique, they had a new talent in TN fan Andy Sears. While more straightforward, he had a strong voice with great range, and was not averse to putting in odd inflections that meant that he was not a straightforward rock singer.

The title cut is up next, a song already well known to TN fans, as it was a number performed by Geoff but not recorded. This is one of the band's bounciest numbers, full of energy and enthusiasm. Instrumental "C.R.A.B." showed yet again that the band had an extremely solid bassist in Clive Mitten while Brian pinned down the beat, which allowed Rick and Andy Revell to move away and move the melody around. "Kings & Queens" has probably the heaviest section on the album, although the introduction does not give that impression. It cuts and changes, moving from dynamic rock to soaring vocals with a sparse background, solid from start to finish. "First New Day" is one of my favourite TN numbers, simple and pleasant, yet strikingly dynamic and hard-hitting at the same time. While the atmosphere is mostly in the music, it is the vocals that combine with it to give this song such a strong edge.

And this is where the album finished, but not now. What follows are the three tracks that the band was paid to record as demos by MCA in May 1984. If 'Art & Illusion' had been a full album, then these would probably had been on it as well. These three were "Blue Powder Monkey", "Blondon Fair" and "Take A Look", two of which were re-recorded for 'XII'. The first of these has a rather lightweight guitar riff, and is not one of my personal favourites, but that gives way to the very much Japan-esque "Blondon Fair" which is a classic in every sense of the word. This is total atmosphere, yet after the introduction seems to take on a life of its own. "Take A Look" comes in at twelve minutes, and not a second of it is wasted. Yet again this is one of their best songs, although this version sounds recognisably different to their later version, particularly in the vocals which were strengthened. As if that was not enough, the album closes with alternate versions of four of the original songs. The booklet is crammed full of photos, information by Andy Sears and Brian, as well as all the lyrics. So, what are you waiting for, if you are a proghead buy now!!!!!
#76, Oct 2003

TWELFTH NIGHT
LIVE AT THE TARGET

Following the departure of Elektra Macleod, the band felt that they could continue just fine as an instrumental act but that they had to re-establish themselves so decided to release their first full-length album. Recorded over two nights at The Target in Reading in January 1981 and released a month later it made it into both the Hippy and Heavy Metal charts in Sounds and gained them their first publishing and distribution deals. Although this album had previously been unofficially released on CD by the French label MSI, this was the first time I had heard the album myself and was certainly intrigued as to what it would be like.

The original album contained four songs, but as one of these took up all the second side (this was vinyl after all) that is probably not surprising. Musically they are tight, as one would expect given that they had just played 31 concerts in 50 days, and come across very similar musically to how they would sound when they were joined by Geoff, but also at times with elements that one would probably now associate more with Ozric Tentacles. While they could be dreamy, they also prove what a powerful rock band they were. The extra element to the music is provided by Clive Mitten who was an incredible bassist and while the others are certainly no slouches it his playing that gives them the edge. It was "Sequences" that I wanted to hear, and I am amazed at how little the arrangement had to be adapted to allow for Geoff's vocals and lyrics when he joined. This release contains notes from Brian and loads of photos but also three bonus songs from the same era which combines to make this an indispensable release for any fan. Next in the Cyclops reissue series should be 'Smiling At Grief', which should then be followed by two CDs of previously unreleased material.
#82, Jan 2005

TWELFTH NIGHT
SMILING AT GRIEF – LIVE

This is the first in what is planned to be a series of limited-edition CD-R's being put together by Brian Devoil and Mark Hughes. I am afraid to say that if you have not already got this then you are too late, as it has already sold out, so if you are a fan of one of the UK's finest ever progressive rock acts then get onto the internet and join one of the mailing groups such as the Yahoo group 'Fact and Fiction'. Brian is a regular contributor to that one, and Andy Sears has also been known to take part. There was lot of excitement about this on the mailing group when it was released, the reason being that this is the only known live recording by the four-piece line-up of the band when it was Geoff Mann, Andy Revell, Clive Mitten and Brian. With the departure of keyboard player Rick Battersby, it obviously affected the way that they could play live, as although Clive could play keyboards it is a bit difficult to do that and attack a bass at the same time (although he does try). Geoff does assist on 'two finger' keyboards, but this was a band very much still finding their feet as Geoff had still only been in the band four months at this point. The result is a set list that includes songs that were quickly dropped, to some that stayed

in the set all the way to the end, so it is interesting to hear them in their formative stages. Each fan of the band will look to this recording for different things, but for me it is hearing two songs in particular that make this essential. The first of these is "Creepshow", ten minutes of Geoff firmly stamping his persona into a song which somehow becomes much more than that. The second is "Sequences" – this twenty-minute epic was already a firm instrumental favourite before Geoff joined, but by adding his lyrics and his vocal trademarks he definitely took this song to the next level. It is interesting to compare this to the 'Live and Let Live' version as by then it was polished and with Rick back on board it became a different beast but here it is a rough diamond.
#84, July 2005

TWELFTH NIGHT
A MIDSUMMER NIGHT'S DREAM

TWELFTH NIGHT
THE CORNER OF THE WORLD TOUR

TWELFTH NIGHT
XII

It has been quite a year for Twelfth Night fans, with Brian Devoil and Mark Hughes raiding the archives and releasing limited editions of gigs that they felt were important. In fact, they have been so popular that the number being produced has had to be increased. 'A Midsummer Night's Dream' captures the band as an instrumental four-piece at Reading University Student's Union on June 27th, 1980. This was where the band first got together so it is of no surprise that they feel very much at home. Given the complexity of the music that they were performing it was not surprising that there no vocals, there just is not the room (or at least there does not appear to be). This is a recording from the soundboard, so it means that the music is very clear, even if some of the audience noise has been lost. In many ways, they remind me of Ozric Tentacles, or at least how the Ozrics would sound like if someone lit a rocket behind them and turned them into a more in your face rock act. This is instrumental progressive rock as its best; it does not get much better than this. And to hear Andy say that the band will be supporting a band called The VIPs at their next gig is just priceless.

From the early days, then up to the very end. The 'Corner Of The World' tour in May 1985 saw the band road testing songs that had been written during a four-month break. The two-album deal with Music For Nations was complete, and they were now looking for a major record deal. This double CD set uses songs from four venues, as for some reason not any recording from the tour contains the complete set so this has now been lovingly recreated. The first disc features the main set while the second contains the encores and some additional versions, and it is stated on the disc what is recorded where. By now the band's sound had expanded, with Rick bringing his keyboards to the fore. Musically they had changed; they were now a band with a singer as opposed to instrumental so there had to be room for the vocals, but this hadn't changed their outlook. Listening to "We Are Sane" still brings shivers down the spine, with Andy doing justice to Geoff's words. But Andy Sears was chosen because he had a great voice and presence and this shines through particularly on his own numbers such as "Take A Look". Here was a band that were again building on the momentum they had lost when Geoff had departed, no-one ever thought that the version of "Love Song" that closes this set would be the last song that Twelfth Night would ever perform onstage.

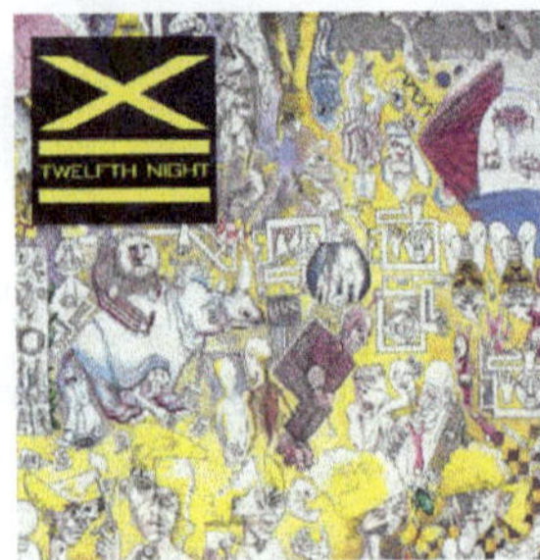

Take a progressive rock band and put them in a studio with a producer and give them fifty-four tracks to play with and the chances are they will use all of them and that is exactly what happened with 'XII'. Signed at long last to a major the band were going to go all out to produce a seminal work – but it did not sell as well as the record company would have liked and soon the band were no more. Strangely it has taken until now for this to be released on CD, although there has been a lot of pressure from fans for years who always refer to this album not as 'XII' but as 'The Virgin Album'. But here it is, remastered, with all the completed songs that they ever recorded for Virgin, combined with three rough mixes which takes the original nine songs up to fifteen. There are times here when Andy comes across as quite Gabriel-esque, but it easy to see that this is an album from a band that have been plying their craft on the road for many years.

It is complex and complicated with a lot going on (remember those 54 tracks) yet also in many ways it is quite simple. "Blue Powder Monkey" is a powering rock song featuring great vocals while in album closer "Take A Look" in all its eleven plus minute glory there is a progressive classic. The sound is superb, and the booklet now contains extensive notes from Andy Revell, as well as from Andy Sears and Brian Devoil. It is a very different TN album to those that had gone before, and while to my ears it does not contain the power and emotion of 'Fact And Fiction' there are very few albums that could ever compete with that.

So, here are three 'new' releases from a band that never had a hit single and broke up nearly twenty years ago. These are reminders of just how good this band was, and the way that fans have reacted show that there is still a place for their music today. Listening to this in the car, I was driving through Bradford when I saw a poster advertising a lavish performance of Twelfth Night. Sadly, it was for a play, but if only it were for a gig……
#85, Nov 2005

TWELFTH NIGHT
ENTROPY

TWELFTH NIGHT
FLASHBACKS

TWELFTH NIGHT
NIGHT VISION

Here we move onto numbers five, six and seven in the CD-R series being co-ordinated by Brian with the assistance of Mark Hughes. 'Entropy' is first up, recorded in Northampton on 29th March 1981. The band were still an instrumental quartet at the time and were touring to promote their 'Live At The Target' and second tape album. It was during this period that they played at The Marquee for the very first time. Songs were often being redeveloped and changed back then, but what is particularly important about this album is that it marks the first time on CD for the song "Entropy", a fourteen-minute workout that had been around since the earliest days of the band but this was the first time that it had been performed in a completed form. There still are not many bands within the progressive rock genre that are brave enough to perform as an instrumental act but the reason that Twelfth Night could do so was because they were playing well-structured songs, not just workouts, it was just that they did not have a singer. This set also includes other well-known numbers such as "Afghan Red" and "Sequences", and I do enjoy Andy asking the audience not to leave between sets but to go and buy some merchandise from the lovely lady "wearing very tight blue trousers".

'Flashbacks' is taken mainly from a show at The Marquee in July 1983, plus three more songs recorded in Gwent exactly a month later. The reason for this is that The Marquee show was heralded as being the first ever performance of the epic "The Collector" (in fact it had been tried out nine days earlier at Woolwich Tramshed), but the recording of that song is incomplete so there is a full version from 7 days later (the version from the Marquee is less than 17 minutes long and the Gwent one is over 20). I bought a tape of this gig from Brian many years ago and have lost count of how many times I have heard it, but it is great to have it in this format with the sound cleaned up. This CD includes the infamous "Saatchi & Saatchi" piece, where Geoff reads out a script for a TV ad prior to dedicating the next song to them, "We Are Sane". The band were really cooking, and the crowd were well into it. There is a real power and passion to an early "Art & Illusion" (which has different lyrics to the final version) while "The Collector" still stands up as real highlight, alongside other classics such as "Sequences", "We Are Sane" and "The Ceiling Speaks".

Unlike the other two albums, 'Night Vision' is not taken from just one performance but instead various sources have been used to provide a complete set list from the 1984 'Art & Illusion' tour. The band are as tight as one could imagine, while Andy Sears is in fine

voice. The first disc ends with the longest song (caused by equipment problems which means that they have major issues with the guitar), "Take A Look". It may have an unusual start but possibly due to this the band kick it into gear when these have been resolved. This has always been one of my favourite songs from this era of the band and when Andy finally makes it to the chorus it feels as if the roof is going to be lifted off Hemel Hempstead. He was a very different singer to Geoff and uses his range here to best effect. There is also a bonus here as on the second disc there are also the songs broadcast by Radio 1 of their set at the Kerrang! Festival at Caister. These releases are indispensable to fans of the band, and thanks to the guys for putting in so much work to make these available.
#86, Feb 2006

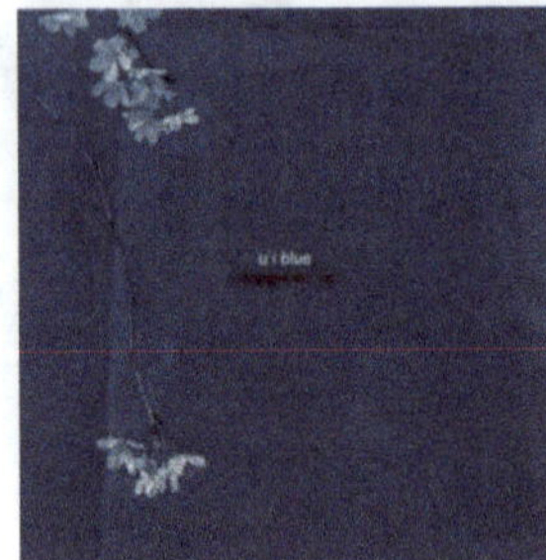

U I BLUE
SONGBIRD'S CRY

U I Blue is a new band, formed around the husband and wife team of Jon Paul and Laura Lindstrom. It is interesting to read the comments by Jon Paul on their website as he says that in his wife Laura, he has found his muse, "it is with her in mind that the album was written, recorded and now performed. Without her, U I Blue is but a meandering musical effort amounting to nothing." Among the guest musicians who are have assisted in this recording I noticed the names of Terry Clouse, Steve Babb and Fred Schendel from Glass Hammer, but first and foremost this album is built around the vocals of Laura. Imagine a Kate Bush who has been calmed down and added to Enya and Sandy Denny then you may just get close to her voice and the feel of the music. Although the backing can be dreamy and reflective, or more in the face with the use of acoustic guitars as well as the swathes of keyboards, it is her vocals that stand out. Jon Paul also has a very effective voice and he combines well with Laura but often the effect is to make hers stand out even more. Although one would expect there to be many progressive influences on this album due to some of the personnel involved, this transcends any sort of categorisation and refuses to be pigeon-holed.

She may not have the overall clarity of Maddy Prior but there are times when Laura has a similar style in the way that her voice is pure and without strain of any kind. There are some gorgeous little musical interplays, such as the delicate electric guitar solo on "The Songbird's Cry Part 1", and the way that it switches from pure acoustic to pure electronic can be inspiring. The only word that can be used to describe this album is "beautiful" and I recommend it without hesitation.
#84, July 2005

ULTIME ATOME
DARK VISIONS

This French act has been together for ten years, but this is their debut album. With two epics, there are going to be quite a few progheads who will look at this and think that it is worth hearing just to see what is going on. As for me, well the jury is most definitely out, and the verdict well may not be in the band's favour when it is returned. Although the press release points towards early Marillion and Chandelier as musical reference points, I would instead turn to Aragon, with more than a hint of Twelfth Night. It has been years since I reviewed Aragon's 'Don't Bring The Rain' yet it is still a frequent visitor to my CD player, and I am convinced that the same thing has been happening over in France. Is that why the music does not seem to sit quite right with me? The guys can all play, and they have some interesting ideas with a good singer, but there are times when it just does not gel as it should. I have noticed that going back to it a few times helps, but the first time I listened to it I had problems getting all the way through it. I am not sure about this – and this is one for progheads to decide by listening prior to purchase, if possible.

#76, Oct 2003

UMPHREY'S MCGEE
ANCHOR DROPS

Apparently, this is the fifth album from Umphrey's McGee but is the first to be released in Europe. They are a rock band that jams and improvises a lot on stage (playing an average 160 gigs a year) and per the press release the music sounds as if "Steely Dan and John Coltrane cooperate to honour Frank Zappa. Mahavishnu Orchestra meets Scritti Politti. Dixie Dregs fight Police with Pearl Jam. One can hardly imagine all that. Yet there exists music that can hardly be described in a different way. This music is made by six people from the United States who act with skill rather than with a crowbar, and who obviously have a lot of fun impressing their audience repeatedly". Okay then. What we have here are six guys who very definitely know their way around their instruments, and know how to bounce ideas off each other, but to these poor jaded ears of mine there is something missing. That missing element is probably the consistency of ideas – that is not to say that they are not good, it is just that they keep blasting off musically not so much of a tangent but often in a totally different direction. Take "Uncommon", this is a great rock single which mostly contains huge homage to The Eels as well as Zappa. On its own this is a great song, but it does not seem to fit in with the rest of the album. It takes a lot of work to get through this, not because the music is bad, but just because there is so much going on and in so many different styles. Just because of the effort it is not one that I will often be returning to (and "Jajunk Pt. 1" reminds me of "Smoke On The Water" each time I play it, although it is very different), as this is more of an exercise than it is a pleasure.

#83, Mar 2005

UMPHREY'S MCGEE
SAFETY IN NUMBERS

When I reviewed the last album by Umphrey's McGee ('Anchor Drops') I possibly was not as favourable as I could be. For me it was all very clever but there was something missing, but I could not work out what it was. Obviously, the band have managed to do what I could not, as now the music is whole and complete and is something that is extremely interesting to listen to. Umphrey's McGee are one of the jam band scene, mixing blues with country, folk, bluegrass, prog, rock etc. and then taking it out on the road for 160 dates a year. Live they are heavily into improvisation but here they have reined in their natural instincts and are producing music that is complex yet also concise. Where previously they were showing just how clever they were and how well they knew their instruments now there is plenty of musical intricacy but only where it belongs within the music where it makes sense. The vocals are strong with good harmonies, and there is a far greater sense of melody throughout the album. It is extremely accessible and all the extra elements (such as the judicious use of slide guitar) and note density now add to, instead of detracting from, each of the songs. It is never going to be straightforward but here there is much more sense of purpose and direction and the result is an album that is more enjoyable that I could have expected from the guys.

#88, Jun 2006

UNBROKEN SPIRIT
DRESSED FOR DINNER

It has been quite a while since I heard so much about an unsigned band, and everyone who has heard Unbroken Spirit seems to of the same opinion: they are great and are going places. I hate being the odd one out so I suppose that I should agree with them. The band only came together at the end of 1994, with this demo being released in November last year. Unusually for a band that is being picked up heavily in prog circles, the keyboard player is notable by his absence! There is just so much going on musically that there wouldn't be room for him. Mike Barlow (guitar), Matthew Cohen (bass), and Allan Mason-Jones (drums) kick up such a wonderful hybrid of progressive and technical rock that a keyboard player wouldn't get a look in. The icing on the cake is the wonderful vocals of John Vaughan. Whether he is singing soft and quietly (as on "She Can Cry") or letting rip (as in "This Boy's Life") you know that you are in the presence of a master. Probably the band that they have most in common with is Mr So & So, not at all a bad thing in my book. They have a CD EP 'Tabula Rasa' (which means "blank scroll") coming out in June, but if you would like to hear these three songs for yourself then just send a blank tape and an SAE to the band.

#35, June 1996

UNBROKEN SPIRIT
TABULA RASA

So, four songs from the guys who are trying to prove that technical rock is alive and well and living in Wales. Wales?! Oh, well, I said in #35 just how much I was impressed with Unbroken Spirit who seem to have been picked up by the prog crowd just because they are so different to most of the hard rock acts around. Make no mistake, Unbroken Spirit are first and foremost a rock band, but the high technical aspect of their music lends itself to those fed up with three chords and loads of dandruff. "Immaculate Friends" sears along at great pace, and John shows that he is not afraid to use falsetto as an effect to totally change the feel of one line of the song. Matthew and Allan manage to keep the rhythm section tight (although there is a great deal going on), which just leaves Mike to provide some roasting lead breaks. What makes them so good is that there is so much going on from each player, but it all makes sense when combined: it is not a major ego trip on behalf of everyone. If you like Mr So & So or Rush (particularly on the beginning of "Heal"), then you will surely love this.

#36, Aug 1996

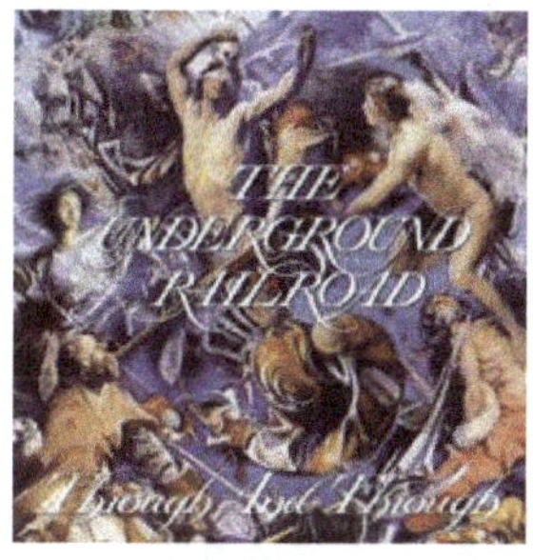

THE UNDERGROUND RAILROAD
THROUGH AND THROUGH

Bill Pohl and Kurt Rongey, both of whom have graced these pages before, with their debut releases 'Solid Earth' and 'Book In Hand' respectively, formed the Underground Railroad. In fact, they have been playing with each other for over ten years, but it was only in 1994 that they joined forces in the Bill Pohl Group. By 1997, they had the album written and felt that it was time to change the name of the band. It was not completed until the end of 1999, and was named after the longest piece, 'Through and Through", which is over twenty minutes in length. This is a very complex and complicated album, which takes a great deal of listening to. They have obviously been influenced by the UK Canterbury scene, and have also taken on elements of King Crimson's more experimental work and some jazz. The result is that while undoubtedly clever, it sometimes takes the listener into areas that are unexpected. While this is not in itself a bad thing, I did sometimes get the impression that this was complexity just for its' own sake instead of following a musical thread. This is a difficult album, but one that someone into experimental and jazz-based prog may enjoy.

#60, Oct 2000

UPRIGHT
OPINION

Upright were originally formed in 1996 but soon broke up. Seven years later bassist Eric Martin decided to put the band back together, and although two of the original line-up were unable to re-join, suitable replacements were soon found. 'Opinion' is their debut album, and is within the genre favoured by Unicorn Records, namely jazz with a hint of

prog about it. This is an instrumental album yet even though all the music has been composed by Eric, it is not as bass led as one might imagine. The sax is as often the lead as the guitar, with the keyboards generally playing a secondary role. However, although there is no doubting the musicianship of those involved, I did find that my attention was soon wandering. This is background music, or music that should be in smoky club. Production is good, but this is not likely to be an album that I often return to.

#79, May 2004

VAN & BORNER
MIRACLES

Barbara Zielińska-Van and Sabina Borner both play synth, and with some guests on guitar and bass have released this album through Ars Mundi in Poland. It is an electronic album and I found that the artist that I was most reminded of throughout was Enya, very much so. But although the first song does seem interesting, by the time that one gets through to the third or fourth there is a little voice just crying out for something different, like Sepultura for example! It is just so bland, that it becomes an effort to listen to it all the way through. Not one that I will be returning to in a hurry. *#80, Jul 2004*

VANDEN PLAS
THE GOD THING

This is German band Vanden Plas's third full album, following on from the debut 'Colour Temple'. The same line-up has been together since 1990, and this shows in the tightness of the music. One thing the band has done, which is different to most of their contemporaries is that they have been heavily involved in the theatre, and from October 1992 until April 1994 the whole band were participating in "Jesus Christ Superstar" at the State Theatre in Saarbrücken, which they then followed with several performances of "Little Shop of Horrors". If that was not enough, vocalist Andy Kuntz then took on a leading role in "The Rocky Horror Picture Show". So, you have probably decided that this is a bunch of wimps, happiest when playing their version of Andrew Lloyd Webber's Greatest Hits. Nothing could be further from the truth. Vanden Plas inhabit the same music area as bands such as Threshold or Dream Theater and while arguably it could be described as 'progressive rock', in reality this is melodic hard rock with some bombastic keyboards thrown in for good measure. Opener "Fire Blossom" starts life as a repeated piano melody which is soon joined by the bass, then the guitar, and suddenly the band are playing as one with the guitar crunching out the original melody while a new keyboard line is provided over the top. Not afraid to change the mood with acoustic guitar halfway through, they can totally change the manner of the

music at the drop of a hat. This is an instrumental, which leads into “Rainmaker”, which is even more in your face than the previous number. There is a great bass riff and then just when it could not possibly get any more frantic, it all becomes gentle so that Andy can sing quietly. This is just a brief respite as it turns into a catchy hard rock song. If you want to discover a great progressive melodic hard rock band, then now could not be a better time to do just that.
#51, Jan 1999

VANDEN PLAS
FAR OFF GRACE
Although released on Inside Out and being described as progressive metal this album has little to do with the world of prog. This is a melodic hard rock band that has far more in common with Stratovarius than they do with IQ, and a band they sound quite like is Savatage, who they have toured with in the past. Although they are clever, and I know that I ought to like this, I could not get a handle on it somehow. There is a spark missing somewhere. That is not to say that this is a bad album, far from it, but even though the guitars and keyboards sometimes rattle along at breath-taking speed and intensity I found myself easily distracted. Perhaps it needs to be played a great many times to be fully admired, but as I probably will not be returning to it again, I do not think that I will ever find out.
#57, Mar 2000

VANDEN PLAS
BEYOND DAYLIGHT
This is prog metal at its very best, nothing more, nothing less. From beginning to end this is the album that Vanden Plas have been threatening since their debut. Just playing the first song, “Nightwalker”, was enough to convince me that I was listening to a winner - everything about it is top quality, from the melodies to the harmony vocals, from the keyboard runs to the riffs to the drumming powering the song from the production to the sheer quality that shines throughout. They have toured with bands like Dokken and Dream Theater in the past and those bands need to keep an eye on what this band is doing. It is the sort of prog technical rock that the Germans can be very good at and this is certainly better than most. They are not all about brashness of course, there is piano and, sometimes, acoustic guitar, but it is when they are combining all the elements such as during the introduction of “Cold Wind" that sets the scene. There is a power ballad in the beautiful “Healing Tree”, and the gentle acoustic guitar at the beginning of “End Of All Days” is literally blistered off the CD by some stunning electric guitar runs. The band show that they are brimming with confidence as they are not afraid to approach an anthemic rocker like “Free The Fire” or even the bonus song “Point Of Know Return”. This is a great album that will be getting some serious airtime in my house.
#67, Apr 2002

VANISHING POINT
TANGLED IN DREAM

This is the second album from the Australian progressive metal band, but the first since they signed to Limb Music and consequently the first to be easily available in Europe. Having already kicked up a storm with a dynamic performance at Wacken, the German press have been eagerly awaiting this album, and it is easy to see why. This six-piece just oozes confidence and puts hard rock melodies and styles against more progressive and melodic ideas that crafts a sound that will be enjoyed by anyone who thinks that Stratovarius are the high point of this genre. They are not afraid to bring in ideas just for a few bars to make a difference to a song, yet never moving away from their hard rock roots. Vanishing Point certainly sound more European than any other Aussie outfit I have heard and are in a class far removed from Skyhooks or Rose Tattoo. Superb.

#61, Feb 2001

JANOS VARGA PROJECT
THE WINGS OF REVELATION I

This may be an instrumental progressive album that tinges on ambient at times, but there is no way that this called a relaxing album. In "Fight Of Mind" drummer István Király starts by setting a blistering pace, then Janos on guitar and Zoltán Lengyel on keyboards swap solos, trading off each other. The music keeps melding and moving, sometimes slowly and reflective while at others dynamic and powerful. The use of different musical styles and rhythms, as well as different keyboard and guitar sounds, all driven along by powerful drumming, makes this an album that is exciting to listen to. It is never boring and while as an instrumental album it can be played as background music, the listener gets far more out of it if he pays careful attention. There is little in the music to suggest its' origins, and this is a good place to start discovering just how good some of the prog music is that is coming out of Hungary.

#66, Feb 02

CSABA VEDRES
EPHATA I

Csaba Vedres was a founder member of After Crying, one of Hungary's most well-known progressive rock bands. Since leaving that band he has embarked on a solo career and this is his fifth solo album. While Csaba in the form of one keyboard or another provides most of the instruments, he also has guests who add violin and brass. The vocals are in English, with both English and Hungarian lyrics provided in the booklet. This is in many ways more of an orchestral or classical album than it is a progressive rock album, and in fact the only piece on the album not written by Csaba is an adaptation of the final scene of the opera 'Boris Godunoff'. But the music does vary quite a lot, with "Hitch-hike To Las Vegas" having a much funkier modern style, while "Lay Down" is almost Gregorian in its' delivery but also contains spoken sections. There is a lot going on in this album, and it is truly progressive in the way that it moves from one style to another, while maintaining close links to classical roots.

There is little in the way of rock but in some ways, it is sometimes like some of Wakeman's work without the overblown grandiose pomposity, while at others it has a much more modern bent. Because it moves around so much, I found that I could only play it in small chunks, as opposed to listening to the album in its' entirety but feel sure that this is down more to my personal taste in music than in any failings on the album's part. Probably not a record I will listen to a great deal, as I know that this label has many more albums that I would rather listen to instead.
#68, Jun 2002

VERTICAL ALIGNMENT
SIGNPOSTS

Vertical Alignment are the first band that I have reviewed where I have no physical product, but rather this release is currently only available as a download. What is also interesting is that this is a debut album, yet the band has managed to gain a lot of support from other members of the prog community. The band itself is Jim Braunreuther (vocals, keyboards), Monty Pierce (guitars and bass), Mike Adams (drums), Terri Jorgensen (bass and djembe) and Pete Jorgensen (vocals, guitars, keyboards, ethnic flutes, sequencing). But then on top of that there have been contributions from Randy George and Wil Henderson of Ajalon, Steve Babb, Fred Schendel, and Eric Parker of Glass Hammer, David Wallimann of Glass Hammer and Young Earth, Carl Groves of Salem Hill, Mike and Shaun FitzPatrick of FitzPatrick, Eddie Jerlin of Everlasting Arms, Kevin Jarvis of Farpoint, Lenna Pauley of Progressive Positivity Radio and The Radiant Flow, with lyrics by author Stephen Lawhead!

This is a Christian album, based on the concept that sometimes God uses major world events to point to a higher way; a better way, but even if you are not a Christian this is an album that you need to hear. This is prog that has been multi-layered and incredibly well-arranged with wonderful vocals and hooks. Musically this is a band that has taken many influences from Yes and Gentle Giant, as well as most Glass Hammer (so it is interesting to see the key players of that band involved). The first time I put this on I was captured and knew that I was in for a treat. I have played this album countless times already and am sure that I will continue to do so. It is currently available as a download only, but I think that it will also be available as a physical product if that is what you would prefer. If you enjoy your prog symphonic with great vocals and music, then you simply must investigate these guys further.
#89, Sep 2006

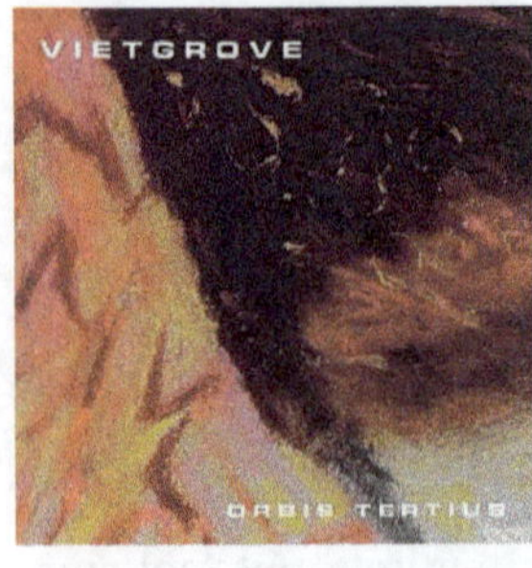

VIETGROVE
ORBIS TERTIUS

Norman Fay has been using the name Vietgrove for a number of years now, and prior to this debut CD has released four cassettes. Specialising in progressive electronic music he has himself an imaginative guitarist, Mark Bailey, who has made a big difference to the way that the band can operate. They have recently been playing support to World Turtle and will be on television in Russia later this year. Norman is from a similar school of electronic music as Paul Ward, as he uses electronic music as a base to build from but not as an end in itself. The songs are exactly that, songs, and not just self-indulgent knob twiddling. Like Paul, Norman has also been experimenting with a guitarist and has added shades and depths that he can also now recreate live. Although not as rocky as Paul or Michael Shipway, this is electronic music that will appeal to many. If you enjoy electronic keyboards (and "The Babylonian Lottery" is a must, trust me) then you will find a lot in here to enjoy and if you are a prog fan wanting to explore a slightly different area, why not start here?
#33, Feb 1996

PÄR VILLSÉ
BLICKAR

PÄR VILLSÉ
PANORAMA

I have been sent a load of information about Pär Villsé, along with some reviews but unfortunately everything is in Swedish, so I am none the wiser. All the lyrics are also in Swedish, so it's not a promising start. 'Blickar' only contains four songs, and was released in 1994, while 'Panorama' was released in 1995 and contains twelve (two of which also appear on the former). For the most part it is interesting progressive rock, especially those that link in Middle Eastern influences such as "Pendel", and "Carmina" shows some good melodic touches. Some of the songs are more in the singer songwriter vein, and I get the impression they would come across a lot better if I could understand the language. Overall, this is interesting, but there are many more progressive releases that deserve your consideration before these.
#38, Nov 1996

VIOLENT SILENCE
VIOLENT SILENCE

Don't you just love press releases? This one states that this is one of the best Swedish newcomers in years, and that the guitars just do not get missed. Okay, there is probably no room for guitars, as there are stacks of keyboards, as well as drums and bass, but

personally I found the flat vocal style very wearing indeed. Some of the singing is so atonal that it takes any edge that there was from the music. They do go through various styles, but the result is that the listener just can't help but feel that there is something missing from all of it and although Record Heaven do release some very fine prog albums, this is not one of them. In many places, it has more in common with early Eighties pop than prog, and this mismatch of styles certainly does not help.
#78, Apr 2004

VIOLENT SILENCE
KINETIC

Since I last heard from the band, they have added a second keyboard player and have also changed record labels from Record Heaven for their follow-up album. This is a band that is brave enough to put their toes into the water of progressive rock, but without a guitarist to hide behind. Those with long memories may just be able to remember that when I reviewed the debut in #78, I was not as kind about it as I might have been, and the same is going to be the case here. Now this is only my opinion, and there are loads of very positive reviews about this one the web, but for me the singing is very flat indeed. Add to that a lack of depth or dynamism in the music itself and the result is something for me is never going to anything more than background muzak. This is not something to play for a bit of get up and go, more like lay down and go to sleep, apart on "Subzero" which is not too bad. They have been likened to Genesis and Greenslade, and while I suppose the latter is the closest and I admit that they are more prog than just electronic, and there is some clever interplay between the musicians, this is not for me.
#86, Feb 2006

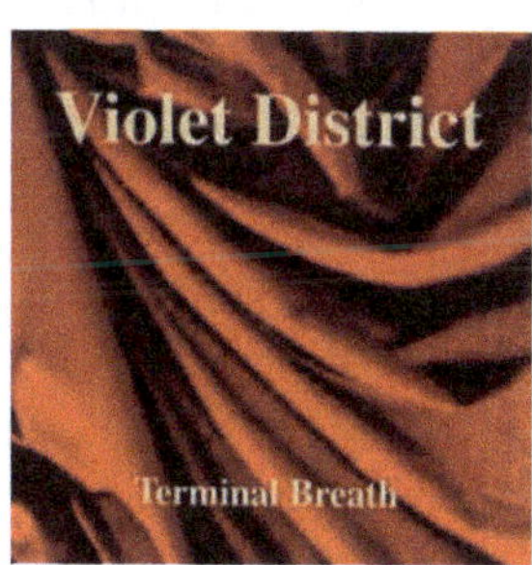

VIOLET DISTRICT
TERMINAL BREATH

Violet District are a German prog band that I have just been introduced to by Artur, and I was surprised to see that this album came out in 1992, and there hasn't been a follow-up. That is a real shame, as this is a joy to listen to: one that will be enjoyed by fans of old-style prog as well as neo-prog (don't you just love these labels?). There is much depth and maturity displayed, with the band at times sounding a bit like Pendragon while at others more like 'Animals' era Pink Floyd. "The Lost", for example, starts with some very powerful guitar lead lines and some almost military drumming, but when the vocals start Mischa is virtually unaccompanied apart from some very delicate keyboards. The booklet does not contain the lyrics, which is a pity, but I believe that they are/were available separately. This is an album that will be enjoyed by the proggers and I only hope that Violet District get back into the studio and record a follow-up. Apparently, this has been

very popular on mainland Europe and it is time that the British prog scene woke up to the joys of Violet District.
#38, Nov 1996

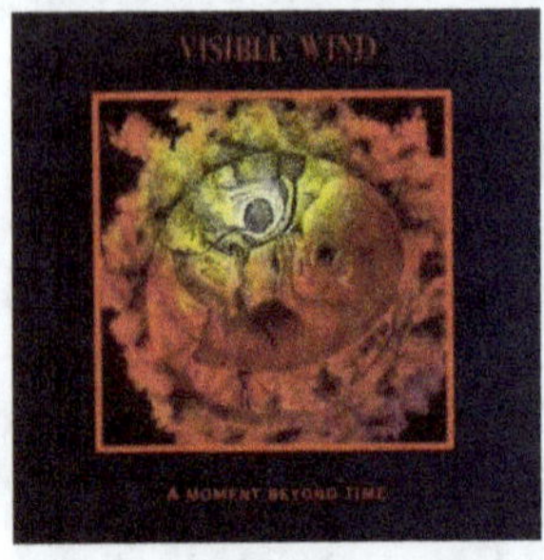

VISIBLE WIND
A MOMENT BEYOND TIME

Visible Wind came together with Luc Hébert (drums), Philippe Woolgar (guitar) and Stephen Geysens (keyboards). It was not a serious affair to begin with as they were all students, but gradually their music expanded and they were joined by bass player, Louis Ray, in time for the recording of their debut album, 'Catharsis', in 1987. At the time there was no lead singer, so the vocals were added by Christopher Wells a few months later. The album was released in May 1988, and Christopher gigged with them for a while, and then left in the September when a decision was made not to replace him but instead have the vocals taken care of by Philippe and Stephen. The second album, 'A Moment Beyond Time', was recorded by this line-up between July 1990 and March 1991, and saw the light of day on the Progressive Records label in May 1991. Since then, Philippe has left the band to be replaced by Claude Rainville and they have been working on the third album. So, what is this like? Firmly and definitely prog, the heavy use of a Hammond Organ sound in their keyboard parts, together with other Seventies keyboard styles, gives the band a unique sound. Very much a modern outfit, with some great guitarwork, there is also this link with the older style of prog. Seeing as how the band is from Quebec, it is perhaps a little surprising that there is only one song with French lyrics, "Soleil d'Aube", where the lead vocal is taken by Phillippe (on all other songs it is Stephen). Overall, this is very listenable, without a duff track on it. Unlike many of their North American counterparts, Visible Wind sound like a European prog outfit, and are not trying to mix prog with AOR. Highlights? Well the songs are all so good that it this is a more difficult task than normal, but I would have to say that the instrumental "Chasing The Skyline" is brilliant with loads of mood changes and great musicianship, and "Ulysses' Return", which has some very strong lyrics. It is a shame that Visible Wind have had very little coverage over here: the only magazine I have seen even mention them is Acid Dragon. They are a band looking out for, and I will be awaiting their third album with much interest.
#16, Dec 1992

VISION
INDEFINITE AND MYSTERIOUS

The full name of this Dutch band is 'Ettema and Van Gulik's Vision', so it is no surprise to discover that this is a duo with various guests. With Bert Ettema providing guitars and Martin van Gulik the keyboards, it was a little surprising that neither of these was the lead vocalist (provided by guest Ernst Strubbe) and it was a shame that the use of guests could not stretch to a drummer. I can't help hating programmed drums, and I cannot be the only one. This is an enjoyable album, most of the prog here on offer is upbeat with a lot of pop sensibilities coming through and it is the more up-tempo numbers such as "Mother" that work best. There is no way that the music can be viewed as 'serious' as the music is way too lightweight for that, but it shouldn't detract from the album as a whole. This took three years to record so I do not think we are going to see much more from these guys but if you want a prog album in your collection that you will enjoy playing from time to time and very few of your friends will have then this might be worth looking for. *#54, July 1999*

VOLARÉ
THE UNCERTAINTY PRINCIPLE

Formed in 1984, and named after a type of American car, this is the debut (and possibly only CD as Volaré are currently dormant although keyboard player Patrick Strawser is active in other bands) album, which was released in 1997. It is instrumental, and although it has been put into the prog genre it could also fit into jazz-rock. At times, there is a great deal going on, with guitarist Steve Hatch playing furiously while the lead is often taken by the keyboards. Although there is at times a real feeling of aggression and dissonance, for a lot of the time it is very laid-back affair, perfect mood music. Not knowing what to expect I was a bit surprised to find that they owe more to the Canterbury scene than I have come across from an American band before. The result is an album that is not recognisably American, having much in common with Seventies UK prog. Some of the guitar sounds are similar to Steve Hackett's, but in no sense could Volaré be thought of as yet another Genesis copyist outfit. This is an album that needs many plays, as after the first few times I was not too sure, but gradually it won me over until I discovered that I was playing it a great deal. If you want prog that is jazzier and a bit different to most of what is around at present, then you may find this worth a try.
#52, Feb 1999

VON DANIKEN
NEW WORLDS

Von Daniken were formed in 1989 by ex-Haze keyboard player/ bassist Chris McMahon and ex-Haze engineer Warren Jacques, and they released this album on cassette in 1990, and here it is now available on CD with an additional song, "Electrick Fish Music". Each of the three songs are more than twenty minutes long, although they are sub-divided and each can be played separately, so the album has nineteen songs if broken up. Paul McMahon makes a guest appearance on guitar in a couple of places, but for the rest of the time it is just Warren (guitars, vocals, programming) and Chris (keyboards, fretless bass, vocals, programming). Those who are fond of electronic music in a New Age style will find much here to enjoy, as will those who like the softer more keyboard led areas of prog. That is not to say that there is no guitar, but rather that it is used sparingly and to great effect, adding nuances here and there in a way not dissimilar to Pink Floyd. It is not

a rumbustious album, but one that is reflective and moody. The twenty-four minutes of "New World" were composed and recorded on 19th April 1989, with the dawn chorus that features on the final section ("The Farthest Worlds of Space") recorded at 4:30 am the next morning! A dream album that will be enjoyed and played by many.
#33, Feb 1996

VON DANIKEN
TRANSIENT

Only three and a half years since the last VD release, Chris and Warren are back. Of course, they might rightfully complain that they have been busy (Chris is in at least four other bands, Haze, World Turtle, Strongheart and Satsuma!), but it is nice to see them back. Chris provides the keyboards while Warren does the rest. It has been quite a while since I played the last VD album, but I think I will be returning to this one far more frequently as there is a depth to it that was missing from the last. I commented to Chris that the guitars in places are far heavier than I would ever have imagined hearing from VD. That is one of the best things about this album; it just has so much going for it in terms of style. When they rock, they really rock, but also go to the other extreme, which is laid back and almost ambient in style. The title song is the closing piece, divided into three sections and managing to clock in at almost eighteen minutes in length. There is space and thought, something to relax into (and just as you do so a guitar lead comes seemingly out of nowhere). It may not be as dynamic and hard hitting or even as commercial as some of the other bands that Chris is linked to, but this is an album for theproghead to savour.
#54, July 1999

VOYAGER
ELEMENT V

I have heard quite a few Aussie rock bands over the years, and although I will always maintain a special part of my affection for Skyhooks and their 'Guilty Until Proven Insane' album (for the uninitiated this is where Iron Maiden borrowed "Women In Uniform"), I can see that this is going to feature in my Aussie playlists in the future. This combines power metal and prog metal in almost equal proportions which means that while the songs contain a lot of melody and structure it also means that there is plenty of balls and aggression. Twin guitars combine to provide plenty of shredding while the keyboards provide that touch of distinction – it is blasted along from the back with some very powerful drumming while Daniel Estrin proves that a keyboard player can be a rock singer. It will be interesting to see these guys in concert as the stage set up must be different to the norm. Keyboards in the middle of stage with the bassist and drummer back left and right perhaps and the two guitarists wandering around the stage? Don't know, but I can state quite firmly that this is a cracking rock album that while may be too heavy for those who enjoy melodic rock nevertheless is very melodic

indeed and shows that the Aussies can do something apart from cream us at cricket, again.
#84, July 2005

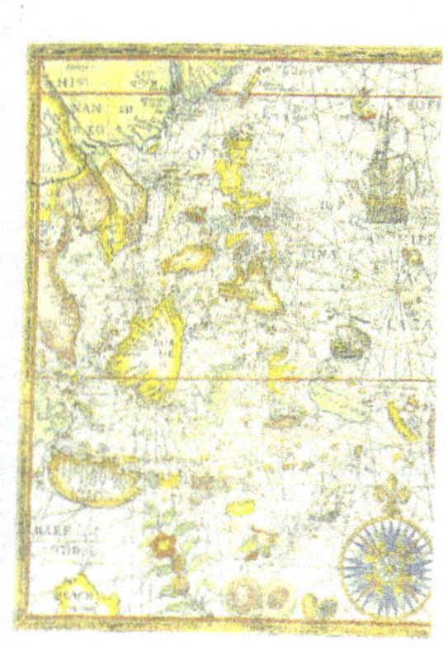

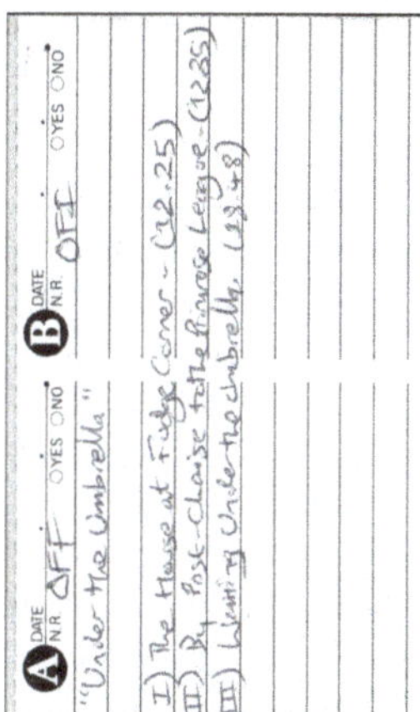

VULGAR UNICORN
THE HISTORY OF THE WORLD

VULGAR UNICORN
UNDER THE UMBRELLA

When talking to Graham Younger of Blindsight sometime last year he told me all about this great new prog band, but unfortunately, he had lost their address and all he could tell me was that they came from Yeovil. I mentioned this to Stu Nicholson a couple of months ago and he promptly gave me Neil Randle's phone number. A couple of calls later and I was in possession of both of their demo tapes ('Umbrella' was not even available at the time of writing, so Neil kindly sent me his own copy). The name Vulgar Unicorn is taken from a series of books called 'Thieves World', where The Vulgar Unicorn was a seedy pub in the middle of Sanctuary, which is a disease and crime-ridden city. The name was chosen because, like Iron Butterfly, the name is a contradiction and it was also hoped that the name would help express the diversity and potential of the songs. Neil Randle and Adrian Soord met at school when Neil was taking GCSE music and playing the saxophone. Because of Neil's interest in music, Adrian decided to learn an instrument and took up the guitar. Neil decided to diversify and worked on bass and keyboards then gradually, as they improved musically, they wrote songs and gathered together a group of musicians all influenced by different sources to form the band. Dave Hutchfield (drums), Paul Hilditch and Richard were all involved in the first demo, 'The History Of The World', which for me was quite an ear opener.

The demo has a very involved cover with full lyrics to the three songs, two of which are more than ten minutes long, and this was their first attempt at recording! Not only that, but they dare to break with normality and use a brass section. Well, what can you say except that at long last here is a prog band that is reminiscent of the early Seventies when every prog band sounded totally different from the rest because they were all using different instrumentation in new and imaginative ways. The brass section is very much a key part of the overall sound, not added as window dressing. For a first demo, it is in many ways surprising that such a young band could produce work of such breadth and imagination. It is not possible to say Vulgar Unicorn sound like anyone else: yes, there are parts of songs that can be said to sound like others but because their influences are so diverse the sound is likewise. With trumpets and sax being such an integral part of the overall sound there is no-one else like them in the current underground scene.

By the beginning of last year, the line-up had settled down with Neil, Adrian and Dave being joined by Nick Reyland, who had guested on 'History' while Richard and Paul were still helping the band out with gigs. Again, this is a three-track demo, with the two short songs clocking in at more than twelve minutes and "Waiting Under The Umbrella" nearly nineteen minutes in length! Adventurous or what? The lyrics to all three songs are linked and tell a story: the Montgolfier brothers move into Semi 36A, or at least they're supposed to, but a mystery letter tells them they cannot. However, this letter contains the first of many clues that lead them on a cross-country goose chase, the purpose of which is to stall them so that a mystery person can move out of 36A in time. Eventually they catch up with this person, but his/her identity can only be arrived at by using the clues in all three songs, a bit like a musical whodunit. Nick provides some soaring trumpet which fits well into the complicated and complex nature of their music, which is sometimes rocky, sometimes mellow or acoustic, always full of contrast. I enjoyed 'Umbrella' even more than 'History' and am very much looking forward to hearing and seeing the full package. Challenging, yes. Inventive, certainly. Intellectually stimulating, definitely. This is not background muzak, it demands to be taken seriously with lyrics as complicated as the musical forms. Intrigued? You should be.
#17, Mar 1993

VULGAR UNICORN
UNDER THE UMBRELLA
It seems ages since I first reviewed the demo tapes that had been sent to me by this young band from Yeovil. One thing that struck me at the time was that here was a band totally different to the rest of the prog scene. The reason for this is the unusual band line-up of Neil Randle (bass, keyboards), Bruce Soord (guitar) and David Hutchfield (drums) to which are added the session musicians of Tony Busby (lead vocals), Matt Burge (trumpet), Greg Willis (alto and tenor sax) and Richard Hunt (violin). Yes, you did read that correctly, Vulgar Unicorn must be one of the very few prog bands that use brass instruments. One thing that is the kiss of death to prog bands when reviewed by critics is the length of some of the songs. Bearing that in mind, the first track of the CD runs in at a mere 44 minutes (the other, "Thief Of Clubs" seems very brief at ten minutes).

The vocals are very good, but it is in the long instrumental passages that Vulgar Unicorn shine. There are loads of influences and dynamics at work as they switch and change. Jazz is very much in evidence at times (with some great trumpet and sax work), while at others it is Twelfth Night or Pink Floyd. Bruce rings the changes as well, as at times it is gentle acoustic while at others it is ringing power chords with some brilliant soloing in-between. To play music as complex and complicated as this takes a lot of skill, but to make it enjoyable to the listener needs something a little special. Vulgar Unicorn have this element and have produced a very enjoyable album. It is very different, and I am sure that many will agree that this is a band and album worth investigating.
#29, Jun 1995

VULGAR UNICORN
SLEEP WITH THE FISHES
The first thing you notice when you open the CD case is the fact that the CD itself has a bright pink spiral, which matches the pink tray ("Yuk" is possibly the most appropriate word here). What I did not notice initially, was that there appeared to be something on the reverse of the tray insert, i.e. under the tray itself. On removing the tray, I found that there was indeed something underneath, a story. The pink tray is effective, the story is effective, but the planning has gone a little awry because it is easy to miss the story altogether. Anyway, this is only nit picking on my part. Vulgar Unicorn are quite unlike any other prog band around as they are truly progressive, mixing jazz, ambient, prog, rock, and a host of other influences while they are also based on a nucleus (Neil Randall and Bruce Soord) who utilise others as they see fit: this can mean an oboe on one track, a clarinet on another, a trumpet on yet another and so on. Most songs are instrumentals, with the album being divided into four pieces, with four songs to each set. This is a wonderfully diverse album, as not feeling bound by any musical form they have given their complex music a freedom that many other bands could not possibly have. I know that 'Under The Umbrella' has been a huge success and am sure that the follow-up can only increase their following.
#37, Oct 1996

VULGAR UNICORN
JET SET RADIO
The two guys from Yeovil have finally returned with their third album, which seems to have been 'nearly ready' for ages. They have utilised some guest musicians and vocalists (if you can honestly believe all the credits on the insert), but for the most part, it is just Neil Randall and Bruce Soord in the studio. They boast of being one of the few truly progressive bands left in the UK, and they certainly sound very different to the norm. Very keyboard based, although not New Age, it is an album that takes a lot of listening to. It is not New Age, but at times, there is the danger that they could disappear in a puff of complexity. Being progressive for its own sake is not an end to itself, although these guys obviously do not feel that this is the case. Very interesting, but sometimes too damn clever for its' own good. Treat with care.
#59, July 2000

ADAM WAKEMAN
100 YEARS OVERTIME
I played this immediately after 'Romance of the Victorian Age', and to say that I was surprised is something of an understatement! "See What You See" kicks off as a funky rock number totally removed from what he has been doing with his father. Not only does Adam provide keyboards and acoustic guitar, but he sings as well! John Lovell provides some sterling electric guitar while Chris Wortley provides trumpet on some tracks.

Having got over the initial shock (I have not heard any of Adam's earlier solo work) I settled down to listen to a pleasant and enjoyable album. He hasn't got a large vocal range, so instead concentrates on breathy emotion which works well. The best song is "Take My Hand" which kicks off with some superb guitarwork and moves and grooves in a very enjoyable Dan Reed Network fashion. If all the songs were up to this standard, then I would be screaming about it from the rooftops as it is not possible to listen to this without moving and having a good time. Some of the songs have a more orchestral feel, as I would have expected, and the ballads also work well, particularly "More To Say". Obviously the diehard Wakeman fan will just have to purchase this, but there is a lot on offer here and to anyone who likes good songs and the softer side of rock will find plenty here for them. This may be his last solo album for a while as his contract with President Records has expired and he is currently working on a new project.
#26, Dec 1994

ADAM WAKEMAN
REAL WORLD TRILOGY

Having a world-famous father is never easy, and Adam is still finding it hard to shake loose from being known as Rick's son. Even the press release makes mention of his father and why not? The name Wakeman is synonymous with brilliant keyboard playing and, in this case, it truly is like father like son. This triple CD set sees Adam attempting a different musical style, although it must be said that his father has been down a similar musical path before. After a soft rock solo album, a few that he shared with his father that were classically based, and a stunning live set with his father (captured on the brilliant Cyclops release 'Wakeman with Wakeman') and the harder Jeronimo Road experiment (which featured Damian Wilson) Adam has moved into a softer area. This could be termed 'New Age', as layered keyboards gently guide you along. It is soothing and restful and is perfect music to relax to in the evening or just to have playing quietly during the day. No, you will not go away humming tunes but that is not the purpose of this; even Sara thinks it is good! While I cannot say that it will become a frequent visitor to the deck, I am sure that there are times when the lights are out that this is the only album that will do. And this is a triple CD digipak that you should be able to purchase for the price of a normal single CD.
#44, Sept 1997

OLIVER WAKEMAN
3 AGES OF MAGICK

Oliver seems to be busier than his brother these days. In the next issue, I will be reviewing his new album with Clive Nolan, but first here is an instrumental album that he has recorded with Steve Howe providing all the guitar parts. I am indebted to Dave Wagstaffe (Landmarq etc.) who plays drums on this album, as it was only through his

contact that I knew it had even been released. To have not heard this would have been a shame as it contains some glorious 'songs' while Steve seems inspired and produces some of his finest guitarwork for a long time. The music is extremely emotive, and the keyboards drive along in songs such as "Mind Over Matter" that make one feel that vocals would be an unwanted distraction. When reading the booklet, it transpires that Karl Groom mixed the album and Rob Aubrey mastered it which is why the sound is so good. The only disappointing thing about the album (love the front cover) is that it was released on Resurgence, which is an imprint of Voiceprint. This album deserves to be heard, and many prog fans would snap this up if only they knew that it was available. This is a prog album that can be enjoyed at all levels, first time.
#65, Dec 2001

OLIVER WAKEMAN
MOTHER'S RUIN

When I first put this album on the player my initial reaction was to let my jaw drop until it hit the desk – the reason is that this is never the sort of album that I would expect from Oliver, and it's bloody good to boot. This is melodic rock, neo-prog, classic rock, call it what you will, but Oliver has surrounded himself with a rock band and produced something that needs to be heard. At the back there is Dave Wagstaffe (Landmarq among numerous others) who, as always, does a very fine job and on bass there is Tim Buchanan with David Mark Pierce on guitars and these guys obviously know how to rock. Then on vocals there is Moon. I have always thought that he is one of those singers who has somehow never gained the recognition that he deserves – I can remember seeing him front Landmarq before Damian Wilson came back yet he has never managed to get involved with a band where he can shine – now he has. In some ways, this is like a hard rocking Asia, but with the emphasis on keyboards and vocals – "Walk Away" is a case in point and is a great singalong rock number that is going to have crowds jumping up and down. Simple repeated keyboards lead the way into the drum patterns, and the song starts to take off with the guitar lead, but it is Moon over the top that makes this what it is.

This is an album that can just be played time and again with the listener never getting bored – Oliver has managed to produce music that is both accessible and enjoyable, rocking enough for those into guitar but plenty melodic enough for those who expect him to be producing prog as he is his father's son. Do not get this if you are expecting another 'Hound Of The Baskervilles' which is a fine album, as this is a very different piece indeed – but bloody good all the same. If you enjoy strong melodic rock with powerful keyboards and great vocals, then this is something that you cannot live without
#86, Feb 2006

RICK WAKEMAN
THE PRIVATE COLLECTION

This is a collection of music that was thought either to be lost or destroyed and while some of the pieces were not actually meant for public consumption, others relate to the classic 'Journey To The Centre Of The Earth' era. First track is the brilliant "The Battle", which is an adapted version of the 'Journey' song and features full orchestra and choir. The tape was damaged, and it took a lot of work to restore it, but the result was certainly worth the effort. Vocalist Gary Pickford-Hopkins is at his very best (for further examples of his wonderful vocals then search out the excellent Wild Turkey albums), and the song is vibrant and powerful. It contrasts well with "Penny's Piece", a solo piano movement composed for Rick's wife Nina (Penny is her real name). Delicate and lilting, it is almost like listening to a running stream. "The Pearl and Dean Piano Concerto" is taken from the 'Journey' concerts and was the original encore. It contained a one movement piece where Rick, along with orchestral accompaniment, raced through the adverts of the day. The crowd cheers at each new recognition, and while it is not possible to remember the adverts some twenty years on it still stands up as a piece in its' own right. There was an American and UK version, and "Now A Word From Our Sponsor" closes the CD. Some of the piano pieces are haunting. "Piece For Granny" was intended solely for Rick's grandmother and it is now only after her death that it is publicly available. These contrast well with "Steam Hole Dance" and "Warmongers" which were originally written for a film that was never made called 'Missing Links' in the early Eighties and are powerful analogue pieces. All in all, this is an important collection, bringing together as it does songs unavailable anywhere else. For the Wakeman completist it is a definite must purchase, as it is for those who love 'Journey'.

#23, May 1994

RICK WAKEMAN
THE OFFICIAL BOOTLEG

Well, just what can you say about an album that is absolutely an essential purchase for anyone interested in either the music of Rick Wakeman or who just loves superb keyboard playing? The full title of this double CD is 'Wakeman with Wakeman: The Official Bootleg', and the reason for this is that Rick has been joined by his son Adam for this live set. The only other musicians are Tony Fernandez on percussion and Alan Thompson on bass, quite a different setup to the one that he has been using recently. We are treated to renditions of some of Rick's most favoured compositions, namely "Catherine Howard", "Catherine Parr" and "Myths and Legends" as well as some covers but the highlight is "Journey of the Centre of the Earth", which clocks in at the best part of forty minutes in length. It takes up most of the second CD and shows just what two keyboard players can produce in terms of orchestral music. It had to be rearranged due to the lack of vocals, but with first one keyboard player taking the lead and then the other, these are not missed at all. I have been playing this album a lot recently and find that whichever track I am listening to is the current favourite. The first of the two covers is "Eleanor Rigby" and I

am sure that The Beatles never imagined that their music could sound quite like that as it is stretched, and the themes explored until it becomes a totally different entity. Logical progression and brilliant keyboard work combined with perfect bass and drums to make this music to be proud of. The final song is the other cover, "Paint It Black". Who says you need a guitar to be able to rock? Up to the minute keyboard sounds take the vocal line as the song bounds along with great intensity. As with "Eleanor Rigby", I prefer this to the original as the bare bones of the songs are taken to bits and then reconstructed. This is not a cheap album, as it is a double CD, but if you are all interested in Wakeman then this is an album you simply MUST have.
#24, Jul 1994

RICK WAKEMAN
VISIONS
This is the latest release from Rick and is similar in ideas to the three Aspirant CDs he released a few years ago. In one sense it is easy listening, yet orchestral in its writing and sound. Rick is a solo performer on this, and it is worlds away from the music he has been creating with his band. It was written to enable the listener to relax and use their imagination to "provide a unique musical experience". It should be said that on this level it works very well indeed, but those who enjoy Rick's more bombastic side, either solo or with a band, may feel disappointed as the music is all very much on the same level. It creates a very dreamy mood, and is very 'New Age" in concept, and if this is what you are looking for then this is the CD for you. However, if you are looking for some rock keyboards from one of the masters of the art then I suggest you look elsewhere. *#31, Oct 1995*

RICK WAKEMAN
OUT THERE
Rick Wakeman is one of the most prolific musicians of modern times. Looking at his web site it looks like he has released over 100 solo albums, let alone his albums with Yes and so many sessions that even he is not sure how many he has played on. This album is credited to Rick Wakeman and the New English Rock Ensemble and hearkens back to the Seventies when Rick played with a full-on rock band. The line-up is completed by Tony Fernandez (drums), Ant Glynne (guitar), Lee Pomeroy (bass) and one Damian Wilson on vocals. The album reeks class from start to finish, from the artwork in the booklet to the final notes of the concept album drifting away. Rick has used some fine singers in his time, both male and female, but Damian has the power and range to put many of these in the shade. Although this album has been written solely by Rick, the impression throughout is that this is a group that just happen to be led by a keyboard maestro as opposed to just a keyboard-fest. Damian has fitted into the role being asked of him and the result is a vehicle that allows him to shine, whether he is singing with a choir or fronting the rock band that this outfit so readily can be. I have

been trying to rack my brains and think of a studio album by Rick that I have enjoyed more and while I can look back at the Seventies with great fondness I should say that this is even better than those and is one that I will be playing a great deal in the future. I have also found myself singing bits of this to myself at work, certainly an unusual state of affairs, let alone for a Wakeman album! Rick is on tour throughout April to June so why not go and see him. Based on this it is definitely worth the trip.
#73, Apr 2003

RICK WAKEMAN & HIS BAND
LIGHT UP THE SKY

Rick's new single has him working with his son Adam, as well as singer Chrissie Hammond. The four tracks are all new and have been put together for a firework spectacular taking place in the North East at the end of the month. This will also be using two other pieces from the 'Journey' and 'Henry VIII' albums. The first two songs feature vocals, with the other two being instrumentals. Chrissie's voice is just so powerful that it amazes me that she is not better known as a star in her own right. "Light Up The Sky" has an awful lot of keyboards on it, but it is just a wonderful number, possibly one of the best actual songs that Rick has performed. The emphasis is on Chrissie with only small instrumental passages, but it is what is going on behind her voice that matters, with Adam and Rick in perfect harmony. Those of you who love Wakeman's instrumental work as well will be pleased to know that the instrumentals are of the highest order (as one would expect) and conjure up images of Wakeman at his classic best. The speed at which he goes up and down the keyboards are amazing, but which is Rick, and which is Adam? I get the impression that these tracks will not be available on album so if you are a Wakeman fan and do not want to miss out then I urge you to get this now.
#23, May 1994

RICK WAKEMAN & ADAM WAKEMAN
ROMANCE OF THE VICTORIAN AGE

The only other CD I have reviewed by this father and son team was the bombastic live album which came out on Cyclops earlier this year, and it is as removed from this as can be imagined. There are virtually no other musicians on this CD, and Rick and Adam take it in turns to lead on an acoustic grand piano, and they share the keyboard overdubs. The Victoria and Albert Museum have been involved, and each title in the sixteen-page booklet is accompanied with the reproduction of a painting. "Burlington Arcade" opens proceedings in a bright and bubbly manner, with the emphasis very much on synths. It is a lovely tune that owes more than a hint to jazz and is very different to the rest of the songs on the CD. "If Only" is next, with Adam on the grand, and the slow romantic nature of this song is indicative of the rest of the album, with synths making only very sparing and subtle entrances. One thing the album does is

provide easy comparison between the master and the pupil, and while Adam is an amazing keyboard player, he still has a long way to go to catch up with his father. I found that after a short while it became very easy to distinguish who was playing lead, as Rick has a superb touch. Possibly this is because he grew up in an environment where the piano was basically the keyboard instrument, whereas today in popular music it plays second fiddle to others? Anyway, 'Romance Of The Victorian Age' owes far more to classical music than it does to rock, but overall, is very enjoyable indeed.
#26, Dec 1994

RICK WAKEMAN & ADAM WAKEMAN
TAPESTRIES

As with their 1994 album 'Romance of the Victorian Age', this collaboration between Rick and Adam is a collection of piano pieces, inspired this time by tapestries in the Victoria and Albert Museum. They have also utilised some bass and acoustic guitar to add some extra touches to proceedings when needed and as in the last album Rick and Adam swap lead piano roles, according to who wrote the song, with seven from each. The difference between the two styles is not as apparent as it was before, but Adam still has a long way to go to catch up with the master. Many of the songs are straightforward 'classical' numbers, but there are some more up-tempo pieces as well such as Rick's "The Garden Party" which is a great fun number. As I said for 'Romance...', if you are searching for one of Rick's epics then you will not find it here. However, if you to hear some beautiful piano combined with some classy guitar (Adam's "Portraits In A Gallery" is particularly worthy) then you need look no further.
#34, Apr 1996

RICK & ADAM WAKEMAN
VIGNETTES

Unlike the last two Rick and Adam albums recorded for President, this one contains singing with Adam providing vocals for five of his songs, and Chrissie Hammond singing on two of Rick's. The English Chamber Choir are also involved, and there is acoustic guitar. In fact, I'm not sure why this has been released as a joint album as Adam and Rick provide six songs each and do not play on each other's material. Adam's songs are more AOR-oriented, with gentle soft singing, while Rick has a more classical bent. The overall result is an enjoyable, if very laid-back, album. It is something to be played quietly in the evening and although it is a move in the right direction after the last two joint albums, I would prefer to hear more of Rick's rockier material, as amply demonstrated on their brilliant 'Wakeman With Wakeman' CD released through Cyclops. If you are an ardent fan then of course you must get this (this is Rick's thirtieth album through President alone), but even if you are not and fancy something light and refreshing then this may be for you.
#40 March 1997

WALKING ON ICE
MORE THAN HEAVEN

Just when you thought that hard rock pomp was dying, then Walking On Ice come along to shatter the illusions with a great demo. Actually, 'More Than Heaven' is their second tape and I feel extremely remiss about not discovering this band earlier. Walking On Ice were formed in 1989 as the brainchild of bassist Andy Faulkner and original keyboard player Steve Smith, who both wanted to write and perform intelligent yet accessible rock music. Lyricist and singer Mark Barrett and drummer Pete Salt were brought into the fold and songs were written while they tried to find a suitable guitarist. After countless auditions, Justin Sabin was discovered, and the line-up completed. From their first gig at Dunstable in March 1990, they proceeded to gig hard and their first official release, 'More Than Heaven', was ready by Spring 1991 ('Whitehall Warrior', their first actual tape, was made available as an afterthought due to demand).

'More Than Heaven' contains four songs and comes in a package that includes lyrics and full colour photos and wouldn't look out of place in a shop. Kicking off with the title cut, it shows that the lads can play, write and sing. The songs all have a commercial element to them, and could all do well as singles, even with the limited radio airplay this type of music gets in this country. Of the four, my favourite is "You Want It All", which has a great hook and just drives along. Kent Custom Bike Show on July 13th, 1991 saw the last performance of the original line-up, as both Pete and Steve left the band. Pete was quickly replaced by Jason Clark, who had previously been in Casual Affair, with whom he had recorded the excellent 'Well, What Did You Expect?' cassette. Steve was replaced by Graham Leeson who had worked with Andy previously. The new line-up rehearsed hard for four weeks, and then supported Saxon at The Standard, getting a good response from the 500 or so Saxon metalheads. New material is being written, and another recording stint is in the offing with a CD released planned for the Autumn. They also have an excellent monthly newsletter, 'Icebreaker', which is along the same lines as 'Night Moves' used to be for Twelfth Night.
#13, May 1993

WALKING ON ICE
NO MARGIN FOR ERROR

Many, many moons ago I reviewed a demo tape that I had been sent by Walking On Ice, 'More Than Heaven'. I was bowled over by the four tracks and then sat back and waited for great things to happen. Unfortunately, they were beset by major personnel changes, and I thought that they would never release anything else. But they have struggled on and Justin Sabin (guitar) and Andy Faulkner (bass) have been joined by Steve Mansfield (vocals), Chris Puleston (drums) and Jez Newton (keyboards). Although I hear through the grapevine that even though this album has only

just been released, Jez is no longer with the band. The weak point for me on this album is the vocals, although I must confess that they have grown on me the more I have played it. Steve has a voice that sounds as if it is just about to go off-key, especially on the long-held notes, but from actively disliking the vocals I am getting more used to them and finding that in places they work well with the harmonies. Walking On Ice were always a good tight band with strong melodies to boot, and the same is true of this CD. The best song on here is the driving "Today, Tomorrow?" which is full of inventive ideas as it belts along, twisting and changing many times. Justin is a fine guitarist, and when given the opportunity comes out with some great lead breaks. All in all, this is an album that requires careful listening to, and is worth it. Maybe not the album I expected after hearing 'More Than Heaven', but they deserve a break. Let's hope that this sells well and that they soon sort out their personnel issues.
#27, Feb 1995

WALRUS
IN THE ROOM OF A SINGULAR POINT

WALRUS
COLLOIDAL

Look carefully at the artwork for 'In The Room..', and it may appear that there is a face coming out of the cabbage leaves. You would be correct, as when it comes to visual presentation then Shiiba (who also plays flute) has been paying attention to a certain Mr Gabriel of the early Seventies ilk. He is joined by Hideki (guitar, Mellotron, backing vocals), Goro (bass, backing vocals) and Okabe (drums, backing vocals). But before we dismiss these guys as yet another Genesis wannabe band, take a close listen to the music. Yes, there are influences, no doubt at all, but these guys punch a lot harder than Hackett ever used to – Walrus have taken Genesis as a starting point and due to that the musical references are still there, but they have moved a long way from the original even if the singer still likes dressing up (there are some great photos on their site). Like the follow-up, this debut mini album is sung all in Japanese, but it is still accessible yet musically complicated enough to whet the appetite of any proghead. There is also the heavy use of Mellotron, which certainly adds a distinctive flavour to proceedings.

The mini-album came out in 2004, but by 2005 the band had their debut full-length album out, which sees them taking a musical shift as they have cut down on the Mellotrons and 12-string guitars and have moved even further away from the Genesis sound (although Shiiba still likes dressing up). They start the album with one of the longest songs, the nine minute plus "The Parade Of Hoshikui" which is still complex but much rockier, with angular riff patterns being developed, and the flute break in the middle only emphasises the power of the guitar when it comes back. In some ways, the staccato reminds me of Talking Heads, but they never sounded like this as Walrus are proving that prog in Japan

very much has a point to make with a sound that is certainly different to what else is around. It is melodic and makes perfect sense and is very approachable, even though it is being sung in Japanese, and I would have thought that it would be guaranteed to get a crowd going at any gig. Of course, not all the album is going to be as powerful as this, and it does slow down for “Somewhere and Nowhere”, but they still manage to bring in something complex even into the most normal of songs that one is prepared to forgive them when Hackett style guitar appears on “A Dark Side House”.
#86, Feb 2006

WAPPA GAPPA
GAPPA
This is the third album by Japanese outfit Wappa Gappa, and I know this because it is possible to view their web site in English! Although the lyrics are in Japanese this is not a major problem, as the female voice becomes just another instrument, but they do kindly offer a translation for all the lyrics in their booklet. This is a prog band that has a lot going for it, with some great guitar leads. It is difficult to describe how they sound as they are quite different to most bands around, but that is very much in their favour. There are elements of Gentle Giant and other Seventies bands due to some of the keyboard sounds they employ, but also, they often go off at tangents into a musical free for all as they open up and have fun. This is easily one of the best Japanese prog albums that I have come across. There are gentle quiet passages, then off they go on another rock out. It’s all quite fun really. Although initially released in Japan it is now also available in Europe through Musea. As for the name? On the site, they tell us that “"Wappa" means handcuffs in Japanese policemen’s slang. “Gappa" in Chinese characters can be read with a meaning of "I break it". There is a hidden hope behind our name which says, "Be free, be yourself".” Now you know!
#79, May 2004

PAUL WARD
FOR A KNAVE
Paul was born in Sheffield in 1961, and his first musical instrument was a descant recorder (but the least said about that the better). At the age of thirteen he was to see a television programme that was to, quite literally, change his life. The show was about Rick Wakeman, and Paul was so impressed with the sounds he made that he quickly built up a collection of Wakeman’s music. He was desperate for an electronic organ, and eventually his parents bought him a small fan-driven chord organ on which to learn the basics. After several attempts at building synthesisers (including a Mellotron out of a vacuum cleaner and some old tape recorders), Paul eventually obtained his first electronic keyboard in 1977. This was a Thomas copy of a Vox Jaguar that Paul amplified using his mother’s radiogram. As his income grew with weekend jobs, Paul gradually bought more effects and proper amplification which led to

him forming his first band, Altimis, with a friend who used to build synths with him (but now played guitar).

Altimis got as far as recording a single, but eventually died as members drifted away. Paul, together with Neil Thompson (the sound engineer) and Geoff Smith (the singer), experimented with recording using Paul's old tape recorder and this proved to be an important period of learning. In the early Eighties Paul played with several other bands, anything from heavy metal to clubland cover songs, but eventually he and Neil decided to go it alone as a studio-based duo. Paul played all the instrumentation and wrote the music while Neil handled production. At around this time Paul wrote a letter to a UK electronic music magazine asking musicians in the locality to contact him. One of the many who did was John Dyson, who along with Anthony Thrasher formed Surreal To Real (a record label dedicated to releasing the best of UK electronic music on CD). Paul and Neil opened a commercial studio in Sheffield and used the studio's spare capacity to produce their own material. As Quiet Point, they released 'Beyond The Quiet Point', which to their surprise was very successful. Back in the studio they produced Wavestar's album 'Moonwind', which led to Paul playing live with them for a few years. However, on the Quiet Point front not everything was going according to plan. They had to move out of the studio premises, and it was difficult for them to find new accommodation. Due to many differing non-musical factors, they were unable to follow up the initial success and after an acclaimed appearance at the 1990 UK Electronica, Neil decided to call it a day.

Paul decided to proceed, and duly recorded his first solo album 'For A Knave', which was released on Surreal To Real in 1991. It has established Paul as one of the UK's leading exponents of electronic music, with both Space Rider and Zenith magazines giving the album a five-star rating. After his first appearance at the Dutch music festival, KLEMdag in Breda, the Surreal To Real stand completely sold out of the album. In the first half of 1992 Paul was asked to contribute to the 'Seed' project, which involved many musicians who were asked to submit their own interpretation of a pre-written melody. Paul's version is widely regarded as the best and has won him many friends in continental Europe. Also last year, Paul played to a sell-out audience for BBC Radio Derby, and along with John Dyson was asked back to KLEMdag for an unprecedented third time (the festival's policy has been to never have the same artist two years running). Well, what of the album? I must confess I knew I was going to like it before I had even heard a note. The reason being is the following, which is printed on the insert "To ensure the highest quality this album was mastered on state-of-the-art digital audio tape and was processed throughout the recording project using noise suppression systems. The click on the fade-out of track nine must, therefore, be a figment of our imaginations and is each individual's own responsibility to deal with in any way they see fit. To avoid susceptibility to this mass hypnosis and consequently hearing the anomaly please disregard this note".

There is no doubt that Paul is a master of his craft, using many different sounds and layering theme in a way that is both melodic and captivating. Each track has very much a separate identity, and the ears cannot believe the amount of sounds available for Paul to paint his audio landscape. I enjoyed the album immensely, but there is one song that stands head and shoulders above the rest, "The Alchemist". This is the only song to

feature another musician, Phil Easton, on guitar. I love this song; it is immediate and annoyingly catchy. The guitar is used to add a sense of dynamism to the song, and it works extremely well. I am not used to describing all the sounds that can be produced by a keyboard player with a long list of instrumentation, but I know what I like, and I like this. Paul will hopefully be producing a new album later this year, and it may well feature the vocal talents of one Stu Nicholson who is tremendously impressed with Paul's work. Personally, I think that is a combination that could work extremely well.
#17, Mar 1993

PAUL WARD
THE FEAR OF MAKE-BELIEVE

Hot on the heels of his 1991 'For A Knave' (Paul tells me he has been busy), come keyboard player extraordinaire Paul Ward's second solo album. I have never been the biggest lover of electronic music, but I fell deeply in love with his debut and I have eagerly been awaiting this one. I was intrigued by the CD even before I put it on as it has one of the most interesting covers I have seen. Instead of artwork we have a short story that commences on the front and continues inside the insert. It fits in perfectly with the album and is certainly different. So, onto the music. Paul manages to put together keyboard sounds in a way that enables you to forget that you are listening to instrumental music. These are songs, not some meanderings created in a studio never to be performed live. Paul has been joined by guitarist Shaun Michael d'Lear for three of the tracks, and this gives a harder edge to the proceedings: more like Marillion than Kraftwerk! Paul is attempting to crossover the boundaries that exist between electronic music and progressive rock, and in 'The Fear of Make-Believe' he has managed to create an electronic world that any lover of good music should investigate. Do not be afraid of the unknown. Also, Paul's classic Quiet Point album (recorded with Neil Thompson) 'Beyond The Quiet Point' is going to be made available on CD and if you place an advance order you will receive an additional CD containing special remixes and live versions of Paul Ward and Quiet Point material. Do not hesitate, do it today!
#27, Feb 1995

WASTEFALL
SELF EXILE

I am not aware of that many prog metal bands hailing from Greece, in fact I think that before listening to this album I was not aware of any, but here we have the third album from Wastefall. Prior to this album they had been signed to the Greek label Sleazsy Rider, but now that they are with Sensory (which is part of Laser's Edge) in the States then surely their profile is going to increase somewhat dramatically. The guys can play, and there is a certain sense of drama about what they are doing, but there are times when this album does not quite shine as it should. That is not down to the production (which has been handled by Tommy Newman), but rather that the guys are

not always exactly sure in which direction they should be going. It is almost as if they are trying to be Pain Of Salvation but with a little more chaos. I am sure that we are going to be hearing a lot more from these guys in the future and it will be interesting indeed to see how they do now that they are going to be in front of a much larger audience.
#89, Sep 2006

THE WATCH
VACUUM

'Vacuum' is the third album from Italian progsters The Watch – it would be very easy to write a one sentence review of this album which would be most unfair. All the average punter needs to know is that these guys have been listening to 'Trespass', mixed in some 'Nursery Cryme' and possibly 'Selling England By The Pound' and there you have their influences. So, we have five guys, not only with a singer who can easily pass for a young Gabriel but a keyboard player who is Tony Banks reincarnated. Some of the shuffles and changes that he comes up with underneath the guitars are the original sounds perfectly recreated. Ah, but there is the rub, unlike bands such as ReGenesis who see fit only to attempt to reproduce songs note for note, these guys have taken the influences and proudly display them for all to hear but then go off and create something that is very new indeed. Yes, they have been influenced dramatically by one group, but for them that is the starting point and none of these songs contain passages that one could say has been lifted from a Genesis song, but rather the stylings and tones are very like what that band created thirty years or more ago.

In many ways, this is refreshing as no-one plays music like this anymore – if Genesis were going then one could guarantee that they wouldn't sound like this, and Gabriel has long moved on – so, why shouldn't they? If you enjoy Gabriel-era Genesis then you will love this, and everyone who has heard this seems to be of the same opinion. This is a very enjoyable album indeed.
#85, Nov 2005

THE WATCH
GHOST

'Ghost' was the 2002 follow-up to the band's debut 'Twilight', and the precursor to the excellent 'Vacuum' that I reviewed in the last issue. As with the latest album, this shows the band wearing their influences proudly on their sleeve, and in some ways, this is even closer to classic Genesis than what they are doing now, and part of "DNAlien" seems quite familiar. But again, that is probably unfair as while they have taken that band as a starting point they have instead moved on and have created something that is vibrant and in the current market quite refreshing. While other bands tip their hat to the golden days, few have fully embraced them as have these Italian progsters, so that there are very few bands who are tackling this musical style and The Watch are

setting an extremely high standard indeed for others to follow. To put it simply, if you enjoy Gabriel-era Genesis then this is a band that you certainly need to get closer to. They are not clones but have taken a musical identity and moved with it and developed it into something that in some ways is very dated but in others is very relevant and now. They are a very interesting and to me very exciting band.
#86, Feb 2006

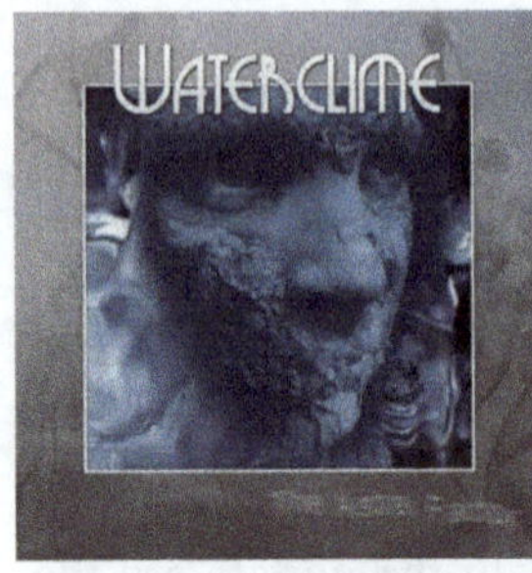

WATERCLIME
THE ASTRAL FACTOR

Waterclime is a new project by Mr V (Vintersorg, Borknagar, Fission etc.), and he provided all the instruments himself apart from a couple of guest guitar solos from Matthias Marklund (also from Vintersong) and an appearance on one song by Magnus Lindren (Black Bonzo). The first time I played this album I was not too sure, as initially I felt that the vocals were not always all that they could be – but the more I played it the more I realised what an integral part they are of the overall sound. This is an album that wouldn't have sounded out of place the best part of thirty years ago, as he mixes melodic rock with prog and creates something that at times sounds a bit like Rush, or a bit like Genesis, or more normally an amalgam of lots of different styles. It is rooted in melody, but with lots of different things being used, such as old-fashioned keyboards but it is all layered and arranged so that it all comes together like a wonderful comfortable blanket. This is not in your face melodic rock, nor is it 'traditional' prog rock (if there is such a thing), but something that is song based and not overtly complex, and the more that I played this the more I enjoyed it.
#86, Feb 2006

JOHN WETTON
LIVE IN TOKYO 1997

Now, I like John Wetton, have long been a fan of various of his groups, but was disappointed when I saw him myself in concert. This CD is of a gig that took place in Japan on 5th October 1997 and has been produced by John himself and I had high hopes for it. But, in this case it is the production itself that is problematic, as the sound levels go up and down. In the opening "Sole Survivor" it is just possible to hear that David Kilminster is playing the guitar line, but this is at a point where it should be right in your face. Some of the songs, such as the stripped-down version of "Heat of the Moment" work very well indeed, apart from when David totally loses it for some reason, but there is the impression that due to the mix this album is not nearly as it should be. There is a bonus CD that contains an extra four songs, but I must say that I would rather wait for the live album that has been produced recently by IQ's Martin Orford. I look forward to that with great interest but doubt if this will be getting many more visits to my player.
#52, Feb 1999

JOHN WETTON
LIVE IN NEW YORK

While I was bitterly disappointed with John's last live release, here I find myself with the opposite response. This is mostly an acoustic album where John accompanies himself on acoustic guitar, and he is joined by Martin Orford on keyboards and vocals and Ian MacDonald on flute and vocals. All the songs are taken from just one gig on 27th May 1997, and while the sound quality leaves a little to be desired, more a very high-quality bootleg than a standard release, the quality of the music in this case makes up for it. Fans of King Crimson will need this album as it features no less than five songs from his period with them, while lovers of IQ will also have to be on the lookout as it features a solo piano instrumental from Martin called "Quilmes". Overall the album shows John's powerful emotional vocals of to the full. His next release will be a full-blown live recording that I have been assured is truly awesome. I can't wait, but until then I will keep playing this.

#53, May 1999

JOHN WETTON
SUB ROSA LIVE IN MILAN 5 JULY 1998

JOHN WETTON
NO MANS LAND LIVE IN POLAND MAY 1998

Even the most hardened Wetton fans must surely be wondering what is going on, as there have been four live CDs now released in as many months. 'Sub Rosa' is an acoustic album in a similar vein to the recent 'Live In New York' and here Martin Orford again joins John, along with guitarist Dave Kilminster. Dave proves that he is very adept on the acoustic and the trio all sing well and along with the all-acoustic, no bass; no drums (or programming, Hallelujah!) instrumentation provides a new insight to many of the songs. This is particularly true of "Sole Survivor" which has totally different dynamics and John and Dave trade acoustic runs with seeming ease. The production is good and there is much on here to enjoy, with all the songs benefiting from a fresh and new hearing.

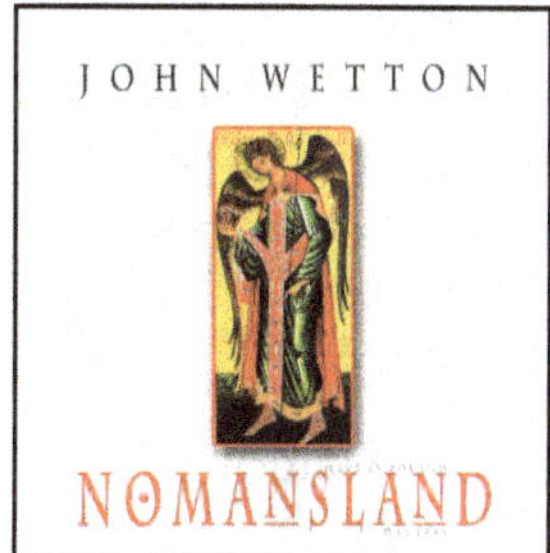

But if you want to know what John is like when playing electric then look no further than 'No Mans Land', which was recorded in Poland just two months earlier. The guys have been joined here by Jadis sticksman Steve Christey and the result is a much harder album with Steve driving the guys along and Dave relishing the chance to crank out riffs when he gets the opportunity. There are some acoustic numbers on here as a respite to the stronger material, but here it is a contrast. Whereas John has been releasing many albums through Blueprint, for this one he has signed to GEP and a lot of work has gone into the production by Rob Aubrey and Martin Orford. Which to choose? The answer would be to

buy both (there is quite a variance between the songs on each CD, and many of those that are duplicated sound totally different), but if I had to pick just one then it would be 'Sub Rosa' as there is something about John, Martin and Dave performing acoustically that has a special magic.
#55, Sept 1999

JOHN WETTON
LIVE AT THE SUN PLAZA

JOHN WETTON
SINISTER

Not long after the gig in Tokyo that has now been released as 'Live At The Sun Plaza' I had the pleasure of seeing Martin Orford perform at Whitchurch. I do not know how anyone that jet-lagged could stay awake, and he did have problems staying on the stool. Martin was keyboard player on August 5th, 1999 and was joined by the usual suspects (David Kilminster guitar and Steve Christey drums) in playing with John Wetton. There is some good stuff on here, but I am not sure what John is trying to do in releasing so many live albums (I have lost track of how many I have reviewed, and that has not been all of them). There is a danger of material being lost or overlooked and although this appears to be a full concert (double CD) there is something much more pressing to purchase.

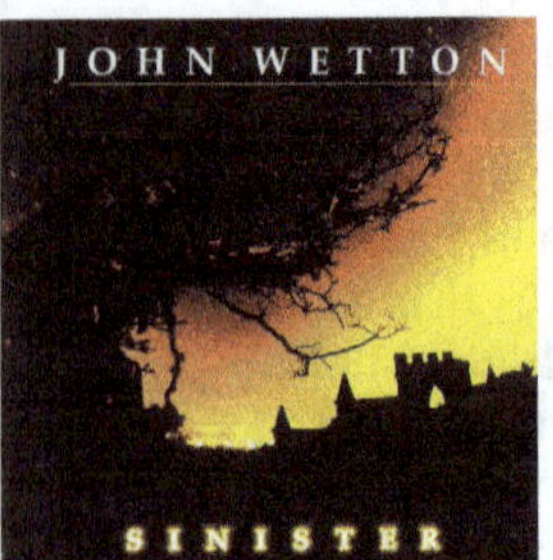

'Sinister' is John's new studio album, and it is simply the finest thing that he has recorded since the debut Asia album all those years ago. The worry is that it may be ignored as there is so much Wetton material flooding out but take it from me this is one of the best driving albums you are ever likely to hear. John has been working with some very strong writers, including Jim Vallance (Bryan Adams), Jim Peterik (Survivor), Dick Wagner (Alice Cooper) and David Cassidy (!!) among others. In addition, he worked on one song with Martin Orford and Steve Christey (where instead of using Dave Kilminster he has brought in Gary Chandler). The first song, "Heart Of Darkness" begins and ends as a gentle number, but in-between it is a fine AOR rocker. Having already been shocked by the quality of the opener, I was not ready for "Say It Ain't So" which is a classic. Imagine Asia mixing with Bryan Adams in a power ballad that can also belt along, then you may have some idea of how good this is. "No Ordinary Miracle" is much more in line with his ballads and slows the album down a little. Then it is back with the third Vallance co-write, which again ups the tempo. A gentle instrumental (featuring Robert Fripp and Ian McDonald) leads into the hardest number on the album. This is "Another Twist Of The Knife", and Dick Wagner riffs the song along, as John gets heavy. This has great hooks and features some of John's best singing – it is worth getting the album for this song alone!! The song featuring Jadis, "Silently", is the most 'progressive' on the album, and features some very characteristic guitar work from Gary. It comes a close second to being the best song on the album. Both "Before Your Eyes" and "Second Best" are slower numbers, and then it is time for the

closer "Real World". This is John with a twelve-string, joined by Steve Hackett (on harmonica!). Overall, it is an awesome album, one that I took out of my CD interchanger with much dismay. If you have ever enjoyed any of John's work, or just want to hear great melodic rock then this is one that you simply must get.
#62, May 2001

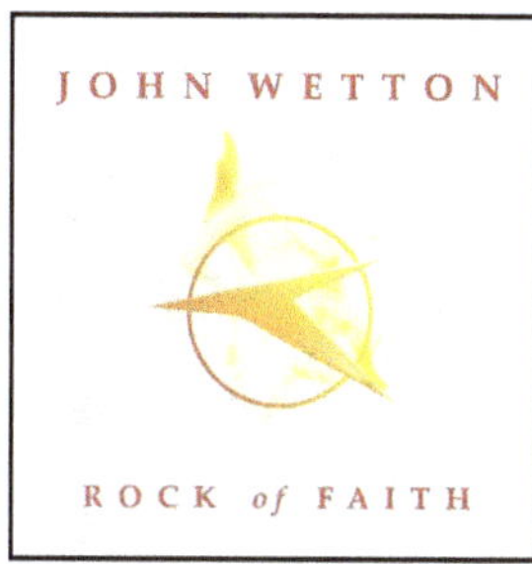

JOHN WETTON
ROCK OF FAITH
It was back in #62 that I raved about John's latest album, 'Sinister', and said that it was his finest work since he had left Asia and here I am now saying the same thing again, because although 'Sinister' was good it was not as strong as this which has to be one of the best albums John has ever been associated with throughout his long career. The core of the band was John himself, Steve Christey (Jadis) and John Mitchell (Arena) who are both in his touring band and one Clive Nolan (Arena, Shadowland, Pendragon etc.). John Wetton had gone to Thin Ice to record the drums and liked it so much he stayed! Clive's partner in crime, Karl Groom, engineered the album and the Thin Ice guys co-produced it with John. There are also a few guests, including one Geoffrey Downes who he hadn't worked with in years, but for this album they also co-wrote two songs together. Something that will most definitely be of interest to all Asia fans. But what makes this such a strong album? The songs are much more in the melodic, hard rock field, but slower, with an emphasis on orchestral overtones with the main listening point being the vocals. Each song is aimed at maximising the power of the voice, with the music as a vehicle, and this has allowed John to shine. The album starts with an atmospheric instrumental, where Clive and John Mitchell combine to good effect to build on the emotion, which in turn leads to the title cut which segues in gently, gradually building on John's vocals. It is an album that hearkens back to old times while also showing the future and based on this album that is very bright indeed. It is immediately accessible and enjoyable and one that I have enjoyed playing a great deal.
#73, Apr 2003

WHISTLER'S MOTHER
THE GRACEFUL ART OF FALLING
Whistler's Mother is the vehicle for the songs of Chris Smith, featuring Chris on vocals and acoustic guitar and Miles Evemy on keyboards. Some tracks also feature Sarah Midson (bass), Michael Brown (drums) and Jeff Ward (lead guitar). Jeff also produced the album, which was recorded, at his studio in Ireland: some of you may recognise his name, as he was the original guitarist in Arena. Both in musical and vocal style, Chris reminds me of Jay Turner, although there is a greater use of keyboards. Miles and Chris obviously have a wonderful understanding, as the keyboards are a very important part of the music but are never overpowering or a detracting force. Songs are the order of the day and the result is an album that is extremely pleasant on the ear. I

think I expected a far more proggy album, especially as Chris was put onto me by Karl Groom, and seeing Tony Grinham's name in the thanks column. However, the album is far more folk-based, with just a few deft prog touches to give the songs balance. I enjoyed listening to the album; one that proves that you do not needs loads of amplification to deliver the goods.
#37, Oct 1996

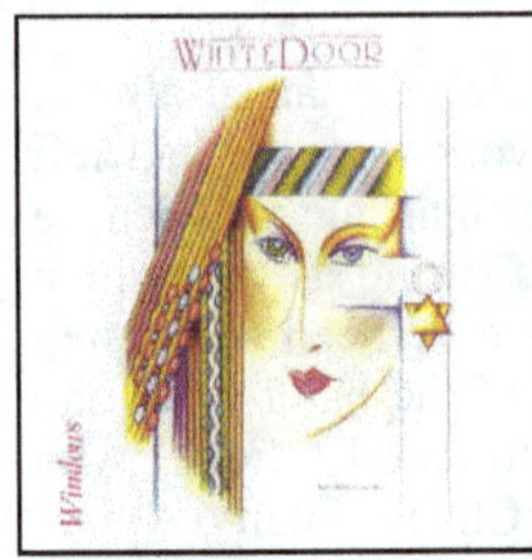

WHITE DOOR
WINDOWS

Grace are one of the top prog bands in the country and have been around for a long time. But, after the release of their second album, 'Grace Live', back in 1980 they split up. Vocalist Mac Austin and flautist and madman Harry Davies had been playing together since the very early days of Grace, back when the band was known as Jim Crow in the early Seventies, and they decided to keep their music association going in a project called White Door. I was kindly sent a copy of the album, and when I was in Whitchurch recently, I caught up with Mac and we spent some considerable time discussing the band and its history. Initially White Door was an outlet just for songs, and in the first twelve months after the break-up of Grace, Mac and Harry wrote twenty to thirty. Harry's brother John was recruited, and with Mac singing and John and Harry both playing keyboards, a synth band was born. Mac knew Andy Richards (ex-Strawbs, and occasionally keyboard player for Sad Café), and it was decided that he would help on the album. Apparently, Andy had lots of ideas and was extremely knowledgeable on the programming side of things, but he needed songwriters to be able to put his ideas into place. The album was initially programmed at Andy's house, and was then recorded at Pluto Studios in Manchester. White Door were signed to Clay Records, Grace's old label, and when Clay heard the album, they were pleased but felt that it needed remixing. A decision was taken to go to Trevor Horn's SARM studio in London.

Halfway through the recording of the album Trevor came into the studio and he was so impressed with Andy that he signed him up to work on 'Welcome To The Pleasuredome'. Some of the ideas that had been used with White Door were then taken into Frankie Goes To Hollywood. The middle eight riff from "Flame In Your Heart" (a single not on the album) was later used in "Relax". The album came out in 1981, and the single "Windows" became Single Of The Week for Simon Bates, but it did not make any impression in the charts. White Door were signed up by Passport Records to release the album in America, as well as for some singles. Magnet Records then decided that they would like to sign them up and everything seemed to be going well until Magnet discovered that White Door were signed to Passport. As Magnet wanted a worldwide deal it was all put on hold while things were sorted out. Unfortunately, Magnet took a year to decide that they wouldn't sign the band after all, and White Door left Clay due to lack of money and the band gradually folded by 1986. They left behind some singles, including "Way of the World" and "Kings of the Orient", which are now very collectable. 'Windows' sold five thousand copies in America, and about two thousand in the UK. With the right backing they would have done extremely well as they had a good commercial sound right for the pop charts. 'Windows' is now very difficult to find, but John Davies is currently working on the material, updating the synth sounds, and it may well be available on CD in the future. Interesting for those into Grace, or even FGTH, it is an album that deserved far more, with good pop songs and some great singing from Mac. Grace perform one of the songs, "Windows" from time to time and it is an album worth searching out in collector's shops. *#18, May 1993*

WHITE WILLOW
SACREMENT

This is the third album by Norwegian act White Willow but is the first that I have heard. I know that the debut 'Ignis Fatuus' caused quite a stir when it came out in 1995, but I never got around to getting it. I am now wondering what I have missed as this is a prog album of some depth. Vocalist Sylvia Erichsen is like Annie Haslam, and the music comes across as a mixture of King Crimson, Jethro Tull and even Gryphon. There is a lot of space in the music, and although there are three keyboard players in the band the music is still very guitar based. Lots of acoustic guitar (and as the press release states that this is their heaviest release, I wonder what the others were like), and reflection but this is not New Age at all. Jacob Holm-Lupo (who provides much of the material, as well as playing guitars and keyboards) harmonises well with Sylvia, and songs such as "The Last Rose Of Summer" are a sheer delight. One to savour.
#60, Oct 2000

WHITE WILLOW
SIGNAL TO NOISE

White Willow's fifth studio album, 'Signal to Noise', was mixed and produced by Tommy Hansen (Helloween, TNT, Pagan's Mind, Circus Maximus). The line-up features new singer Trude Eidtang (vocals), Lars Fredrik Frøislie (keyboards, electronics), Jacob Holm-Lupo (guitars), Ketil Vestrum Einarsen (woodwinds), Marthe Berger Walthinsen (bass guitar) and Aage Moltke Schou (drums, percussion). Before I get onto the music, I must mention the group photo, as they are sat around the table on which is a pile of albums – the top one of which I recognise as being 'The Day The Earth Caught Fire' by City Boy. Any band that recognises just how good City Boy were, are already ahead in my book. Well, the band took three weeks to record this instead of one year, and have a new singer on-board to boot, but they have still managed to produce a multi-layered progressive rock album that twists and turns through many different styles yet still contains loads of Mellotrons. Trude's voice has a good range, but there is an almost ethereal quality to it – a breathiness that adds to the overall feel of what is a very strong rock band with lots of ideas. White Willow are going to be playing in the UK at the Summer's End Festival, and I know that there are going to be many progheads who are going to be very pleased to see them indeed. This is good solid symphonic prog from the Seventies with loads of ideas. *#89, Sep 2006*

ALAN WHITTAKER
WAKE UP AND WELCOME TO THE REAL WORLD
Alan used to be in Mancunian proggers Moriarty in the early Eighties, where he provided guitars and vocals. With the impending birth of his son in 1995, Alan decided that if he was going to make a solo album it was now or never. How many of you read the credits on a CD? I do, as I have often found little gems which give me an insight to the band, and here are Alan's comments to his wife: "And most of all to Sally for putting up with me spending ludicrous amounts of time locked in a pair of cans cursing the machinery, cats and my own inability in varying degrees". Now even before playing it I knew that I was going to like this album as anyone who laughs at themselves normally produces the goods. I am still not quite sure how Alan ended up in the Progressive Rock Directory, as quite a lot of this is singer-songwriter material, albeit sometimes with proggy instrumentation. What is blatantly obvious is that Alan is a songwriter and lyricist of no mean achievement and he can also belt it along at times as well, just listen to the funky rock of "Master of the Universe". True, Alan hasn't the purest vocals in the world, as I am sure that he would be the first to agree, but this is a classy album. A real home release this, with no attempt to give it a number or record company, not even a barcode. For only £10 and an SAE this joy can be yours to behold.
#33, Feb 1996

ALAN WHITTAKER
TOP OF THE WORLD
This is a dreamy album, as Alan drifts along in a style not too dissimilar to Crowded House. Fourteen songs, and they are all pleasant, guitar-based with plenty of keyboards. It is music to let bubble away in the background or take a bit more seriously and listen to intently. This is not music to be played at high volume, although some such as the title cut do have a lot more in the way of guitar. It is not a totally solo project as he does have a few guests, but for the most part it is Alan singing and accompanying himself in one way or another. This is music that those who enjoy the lighter side of prog or AOR would get a lot from; he is not the greatest singer in the world but knows his strengths and limitations and works with them. The melodies are good, and it is an album that I play when I do not want anything too intrusive. Alan has been making a lot of his music available as MP3's through the internet, but amazingly enough also gives away his CDs! This is his third album, with a professional booklet and tray card, and does not appear to be a CD-R. If you ever wanted to discover some fresh new music but did not know where to go, what is stopping you from starting here?
#78, Apr 2004

WICKED MINDS
FROM THE PURPLE SKIES
As soon as I put this into the player a smile started to creep across my face, as here is a

modern band that has taken The Nice, mixed it with early Uriah Heep and managed to put some serious heaviness into some classic rock. I hadn't looked at the booklet when I was first playing this in the car, so it was some surprise to find that there are two covers in Pentagram's "Forever My Queen" and Uriah Heep's "Gypsy". The Hammond Organ is bang on, and singer J.C. certainly has something of David Byron about him. But if all this was not enough, they end with the eighteen-minute long "Return To Uranus". It starts delicately with acoustic guitar and flute, but gradually some Jon Lord, Keith Emerson style noodlings come in and the guitar is gently soloed until soon the whole band are kicking in with a Heep, Purple style classic. This is an album that needs to be more widely heard as there is not a duff sound to be heard and while they may not be creating anything drastically new, it's such great fun to listen to. I have had problems getting this out of my player as it is so strong – easily one of the best albums I have ever heard from Italy. As with all Black Widow releases this is also available on vinyl and that is probably the correct way to play this as it brings together lots of styles from a bygone age and is all the better for it. *#83, Mar 2005*

HARRY WILLIAMSON
LIFE IN THE WORLD UNSEEN

Harry is a very adept musician, who seems to delight in discovering new stringed instruments to play with, and the result is an album that was recorded over a period of four years. Some of them are solo, some just with Guy Evans, while others are recorded with many friends playing more weird instruments. Harry attempts to capture moods and styles in a very varied manner, and the result is intriguing and sometimes hard to listen to. This is music that certainly will not appeal to many but if you enjoy music that can be challenging then you could do far worse than this. *#63, Jul 2001*

WILLOWGLASS
WILLOWGLASS

Amanda was in the car listening to this with me and after a while she turned and said "this is the perfect album to listen to at the end of the day, isn't it daddy?". Now I must be training her right as I think she has wisdom beyond her eight years as although there are some very upbeat sections it is indeed an album to be enjoyed with a glass of fine wine and the lights turned down low. Willowglass is Andrew Marshall on everything apart from drums, which are provided by Dave Brightman. I am glad that there are no vocals, as I think that may spoil it and I really enjoy having this on and just drifting away. It contains elements of Floyd, Genesis, Camel, Jadis, Steve Hackett and so many more but whether the lead melody is being picked out delicately on electric guitar or keyboards, then this is an album of peace, tranquillity, and in that respect the cover art is bang on. An extra element is that Andrew also plays flute, so instead of the synth version there is a breathy realism that feels far more organic and in keeping with the overall tone. There are Mellotrons aplenty, and one word that really sums this up is "lush", as it is full of life and somehow a return to a bygone age where it was not unusual for singers to wear dresses and put on a fox's head yet is also very much an album for now. This is not some sad impersonation of something that has been before, begging to be left a crumb from the table of musical acknowledgement, but is instead demanding a full-blown feast. This is a wonderful album that I have thoroughly enjoyed and highly recommend to those who enjoy good music, whatever the genre. *#85, Nov 2005*

DAMIAN WILSON
COSMAS

Damian's solo album has been a long time coming. I remember him filling in for the ill Geoff Mann at The Marquee years ago, accompanying himself just on acoustic guitar, and can even remember him playing one of the songs that now appear on this wonderful album, "She's Like A Fable". I have long been telling anyone who will listen about Damian's vocals, as to me he is probably the best singer to come out of the UK underground. His power and range are second to none, and he has proved in the past his ability to cope with different styles in the hard-edged technical rock of Threshold and the progressive Landmarq. He left both bands a few years ago to front La Salle, which also featured Neil Murray (Whitesnake), David Palmer (Jethro Tull) and Guy Fletcher (Dire Straits). On his return to the UK he auditioned for Iron Maiden and made it through to the final three (I still believe that it would have been better for Maiden if they had chosen him instead of Blaze) and he has recorded again with both Landmarq and Threshold as well as joining Adam Wakeman in Jeronimo Road. It is rather surprising then that his solo album is not packed full of 'names' or rockers, but instead is just full of wonderful songs which are mostly slower, allowing Damian to shine. Great thought has been given also to the accompaniment, which is varied; sometimes orchestral while at others it is gentle guitar or piano. Overall this album is a delight and should appeal to anyone who loves songs that do not require a stack of Marshalls.
#44, Sept 1997

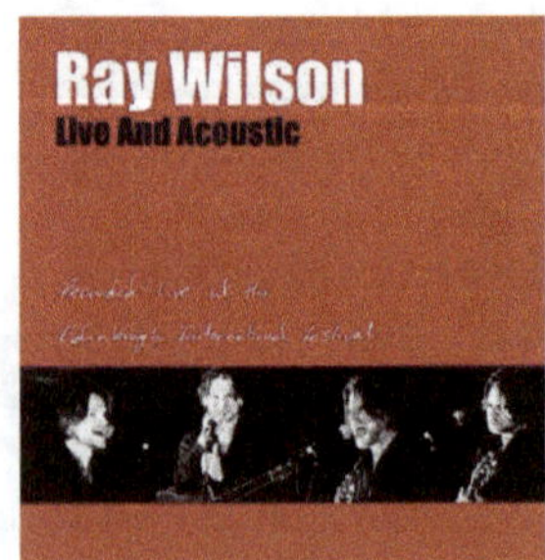

RAY WILSON
LIVE AND ACOUSTIC

RAY WILSON
CHANGE

I was one of many who wondered what on earth Mike Rutherford and Tony Banks were thinking of when they replaced Phil Collins with the ex-singer of rock band Stiltskin. Sure, they had a number one in the UK on the back of an ad for Levi's, but he was a rock singer! And so, it came to pass that I was given a copy of 'Live and Acoustic' and told to go away and listen to it. This is Ray at the Fringe

Festival with an acoustic guitar, a few friends behind him, lots more in front of him, and his voice for company. Looking at the track listing I knew that Ray had to be either crazy or truly gifted. Anyone attempting to produce an acoustic version of "In The Air Tonight" must be certifiable, doesn't he? But it's good, as is the next song, a dramatic version of "Inside" that sounds totally different without the rock guitars. By now I was hooked and looking forward to each new song with great interest. There are a few that are not quite up to the mark, but even these are carried through by his great vocals. I just hadn't realised how well this guy could sing. Of his own, the highlight had to be "Sarah", but there are just a few covers in there to make any Genesis fan salivate. How about a stunning version of "Lovers Leap" and a stonking "Carpet Crawlers"? He closes his set with an emotive "Biko", showing that he can do solo Gabriel as well as he can solo Collins. But the real joy is to be found on the 'hidden' track after an amazingly successful "Mama". This is when he performs "Desperado" with no accompaniment whatsoever – just his voice and a little reverb. Astonishing.

Now that album sort of crept out, having originally been released by Ray himself, but that cannot be said of 'Change', which has had a lot of publicity. Just one of the songs from Ray's live album finds its way onto the studio, "Another Day", which comes towards the end. But again, the main feature of this album is Ray's vocals, but here they are just slightly more hidden away by the layers of instruments. Even though the songs themselves are good, I found that I was wishing again that it was just Ray and his guitar. It is not a bad album, it is one that I have enjoyed playing time and again, but there is an honesty and raw passion on the live album that is sadly missing here. The latter may be easier to find but if you want to know just what to expect from Ray Wilson then look for the live album as it is superb.

#74, Jun 2003

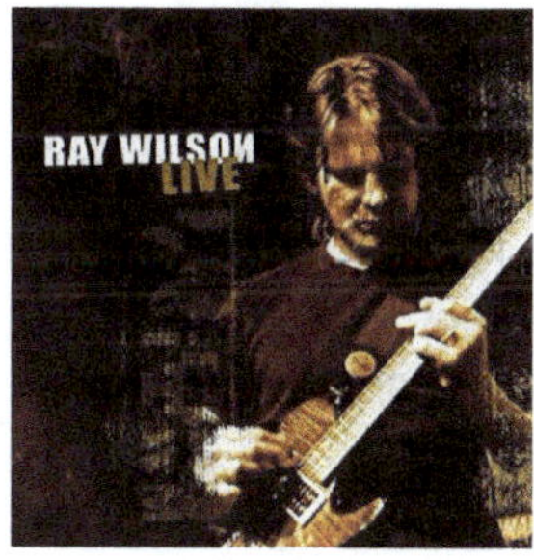

RAY WILSON

LIVE

It was not that many years ago that I was raving about Ray's acoustic live album, and now here he is back with a full band in front of an avid German crowd in November last year. This is a double album, and Ray proves yet again that he is a fine singer and exactly why Mike Rutherford and Tony Banks felt that he could fill Phil Collins' sizeable shoes. Of course, in many ways that career move was a huge blessing for him, but in other ways it can also be a millstone that Ray is happy to carry around with him. He recorded just one album and completed one tour, so why in a 32-song set are there eleven songs that are Genesis or Genesis related? He even covers "Biko" and "In The Air Tonight", but he knows that he is guaranteed a response. The same can be said for the song that follows "Air". The crowd had been enjoying the gig up until then but when the keyboards start for "Carpet Crawlers" they start to sit up and take notice. I think that what annoys me is that I am the same as those in the audience, I want him to be playing his own material but he sounds just so good on this, probably better than Phil did

as his natural voice is that bit lower, much more like Peter's. That he can write good songs in his own right is never doubt, as is proved on numbers such as "These Are The Days" and the gorgeous very tongue in cheek "The Airport Song". But of course, he did have a number one single in the UK, and not with Genesis, so it is of no surprise that "Inside" is also performed and overall there is a good feel to the set, a good balance as he moves from one style and period to another. Favourite? I would love to say that it is an original, but his version of "Ripples" is inspired, and an interesting choice, while "The Lamb Lies Down On Broadway" and "Lovers Leap" do justice to the originals. Maybe in years to come Ray will feel that he has moved far enough away from the huge Genesis shadow that has fallen over to him to play more original material but overall this is an album for the Genesis and non-Genesis fan alike.
#84, July 2005

WINGDOM
REALITY
Wingdom are a new Finnish band that was formed by ex-Sonata Arctica members Mikko Harkin and Jukka Ruotsalainen. They were then joined by Sami Asp (Derek Sherinian, Virgil Donati), Markus Niemispelto and Alessandro Lotta (Rhapsody). Given the backgrounds of most of the band it is of no surprise to find that Wingdom are musically firmly into progressive metal with power metal tendencies. It is also not surprising to find that this album was originally released on the High and Loud label, which is owned by Timo Kotipelto of Stratovarius. In this country, it is available on the new 'The A Label', which is distributed by RSK Entertainment. Pick any of the aforementioned bands and one will discover similarities. When they want to they can blast along like good 'uns, but do not fall into the trap at the beginning of the album where it sounds as if the band are playing through layers of material: certainly, do not feel inclined to turn it up as at twenty seconds there is an explosion and the full force comes blasting through.

What does make this an interesting album is that they want to mix styles within the same song so they can be at full bore one second and then into a reflective power ballad mood the next, and of course vice versa. The keyboards play an important role in providing lead melody lines over the top of what can be some aggressive guitars. The vocals are spot on and it is only the lack of truly memorable songs that stops me from raving about it. Interesting certainly, and enjoyable, but not totally essential although fans of the genre may disagree with me.
#84, July 2005

WINGS OF STEEL
HOMESICK
Dutch band Wings of Steel were formed in 1988 and are one of those rare things in rock music, a trio. Not content with that, their vocalist Jan Van Heumen is also the drummer, which is also unusual. Along with Roland Kok (bass, keyboards) and Peter Van de Ven (guitar, keyboards) they released their first demo, 'Running On The Edge' in 1991 and it

was well received in both Holland and elsewhere. They supported Saga in June 1992 and Galahad in the September. In fact, Stu remarked to me at the time that not only could the drummer sing well, but still played and kept time. This is the full -length debut, and very good it is too. One thing that surprised me was the fact that the band sound as if they come from the other side of the Atlantic. The songs are well-crafted and performed, but although they are all enjoyable, none of them stick in the mind after the album has finished. Good melodic rock a la Asia, or even Saga. The guitar is mostly kept under control, but at times is allowed more of a free rein such as "Running On The Edge", which is one of the more powerful numbers. The best song is "Make It Alone", which is an acoustic number with gorgeous harmony vocals, a song that any band could be rightly proud of and could even be a hit single following in the footsteps of Extreme and Mr. Big. If you like American-style rock that is on the prog side of AOR, and with great vocals, then Wings of Steel are worth discovering.
#17, Mar 1993

WINGS OF STEEL
FACE THE TRUTH
It has been three years since their debut CD, 'Homesick', and although they are still a trio, they have a new bassist in the form of Orlando van Swaay. They have also changed musical direction as well, becoming a far heavier outfit than they were before. The press release says, "it would never occur to a lot of fans to categorise them as progressive rock". I would have to agree with that, because what they are doing now is not prog but more a heavy melodic rock clearly influenced by American styles. I have only had the opportunity to play this album once, and while it is enjoyable, I must say that on first listen there is nothing that stands out. I think that this is possibly because Wings Of Steel have tried to get heavy while retaining the melody, and it does not quite fit together as it should. At the same time, I have enjoyed listening to it, but is it one that I would have gone out and bought? Hand on heart I must confess that I probably wouldn't. To hear heavy melodic rock at its best I would point to Everon or Threshold, and not Wings Of Steel. This is a shame as the last song I heard from them ("Thoughts Of Change" on 'SI Compilation Too') showed real promise and I was looking forward to this, but the debut is better. We must wait and see what the Dutchmen come up with next.
#28, Apr 1995

WINTER
ACROSS THE CIRCLE'S EDGE
I am glad that I was told to check out this band, as not only are they brilliant live, they have an excellent album out as well! But I am probably getting a little ahead of myself and should tell you something about the band first. Winter were originally formed in January 1988 in Newtownards, Northern Ireland with a line-up of Johnny Lennie

(vocals), Richard Loyer (bass), John Murphy (drums), Phil Murray (keyboards) and Rab Beggs (guitar). They gigged consistently in Ireland where they built up a devoted and noisy following around the local pub and club circuit. Their first demo was runner-up on the Friday Rock Show in September 1989 and this, combined with Tommy Vance's comments, gave them the impetus to record the album 'Across the Circle's Edge', which was released in October 1990. Although there were good sales locally, Winter realised that they were never going to reach a large audience while based in Northern Ireland, so the decision was made to relocate to London. Phil and John were unable to make the move due to personal reasons, and the final gig of this line-up took place in March 1991. Tim Wilson was recruited on drums and Tony Brady on keyboards, and the band moved to... Holland! Many people see this as the only country where prog is appreciated (aided by the excellent SI magazine), and they played many gigs up and down the country. Unfortunately, Rab was unable to settle, and returned to Ireland. But the band were still very confident in their own ability and moved to London in September 1991 and soon recruited Andy Ryan as a replacement. Due to musical differences Tony Brady was asked to leave the band, and he was replaced on a temporary basis by Mario Giodalides, who himself was replaced by Stuart MacDonald who made his live debut with the band only last week.

So, what about the album? I only have the tape at present as the CD is not yet available (it has just been released by SI), but that hasn't stopped me from playing it a great deal. It kicks off with "Technocracy", a song that shows that Winter belong strongly in the melodic rock camp, and arguably shouldn't have the prog label thrust upon them. This is good decent rock that happens to use keyboards as well. The driving riff and powerful drumming needs an outstanding vocalist to stand up to it, and it is much to Johnny's credit that he does so with great aplomb. His voice is extremely melodic, probably most like Geoff Mann, which soars or menaces as the need arises. Lyrically, it is intelligent as Johnny says that this song tries to state that "most bands have stereotypical images and produce facile music, yet through their high media profile they have been treated with a ridiculous and undeserved reverence". I'll agree with that, as I'm sure you will. "The Betrayal of Reason" is no less rocky, but with a much slower tempo, at least until the guitar break when all hell breaks loose. The band are tight and can rock with the best of them. "Close Your Eyes" starts off with a keyboard-driven rock intro, but this gives way to some acoustic guitarwork, which allows Johnny to use his voice to the full. As his voice takes on a rougher edge the electric guitar makes itself known again, and gradually the tempo and volume builds until we are in a full-blown rock song and the riffs drive along with Johnny alternately singing and growling over the top. "Evengate" is a gentle interlude, a piano-driven ballad, which shows how Winter are a band of contrasts.

This leads into "Toybox", a song about guilt, where the character in the song personifies an external conscience who prowls in the quiet moments of the mind. Crashing drums, riffing guitars and soaring keyboards lead the way with the bass driving it all along. Over its' course, the song changes many times, creating new melodies and returning to old themes. There is a passage filled with menace, both lyrically and musically, as the

keyboards take over, although the others gradually make their presence felt. It is a real epic, with great depth, and at nearly nine minutes long is a song that the listener can get lost in. The album closes with "Winter", an instrumental that displays all the best parts of the band. Winter deserve to be taken seriously, both on record and onstage. They have given up a lot to make it, and truly deserve to do so.
#15, Oct 1992

WINTER
MARCHING OUT OF TIME
At long last we have some new product from Winter: this is the first time they have been into the studio for something like four years. I rated their debut CD and have been looking forward to hearing something else from them and what we have here is a two-track tape, which at least means that something is available again. Winter's greatest asset is the vocals of Johnny Lennie, which is outstanding. He shines on the second track. "Three Thousand Candles" which is about the deaths in Northern Ireland (Winter hail from Belfast). At times, there is real anger as the music switches from ballad to rock and back again and again. Neither track lives up to "Toybox", but then again there are not many that could. If you have not heard the rock prog of Winter, then this an ideal opportunity.
#21, Jan 1994

WITHOUTENDING
WITHOUTEND
This is the debut album by Australian trio WithoutEnding, but when I say trio that is with the understanding that they have guest keyboard players and given that the keyboards are very important to the overall sound I am a bit surprised that they do not have a full-time member on board. Something else that is unusual about this band is that the singer is also the drummer, both roles he fills with power. Having played this album quite a few times now I still can't decide if I like it or not. I mean, it is interesting, and they are obviously extremely musically adept and have some good ideas, but I still do not know if it gels as it should. I saw one review where it was said that they brought together the best of Marillion and Dream Theater and I must say that this is just a little bit of an over exaggeration. Some of the songs, such as "Analyse", show that there is real promise, but I am still not sure as to whether it has been fulfilled on this album. It is not so much prog by numbers but something that possibly does not inspire or captivate quite as it should.
#84, July 2005

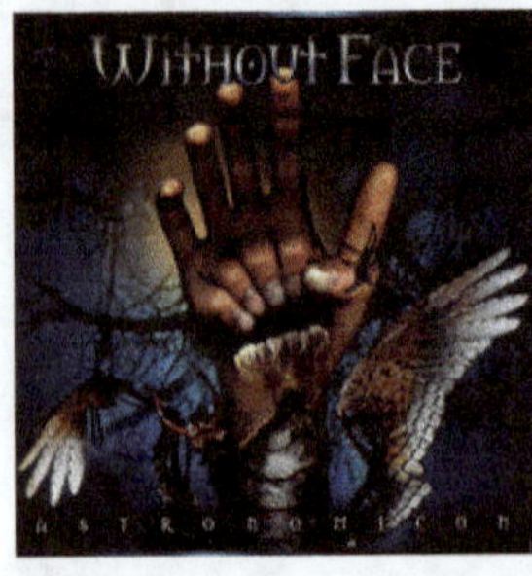

WITHOUT FACE
ASTRONOMICON

Unless Elitist are very careful, they are going to build themselves a reputation of releasing some of the best technical progressive rock albums around. Following on from Rakoth, I have also been listening to the second album by Hungarian band Without Face (following on from 'Deep Inside', which has just been reissued by Dark Symphonies in the States). The band utilise the unusual (within prog circles) tactic of employing two vocalists, and while Julie takes most of the lead roles with her pure clear vocals the band shine at their brightest when she is harmonising with András who generally provides a deeper style. Melody is very much the order of the day, and with the lyrics in English the album is extremely accessible. Musically this is a hard rock band that can crank it out with the likes of Threshold or Pain Of Salvation while maintaining the complexity and twists of out and out prog. They can be very heavy indeed, or conversely be musically heavy but having the whole thing lightened by Julie's vocals. In many ways, they are a heavier version of Legend, the much-missed pagan rock band, but with more shape. An album I have enjoyed listening to immensely and although it may be too heavy for some prog fans it is one that I heartily recommend to those who enjoy the mix of prog and metal.

#69, Aug 2002

WITHOUT WARNING
STEP BEYOND

Having only a promo with a cardboard sleeve, and no press release, there is very little I can say about this band apart from the fact that they are a five-piece. As I started listening to the album (which commences with the title cut) I thought to myself that there was a real groove going on, reminiscent of Dan Reed Network or possibly Electric Boys. However, with the next track being more straightforward hard melodic rock, and with the second longest song "Gracefully" (nearly eight minutes) being guitar-oriented prog I was finding it hard to work out where these guys were coming from. The problem is that although some of what they do is very good indeed, other parts are just okay. There is nothing wrong with the album, but I got the impression that the band themselves are confused over what musical direction they wanted to pursue. I am all for diversity within an album but there is no overall cohesion, which robs the album and music of an identity. It would be hard to say that Without Warning have a sound of their own, one which makes then instantly identifiable which is a shame as I feel that they have a lot to offer, just not this time. Some good things, some not so good, which equates to an album I am unlikely to be playing much in the future.

#51, Jan 1999

WOOLLY WOLSTENHOLME
SONGS FROM THE BLACK BOX

Stuart John Wolstenholme, forever known as Woolly, was a founder member of Barclay James Harvest in 1967 when he and John Lees teamed up with Mel Pritchard and Les Holroyd. With them he recorded nine albums before leaving in 1979. This was because he was feeling frustrated at working in a band that had two other songwriters, and as he had no time to record his songs outside of the band, a solo career was his only option. 'Mæstoso' was recorded in early 1980, with guitarist Steve Broomhead and drummer Kim Turner, both of whom had worked with Woolly on the second Mandalaband album. Some of this material was originally written for BJH, and in fact the title track was recorded by them in 1974 but was never released. Two other songs had been selected for the next BJH studio album, while two others had been rejected by them. The release of 'Mæstoso' was overshadowed by a good period for BJH and was largely ignored. Terry Grady joined as bassist, and Mæstoso hit the road, supporting acts such as Judie Tzuke and Saga. Prior to the tour Woolly had already begun work on the second album provisionally titled 'Black Box' and had recorded several eight-track demos. However, after the tour Steve departed and Polydor decided not to release a second album, so Woolly left the music business altogether and instead concentrated on running his organic farm in Wales. Voiceprint managed to persuade Woolly to get involved with the mastering of the CD, but he has no plans for a musical comeback.

This CD comprises the whole of 'Mæstoso', as well as those songs that would have appeared on 'Black Box'. For the most part these are not completed songs, as some musical parts are missing and the lyrics may well have changed, but it gives an idea of what would have been on there. There are eighteen songs on the CD, and it kicks off with "Has To Be A Reason". I did not realise just how strong a voice Woolly has, he takes lead vocals on all tracks, thinking that many of the harmonies on the BJH albums were double tracking of John and Les's vocals. It is no surprise to discover that many of the songs sound as if they would not be out of place on a BJH album, given that Woolly was an integral part of their sound for most of his musical career. Because of the large fanbase still enjoyed by BJH I am a little surprised that this music was not better received at the time, as it compares very well with the standard being achieved by BJH (personally I feel they were at their peak with 'Time Honoured Ghosts' and 'Octoberon'). This music is melodic and enjoyable, and of obvious historical interest to anyone who likes Barclay James Harvest. The sleeve notes are comprehensive, and all in all it is a good example of another re-release handled well by Voiceprint.
#24, Jul 1994

WOOLLY WOLSTENHOLME
BLACK BOX RECOVERED

In 1980 Woolly was recording his second solo album, which was to be called 'Black Box'. However, he lost interest in the music business and decided to farm instead. Tapes from these sessions along with the complete 'Mæstoso' album were released in 1994 as 'Songs From The Black Box' (reviewed in #24). That album has long since been

unavailable, and due to demand Woolly has now cleaned up the tapes, found some rarities and this is the result. Perhaps unsurprisingly, this album has much more in common with BJH than his new album given that the sessions for this was only three years after departure, not twenty-five, but they still show that Woolly was also looking for other musical ideas. Mæstoso had been touring as a band and this is very much a band album, although issued under Woolly's name. It is prog with a melodic element, music that is easy to listen to yet also there are hidden depths to be discovered. BJH fans will state that this is an essential purchase as it is historically important, but better than that this is an album that certainly should have been released at the time and is a fine listen.
#80, Jul 2004

WORLD TURTLE
HAZE

Haze were formed in 1978 by Chris and Paul McMahon and established themselves in the Eighties as one of the top 'underground' prog acts. After some ten years, four drummers and some seven hundred gigs the band called it a day. Paul and Chris then formed World Turtle with Fudge Smith (Pendragon), but the band was short lived and split up in 1989 when Paul quit, disillusioned with the music business. Two years later the brothers were back as World Turtle, which ended up as a duo with Chris providing keyboards, bass and programming while Paul provided vocals, guitar and programming. This album contains new recordings of songs that would have appeared on the third Haze album, songs from the two World Turtle cassettes along with re-recorded Haze tracks and the previously unreleased "Epitaph". These guys are quite unlike any other band as they mix prog, jazz, dance and pop into a glorious whole, in fact, one of the real joys of this album is the fact that each track is so different from the one that has just finished playing. "The Ember" was written as long ago as 1982, but not originally recorded until 1985. A repeating guitar pattern sets the scene for the strong vocals of Paul. This is a prog rock song, certainly, yet it manages to be totally accessible and commercial at the same time. It is this commerciality that runs through much of the music, provoking the amazement that they were not/are not a much bigger band. I must admit that due to the arrival of this CD just before the deadline I am reviewing it having only listened to it twice, something that I would never normally consider but this is just so good! Listen to the "Ship Of Fools" that could and should be a hit single as it grooves along, or my personal favourite "New Dark Ages". One of the joys of the insert is that along with the lyrics, the thinking is explained behind each song. "At the time this song was written, the news headlines were full of the civil war in Armenia, and Azerbaijan and the thought occurred to me that it's impossible to justify hatred based on ethnic, national or religious differences because no-one has any choice of what country or ethnic group they are born into. Sadly, the song seems to become more relevant each time I watch the news". It is a driving rock number with some great bass and guitarwork yet has a totally infectious chorus. Just to prove their diversity the following track "Safe Harbour" is a ballad of sheer beauty. The only

criticism that I can level at this CD is the lack of 'real' drums, as at times I found the electronic percussion just a bit too much. However, this is a small moan about an album that I will be returning to time and again.
#24, Jul 1994

WORLD TURTLE
WILDERNESS OF EDEN

There can be few as dedicated to the cause of progressive rock as Chris and Paul McMahon. The hippie and the straight love their music, and when on stage they are a joy to behold. However, one thing I have said in the past is that I wished that they would use a drummer (as they did in the olden days, when they went by the name of Haze), instead of relying on programming. Not only have they used a guest drummer for this CD, but they have also brought in other musicians to add touches here and there. The result is a class album, and while it will not reach the same number of people as IQ, there is no reason for that. This is totally accessible on first hearing, and the class oozes out of every note. Many will always view them as a prog act when in truth they are far more than "just" that. This is a song-based outfit, with great melodies and vocals. Some of the songs, such as "Kickback", sound so layered and all-consuming that it is hard to believe that it hasn't cost hundreds of thousands of pounds to produce music of this quality and majesty. This is a legal natural high, and when music is as good as this the only thing to do is release your grip on reality and just go with the flow. Listen to it and defy yourself not to smile and have a good time. Whatever you do, do not join in on the chorus to "Let Go" as it's not right to enjoy music as much as this. There is something here for everyone (even an old Haze number, "Rip Van Winkle", which has been greatly revamped), and at times I found myself thinking of Level 42, as they funk and soul along. Not all of it is energetic, there are mellow times as well, but it is the way that the many pieces of the puzzle join that make this one of the best damned albums you are likely to hear this or any other year. The McMahon brothers have been making concertgoers happy for many a moon, but if you are one of those who have missed out on a show then grab a piece of the action. All those I have spoken to about this album agree on one thing, it's brilliant! There is also a limited-edition cassette of outtakes available if you get this directly from the band themselves – you owe it to your ears.
#45, Nov 1997

WYXMER
FEUDAL THRONE

This release is somewhat unusual, as the first six tracks were recorded in 1991, four of which appeared on an EP back then, which has the same castle photograph that appears on the new album. But it is being marketed as a new album and given that virtually no-one outside (or possibly inside) of Italy would be aware of them that is probably a good move. The one thing that I do hope is that this is still a viable band as opposed to a historical remnant as it is very good, very good indeed. In many ways, they are reminiscent of the much loved and sadly missed Winter, whose album still finds time on my player. It is atmospheric, packed full of emotion and layers, with a very Seventies feel – darkly progressive with some elements of folk. Add to that the powerful and clear vocals of Astor Pride and this is a winning combination. It is something that will appeal to those who enjoy their prog with a solid dose of rock guitar without ever falling into prog metal and is certainly one of the most exciting Italian albums I have heard for a while. This is an album that I have enjoyed, class dark Seventies prog from start to end, and is well worth investigation. *#86, Feb 2006*

XAAL
ON THE WAY

Xaal are a French instrumental outfit, originally releasing this album last year, although Progressive International released it on CD earlier this year. The trio of Patrick Boileau (drums), Nicholas Neimer (bass) and Jad Avache (guitar, guitar synth) were joined by Yvon Guillard (trumpet), Alain Guillard (tenor sax) and Stéphane Jaoui (keyboards) to produce a very listenable album. There are very firm influences from outside of the normal rock sphere, and in this case the biggest is jazz, but unlike some this is still very listenable. Obvious comparisons that spring to mind would be Brand X or Colosseum II, but at times there is a more orchestral theme. Highlights? Well, there is some phenomenal jazz bass to be heard, particularly on the opener "The Child". If you like jazz rock, then this is an album for you. *#16, Dec 1992*

XINEMA
DIFFERENT WAYS

The three members of Swedish outfit Xinema originally played together in a band called Madrigal in the late Eighties. It was only when meeting up in the late Nineties that they thought that it might be fun to go back and revisit some of the Madrigal material and record a CD for themselves. But as time passed, the very fact that they were under no pressure meant that they had produced an album that they felt might be appreciated by a wider audience than just the band themselves and it is this album that has just been released by Canadian label Unicorn Records. This is prog that has a light heart; it is music that needs to be taken seriously but not so seriously that it is not enjoyed. My initial feelings on the album was that they were influenced by Saga and while that is still the case there are also some more commercial elements which give the album a more acceptable air to some progheads. It is 'respectable' music, music that is pleasant and complex while not being hard work, much closer to Nineties Genesis than to that of the same band twenty years earlier. Because it is such an easy album to listen to, I am sure that this is going to gain them a large following. If you enjoy prog that has stacks of space within it, and from a band that are not afraid to play a ballad when they must, then this is an album to investigate further. *#72, Feb 2003*

XINEMA
BASIC COMMUNICATION

This is the second album from this Swedish trio, who comprise Mikael Askemur (vocals, bass, keyboards, and guitars), Sven Larsson (guitar) and Jonas Thurén (drums). It has been a few years since the debut, but the wait has been worthwhile as here we have yet another solid symphonic prog album that also contains a few elements of AOR and happily straddles both camps. The vocals are very strong, and the music is very powerful indeed with the band certainly understanding the need of dynamics and creating music that has plenty of holes in it which allows the different elements to shine through. There is never the impression that they are a trio, and never the feeling that this is a small band working for a specialist Canadian label as this is music that is full of confidence, as if the band were already major players in the market. This was the first non-Canadian act to be signed to the label, and this album has certainly repaid the confidence that Michel St -Père had in getting them on-board. Powerful and full of impact, this is something that fans of Marillion and IQ will certainly get a lot out of. It is possible to listen to some of the music by visiting the Unicorn website, so why not immerse yourselves in some great progressive rock music. *#89, Sep 2006*

YOU AND I
EXIT

It is nice to see that prog bands from Hungary are no different to those from the rest of the world. The album is "based and inspired by the knowledge found in the Tibetan Book Of The Dead, the eternal wisdom of Siddhartha Gautama, and the words of Lebanese writer Kahlil Gibran" (so there). The album is in Hungarian, with a narrated passage between some of the songs, but all the words, lyrics and song titles are provided in both Hungarian and English. I found that the only time that the language was a problem was during the narration, as during the songs themselves the pure clear vocals of Fanni Völgessy Szomor become another instrument. Musically they have much in common with Eighties Yes, and the result is an album that any prog lover will enjoy. *#63, Jul 2001*

YWIS
YWIS

Back in #17 I reviewed the album by Timelock, and here is the 1983 album by the direct forerunner of that band, Ywis, which has just been reissued by SI Music. It is of little surprise that the music contained herein is of very similar content and quality to that to be found on 'Louise Brooks', but on the whole, I found this album more enjoyable. The songs seem to be that touch more commercial, certainly to the American AOR/Saga fan and this is very much in Ywis' favour. The one real weakness is the command (or lack of it) of the English language, with the English lyrics being penned by an outsider. Still, even though the guitar is sometimes over-sanitised (e.g. "The Flasher"), there is still enough of it to make the album of real interest to the rocker who likes keyboards used in a rock setting but is not overly found of keyboard-dominated prog rock. I do not think this album will set the world alight, but due to the recent interest in the band there is talk of them recording some of the songs they wrote but never laid down. With some more guitar to go with the excellent vocals then they could be onto a real winner. *#21, Jan 1994*

YWIS
LEONARDO'S DREAM

In 1993 SI Music re-released the debut album by Ywis, which originally came out in 1983. Encouraged by the reaction to this, the band decided to get back together again (they originally split in 1985). Keyboard player Juliean Driessen decided to stay with Timelock, so Rene van Spanje who had previously done the same on some foreign tours replaced him. So, ten years down the road, would the band still be able to perform as a unit? The answer to that must be a resounding yes – most of them had stayed active within the scene and the renewed interest in Ywis had given them a real buzz and motivation to continue where they had left off. They have a very American AOR style mixed with prog, which means that the music is easy listening, although the guitarwork (care of Rinus Hollenberg) does manage to break through at times. The album will appeal to those into American soft rock, as it is melodic with good vocals, while not being too proggy. By the same definition, some prog lovers will find it too 'American' for their tastes. Still, it does work, and considering that it is their first work together for ten years I look forward to the next one with interest. *#32, Dec 1995*

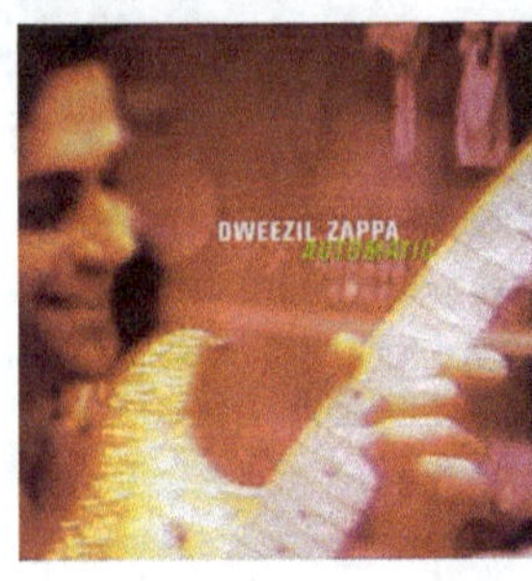

DWEEZIL ZAPPA
AUTOMATIC

This is Dweezil's first album under his own name for nearly a decade and is the first predominantly instrumental guitar album he has released. He is now working under the musical ideal of "Anything at Anytime for Any Reason at All", which has certainly meant that this album has many different ideas and approaches. In the sleeve notes, Dweezil says that he thinks that Frank would have enjoyed it, and I think he's right. There are some very bizarre numbers such as "Shnook" and opener "Fwaktension" where Dweezil proves that he is one of the fastest guitarists around. He can also put rhythm into seemingly impossible time signatures, as well as letting his fingers fly off at tangents. There are also some more serene numbers that are cover versions, such as the all-guitar takes on "Hawaii Five-O" and "Les Toreadors". Possibly one of the most typically Zappa-esque numbers must be "You're A Mean One Mister Grinch" where brother Ahmet provides lead vocals. It rocks and moves with some great music behind the 'delicate' singing. A great album filled with a sense of humour to just take the edge off what is quite pretentious. Wonderful.
#62, May 2001

ZARAGON
NO RETURN

Zaragon were formed in Denmark in 1979, and released this their only album in 1984, but after this CD release was agreed with APM, they reformed and recorded an extra track for inclusion. The result is an excellent album, heavily rooted in the Seventies but much more in the American prog style, most notably Kansas. They have managed to capture a feel very like "Point Of Know Return", yet at the same time they are no mere copycat outfit. This is the third CD I have received from the Swedish APM label, and it is far and away the most listenable and enjoyable. Apart from the two minute "Exit", which originally closed the album, the other five are very respectable in length with two clocking in at the twelve-minute mark. Zaragon are a band that could create an impact in today's prog scene, and I hope that this re-release will provide the band with the impetus to get going again and record a new album. Music as good as this should be more widely heard and all power to APM for discovering it. *#28, Apr 1995*

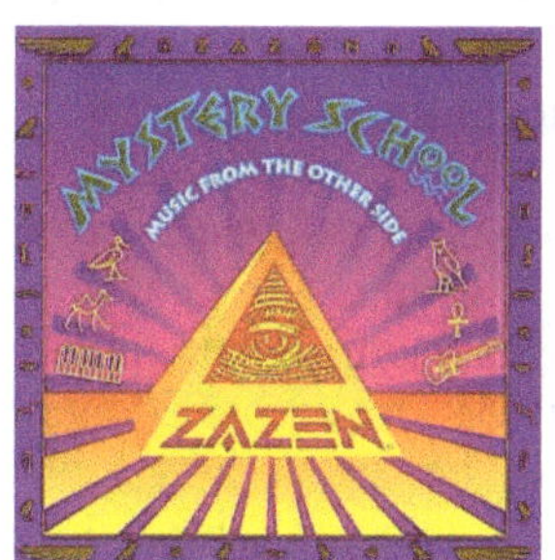

ZAZEN
MYSTERY SCHOOL: SONGS FROM THE OTHER SIDE

"Zazen" is a Japanese word that means "to sit in stillness", but the band do not believe in the philosophy that stillness must be totally mellow. Keyboard player Steve Kaplan says "To get to heaven you sometimes must experience a certain intensity, and our goal is to take listeners on a journey – start out pretty and soft to lull them into a false sense of security before increasing the intensity to shift their state of awareness". Zazen are comprised of Steve, bassist Andy West, guitarist Joaquin Lievano and producer Rama. The individual members of the band all come from very diverse backgrounds, which goes some way to explaining why the music combines so many influences. Steve is at home on a synthesiser or a piano, and after gaining a degree in piano performance from California University he went on to appear as featured piano soloist with Jack Elliott's New American Orchestra and the LA Philharmonic. Since then he has progressed through acoustic jazz and is now an expert electronic keyboard player. Joaquin came to the fore as a jazz fusion guitarist and worked with several artists as well as releasing his own solo album on CBS in 1987. Andy will probably the most familiar, as he was the bassist and co-founder of the rock instrumental band Dixie Dregs. The band all initially met up through a mutual interest in Buddhism: it was evident from the beginning that there was a musical chemistry between them, and they experimented with sounds, textures, melodies and compositional structures before coming up with the style that is recognisable as Zazen. The songs on this album began when they discussed among themselves themes such as the ancient Mystery School of Egypt and Atlantis. The songs were then structured in musical triangles, starting with a soothing piano or synth melody and edging into an explosive dimension of rock guitar before coming down for a relaxing crescendo. The musical identity of Zazen is very much one of their own making. The only word that could be used to describe it is "fusion" as they fuse together a myriad of different influences from chamber music and tribal rhythms to acoustic guitar or soaring

rock. To my ears it is an album that takes a lot of listening to, not one to be put on while doing the housework, as there is a lot going on and it pays not to miss it. To say that these guys can play is like saying that Michelangelo could draw a little. For me it is the guitarwork that is the big bonus: Joaquin is content to keep it under wraps for the most part, but when he takes off, boy is it worth waiting for. It would be interesting to put him in a room with Steve Vai or Joe Satriani and see who is the fastest, because when he goes down the frets you feel that the guitar is going to melt as he is so quick. This is an album to listen to only when you have the time to fully appreciate it: keyboard dominated for the most part, it is full of strength and diversity.
#16, Dec 1992

ZENIT
SURRENDER

Swiss band Zenit was formed in 1998 by ex-Clepsydra bassist Andy Thommen. Their debut album was released in 2001 and they have now come out with the follow-up. This is extremely strong neo-prog, and they have been looking over to the UK as there are elements not only of Marillion and Twelfth Night, but also some Floyd and IQ and possibly even some Pallas thrown in for good measure. This is a style of music that Aragon have also been following with extremely strong songs, great vocals and some impressive instrumental moments. There is a section in "Yin and Yang" where Andy is sliding some notes on the bass and it is so delicate yet is just right for the music as it brings in emotion and quality in equal measures. The album was mixed by Etienne Bron who also worked on the first three Clepsydras albums, so he has a long-term relationship with Andy, and it shows. There are some great piano moments on this album, and the interaction with the guitars is very powerful indeed and will appeal to all those into neo-prog. It has been released in a three-fold digipak with strong artwork and presentation. *#87, Apr 2006*

ZEN ORCHESTRA
SHE SAID TO ME...

This is a one song demo from Mark Barrett and Steve Smith (both ex-Walking On Ice) along with Stewart Milner. The idea is to have these as core members and then recruit others for live work when needed. It is going to be very much a studio-based outfit, with the band members not feeling restricted to playing one instrument in each style. "She Said To Me..." certainly bodes well for the future as it is an extremely powerful song, with elements of both Peter Gabriel and ELO. Expect to hear me talking a lot more about these guys in the future as if they can keep this standard up then they are quickly going to become major players.
#38, Nov 1996

ZIFF
STORIES

'Stories' is the debut album by German band Ziff, and what a find it is too as they produce some top-notch prog, combined with great musicianship, while remembering the importance of tunes. Sometimes bands seem to be wrapped up in their own musical ability and forget that music should be enjoyable to listen to and these guys come across as a mix of Galahad and IQ with some GLD thrown in for good measure, a great recipe by anyone's standards. Songs such as "Story Of A Jew" are powerfully both musically and lyrically, "His parents were stripped naked, like so many others, but it was not so much their death, but their nudity that hurt him, and no one said Kaddish to them, he was the only one who was left alive". The strength and depth of the material is quite amazing for a debut, and it is of no surprise that they are attracting good press throughout Europe. 'Stories' is the first release on the German label Angular Records, a subdivision of Musea, and on the evidence of this release both Angular and Ziff have a very strong future ahead of them.
#34, Apr 1996

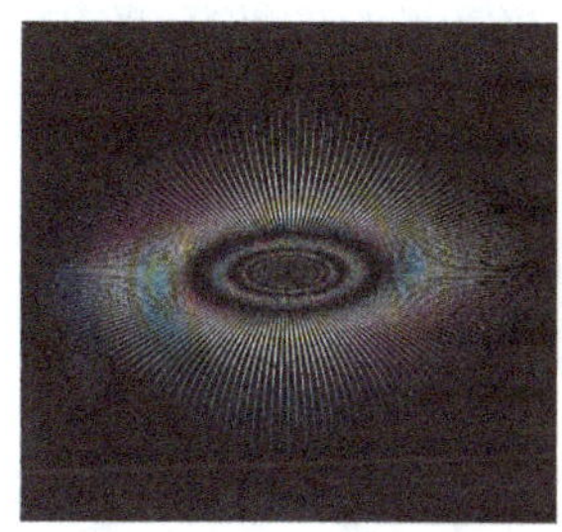

ZONE SIX
LIVE WIRED 2004

On the front page of their website, underneath a psychedelic photo of the band performing that looks as if it was taken in 1969 at the very latest, it says 'IMPROVISATION - SPACEROCK - PSYCHEDELIC - TRANCE - FREAK OUT', and that tells you all that you need to know about this album. Want more? Okay, not only has this been released on digipak CD but also on double album vinyl, which contains an extra nine minutes which is not on the CD. Also, if you want to try out some of their music then they have live albums available on the site, with tray cards etc., downloadable for free! But this recording is spot on production wise, which according to the site comments is not always the case with the others. Zone Six are a four-man German band who have an incredible understanding of what each one is doing musically, and it is hard to believe that these pieces are not rehearsed time and again. There is a lot of space in the music at times, as they are very conscious of dynamics. One 'song' is only just over five minutes long while another is nearly twenty-three, but as they all seem to virtually run into each other this does not seem to matter. This is powerful improvised space rock that any fan of the genre will certainly enjoy.
#86, Feb 2006

Smaller Reviews

Originally, I was in two minds as whether to include both these and the Various Artists reviews which appear in the next section, but eventually decided they do tell an important part of the underground story. This is how the reviews originally appeared in Feedback, mixed together for no reason apart from this is how I received them. They are presented in chronological order – no artwork as these are just tasters, but some of the bands mentioned don't feature anywhere else in the series so need to be here for completeness.

TRISTAN PARK ***AT THE END OF THE DAY...***
LANDS END ***PACIFIC COAST HIGHWAY***

I know very little about these two American bands, apart from the fact they have both been signed to Cyclops and that their new recordings will be out later this year. Malcolm has kindly sent me these earlier releases to discover why he signed them up.

Tristan Park have a six-man line-up, with two guitarists and two keyboard players. Added to that, everyone sings so it means that there is plenty of room for harmony vocals. This is immediate music, more Pomp/AOR than prog, with infectious melodies. I found that the more I played this the more I thought of Shooting Star, one of the top American bands of the Eighties (if you have not heard any of their stuff then you ought to search out their debut, or 'Silent Scream'), along with Kansas. These songs are just so good, full of little bits and pieces that add and do not detract from the whole. I am especially fond of the use of sax in "Precious Designs", a song tailor made for American radio if ever I heard one. All in all, with songs ranging from ballads to American rock this album is a real joy and I look forward eagerly to the new one.

Lands End appear to be primarily an instrumental band. That is not to say that they do not sing, but most of the songs are very long (three over ten minutes) and the vocals are

rather sparing. Only a four-piece, with the bassist also being the keyboard player, the music is complex with a more European feel than Tristan Park. In fact, this is a much 'proggier' album, heavily influenced at times by IQ (the beginning of "Conspicuously Empty" is an IQ steal I can't place) although the guitar never rocks like it should. At the end of the CD I felt rather disappointed as I had listened to a band with lots of potential and masses of musical ability yet was rather too laid back and meandering for my taste. It may also be that played back to back with Tristan Park, there was no comparison. While Tristan Park is worth looking out for, I will reserve judgement on Lands End until I hear the new CD later this year.
#28, Apr 1995

THE MOOR ***EVERY PIXIE TELLS A STORY***
SIMON SAYS ***CEINWEIN***
Bishop Garden Records was set up in Sweden primarily to release music by The Moor, although some other artists are now being involved (Simon Says has a link with The Moor as it is fronted by The Moor bassist Stefan Renstrom). The Moor describe their music as progressive space-rock, and this is as good a label as any. The lyrics are certainly bloodthirsty enough to satisfy the death metal follower, and at times the guitars are as well: no namby pamby widdly-widdly here. The music is set at a very slow pace for the most part, like classic Sabbath, and the vocals are sung in a low register. The one cover version shows where they are coming from, as it is Hawkwind's "Angels Of Death", one of the most upbeat songs on the album. Hawkwind have obviously had a major effect on The Moor, who for the most part try to be heavier but have also lifted quite a few influences. All in all, it is an interesting album, certainly different from much of today's prog, and one that will be enjoyed by spaced out Hawkwind freaks everywhere.

I quite enjoyed The Moor and was expecting something similar from Simon Says, but to say that I was amazed is something of an understatement. From one album that is all very enjoyable but is all on one level, I am now listening to an album of great depth and of interest to a great many people, not just a minority. It is an album firmly rooted in the Seventies as it moves from one theme to another, yet also brings in ideas from the Eighties and Nineties as well. Stefan Renstrom has built a band more than happy to move through extremes as a song that has driving electric guitar gives way to a wonderful acoustic song like "Devonian Forest" which contains some beautiful reflective keyboard work. There is just so much to listen to and enjoy with this album, and I only hope that Bishop Garden Records can do justice as this is a CD that could do very well in the UK. The switching through different styles gives the listener plenty to enjoy and in my opinion 'Ceinwein' is one of the top albums to come out of Scandinavia this year.
#31, Oct 1995

THE WISHING TREE ***CARNIVAL OF SOULS***
IRIS ***CROSSING THE DESERT***
These two albums are the result of Marillion members at play. Firstly, The Wishing Tree is Steve Rothery's solo album; where he is joined by Pete Trewavas, with the line-up

being completed by Enchant drummer Paul Craddick (some of you may remember that Steve produced their album 'A Blueprint Of The World') and vocalist Hannah Stobart: the Marillion connection is also strengthened by the lyrics of John Helmer. The result is an album that is not a progressive rock album in a sense that many would understand, but instead is one that covers many differing styles, playing to the strengths of Hannah's vocals, which sound a bit like Judie Tzuke crossed with Steve Nicks. This is a truly beautiful album, and one that could find Steve Rothery a whole new section of fans. He provides electric or acoustic guitar as the need arises, and while "Hall Of Mirrors" has a folky feel, "Midnight Show" is more Floydian while "Night of the Hunter" is down and dirty. I cannot praise this album too highly.

Iris is the vehicle of Sylvain Governaire (guitars, keyboards) who has played with Arrakeen and Casino, along with Ian Mosley and Pete Trewavas (again!). 'Crossing The Desert' is an instrumental album and not as immediate as 'Carnival'. This is self-indulgent, and although interesting it does seem to fade into background/New Age. It is enjoyable, but not a patch on 'Carnival of Souls' and if you enjoy female vocalists then I can assure you that you will love this.
#37, Oct 1996

GEOFFREY DOWNES *EVOLUTION*
JOHN WETTON *AKUSTIKA – LIVE IN AMERICA*

Geoffrey Downes and John Wetton were founder members of Asia, who released one of the most important debut albums of the last twenty years and although Geoffrey still performs in a band of that name, John is now a solo artist. These two albums are their most recent solo releases, so how do they compare to each other?

I rate Geoffrey highly as a keyboard player: he had a difficult job filling Rick Wakeman's shoes in Yes, and his previous work with Buggles was also of merit. Why on earth he has seen fit to release one of the worse albums I have ever heard is beyond me. Imagine James Last using keyboards and playing rock hits, and then you may have an idea of just how bad this is. Bon Jovi never imagined that "Living On A Prayer" could be like this. How about "Alone", or "Who's Crying Now?". Yes, it has all been very well done, but this is background muzak of the very worst kind.

However, John has managed to produce one of the albums of the year. Accompanying himself on piano or acoustic guitar he has given old songs new life and shown them in a totally different light. Stripped from over-production and clinical instrumentation and harmonies, he proves that songs such as "Only Time Will Tell" can be transformed. This works most dramatically on "Heat Of The Moment" which is virtually a new song. Twelve songs, each one a gem, and although I realise that the acoustic bandwagon is one that many seem to be jumping on at present, at times it is justified. This is an album that shows just what can be achieved in an acoustic environment. The question here is which of the two artists deserve to be working under the Asia banner? One is making the most of his talents while the other wastes his.
#37, Oct 1996

QUIDAM *QUIDAM*
ABRAXAS *ABRAXAS*

Both albums have been released by the Polish label Ars Mundi, but are quite different in style. Quidam were formed in 1990, but only settled with this name and line-up in 1995. All the lyrics are in Polish and are delicately sung by Emilia Derkowska. It is for the most part a dreamy album, with heavy reliance on swathes of keyboards although at times folk elements come through, notably on "Bajkowy". Emila also provides cello and with Ewa Smarzynska on flute and whistle they have an unusual edge to the music. The electric guitar is rarely allowed to shine through but when it does then its' presence is definitely felt. This is a prog album full of beauty.

Even before playing the Abraxas album one is impressed as it comes in a cardboard slip sleeve, and on taking out the CD there is also a poster. One side of this has a picture of the band while on the other are English translations of all the lyrics. On taking the booklet out of the case one discovers that each set of Polish lyrics is accompanied by a stunning painting. But what of the music? Although Adam Kassa does not sound like Geoff Mann, he reminds me of him in the way he sings, with occasional strange inflections or vocals. A flute again makes some impression, and they do come across at times as Twelfth Night, mixing with East European folk. This is an album to be played again as again as each time more can be gained from it. Both are worth investigation, for different reasons but Abraxas have brought out an album that is a real find. *#39, Jan 1997*

SIGMUND SNOPEK *NOBODY TO DREAM*
SILENT LUCIDITY *POSITIVE AS SOUND*
GHOSTS OF DAWN *SUNCHILD*
GHOSTS OF DAWN *MEANS & DELUSIONS*
MARYSON *MASTER MAGICIAN*
LANVALL *AURAMONY*
INES *EASTERN DAWNING*
TEA IN THE SAHARA *BOOMERANG*
5:01 AM *21ST CENTURY DREAM*
MYSTERY DE NOTRE DAME *MYSTERY DE NOTRE DAME*
RACHEL'S BIRTHDAY *AN INVITATION TO*
AIRBORNE *THE OTHER SIDE*
QUASAR LUX SYMPHONIAE *THE ENLIGHTENING MARCH*
COURT *DISTANCES*
ANCIENT CURSE *THE LANDING*
IVANHOE *POLARIZED*

It's a bit like waiting for a bus isn't it? I hadn't heard from German label Music Is Intelligence for nearly two years and then a box arrived with eighteen CDs in it! Last time it was twenty-four, so at least this time it is not quite as many.

I was not keen on Sigmund Snopek last time and I'm afraid that this album does nothing to make me want to change that opinion. Sigmund (in the booklet, none of these came with press releases) appears to have a high opinion of himself as a classical composer, not wanting to go back to "prog rock". A lot of the album is made up of classical pieces that have far more in common with that genre while at the same time having an edge of the Sixties about them as well. Some of it is quite reminiscent of The Moody Blues, but for the most part I would have to say that this washed over me. I enjoy some classical music, but this is not one that I would have purchased.

Silent Lucidity is new to me and appear to be German. After a quiet, although threatening introduction, they turned out to be a prog band that are interested in pursuing the heavier side of things. In fact, they seem to switch between Metallica-type heads down and get rid of the dandruff, and material that is more reminiscent of classic Rush, which made for an interesting album, as there was certainly diversity within the songs. A four-piece, with twin guitars, I get the impression that this band will be even heavier live. A good sense of melody and enough changes to interest any proghead makes this one to pursue further.

There are two albums by Ghost Of Dawn, another German band. Although 'Sunchild' is on Music Is Intelligence, 'Means & Delusions' does not have any credits. They are not a prog act, and I'm not sure why they are on Peter Wustmann's MII label as they come across more as a hard rock outfit with leanings more to the indie scene than to the technical. Some songs, such as "There's No Holding Me I Cannot Rest Until The Summer Ends" are quick up-tempo blasters and although they are good at what they do I cannot help but feel that they are on the wrong label, as this has a reputation for prog but I can't see many progheads picking this up.

Maryson are a Dutch outfit (named after their keyboard player), and their album is a concept based on a fantasy novel written by, surprise surprise, the keyboard player, one W J Maryson. And what can be said about such as epic work written by a master of his craft? Yes, I did not like it as it is far too meandering and for a lot of the time just plain boring. Sorry guys.

Arne has come a long way since he first sent me a demo tape, and I enjoyed his last album 'Meloydian Garden' and I presume that this is his second. Lanvall is still pretty much Arne doing most of the work, with a few extra musicians, but this time he has also been joined by renowned multi-instrumentalist Gandalf who plays on three of the songs. The "Overture" has a big choral element, which is a shame as Lanvall is all about great guitar playing. At times, he is very close to Jadis, as second song "Red" amply demonstrates, but here some of the songs are just too dreamy and atmospheric, almost heading into New Age territory. There is the feeling of promise not quite fulfilled, and while I know that Arne will one day produce an album that will be loved by all for his dynamic guitarwork this is not it.

Ines impressed me with their last album and has continued to do so with this one. Ines is the name of the keyboard player, but they are a band (who do not have their own singer). They use four guest vocalists this time, with the most well-known being Harald Barath. As with Lanvall they hint at what they are capable of, but for some reason do not quite pull it off. The melodic vocals work best with the more upbeat almost AOR songs, but the slower ones tend to drag. Still, this may be a grower so I shouldn't be too harsh.

Tea In The Sahara surprised me. I mean, it must be one of the most naff names I have come across, but musically these guys know what they are doing. This is technical prog with loads of widdly widdly and especially good interplay between keyboards and guitar. Track three, "Boomerang", ought to come in for special mention as the lightly sung and backed verse works well with the rockier passages. Mind you, it does demonstrate the importance of the name. This was the last one I played just because I was afraid of what I might have to listen to, and instead it turned out to be a very pleasurable experience indeed!

5:01 a.m. are Dutch and mix prog and a more AOR style that made me think of other Dutch bands such as Ywis, as this is accessible music that will probably find favour in both camps. Edu Arde is an extremely strong melodic vocalist and the production is very geared towards him. No problem with that, especially as the overall balance of the mix is very good and the result is that this comes across as a strong album. The cover artwork is a bit of a let-down, but do not let that stop you from discovering another good album.

Mystere De Notre Dame appears to be Italian, although singing in English like the rest of the acts here. They are a far more rock-based act but mix it with good harmony vocals and very symphonic sounding keyboards. Twin guitars make their presence felt without falling into HR territory, but there is more than enough here for those into melodic hard rock to show an interest. There is plenty of light to offset the heavier moments and is an album that can be enjoyed on many levels. Closer "Amaranto" is worth hearing.

Rachel's Birthday are a little strange, as opener "Birthday Invitation" is acoustic prog while the next is an up and running belter of a rock number: and they do both styles so well. In some ways, they remind me of Credo, and the whole album is one that begs repeated playing. A little strange at times, but worth it, nonetheless.

Airborne are a hard rock band, and not an overly interesting one at that. They do not have a keyboard player, but keyboards are an important part of their overall sound and close investigation reveals that Ines guests while her husband Hansi Fuchs also contributes musically, and they also contribute a song. This is their second album for the label, which means that presumably enough people purchased the debut for them to be allowed another.

Quasar Lux Symphoniae called their album 'The Enlightening March of the Argonauts', and that is definitely the most enlightening thing about it. This is prog a la early Seventies, but worse than that it is not very good! Heavily keyboard based with a vocalist who can sometimes sing in tune, but can't at others, does not make for an enlightening experience at all.

I must confess to not remembering a great deal about Court's 'And You'll Follow' that I reviewed some years ago, and now I have 'Distances'. Court are basically a multi-instrumentalist with a few guest musicians but unfortunately due to the arty design the booklet is virtually impossible to read. Although overall it is better than the album by Quasar Lux Symphoniae it is also very much of the early Seventies and while interesting is not exciting.

Ancient Curse commence proceedings with a real bang and guitar riffs. There are not any keyboards here, as we have a technical rock band out to prove a point. It is impossible not to be impressed, and even the use of acoustic guitar is well thought out and not just dropped in somewhere for effect. "I Am Leaving" crunches out in a very buoyant fashion, with the band even making room for some double bass drum pedals that Megadeth would be proud of. In this country, this album will be ignored solely because of the label it is on, but if you are into good melodic hard technical rock then this is an album you need to search out.

From memory, out of all the bands I reviewed last time, the one that impressed me most was Ivanhoe and their 'Symbols Of Time' album, not only for the music but also for the artwork, which stood out. The same can be said for 'Polarized'. Ivanhoe are a very heavy prog band indeed, heading into the same area as our own Threshold or Dream Theater. Just listen to 'Sunlight" and tell me that it is not heavy enough for you. This is yet another stunning album.
#44, Sept 1997

IN THE LABYRINTH — ***THE GARDEN OF MYSTERIES***
ZELLO — ***ZELLO***
EVIDENCE — ***HEART'S GRAVE***

As with Music Is Intelligence, I hadn't heard from Swedish label Ad Perpetuam Memoriam for some time until these arrived the other day: and they came with press releases!

In The Labyrinth originally released their album on cassette in 1994, but here it is in greatly extended (going from 13 to 22 songs and is now more than 74 minutes in length). There is not much in the way of vocals, but there is a wealth of unusual instrumentation on offer, including a lot from Asia and the Far East, with the result coming across as a compelling mix of prog and World Music. The sound swirls around, developing first one strand and then another, using many influences yet at all time retaining its individuality and purpose. This is the first time that I have heard music melded and moulded quite like this, and although it may sound strange and weird it is very easy on the ear and pleasurable on first hearing. Although it can be enjoyed on a light level, I am convinced that the more I play it the more I will get out of it.

Zello are a totally different kind of fish and while it may have been difficult to conjure up the majesty of the music of In The Labyrinth here it is relatively easy. Zello may not have a guitarist (they make up for it with two keyboard players) but you will not miss that as there just is not any room in their sound and are just about the closest thing I have heard to Kansas, ever. P-O Saether is a great vocalist while Lennart Glenberg fiddles away like Robbie Steinhardt, with the result being that this is one of the most accessible albums that APM have ever released" "Fairy Queen" is one of the most glorious prog songs that you will hear this year. Zello are more than mere copyists, the fact that they do not use electric guitar (an instrument very important to Kansas) demonstrates that, but rather toil through a similar field to that developed by the Americans These guys certainly do not sound Swedish.

Evidence is a French band that has been heavily influenced by Peter Hammill and Van Der Graaf Generator, and 'Heart's Grave' is an opera in twelve parts. At times the music is very dark and threatening, melancholy and moody, while at others it is almost light-hearted. Apparently, this album is the first in a trilogy called 'The Cross' and it takes a lot of work to get into, and although some may feel that the result is worth it, it was taking more time than I could spare. So, there are some definite finds here and it is great to hear from APM again. *#44, Sept 1997*

LANDS END	***DRAINAGE***
FRUITCAKE	***POWER STRUCTURE***

Label boss Malcolm Parker and I have long since agreed to disagree about Lands End, although I did think that their last album had some merits. Here we have a live album, plus a few unreleased studio cuts, mostly recorded at the Mexicali prog festivals in '96 and '97. There is more improvisation and jamming than is apparent on their studio albums and when the band pick up the tempo it becomes interesting although it does seem to be a bit meandering at times and, it must be said, boring. Jeff McFarlan also has the annoying tendency to go off key when he is holding long notes (this must be the "emotion laden vocals" referred to in the press release). They have some great song titles, such as "a castle, mother, nanny & a warm soft bed" or "the revolution like Saturn devours its children". Probably not an album that I will be returning to often.

This is not a statement that can be put against the new release by Fruitcake, their fourth on Cyclops. With roots that stretch back into early Seventies Genesis and Yes, this is retro prog of the highest order. Drummer Pål Søvik, who supplies lead vocals, has a clear and melodious voice, with just the hint of an accent to say that he is not singing in his native tongue (Fruitcake are Norwegian). The strong use of bass pedals provides a solid bottom line and the good keyboard work is accentuated by the soaring guitar lines of Robert Hauge. If you like Flower Kings then it is safe to say that Fruitcake is a band you ought to discover, with their best album yet. *#51, Jan 1999*

VARIOUS ARTISTS	***MOONCHILD '98***
TRUTH IN ADVERTISEMENT	***BALANCE***
MAGUS	***TRAVELLER***
BLUE SHIFT	***NOT THE FUTURE I ORDERED***
NEW SUN	***NEW SUN***
NEW SUN	***AFFECTS***
DELUC	***8th WONDER***
CRUCIBLE	***TALL TALES***
FIG LEAF	***PLAYS BOB W. & OTHER SELECTIONS***
SMOKIN' GRANNY	***SMOKIN' GRANNY***
DIE A TRIBE	***ALBATROSS***

It was with great interest that I put on a new compilation that I had been sent by Jeremy as not only did it contain a new song by him, but also songs by bands that I had never heard of before. I was also interested in the philosophy of the label, part of which was

"We believe that progressive musicians should not have to cater to crass commercialism and the polluting atmosphere of the music industry with its questionable antiquated policies and downright thievery". Only one band had failed to provide an email address, so I took the plunge and contacted everyone I could and had a tremendous response.

Mark Reynolds, of Truth In Advertisement, told me to be brutal as the CD is two years old and the new one is in progress. I did think that the beginning was very amateurish, but after that it settles down quite nicely. Some are instrumentals, others are songs, with Mark displaying a voice fairly like Clive Nolan. As prog goes this is middle of the road, not at all cutting edge, but a pleasant listen all the same. I will be interested to hear his newer work.

Magus is the brainchild of Andrew Robinson, who along with Brian Hirsch of Indeed set up the Moonchild label. Of these albums that I was sent this was the one that made the most immediate impact on me. This is just good, solid, prog, with more than a hint of Alan Parsons Project. It is nearly a one-man band, with Andrew supplying vocals, guitars, bass, bass pedals and keyboards but he did have the sense to bring in a drummer, along with another keyboard player. Magus are now very much a band, and it should be interesting to see what the next album brings after they have completed some more concerts. A very interesting album, with enough mood swings and changes in tempo and approach to make it enjoyable for any prog fan.

The first thing you notice when you look at the CD from Blue Shift is there is a cover version. That is not unusual, but a band is taking its life in its hands when it dares to play Led Zeppelin. As it is, the guys have done a decent version of "Immigrant Song", but that is the seventh song on the album, so how does it start? I was intrigued as an acoustic guitar opens proceedings, which was gradually accompanied by some very delicate keyboards. I needn't have worried though as they soon segued into a harder version of Yes. Not copyists as such, but in Stewart Meredith they have a Jon Anderson sound-alike and they have taken the music of Yes and made it much rockier. Another goody.

The songs from New Sun that appears on the compilation is taken from their second album 'Affects', but they kindly sent me a copy of their debut as well, which came out three years ago. I am amazed that I have not heard of this band before, even though they are American. If Twelfth Night were still around today then this is how I would imagine that they would sound, especially if they had been listening to Rush. Always very rock based, the vocals are very like Geoff Mann, not so much in the actual sound but in the way that the vocals are projected and used. Although they have moved on with the second album, both are worth discovering with strong guitarwork and great melodies. This band would do very well over here in the prog field if only they had more publicity, and are worth investigating.

Moonchild treat progressive music as a very wide term, and feature jazz rock, and this is very much the case with Deluc which is basically a vehicle for the guitar talents of Fred LeDuc. Unlike all the other bands featured so far, Fred is not based in America but Australia! Most of the songs are instrumental, and while many are reminiscent of Coliseum II some others are much funkier with great guitar/keyboard interplay. There is the impression that the musicians are very much at home with each other, each playing to allow the others room to move and to let the music breathe. Comforting as opposed to confrontational this is jazz that is accessible to all and enjoyable for most. Many progressive bands should listen to this album and realise that while musical ability is important, possibly more in this genre than in others, it is also knowing when not to play that is as important as blistering along.

When I saw the cover of 'Tall Tales' I was convinced that Crucible was going to be a Tull copyist outfit. When I realised that the songwriter, Tim Horan, played keyboards, acoustic guitar and flute I was convinced of it. But I was very wrong. There are elements of Tull, but much more of late Seventies Genesis, Yes, Kansas and a host of others. This album is much more about good songs and melodies and damn any attempt at classification. All that needs to be said about this album is that it is packed full of well thought out songs which cross the boundaries of many styles, while at the same time never straying too far from rock. Due to its' very definition the type of music is progressive, but Crucible have little in common with many of the 'prog' bands around.

The song featured from Fig leaf is from the Norwegian outfit's most recent album 'The Humble Poet', but I have in the player their second album from 1995. If I had to guess at the nationality of the band, I would have got close, as the type of music they are playing (or were playing) fits in with most of the Scandinavian prog bands. At times, soft and gentle, at others very much in your face, it varies between acoustic and hard psychedelic rock. The songs are all in English but of all the bands on the album this was the hardest to get into. That is not to say that it is a bad album, but rather that this music takes a bit of work. When they rock, they really do, and "Changes" has some distorted vocals which makes it a very over the top effort indeed. Well worth the effort I thought.

Smokin' Granny's album is only available on cassette and if it wasn't for the fact that it came from the same place, I would have passed this smartly on. This is JAZZ. One reviewer said that it was "an incredible blend of funk, jazz, prog, tonal and atonal improvisations" and I could not have put it better myself. Although this band itself is only five years old, three of the guys have been playing together in bands on and off for about eighteen years. A solely instrumental outfit, the main 'voice' is Todd Barbee who is described as multi-reedist "who has played saxophone since before birth". Some of the music is, um, hard to listen to, and of all those received this would be the one that I would play least.

Lastly, we come to Die A Tribe, who not only are not on the sampler but also are not on the label either! Brian Hirsch thought I might find it interesting so passed it along. A mix of jazz and prog without a keyboard in sight, and a female singer to boot. In many ways, these are like a slightly more up-tempo version of the late Lives & Times and of all the releases is the one that is obviously low budget. It is quite interesting but at the same time there is nothing that immediately makes it essential.

So, there you have it. A sampler album from a label unknown to me has led me to lots of new bands with some bloody good albums

BRIAN HIRSCH *QUEST FOR TRUTH*
INDEED *INTER-DIMENSIONAL SPACE COMMANDER*
J.R.S. *WINGS OF GOLD*
MAGUS *HIGHWAY 375*
JEREMY *SALT THE PLANET*
FIG LEAF *FEARLESS*

It was with no little trepidation that I put on Brian Hirsch's 1994 CD 'Quest For Truth' as over the last few months we have been in contact a great deal. He has been supplying me with CDs that have not only been released on the Moonchild label (which he set up with Andrew Robinson from Magus) but also by bands that he felt I ought to know about. Anyway, seeing that the insert was literally that, and not a booklet, I feared the worst. However, I am glad to say that all my fears were groundless. Although it would have sounded better with a human drummer, it turned out to be a very good album indeed. With a guest guitarist on some tracks, Brian shows that he is a dab hand at Wakeman style finesse and has produced an album that certainly will be much enjoyed by those interested in the 'White Rock' era. This is not ambient or self-indulgence, but an album of tunes and melodies that develop and hold interest.

By 1996 Brian had become a band, so by losing all outside help he was now Indeed. Not knowing any of his past I will assume that this is the follow-up, but if it is then it is quite a different album altogether. The album uses a much rockier format, and some very different keyboards. The key here is in the title, with the music having a "sci-fi" feel. Brian was playing guitar himself by this stage, using it primarily to add some power chords when the time was right. It is difficult to choose between the two as to which one I like best as they are just so varied in approach. Brian has a very quick manner up and down the keyboards, but he uses these runs sparingly, which gives them even more effect when they appear. I found myself likening parts of this album to the instrumental passages of Legend and I am sure that in a pure rock group environment then this album could blast like a bastard. If Brian develops Indeed into a prog rock band that is out there gigging, then I am sure that they will gain a lot of attention.

J.R.S. is Jeffrey Ryan Smoots and his band (which in the case of this album is drummer David Beardsley, with Jeffrey providing vocals, guitar, bass and keyboards). Jeffrey is obviously an accomplished rock guitarist and the possessor of a voice that is friendly on the ear, with the result being that this album sounds quite a lot like early Styx. In all honesty, it is far more commercial than what I have come to expect from Moonchild but that does not take anything away from an album that does have its; moments. One of the problems that J.R.S is going to have with this album is getting it to the right audience. Moonchild is seen to be a prog label, but this does not fit into that category while it also can't be compared to Dream Theater or our own Threshold and is not as heavy as other bands such as Eldritch. A songs-based album with some good rock guitar, it is something I have enjoyed playing and at the end of the day that is all that matters to me.

I reviewed Magus in the last issue, but now Andrew Robinson is back with an EP. Again, he is the sole musician involved, and this time the four songs last less than twenty minutes in total. Completely instrumental, there is again the feeling of Alan Parsons

Project, but this time crossed with the X-Files as Andrew brings in an alien theme. I must say that this did not impress me as immediately as his last work, but maybe this will grow on me.

Jeremy is by far the most well-known (at least to me) artist on the Moonchild roster, and here he is with the follow-up to 'Celestial City', which was released on Kinesis. 'Salt The Planet' is his first album with Moonchild and is another example of a man doing it all on his own. At one time Jeremy was using a 'real' drummer but he appears to have dispensed with his services, using a combination of drum machine and percussion. Jeremy appears to have moved much more into an electronic feel with the music on this album as a lot of the sounds he employs used to recall bands such as Camel, but now it is much more like Tangerine Dream. Consequently, musically it is a little out of the area that I would normally listen to. Jeremy has truly progressed as he has moved on, but in this case, he has left a listener behind: it will be interesting to see where his music takes him, and I look forward to hearing his next development with interest.

Fig Leaf have got to be one of the most interesting Scandinavian bands around and in many ways, they remind me of Anekdoten (what has happened to them these days?), although the instrumentation is different. They appear to be at home either singing a gentle ballad, with just some choice Hammond chords and emotive drumming, or creating a new version of hell with a flute and sax adding to the discord. This does not fit in with most people's ideas of a cosy neo-prog movement, but this is what 'progressive' music should mean, attempting to create something that is quite different to most of the music that is around. I am not sure what the person solely weaned on medicated doses of Pendragon, Galahad or Arena will think of this, but to someone who hears more prog than most this is like a breath of fresh air through a scene that sometimes appears to be stagnating.
#52, Feb 1999

AFTER CRYING — ***ALMOST PURE INSTRUMENTAL***
SOLARIS — ***NOSTRADAMUS: BOOK OF PROPHECIES***

Thanks for the modern marvel that is e-mail, I have recently been in contact with Gregory Boszormenyi who is the owner and manager of Periferic Records in Hungary and he has kindly sent me two of their latest releases. After Crying are one of the most well-known progressive bands in Hungary, bringing together elements of Hungarian folk music and chamber music with King Crimson and Emerson Lake and Palmer. Their first album was released in 1990 and this compilation came out last year with ten previously released numbers and four new ones. To the western ear this is quite a strange amalgam of music, as at times it sounds like a modern orchestra mixed with a rock band, playing something that is quite off the wall. At the same time, it is very compelling indeed. Even for a progressive band the instrumentation is unusual as while there is an innermost cell of six people, they also use other musicians as the need arises. These six are Egervari Gabor (flute, vocals), Gorgenyi Tamas (vocals), Pejtsik Peter (cello, bass, vocals), Torma Ferenc (guitar, bass, keyboards, vocals), Vedres Csaba (piano, keyboards, vocals) and Winkler Balazs (trumpet, piano, keyboards, vocals). Not by any means a normal line-up. The more I play to this album the more I liked it as it is truly progressive, bringing together eclectic rock with orchestral sounds in a way that is unique yet strangely familiar.

Solaris are a different band, more in the western style but still very much grounded in a musical style far removed from our own. While this is much more rock based, Guest musicians are utilised along with Gregorian chanting and heavy use of flute to bring to life their feelings about the prophecies of Nostradamus. Of the two this is the most immediate, and the one that the general progfan would most appreciate: mostly instrumental, in that the vocals are used as instruments. There is the feeling throughout that there was something different about what is going on, but that can surely be put down to the different musical heritage and the way that they approach their music. Both albums are worth investigating and I would hesitate to recommend one above the other, as they are so very different.
#55, Sept 1999

Various Artists

The 90's saw a great deal of sampler albums released, plus a plethora of "tribute" albums. Instead of including every single review I wrote during that period, here are those I feel were the most important of the ones I was sent.

S.I. MAGAZINE COMPILATION DISC TOO

The first CD released by SI Music was a compilation celebrating the first ten years of SI Magazine, and now here is the follow-up. Like the first it features tracks recorded specifically for the compilation and unavailable elsewhere. It comes with a well-presented and informative booklet, which give information and a photograph of each band. The cover is a wonderful colour drawing by IQ's Peter Nicholls, and the whole package is well put together. Most of the artists are on the SI label, although not all, (such as IQ and Jadis). What is apparent is that out of the twelve bands included, eight are British, on a disc released by a Dutch label primarily for European markets. It shows that for the best prog around then Britain is the place to be, it's a shame the mass media tend not to agree.

IQ – N.T.O.C. Resistance. As soon as this blasted out of the speakers, I knew the CD was worth getting for this track alone. IQ are back with a vengeance, and if the album they are currently recording contains material as strong as this then they are going to have a monster on their hands. With Peter Nicholls firmly back on vocals, it is interesting to note that the line-up (apart from bassist John Jowitt) is the same as the one that recorded 'Living Proof' back in 1985. To my ears IQ have put together the two distinctly different musical identities they had with two different vocalists and have come up with a winner. It has great hooks, is catchy, and if released as a single would get loads of airplay and be a smash hit single (my doctor has told me to keep taking the tablets).

Shadowland – I, Judas. Shadowland played this song on their recent tour, and I was looking forward to hearing the studio version. Initially I was a little disappointed as the live version was more menacing, but it has grown on me. It has quite a laid-back verse, relying on Clive's voice, but the chorus lets Karl bring in the dark side. This song would have fitted exceedingly well on 'Ring of Roses' (which all good melodic and prog rock lovers have of course purchased by now).

Wings of Steel – Thoughts of Change. More keyboards on this than on 'Homesick', and I thought this was a better song than could be found there.

Landmarq – Borrowed Mind. A lot of keyboards on this one, much more than on 'Solitary Witness'. Damian Wilson is a stand-out vocalist, and this gives him a great chance to shine: a song to mellow out to.

Pallas – Never Too Late. The Scottish proggers looked ready to take the world by storm in the Eighties, but line-up changes meant they lost their way. However, they are back with a beautiful piece of music which is basically an acoustic song (with some great guitar by Niall Mathewson), featuring the clear emotive vocals of Alan Reed. It's great to see them back on form and I look forward with interest to the new album.

For Absent Friends – Running Scared. This Dutch band have released two CDs, but to my immortal shame I have not heard either. What we have here is good commercial prog with a great hook. The song drives along. But has enough time and mood changes to suit the most discerning taste.

Jadis – This Changing Face. Gary Chandler must have the most easily recognised guitar sound in prog, and their melodic rock stands far above many of their contemporaries. This is an old song that appeared on one of their early tapes, but here it is re-recorded and with real fire to it. This is Jadis at their very best, and who could wish for more?

Chandelier – Itai. To my ears this German band give us the weakest track, not only that but is the only one available elsewhere (taken from their second album 'Facing Gravity'). They seem to mix Japanese influences, but it does not work, and a cynic might point out that they are the only German band on the SI Germany release.

Threshold – Intervention. Threshold are the band of Thin Ice axeman Karl Groom and along with fellow guitarist Nick Midson, bassist Jon Jeary, drummer Tony Grinham and singer Damian Wilson (also of Landmarq) they provide a heavy prog sound. I love Damian's voice, and yet again here is a song for him to shine on, but this time with a moody and at times very heavy backing. It is the longest song on the CD, at 6:39, but annoyingly fades out just when you think it is going to develop into something even more powerful than it already is. I know that the bands were strictly limited to seven minutes' maximum length, and I would like to see this expanded even further, but as it stands it is a powerful entity.

Paul Menel – Let's Hear It For Freedom. Paul is the "other" singer from IQ, with whom they recorded two excellent and sadly overlooked albums, 'Nomzamo' and 'Are You Sitting Comfortably?'. He has a very pure clear voice yet can also convey emotion and power. This song is very like the later work of IQ, being very melodic and effective, which may also have something to do with bassist Tim Esau who was with Paul in that band. It is great to see him back in the music scene and I look forward to his new album with real anticipation.

Timelock – Touchdown. Like fellow Dutch rockers Wings of Steel, Timelock have pulled out all the stops on a song that is better than those on their album. A real killer with loads of melody, harmony vocals, and at times rocking guitar that drives the song along. This is something that wouldn't be out of place on an album by Shooting Star for example, and if you like American rock then you will love this.

No – Quantum Leap. Seeing as how Jadis and Shadowland were touring together last year (and later this), the two top keyboard players in the business, Martin Orford and Clive Nolan, decided to record a track for inclusion: Rick Wakeman it ain't. Unlike much keyboard playing, which can be self-indulgent and meandering, here is a rock song that does not need any vocals. Peter Gee (Pendragon) and Karl Groom (Shadowland etc.) provide the guitars while John Jowitt (Jadis, IQ) is on bass and Dave Wagstaffe (Landmarq) drives it along with some sterling drumming. If anyone thought that keyboards could be boring, they should listen to this.

So, what we have here is the indispensable prog rock compilation album. But it is far more than that, as not only is it a CD that all good music lovers should have, but it is also an introduction to something much bigger. On purchasing this CD, listeners will find themselves deep in the world of Simm Info. SI have a lot to offer the music lover, and there is no better way of finding out just what I have been raving about.
#17, Mar 1993

THE S.I. SAMPLER VOL. 1

This sampler has been released so that listeners can easily discover the delights of SI, featuring songs already available, taken from the first twenty SI releases, which cover the years 1991 and 1992. Twelve songs have been chosen, six of which are by British artists. The main problem with a compilation like this is what to include and what to leave out, but overall the CD works very well indeed. Most of the artists included have already been reviewed in Feedback, including Tracy Hitchings, Shadowland, Geoff Mann, Landmarq, Casino, Winter, Wheels of Steel and Timelock. That only leaves Egdon Heath, For Absent Friends, Differences and Aragon – and of these last four two have already been reviewed for different music. So, there is nothing new on here and why should the hardened progger or intrigued newcomer go out and buy it? Apart from the fact that there is some bloody excellent music on here, it is the perfect way to find out about the prog scene viewed through the eyes of Willebrord Elsing. Twelve songs of outstanding quality, 65 minutes of music, a well-presented insert card but most important of all is the price! This CD can be obtained from The Secret World for only £5. I know that in the past some of you may have been a little reticent about writing away for albums by groups you have previously not heard of, but this a full-length album introducing you to the world of prog at a price that just cannot be beaten anywhere. If you have not already gone out and bought albums by the groups mentioned, then do so today. *#19, Aug 1993*

NOW THAT'S WHAT I CALL PROG MUSIC 3

This is the third tape that has been issued by those nice guys at Silhobbit. For those of you who have had the luck to escape their clutches then I better tell you a bit about them. Silhobbit is basically a pisstake, and no-one is safe, including yours truly. In the last issue, a third of a page was taken over to the story that I was being sued by Clive Nolan. The point is, although they take the mickey out of an awful lot of people, and put more fiction than fact in the magazine, they genuinely eat and drink prog as a way of life and try to positively promote it in whatever way they can. To this end we have their latest tape on show. It comes with a booklet (so they say – I have not had mine) and features eighteen "tracks". It is faIr and honest to say that some of these are more pisstakes (such as the recording of Steve Christey of Jadis setting up his drum kit being billed as a song, "Tug Boat Over The River Styx"), but others are either songs or live renditions just not available elsewhere. Many of these have been featured within the pages of Feedback, while others such as Porcupine Tree with the excellent "Mute" are new. Of the more well-known bands there are live songs by IQ, Shadowland and Grace (with a stonking version of "The Holyman"). Special mention must be made of Moria Falls, whose "Grasping Air" features no less than seven different Mellotrons! Downside must be the different recording levels, but at nearly ninety minutes in length there I something here for everyone. If you are interested in the tape or the mag, which is essential reading (if you use it in the toilet be careful the print doesn't come off) then write to those awfully nice people at Silhobbit.*#23, May 1994*

THE AUDIO DIRECTORY

Dave Robinson is, like me, certifiable. He spends most of his spare time working on prog music, and a few years ago he published 'The British Progressive Rock Directory' to promote all the underground progressive rock bands in the UK. I still find it invaluable and have had bands write to me because of the fanzine section in the back (maybe after this review I'll get half a page all to myself). It seemed a logical step for Dave to put together a tape featuring bands mentioned in the directory, but this took on a separate life force and it ended up being three tapes, each over 78 minutes long. Some of the tracks are long

deleted or never fully available, while others were specially recorded. Steve Paine of Pagan Media was roped in to help get the tapes ready for release. Many, although not all, of the acts are known to me and it is interesting to be able to compare the many different forms of music characterised by the word "prog". Tape one starts with the multi-layered The Guitar Orchestra, which is a totally different band to the one that follows it, Manitou whose track is from the superb 'Looking For The Lost' (reviewed in an earlier Feedback). There is information provided on each song, line-up, a small bio, and most important of all a contact address. The whole idea of these tapes is that not only for you buy and listen to forty odd bands, but then you write to the ones you like and find out more about them. Many of the bands literally live and die through this type of contact. Looking through the bands listed, only about half have released a CD, so they only make money through gigging and demos. Well, the deadline is here, and I must confess that I have not managed to play them all. I mean, four hours to sit and down and play them all at once! To find your way into the underground UK scene then get these now and if you are only tempted into one then I must suggest Tape Three as it features Credo, The Covenant, Red Jasper, Iona, Grey Lady Down and Solstice among others. A work of love deserves support
#24, Jul 1994

PROGRESSIVE & MELODIC ROCK VOL.2
PROGRESSIVE & MELODIC ROCK VOL.3

Following hot on the heels of last year's Vol. 1, which concentrated on SIMPly 1-20, here we have volumes 2 and 3. Volume 2 covers the first three years of SI, concentrating on re-releases and sub labels, while volume 3 covers SIMPly 21-49. They have been issued at a budget price, and a great introduction to the world of SI. Of the 26 CDs featured over the two discs only four have not been reviewed in Feedback, three (Differences, Egdon Heath and Coda) because they came out before I was involved with the label and one (Van Otterdyke) because it is not actually out yet. Each CD contains over seventy minutes of music, and is worth purchasing by anyone who remotely likes either progressive or melodic rock music. It is interesting to hear just how different some bands sound, yet also how similar others are. One surprise I had was that I did not realise that Aragon's brilliant 'Don't Bring The Rain' had been reissued on SI, as when I reviewed it, the CD was out on Progressive International. So, buy them, settle back and crank up the volume. The CDs have been compiled in number order, so put on Volume 3, programme the CD player to play track five first, then listen to Geoff make his entrance to an ecstatic Marquee as Twelfth Night blast out "The Ceiling Speaks". Prog at its' ultimate best.
#24, Jul 1994

THE CYCLOPS SAMPLER

Here is another sampler, this time featuring the acts signed to Cyclops. It is strange to think that the first Cyclops release was just earlier this year, yet already this is release number seven and there are many more planned. The CD insert contains details on every band (most with photos) and is very informative. Unlike some other labels that also heavily feature progressive rock, Cyclops have signed bands that are not direct clones of Marillion or Genesis but are bands in their own right. What this means is that the twelve tracks are very different from each other, and there are also no room for egos as the bands are presented in alphabetical order. Grace is the only band to feature twice, as at the end there is an orchestral version of "Lean On Me". Most of the tracks are taken from albums, but some are remastered or extended.

Abbfinoosty start the ball rolling with "Future", from the album of the same name. For the most part this is a gentle song relying on the bass guitar for melody, but it builds up to a climatic solo. I can guarantee that anyone hearing this would say that it sounds nothing like their preconceived ideas of what prog rock should sound like. In other words, approach with an open mind. Next is Credo with "A Kindness", a gentle ditty about a mass strangler. This powerful live number has transferred well to the recorded medium as the gentleness contrasts with the menace conveyed by vocalist Mark Colton. There are very few tricks here, just good musicianship as the song builds and builds to the extended finish. This is a prolonged guitar solo by Tim Birrell of beauty and majesty, full of emotion and feeling, not unlike Santana. I could go through this album track by track, as each deserves it, but special mention must be made of the inclusion of Grey Lady Down's "12:02" (easily their best song) and Mr So & So's "Circus" (ditto). Epilogue's "Swords & Knives" is the 'poppiest' and the catchiest, while "The Fool" by Grace shows why this band have such as vast following. The other acts are Haze, Steve Hillman, Geoff Mann, Primitive Instinct and Walking On Ice (stable at long last after a period of looking for new personnel).

This sampler is (or should be) in your local record shops at a bloody cheap price. Yes, I know that I go on and on about prog in every issue, but here is the opportunity to hear some great BRITISH sounds being made by up and coming bands. If you like good melodic or progressive rock, then there will be something on here for you.
#24, Jul 1994

MANNERISMS

On February 5th, 1993, Geoff Mann died of cancer. His death affected a great many people, including yours truly. Geoff lived life to its fullest, not only fronting rock bands, writing and performing plays, having major exhibitions of his paintings, writing a book and being a vicar, but also being a husband and father. He released fifteen albums in various guises, but it will always be as Twelfth Night's frontman that he will be remembered. Many people view 'Fact and Fiction' as THE prog album of the Eighties, yet due to the fickle nature of the music business Marillion were the band to make it big while Twelfth Night became the most influential band never to do so. It was felt by many of the current underground scene that it was only right and fitting that a tribute to his life and music should be provided, so bands who had worked with Geoff were asked to pick a song, and Willebrord Elsing at SI agreed to release the album at no cost so that all profits could be donated to Cancer Research and Geoff's family. A lot of work went into the booklet, with many photos of Geoff's career, as well as all the lyrics and information about who played on what. Apart from Eden Burning, Galahad and Clive Nolan with Alan Reed, who were all asked to perform certain songs, total freedom of choice was given to each band. It is a fitting tribute to Geoff's music that not only did each band choose a different song but virtually all of them chose a different album, with only 'Fact and Fiction' being used twice. So, there's the background, but all albums must stand on their own merit, no matter how good the reasons are for recording it, so is it any good?

First track is "Sob Stories" (from 'Prints of Peace' by The Bond), which is performed here by Eh!, Geoff's final band, with Peter Nicholls of IQ on vocals. Peter was one of Geoff's closest friends and in vocal style is also quite similar in delivery. As the song bounces along in a rockier manner than the original, the listener finds themselves deep inside the lyrical world of the Mann. Geoff was one of the finest lyricists in the rock world, certainly far and away the most important working in a Christian framework. This track is just stunning, and it is a case of "Follow that"! Next up is Pallas, who played with Twelfth Night at the Hammy O many, many years ago. Guitars riff, keyboards provide the edge, then Alan Reed's vocals enjoin to make "What In The World" a masterpiece. By now I was amazed at what I was hearing, as bands seemed to be putting their very being into making this tribute totally justifiable and worthwhile. IQ performed a heavily extended version of "Apathetic and Here, I" then Galahad crunched in with the old Twelfth Night opener "The Ceiling Speaks". Not content on singing with Eh! and IQ, Peter Nicholls also sings the emotive art rocker (that fretless bass sounds just like Japan) "Down Here". By the time that track eight came on I was in heaven as Pendragon performed "Human Being", and of all bands on show it was Pendragon who came closest to capturing that element that made Twelfth Night so very special. Jadis managed to show a different way of doing things as "Never Mind" was totally transformed into one of their own, and to my ears is the second-best song on the album.

After Geoff left Twelfth Night, they recruited another vocalist, Andy Sears, and recorded two more albums. The split was acrimonious and apart from drummer Brian Devoil all left the music business. So, this was the first time they had been together for years, and the first time they had been tempted to pick up their instruments for real. "Piccadilly Square" is performed by a band at the very height of its powers, not one that does not exist anymore. British music is very much the loser for not having this band around. Andy proves that he still has one of the best voices, as he puts his heart and soul into this. The last song could only be one, "Love Song". It is one of the most well-known prog songs around, containing some of Geoff's most poignant lyrics, and because of this was always going to be the most difficult to cover. Any album of this type would have to contain this song, but how can you do justice to a classic? Clive provides the orchestration, and Alan Reed the vocals, and all in all it is the perfect version, and the perfect album closer. It is not the last thing on the CD as there is some uncredited talking from Geoff, which shows some of the humour of the Mann.

I feel that I have not managed to capture for you the utter brilliance of this CD. It has been recorded to get Geoff's music across to a wider audience and it succeeds on every level. Get yourself a Christmas present and buy yourself 'Mannerisms'. Your ears will love you forever.
#26, Dec 1994

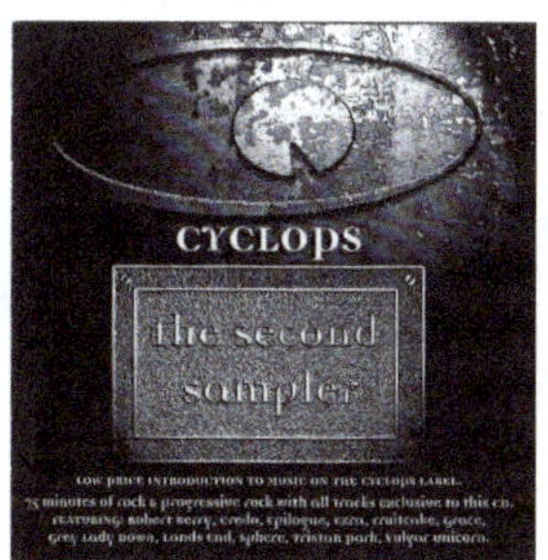

THE SECOND SAMPLER

This is the second sampler from Cyclops Records and again is a budget way to discover some of the joys this label offers to the progressive and melodic rock fan. Eleven bands are featured, all of which provide otherwise unavailable material (although GLD cheat by using a 'live' version of "The Flyer"). The bands involved this time are Robert Berry, Credo, Epilogue, Fruitcake, Grace, GLD, Lands End, Sphere, Tristan Park and Vulgar Unicorn. As with the first sampler (which featured four of the same bands), this is a great way of hearing some of the better progressive bands around. On a personal level, it is good to hear a recording of Credo's "The Letter" which is an absolute killer when played live but does not seem quite right here. My favourite song is Grace's "The Miracle" which was recorded during the sessions for their excellent album 'The Poet, The Piper & The Fool'. The songs here will not be available elsewhere, so now is a great time to discover the world of Cyclops and get some great music for a cheap price.
#33, Feb 1996

PICK & MIX

Delerium Records emerged out of Freakbeat magazine and have their finger on the pulse of the underground scene. This collection has been put together to promote the label, and must be the best value for money offer you are ever likely to see: there are twenty-three different bands on this double CD set, each with their own style, providing nearly two and a half hours of music yet it is at the crazy price of just £5. The most well-known act to many will be Porcupine Tree (who provide an exclusive track), but others such as Omnia Opera and Dead Flowers are also acclaimed purveyors of psychedelia. The folk rock of Suicidal Flowers (which starts with some beautiful fiddle) sits happily after the pop of The Aardvarks and before the far rockier Kava Kava. And as for Boris & His Bolshie Balalaika, their version of "Purple Haze" must be heard to be believed. Anyone into the underground ought to pursue this further.
#33, Feb 1996

THE THIRD CYCLOPS SAMPLER

Head honcho Malcolm Parker continues to promote bands on his label with another budget price sampler. The problem is that while bands such as Pink Floyd and Genesis can sell by the million, the same punters who buy those will not risk forking out a few quid to try a new name. It is extremely frustrating for Malcolm and virtually anyone connected with the UK prog scene to hear a stunning album yet know that its sales are likely to be measured in the hundreds or low thousands, yet if it had a different name on the cover then it would sell by the bucket load. Added to the problem, is that the mainstream press is convinced that progressive rock died out years ago, and if it did not then it bloody well should have and if they do everything in their power to ignore it then maybe it will go away. Unfortunately for them, as this album shows, prog is here to stay. None of these bands featured on the first sampler, and only four on the second, and the songs are all unavailable elsewhere although "Book of Hours" by Anekdoten is live (bit of a cheat this one seeing as how they're not even signed to Cyclops, still, check out 'Vemod'), and a few are remixes. The gems are Still (the band formed out of the ashes of the sadly missed Echolyn) and Sphere, but they are all worth a listen. If you ever wondered about the current prog scene, but were afraid to ask, then write to Malcolm and get this.

#38, Nov 1996

PROGDAY '95

ProgDay is a two-day festival organised by Peter Renfro in the US on Labor Day Weekend. This is a double CD, featuring artists playing at the first ProgDay, in 1995. First up are Ozone Quartet with two songs. An instrumental outfit, with the lead instrument being a violin, I found it interesting but more as an appetiser instead of being the main course. However next up with six songs is Timothy Pure. Although I would have preferred to hear the guitar higher in the mix, it just proves to me what I have been thinking based on their studio albums, that here is a band that deserves to be higher recognised in the UK with their IQ-style prog. Discipline are new to me, although I have had contact with singer Matthew Parmenter who assures me that I will have their new album in time for the next issue. They have five songs in which they managed to impress me. The hard edges are, and they mix good rock guitar with some very delicate piano work. They move from simple melodies to feeling and emotion with songs such as "Canto IV" being extremely impressive. I am not sure who Bon Lozanga is, but he gets one song in which to play guitar and effects. Okay in its way, but it only acts as a prelude to the headline act, Echolyn. I, along with many others I am sure, felt that these guys were going to be huge. I mean, they were signed to Sony in the States, but they are no more. This shows just what they were like as live band and I wish I could have seen them, as there is a real presence that comes shining out of the CD, anger and enthusiasm that is infectious and effective. Listen to the vocal harmonies on "Uncle" and marvel.

#52, Feb 1999

CYCLOPS SAMPLER 4

Malcolm Parker started Cyclops some eight years ago in conjunction with his mail order company GFT. Since then he has released some of the best prog music around and this budget price double CD is an introduction to many of those bands. While there are many British acts such as Citizen Cain and Jump, there are European acts (Malcolm is a big fan of Fruitcake and Sinkadus) as well as some of the best from America (including the awesome Salem Hill and the truly progressive Kopecky). What is interesting about this album is that the bands do sound very different, not as similar as someone not knowing the genre might think. There are a few unreleased tracks or alternate versions for the hard-core fan, but this album is for the outsider to get some insight into what the progressive 'underground' is about.

#62, May 2001

NOT OF THIS EARTH

This is the biggest release ever for the Italian label, Black Widow Records, a triple CD set that comes in a hard cover book format and is also available as a four LP boxed set. Yes, Black Widow is one of those rare labels that also still release vinyl, and this features forty-one bands with a total running time of more than three hours. The concept behind the release was that each band would produce music that was inspired by a science fiction film, and the result is certainly interesting. One of the numbers will already be familiar to many, as it is Hawkwind with a live version of "Sonic Attack" which apparently was influenced by 'When Worlds Collide'. Musically there are almost as many different styles as there are bands, so while space rock may be the order for one, a totally dreamy and effective number may be the rule for another. They are bound together through their love of science fiction and are not constrained to have to play in a particular fashion. I do not believe that all the bands on this set normally record for Black Widow, and while I can't speak for each act, I know that Quarkspace (from USA) and Mr Quimby's Beard (from the UK) have their own label. A lot of care and attention has gone into the complete package: there are long discourses on the history of science fiction in general, and films in both Italian and English with plenty of pictures. I have discovered that I am missing out by not ever having seen any of the Italian porn science fiction movies that are apparently very popular. There is a long explanation and detailed look at 'The Prisoner' as well as a comic book version of the tale. So, having read the information provided in the 'book', and studied the film stills and covers of 'Astounding Stories' etc., turn to the CD booklet itself. This is stuck into the rear cover where the fourth CD would be if there was one and contains full details on each band including who played on which song, as well as which movie inspired the music, and then many more details about the movie itself. I have not come across a compilation of this form before but in many ways, it is as complete as can be imagined, and I can't conceive of anything that could be done to make the presentation any better. With so many bands it is hard to pick out musical highlights as they all need to be heard but Candlemass, Malombra and Standarte are three of my current favourites.

Not all the bands are known to me, and it is a perfect introduction not only to the label and the bands playing for it but also to the genre and movies that have inspired this release.
#71, Dec 2002

FRACTURE MESSAGE

Seeing as how Hiroshi arranged for all the liner notes for this sampler CD to be translated into English it seems somewhat churlish not to use them. To my ears this is a powerful sampler showcasing many differing Japanese acts and all prog fans should be searching this. The first band here is Pochakaite Malko, whose foundations can be found in Magma, Univers Zero, Frank Zappa, Zamla Mamas Manna, the Canterbury musicians, ethnic music and modern, contemporary classical music, delivering "formidable mixture gothic rock" under the principle of "violent repetition on odd meters". This track is taken from the first (and to-date only) album.

The second song is by Quikion (kee-kee-on), an acoustic unit featuring medieval instruments and female vocals. Dubbed as "Pascal Comelade meets Pentangle" as well as "the chansons from the mysterious forest", their early live performances were laden with rich melodies. Next is Round House, known for their musical prowess in the western part of Japan, especially as a regular contestant for the historical rock band contest "8-8 Rock Day" back in the 70's. The structure of the music, dramatic and tight in the vein of Return to Forever, topped with wailing guitar, perfectly hits the weak spot of many prog fans. The fourth track is by Theta. Based on the symphonic rock style, the band nicely blends in jazz-rock elements, which make the music altogether tasteful. The fifth track is by MorSof, short for Morning Machine & Soft Musme. Obviously, the name is a juxtaposition of Soft Machine and Morning Musume (current teen-age craze, a bundle of all-girls pop cute package), though there's nothing of Morning Musume in it, apparently. As for Soft Machine part of it, there's plenty. Twisted theme progresses into exploding improvisations in the vein of Sun Ra, somehow wearing the very colour of Soft Machine, without being self-indulgent but with discipline. The band is yet to release an album, so this track makes a rare appearance.

The next one is KBB's “Hatenaki Shoudou” (“The Endless Urge”) which originally appeared on their debut album from Musea: A tight performance with dramatic opening though tasty ensemble in unison towards the end. Track seven is by Six North from Kyoto. Their live performance boasts hard and tight jazz-rock of high sophistication while this track leans heavily towards the jazzier side, reminding of technical jazz fusion names such as Miles Davis and Weather Report. The eighth, “Roger”, is by Quaser from Kobe. Their history goes back to '75 and this song represents a Jungian perception of the world. Hard-edged performance supports busy developments, giving interesting contrast to subdued whispering vocals. The ninth track presents Head Pop-Up from Yokohama. The song is full of appeal to prog fans with its structure, development, phrasing and odd meters. Cool keyboards, energetic guitar solos are most remarkable in this performance.

The last track on this compilation is by Akihisa Tsuboy and Natsuki Kido Duo. Having collaborated in various units, the duo has performed sporadically since 2000. The improvisation leaves listeners wondering how two instruments could ever make sounds so rich.
#72, Feb 2003

CYCLOPS SAMPLER 5

No other independent label can be said to have done as much for progressive rock in the UK as Cyclops, and with this sampler Malcolm marks his 125th release. This double CD features 19 bands with 20 songs, with only one being previously available in this form. The collection shows the diversity of styles on Malcolm's label alone that can be called 'progressive' from the folk stylings of Mostly Autumn through the classical influences of Karda Estra to the rockier Nice Beaver. The traditionalist may prefer Parallel Or Ninety Degrees, while those who like the old school would want to own the previously unreleased CBS studio version of "Fact and Fiction" by Twelfth Night. There are so many different styles of progressive rock that to the outsider it can be hard to work out who is what, and what styles of music are covered under the banner. There are also some sections of the scene that are quite incestuous with musicians appearing in each other's bands although this only happens a small amount in these acts.

If you have ever enjoyed prog bands then why not try this collection of what is going on now? It is a sad indictment that if Genesis, Yes, King Crimson, Van Der Graaf Generator or any of the other wonderful prog bands that this country developed thirty years ago, were starting life now, then they would be destined to the same fate as the acts on this sampler. Why will hundreds of fans go to see a tribute band but not try something they have never heard before? Many of you have contacted me to say that you enjoyed the Black Widow sampler that was in #71, well why not try out the UK's No 1 progressive label and see what it can offer? You may not like all the bands on here, but you will find plenty you will.
#73, Apr 2003

Video/DVD Reviews

JAN AKKERMAN
A TOUCH OF CLASS

This DVD is basically a one-hour television special that was commissioned in 1984 by Channel 4. It is mostly comprised of footage from a concert at the Venue on 21st December 1983, but there is also some video of Jan playing a lute plus snippets of arguably his most well-known TV performances in the UK where Focus ripped apart OGWT with wonderful versions of both "Sylvia" and "Hocus Pocus". But this was a TV special so as well as the concert footage there is also Jan discussing where he came from and how he got involved with the band that became Focus (as well as two extra bonus tracks). The result is a well-balanced look at Jan, with the concert footage obviously dated but there are multi cameras well edited as the band works their way through songs from both the new (at the time) album 'Can't Stand Noise' and 'Tabernakel'. There is a well-written booklet and although this is not full of bonus features it is exactly what it purports to be, an interesting feature on arguably Holland's most famous guitarist. This is obviously of major interest to fans of the man but is also well worth seeing if you have the chance and ever wondered what he was like in concert.
#87, Apr 2006

ASIA

LIVE LEGENDS

I believe that this is the same DVD as 'Bedrock Live In Nottingham': my rationale for this is that it was recorded in Nottingham, has the same line-up (Downes, Palmer, Wetton and Pat Thrall), and that John thanks Central TV during the gig so it seems a safe bet. Although I have 'Asia In Asia' on video (which features Downes, Palmer, Steve Howe and Greg Lake!) this is the first time that I have seen the band with Pat Thrall. This makes the band even more interesting as although he must follow many of the lines originally laid down by Steve, he attacks this from a hard rock perspective instead of a prog rock one which gives the band much more bite. At the beginning, I was not too sure about John's voice but by the end of "Sole Survivor" he has loosened up and this is a great gig. Most of the songs are from the first two classic albums and any Asia fan will say that this is alright with them. Pat's rocky attack works wonders on "Time Again" which becomes the hard melodic rock track that it always threatened to be and is easily one of the many highlights on the album which sees the line-up gelling onstage. Carl seems to revel playing shorter numbers, playing the drum god to the tee and even his solo is not too long, and the overall feel is that this was a band that had had a great career to date and had a bright future ahead of them. Of course, it was not too long after this that they imploded to a certain extent, but this is a good record of the band they were back then.

#83, Mar 2005

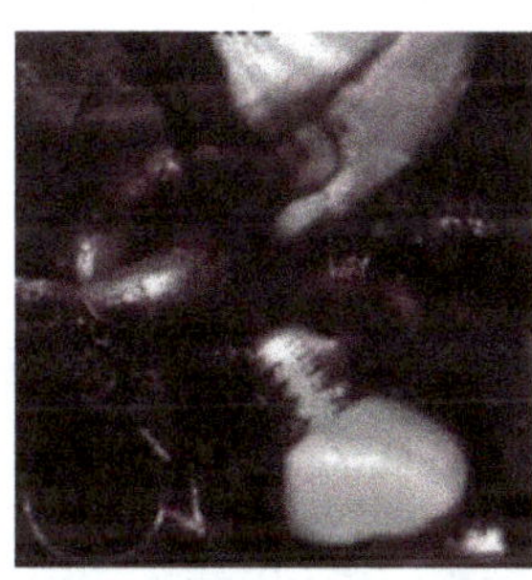

CHAIN

CHAIN.EXE LIMITED EDITION

The wonderful album 'Chain.Exe' that I reviewed earlier is also available as a limited edition direct from ProgRock Records (where it comes with a DVD). If, however, you have bought the album as a single set it is possible to go back and buy this extremely interesting all region DVD. It is 205 minutes long and is just crammed full. The main bulk is with Henning in the studio and all the vocalists and musicians involved with the album. It is a great insight into the way that the music was constructed, and how it was all put together. I found it fascinating, and fans of Saga are obviously going to want to see Michael Sadler at work. But that is not all, as there are interviews aplenty, the video for "Eama Hut" and possibly one of the most interesting things on the DVD, Henning explaining and demonstrating the rhythms of "Cities". He can make playing complex music seem very simple. There is also a gag reel, slide show, concert footage etc., and all in all this may well be for the fans but once you have heard the album you will want to get this so you may as well just buy the limited-edition CD direct from the label anyway!

#84, July 2005

ROGER CHAPMAN
FAMILY AND FRIENDS

Talk to people who love Roger Chapman's music and they will tell you that he is one of the finest vocalists that has ever graced these shores, although to some he may be something of an acquired taste. He first came to fame when fronting Family, but since then has created a strong reputation for his solo material. This live set is taken from a gig last autumn at the Opera House in Newcastle, where it does seem as if Chapman is surrounded by friends. The audience wants to hear him perform and he obliges by singing songs from throughout his career as well as a few covers. It is only a small stage, but he has a large voice, and he works through sixteen songs that seem to be over far too soon. The song that many people will know is "Moonlight Shadow" which he recorded with Mike Oldfield, yet while that is well received, I would rather point to the Family classic "The Weavers Answer" or his take on Dylan's "Blind Willie McTell". It is a warm experience, as if he is playing just for the listener – and the stage is delicately lit. There is nothing flashy, just a man and his voice. As well as a montage of his career, the bonus material also includes a lengthy interview with Roger, which provides an insight into just what he is all about.

#74, Jun 2003

COLOSSEUM
COLOSSEUM LIVES

This is one of those DVDs where everything comes together in a perfect package. The main feature is the complete reunion concert of Colosseum when they played in Germany in 1994. They kick off with "Those About To Die" and play many of their most well-known pieces, such as "The Valentyne Suite". It is strange to think that it was some twenty years since they had last been together – it is as if they had never been away. As a unit, the band are incredibly tight, and produce music that is extremely complex with enough time changes and note density to please even the most unconvinced proghead. Add to that the power and presence of Chris Farlowe, who proves that he is still a vocalist to be reckoned with, and this concert is a joy from start to finish.

But if that was not enough, there is a 90-minute documentary detailing the complete history of the band, which is jam packed with interviews and relevant footage and photos. It is easily one of the best, if not the best, short history of a band that I have seen, and it is worth buying the DVD for this alone. If you have never heard Colosseum before (keyboard player Dave Greenslade also formed, um, Greenslade) then this is a wonderful introduction.

#74, Jun 2003

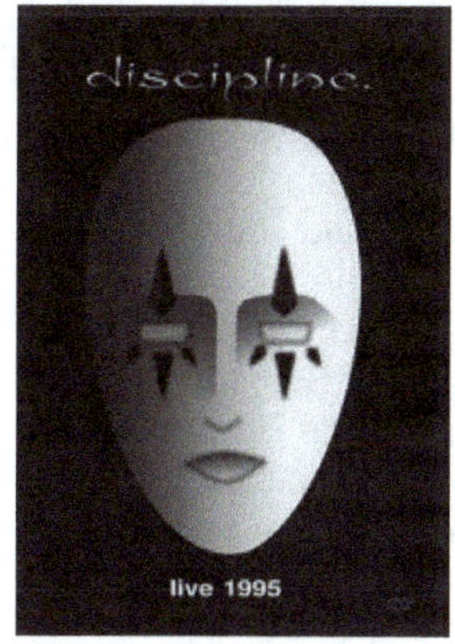

DISCIPLINE
LIVE 1995

I hadn't played any Discipline for a while before putting this DVD into the player – take it from me that was rectified as soon as this had finished. Discipline were a band that created quite a stir among prog fans in the States, but somehow never managed to gain the much wider success that they deserved and the reason for that is quite beyond me. To put it simply they were a band with a wealth of musical ideas which chopped and changed, and in Matthew Parmenter they had one of the most visual and animated frontmen at least since Fish, if not since Gabriel. With make-up and a much larger than life persona he strode the stage totally in control, and somehow managing to dominate proceedings just by the force of his personality. Combine that with great vocals and songs and this prog band should have been a winner, but somehow their abrasive very rock early Genesis style did not give them what they deserved. This DVD captures a multi-camera show from 1995 as well as songs from throughout their career and at nearly 2½ hours long is well worth discovering.

#85, Nov 2005

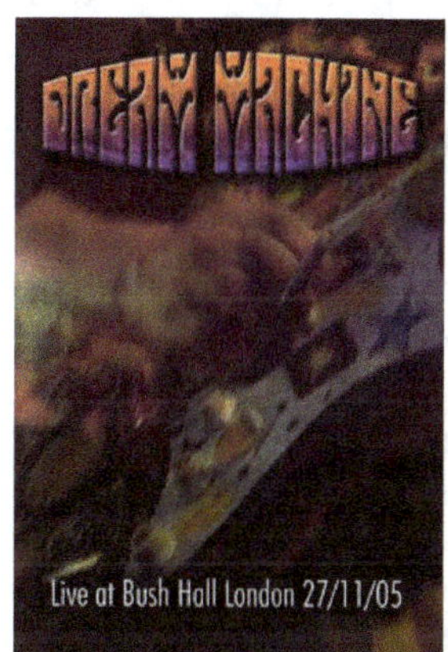

DREAM MACHINE
LIVE AT BUSH HALL LONDON 27/11/05

This DVD was recorded at the launch gig for the album (reviewed earlier), by which time the band had already experienced a change in line-up as Seaweed had decided to leave the band to concentrate on work in the studio and he was replaced by Joie Hinton. No extras, no menu, this is just the guys playing the album in its entirety (well it is only three songs after all) and clocks in at over 70 minutes long (I did not say that they were short songs). Although there are two keyboard players instead of one, these guys are always going to be compared to Ozrics, especially with the imposing figure of Jon 'Champignon' Egan at the front of the stage, but there are subtle differences between the two. There is a feeling of something more spacey in what they are doing, although with the light show tripping away there is the feeling that this is a gig that could have taken place at UFO nearly forty years ago. If you are going to be playing this in the car get the CD, but if it is for home use then get the DVD and play it loud with the lights off and get into the world of Dream Machine.

#87, Apr 2006

ELP
PICTURES AT AN EXHIBITION

This DVD captures the band at their peak, as they perform their version of Mussorgsky's 'Pictures At An Exhibition'. Given that at the time they were already selling vast numbers of albums, the setting could not be more basic with the three of them sharing a

very small stage. The crowd are sat on the floor just listening intently to the music, as if in a trance. Keith of course does his normal showing off, but in many ways, it is strange to see them so laid back – as if they are getting as much out of their performance as the audience. They react and interact, and although they appear subdued the music is not. I was rather hoping that the weird 'effects' that were on the video had been removed but they are still here, unfortunately. But at least it is now possible to watch the band in a digital format, with improved Dolby sound. There are some extras that increase the length of the original film, but there is no extra music although some of the photos are interesting.
#74, Jun 2003

GENESIS
DUKE – ROCK MILESTONES
This is part of a series called 'The Essential Albums Of All Time': now I consider myself to be a fan of Genesis and I was one of those that bought this when it was released which helped it get to Number One in the charts. I also saw them on this tour and still have Phil Collins and Chester Thompson's autographs that I got on the second night at Paignton Festival Theatre. Do I like the album? Yes. Is It essential? No. To many fans this is the beginning of the real end, with the albums after this having some great moments but with a feeling that the band were now far away from their roots. But what gets me annoyed about this is that I get the feeling that here is an attempt at making a DVD that does not exist. This is 52 minutes long, with no extras, and the first time that 'Duke' is even mentioned is half-way through. There is audio of Steve Hackett, and some lovely shots of mixing desks while people are talking, but this is not what I expected at all. The critical look is quite interesting, but I feel that I or any fan could probably have done better. What is interesting are the clips from the Duke tour and it would have been much better to have presented these as a concert DVD, especially as there are some interviews with Mike, Tony and Phil from that tour. This is a DVD that needs to be avoided and certainly does not give any valuable insights into the album.
#87, Apr 2006

GLASS HAMMER
LIVE AT BELMONT
According to the press release, buy this DVD and you will "experience the world's premier progressive rock band in all its majesty". Now, that is a sweeping statement and one that they must substantiate – the only way of doing that is by producing the goods and in this they have very much done just that. The DVD was recorded at Belmont University, on a huge stage. Well, they needed a big stage seeing as how the Belmont Choir joins them on some numbers, and they are 150 strong! There is also a string trio,

backing singers, and Carl Groves of Salem Hill (who opened that night, but are not on the DVD) steps up to the plate as guest vocalist for the night. The cameras are plentiful, the lights are good, and the sound is spot on, so is the band as good as they claim to be? The answer to that is possibly, and that is only down to personal taste. Whatever you could possibly wish for from a symphonic progressive rock band is here, whether it be some soaring guitars, great basslines, incredible keyboards, stunning vocals and harmonies, complex music, or a feeling that here is a band creating something very special indeed. I felt that the choir had more of a visual impact than a musical one, and it is certainly interesting watching as some of the singers obviously get lost within the music, but it is a brave attempt at trying to do something different and Glass Hammer get away with it. This double disc set, which is more than four hours long, contains not only the concert but loads of bonus material such as rehearsals, home videos of other gigs, slideshow with commentary etc. If you enjoy progressive rock music yet have not come across Glass Hammer before then you owe it to yourself to get this.

#88, Jun 2006

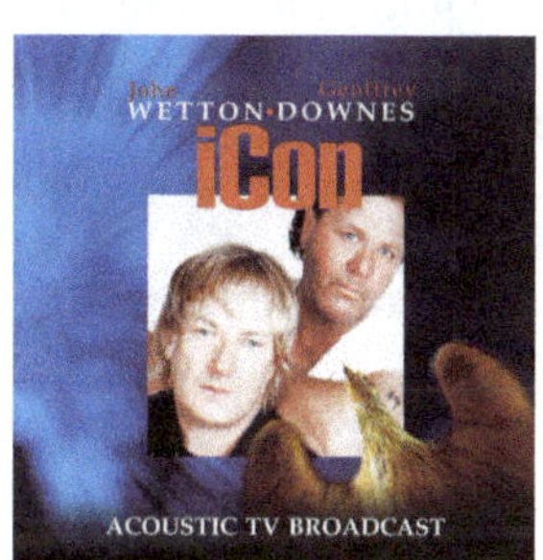

ICON

ACOUSTIC TV BROADCAST

Okay. I am sure that there must have been a good reason for this DVD, it is just that I do not know it. This is a collection of songs performed in a TV studio, with no audience. Hugh McDowell has joined John and Geoff on cello and the result is supposedly an acoustic performance. Well, it is mostly acoustic, but I am convinced that the audio has little or nothing to do with what is being performed in the studio. There are no microphones visible, and while Geoff's piano playing appears constant John appears to be waiting a split second before he starts singing. Also, the harmony vocals have been treated and Geoff manages to play some synth lines on a grand piano. I am not saying that this is a mimed performance you understand; it is just that it appears that way. Maybe it is just as well that we have a CD available as well, as when taking the visual aspect away then this becomes far more appealing. The acoustic bass hardly features at all, but the piano and cello combination works very well indeed, and this is then something that any fan of the guys will want to have. So, the verdict is to not get the DVD, but buy the CD as I for one found the DVD far too hard to watch but to listen to the treatment of songs such as "Voice Of America" and "Only Time Will Tell" is wonderful.

#87, Apr 2006

IQ

SUBTERRANEA THE CONCERT DVD

For many fans the top release of the Nineties was IQ's masterpiece, 'Subterranea'. As well as a studio album, it was conceived as a complete show and they dared to take the

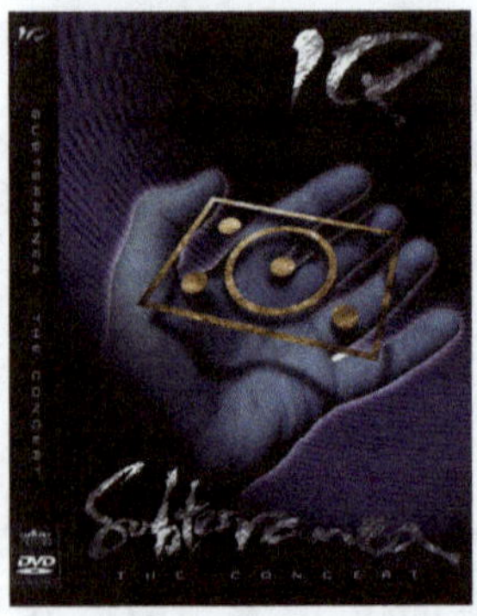

concept on the road. That involved the most lavish show ever attempted by an underground prog band, using back projection, front projection, screens, lights, an actor, stage costumes etc. The concert at 013 Tilburg on 4th April 1999 was filmed and recorded and the project was later released as a CD and as a video. Although the band have moved on since then, the decision was taken to shorten Mike Holmes' life span by entrusting him with turning all the recorded material into a full-blown DVD, with extra material. IQ put their all into making this a rounded show, one that would make sense even if the listener was not already familiar with the material. Peter plays his role to the hilt, taking the audience with him through the story, while the others concentrate on playing their most complex, longest piece of music ever. But why should anyone buy this if they already have the video and the CD? Apart from the much-improved sound and vision qualities, the extras make this worth the cost on its' own. There is bonus material as would be expected in the shape of the two encores "Human Nature" and "The Wake", as well as a documentary detailing the history of the project. But what makes this such an interesting DVD is the band commentary that can be turned on for the whole show. It adds a great deal to the full understanding of the project, some of the nuances to the music and story, and shows some of the relationships that the guys have with each other, in the way that they genuinely bounce off each other. I also was not aware at the time that the concert had to be stopped due to a technical problem. The band then played some songs to keep the audience occupied, then started the whole thing from the beginning again. As it was a seamless show, they could not afford to have a visible join. And just why did JJ dress up as a rabbit???? The DVD lasts for approx. 2½ hours, and it just seems to fly by. For any fans of IQ or progressive rock this is an essential purchase.

#67, Apr 2002

IQ

THE TWENTIETH ANNIVERSARY SHOW

Recorded at The Mean Fiddler on 15th December 2001, this was to celebrate IQ's twenty years of prog nonsense. Strange to think that next year it will be 25! IQ have throughout that time produced consistently strong albums, and their latest is arguably their best yet, and have also played live both in this country and abroad even when other prog bands have removed themselves from the scene. This is a double disc, and first concentrates on the concert. Tim Esau does join as a guest for the odd number, and Tony Wright also guests on saxophones, but for the clear majority of the gig it is four of the original line-up, plus 'new boy' John Jowitt (I mean, he has only been there since 1991). Peter has the make-up back on, as he used to wear in the old days, and it is obvious that there is going to be a party. IQ have long used back projections of films or graphics to add to the show, and they certainly add an extra element.

These guys have been together so long that they can relax onstage more than most bands, just because they know what everyone is doing all the time, which means that Mike and John can be ready to get up to any mischief they can, especially if it involves Peter Nicholls. But all the time they are playing some of the most complex and rock driven progressive music around. They have gone beyond the point of being noticeably influenced by others; these guys are an institution who have influenced countless bands themselves. With such a history, it is always going to be difficult to pick a definitive set list (what, where is "No Love Lost"?) but there is enough old and new to make any fan happy with "The Seventh House" sitting happily alongside "The Narrow Margin" and "Human Nature".

The second disc starts with the encores, for which IQ have become well known. Tonight, after "Subterranea" they treat us to "Jet" and "Crazy Horses" before ending with "The Wake". But of course, that is not all. There is also the support band to enjoy, The Lens, which features certain members of IQ in wonderful jackets and wigs (the last time John had hair this long he was in Ark!). It is possible to access all the intros and outros used by the band at gigs, as well as a tour diary. This last includes various subtitles, which shows the humour of the band. I am particularly fond of the Mice Men of Tilburg, as well as the prog epic being composed by the band on beer bottles! Then there is a Cookie Cam section, delayed time images of the stage set up, a photo gallery and an encore from Holland in 2004 where they managed to run "Mamma Mia" into "Out Of Nowhere" and it makes sense!

Great camerawork, great sound, and most important of all a great band. This double DVD is over four hours long and is a worthy testament to one of our greatest prog acts.
#82, Jan 2005

JADIS
VIEW FROM ABOVE

Recorded in Krakow on 11th April 2003, this shows the current (and the classic when you come to think of it) Jadis line-up of Gary Chandler, Martin Orford, Steve Christey and John Jowitt. It was just before 'Fanatic' was released so it is of little surprise that there is quite a lot from that album on it and the band walk on to the outside noises that start off the album. But there are songs from throughout their career, so it acts as a good retrospective (although with omissions from the set such as "Wonderful World" or "This Changing Face" it means there is the opportunity for a second DVD please!). The guys are cooking, and the whole show is very well shot so there are loads of camera angles, the sound is strong, and it has been very well put together. Not only is there the opportunity to watch one of the best UK prog bands around playing a great set with good lighting etc., there are also some bonus features that are worth seeing. There is a tour snapshot, plus some footage of the band playing "Holding your Breath" from 1994 (see how they have changed, especially Gary's hair!). There is also an extensive interview conducted with Gary and Martin, which is interesting for Jadis fans, I learned

some stuff that I did not already know. If that was not enough there are fully animated menus, an art gallery, photo gallery, desktop images, band biography and member's profiles etc. It is a wonderfully put together package that any fan either of the band or of prog will want to have. This is a DVD that I have been playing often and I know that I will be again in the future and is a strong representation of the guitar-led songs that have made Jadis such a great live act.
#83, Mar 2005

LANDMARQ
TURBULENCE
The main bulk of this DVD was recorded in Poland at the Wyspianski Theatre last November and has been released by the Polish Metal Mind label. As with other DVD productions I have seen from this label this is very professional with lots of cameras and angles, good lighting and excellent sound. This is the first time I have seen Landmarq since Tracy Hitchings took over singing duties, and this line-up also includes Credo keyboard player Mike Varty. Uwe D'Rose is still there on guitars, while Dave Wagstaffe and Steve Gee still make up the rhythm section and the result is a very powerful unit indeed. Mike has added something to the band (as well as reducing the average age, also one of his main roles in Credo) with a modern approach to keyboards and good vocals, and Tracy has always been known to have one of the finest female voices in prog and here they combine to work through nine songs to the appreciation of the audience. This is classic neo prog with a punchy bottom end and good guitarwork, with clever arrangements and strong vocals and melodies. However, as well as the well shot concert video there are also some rarities within the bonus section which are of interest. As well as the discography, interview, band history etc. there are some videos. One of these is the band with Tracy but with Steve Leigh on keyboards, but the gem is the next one which is the original line-up of the band with a very hairy Damian Wilson kicking out "Killing Fields" – I can still remember the first time I saw this line-up, with Tracy and Clive Nolan support at The Standard, those were the days. We also have Tracy with Dave Sparrow, Karl Groom and Fudge Smith performing as Dancing On Stones, while Ian Salmon, Sue Element and Paul Brown join Mike Varty and Dave Wagstaffe for two songs as Janison Edge. Then on top of that there are six bonus audio tracks as well! This is a well-constructed DVD showing just what Landmarq have to offer. Get this and then go and see them playing with Credo around the country!
#88, Jun 2006

LANA LANE
10TH ANNIVERSARY CONCERT
Lana and Erik have been taking their music to the masses for quite a while now and they decided that for the 10th anniversary tour they would revisit the set list and provide something that took songs from every album, old favourites plus some that hadn't been played live before. They also looked at the 'Storybook' live DVD and attempted not to

duplicate the track listing so that the DVD of the show would be quite different. Once the songs were decided upon it was just a matter of performing them, and that these guys can do with ease. The band is very powerful and rocking with Mark McCrite and Peer Verschuren complimenting each other with very different guitar styles (Peer obviously feels that he is a rock god, with some justification), while drummer Ernest van Ee powers his way around a kit, and bassist Kristoffer Gildenlöw also is no slouch. But the musical mainstay of the band will always be Erik Norlander with his wife Lana firmly taking centre stage. There are some wonderful performances here, with my favourite probably being a storming version of "Destination Roswell". Dramatic and sweeping progressive rock music, with strong guitars and great keyboards and on top of that there are stunning vocals. Who could wish for more? Not only is this a multi-camera show, but also there has been some very slick editing and extra images put into the concert. The result is a wonderful celebration of Lana so that if you are a newcomer you will love this as much as those who have been fans throughout. On top of that there is also a video diary from 2005 that also captures some performances, plus a bonus audio CD that includes 17 of the 19 songs. This is a great release and well worth investigating.
#87, Apr 2006

LEGEND
PLAYING WITH FIRE
Last October Legend played a gig at the Castlefields Centre, Runcorn, which was filmed specifically for this video. Unlike some other videos that are coming into the market, this has been 100% professionally treated from start to finish. In fact, the quality of the filming is easily comparable (and quite possibly superior) to that of a television broadcast. Legend work closely with Nu-Light Systems, and the lighting rig in evidence for this gig easily surpasses that of any prog gig I have attended this year. Add to that the pyrotechnics which Legend are renowned for, and all the elements of a stunning gig are in place. Oh, I hear you say, but what about the music? Steve and Jon have worked hard on the tapes to ensure that the sound quality is as good as can be, and it is possible to just sit back and enjoy the great sounds of Legend. The material is a mix of tracks from the first CD and some that will appear on the second, but the major difference on the music front from 'Light In Extension; is the very welcome new rhythm section of John Macklin (drums) and Martin Rouski (bass) who help make great songs even better. Many people felt that the one fault with the debut was the over the top drumming, but I am glad to say that Chris Haskayne is no longer involved so it is not a problem. The gig contains eleven songs, and right from the opener "Pipes Of Pan" you are drawn deep into the world of Legend. They are unlike any other prog band around, having totally different influences: Debbie sings in a style not unlike that of Maddy Prior, and I have said in a previous

review that they remind me of Nineties Steeleye Span. I still think that, but they are also far heavier than I could have imagined. I took a mate to see Legend the other night and he asked me how I could call it prog when it was enjoyable rock music, and I must agree.

It is difficult to pick up highlights on this video, as every song is a winner. I rate "The Chase", which is a stunningly powerful instrumental played at breakneck speed, the lighting rig is stretched to its fullest extent and the effect is visually and musically superb. "Toccata & Blues" is another favourite, being an adaptation of Toccata & Fugue. The closer, "Light In Extension", is possibly the best as the band roar to a climax. After the listed songs, there is another on the video to enjoy. When 'Light In Extension' was released in Japan, Legend were asked to supply an extra song but unfortunately, the band were only a trio at that point, having got rid of the rhythm section and yet to replace them. Undaunted they went into the studio and recorded "Storm Warning" with Paul doubling on bass and guitar and Steve on keyboards and drums. Due to contractual reasons, it should never be released in the UK, but here it is uncredited on the trail out. So, what is the result, video of the year? Well, it is going to have to be a bloody brilliant one to better this. I know that Jon and Steve have sweated blood on this project due to many technical difficulties, but this is something to be proud of. If ever a video captured a band in their element, then this is it. It's time to give yourself a present and get this video now: you will not be disappointed.
#19, Aug 1993

MAGENTA
THE GATHERING

Magenta were winners of 'Band Of The Year' award from the Classic Rock Society in 2005 and this DVD aims to show why. The main bulk is a two-hour concert, shot with 6 cameras, and available in 5.1 sound. In Christina, they have a great vocalist, one that seem to just keep winning plaudits from all who hear her, while in Rob Reed the band have a keyboard player who has loads of experience and knows what is needed when it comes to arrangements and fine tunes. But this is much more than just two people. Magenta are, as this DVD amply demonstrates, a six-person line-up that are very tight knit and the music that they produce is complex, complicated, and just so much fun to listen to. They are not afraid of producing grandiose epics like "The White Witch" which clocks in at over 23 minutes, but my favourite on the album is probably "Gluttony" which is just less than half that. If the concert is not enough then there are interviews, studio clips and a promo video for "Broken". Magenta are one of the top UK progressive bands around who have been making great strides over the last few years and if you have been unable to capture them in concert then you need to get this to see what you are missing and if you have seen them then you must be in the queue for this already.
#88, Jun 2006

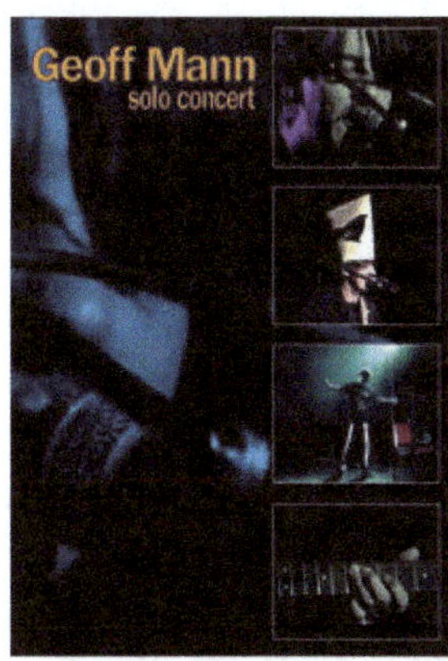

GEOFF MANN
SOLO CONCERT

Over the years Andy Labrow has been doing a lot to keep the name of Geoff Mann in the public eye, not least by maintaining the web site, and through this site he has started offering for sale CDs that are no longer available as well as this DVD. Recorded by a fan when Geoff supported IQ in Germany on 14th September 1991, it was offered to Andy who did not know of its' existence and was surprised at the quality. He already had access to tapes of the gig from the desk (apart from the first song) so all he had to do then was put the two together. Add to it a Frank Bough interview with Geoff and some photos and it was ready for sale at the ridiculous price of £5.50! I never saw Geoff in concert, the one time I should have seen him was at The Marquee, but he was already too ill, and Damian Wilson took his place. Andy says that this was one of Geoff's finest gigs, and now we also can see it.

This gig finds him sat on a chair with his trusty double-neck guitar to hand, and the camera switches between showing him in his entirety or concentrating on his hands or his face. Lots of credit must be given to Kees Nijpels for a) recording the gig at all, b) making it available to Andy and c) doing such a good job. It is steady camerawork from the front row and the result is something that any fan of Twelfth Night or Geoff Mann simply must have. At the end of the set Geoff was convinced to go back onstage for an encore, and although some wags shout out for "Sequences" or "The Ceiling Speaks" he just sits down and starts "Love Song". The Frank Bough interview took place in 1990 on Sky News, and Frank obviously had no idea who Geoff was, and this was going to simply be a piece on rock music and its place in the Church. Geoff launches into "Rest Assured" and the reaction from Frank at the end is totally genuine as at the end he says, "Boy, you can play, you can really play". Overall Andy should be commended for all the work he has put in, and it certainly does not look like a DVD-R. For only £5.50 this is the DVD bargain of the year.
#82, Jan 2005

NEAL MORSE
TESTIMONY LIVE

When I wrote the review of the Mean Fiddler concert that I attended on this tour I said that I hoped that someone had captured this on DVD, as it was one of the best gigs that I had ever attended. My wish was granted, and this DVD captures the complete gig from Tilburg on 17th November 2003. As well as Neal, there were seven musicians on stage that night, but given the multi-instrument status of most of them they managed to create a sound that was even bigger. How Eric Brenton managed to keep track of what instrument he was playing at any point within any song, let alone the correct notes, is beyond me (guitar, violin, flute, pedal steel, mandolin, and he sang as well!). But this gig is about Neal as he is telling his own story, it is his testimony. There has been nothing but praise for the album from the prog press, and for me it is one of the best albums he has released (in whatever guise) and this DVD manages to capture the power of recreating this extremely complex music onstage.

Tilburg is a good venue, so they used lots of lights and there were loads of cameras as well, which means that there are lots of angles within the concert, so it is always interesting. The second DVD contains the encores (including a rousing version of "The Light"), plus a tour documentary. This gives a fascinating insight into the tour and some of the travails they went through. This is worth watching for the first rehearsal alone, where the camera focuses on Mike Portnoy as he plays an extremely complex passage – boy that man can play drums. This is a release that anyone who saw Neal on tour must have, and if you have been wondering what all the fuss is about then I highly recommend this.
#82, Jan 2005

MOSTLY AUTUMN
AT THE GRAND OPERA HOUSE

This DVD captures Mostly Autumn at their most prestigious gig to date, selling out the Grand Opera House in their home city of York. For the occasion, they also brought on stage at different times Troy Donockley (who has of course recorded with the band), a string quartet and a choir. Lots of lights, back projection films (which can also be viewed separately), and the impression is certainly given that this is a band that are ready to breakthrough to the big time. They have been likened many times to Pink Floyd, but that is unfair both to them and the Floyd. Yes, they incorporate many prog elements in their music, but there is also room for folk and by having two very different lead vocalists it means that they can move the sound around. This is a seven-piece outfit, but with strong singers and instrumentalists they come across as far more than that during a gig. Bryan Josh takes stage left and has quite a commanding presence, but when she is singing lead then it is Heather Findlay who is the star and knows it (when she is wearing her hat there is a very striking image). Songs such as "Answer The Question" show why this band is a force to be reckoned with, it is dark and brooding in the verse with riffing guitars and Bryan almost growling out the vocals, but when Heather joins in and then with Angela Goldthorpe takes over, the music stays heavy (there are two electric guitars after all) but moves to a new plane. This is a song that builds and builds, with a piano somehow managing to stay on top of all the power that is the pressure cooker just waiting to explode. Then just when it can't go any further it just gently drifts away, and the piano introduction to "Goodbye Alone" heralds yet another style.

When the band comes back for encores, there is a sense of relief, and they are going to have a good time. With Troy onstage, the three guitarists start the riff to "Smoke On The Water" and it is smiles all round. That and the next encore, "Comfortably Numb", are the only covers and the audience are left satiated, as was I. 90 minutes somehow does not

seem long enough. I loved this band when I first heard them (what seems like) many years ago when they were signed to Cyclops, they have just kept getting better.
#79, May 2004

MOSTLY AUTUMN
THE NEXT CHAPTER
This is a bringing together collection from Classic Rock Legends, containing not only thirteen songs recorded over the last couple of years, in different places, but also a chance to sample "Pure White Light" from 'Passengers'. There is full information on where and when each song was recorded, and while this is obviously going to be more for fans of the band, the casual observer can get quite a bit out of it as well. The sound is strong throughout, and the camerawork also of a good quality, and it is interesting to see the band in different settings from a small but extremely enthusiastic audience at The Mean Fiddler to festivals both in the UK and abroad. There is film capturing the band in less formal settings in the Lake District, with music later added, and the overall effect is one that while it may not be the best introduction to Mostly Autumn (the previous DVD is better for that), this does show another side of the band that is interesting. There is a passion and emotion in their music combined with strong images and musicianship which show that the next chapter could well be the big one.
#79, May 2004

MOSTLY AUTUMN
THE V SHOWS
Recorded at the Astoria on 8th May last year, this shows just how far Mostly Autumn has come in a relatively short while. With the positive reception to 'Passengers' still ringing in their ears this is a band that is always moving forward, working hard to maintain their fanbase by releasing consistently strong albums and touring with a good show. This gig at The Astoria featured not only the seven members of the band, but also guest Troy Donockley and a string quartet. Add to that an impressive light show, back projections and even some lasers and one can see that they are visually at least quite different to other prog bands around. Musically they are always going to be likened to classic bands like Pink Floyd but the one cover here is an emotional and quite rocky version of Genesis' "Afterglow" which they have managed to make into an upfront showstopper instead of something that is quite laid back and more reflective.

Heather Findlay, as ever, is in fine voice and the interplay between her and Bryan Josh is always interesting and opener "Something In Between" is just wonderful. But what makes this band so interesting is the amount of textures that they can bring to play with so many instruments available within the band. With most of the band providing harmony

vocals and especially Angela Goldthorpe switching between second keyboards and flute this gives the band a wide palette and they want to use all of it. Some of the songs are very rocky, being blasted along by two electric guitarists, but against that is the amount of light that is provided either by Heather and Angela or by keyboards. This is band that has yet to reach their full potential, and if you have not had the opportunity yet to see them in concert then this is a DVD that all progheads will enjoy. As well as the gig, it also includes three bonus cuts, and a running length of 114 minutes.
#83, Mar 2005

NEKTAR
PURE - LIVE IN GERMANY 2005
This was recorded for a TV special in 2005, and disc one includes the complete set. The line-up by now was original members Roye Albrighton (guitar, vocals) and Ron Howden (drums, vocals) along with Randy Dembo (bass, vocals) and Tom Hughes (key, vocals) who both joined in 2004 after Mo Moore and Taff Freeman had departed. Nektar are somewhat unusual in that they are a British band who never achieved the success over here that they did in Europe, and to quite a large extent they are still ignored or probably just unknown over here in their home country. But they are still very popular in Germany and since Roye resurrected the band in 1999 after he recovered from a potentially fatal liver disease they have been working hard. This is my first encounter with the band, and I must admit being very impressed. Tom is using a 'proper' Hammond (boosted with some other keyboards) instead of relying on patches and samples and so is moving the sliders to get the sound he wants – not something you often see these days. They have two strong lead singers in Roye and Ron, and I loved watching Ron play drums. He is one of those guys who makes drum playing look totally effortless, just sitting there almost motionless while his legs and arms do all the work. There is quite a cheer when Roye announces that they are going to play "Dream Nebula" from the first album, which came out in 1971!

The second disc captures the band the following day performing virtually totally acoustically at a charity event, plus there is a biography, discography and slide show etc. The sound is very good, camerawork excellent, and the performances are spot on and for a newcomer like me this is an interesting introduction to the band, and I can see that I am going to have to find out about their albums. Good value.
#86, Feb 2006

ERIK NORLANDER
LIVE IN ST. PETERSBURG
Nearly 150 minutes' worth of material, with the DVD also coming with a CD that contains most of the concert plus two new studio songs. Erik was joined here by his wife Lana Lane on vocals, Kelly Keeling (vocals, bass), Peer Verschuren (guitar) and Ernst Van Ee (drums) and together they make a wonderful over the top progtastic sound. As

well as the main concert, there is also an on the road documentary which features songs from some of the shows leading up to the main gig itself along with interviews with those involved. The result is something that is a wonderful introduction to the world of Erik and his great keyboard playing and is something that any proghead can go out and purchase even if they have not come across him before. The songs are superb, the musicianship immaculate and the camerawork strong with good production which means that this is a package well worth seeing. This is easily the best DVD that I have come across for this issue.
#89, Sep 2006

PAIN OF SALVATION
BE
There is no doubt that "Be" is an intriguing project, one that took Pain Of Salvation to a new level and this live DVD captures a very impressive performance. Apparently, the full release contains also a CD and a 48-page booklet. I can't comment on the latter two, as I have not seen or heard them, but I have had the opportunity to play the DVD. The main section of the DVD is a film of the original stage production, where POS are joined by a string section etc. to perform the album. This is a production as opposed to a concert; with the impression that it could have taken place as a West End show if it was not for the fact that the music was just so intense. It is the sort of thing to play when there is no one else in the house as this needs to be played through in its entirety to get the most out of it, and it's not short! After having watched it then play it through again with the audio commentary from Daniel Gildenlöw. There is a photo gallery, plus loads of extra bits and pieces, so much so that there are two bonus menus. The whole thing is very slick, and any POS fan should have this in their collection.
#84, July 2005

PENDRAGON
LIVE...AT LAST AND MORE
This DVD is an extension of the Live... At Last! video that was released in 1997, taken from Polish TV footage of a show in Krakow the year before, when they were on the "Masquerade Overture Tour". This has been extended so that not only does it contain the songs from the show, but there is also a rare video clip (not "Red Shoes" as is stated on the case, but "Saved By You"), as well as an interview with Nick conducted by my good friend Artur Chachlowski, discography, photo gallery, desktop images, web links etc. What of the gig? The guys are having a blast, playing in front of a very appreciative audience, and as the gig was filmed by TV there are numerous camera angles and the quality is very high. As with any gig there are always numbers that the fan would wish

had been captured, but with highlights such as "Guardian Of My Soul" and "The Last Man On Earth" it is hard to pick fault.

I particularly enjoyed "Leviathan", where Nick proves that he knows how to play a full-on rock intro, then taken up by Clive. This line-up has been together for so long that they know just how each other is going to react, and with the crowd on such a high it is difficult to have anything but a good gig. The "Saved By You" promo clip is great fun. I had never seen it before, although I have both the 7" and 12" single in my collection, as well as a vinyl copy of the album from which it is taken, 'Kowtow'. Nick looks so much younger (well, it was thirteen years ago!) and Clive looks quite menacing! The interview is interesting, giving some insights into the way that Nick feels about his music and what has been happening in the recent past. Released by Metal Mind in Poland, this is a DVD that all proggers need to have.
#68, Jun 2002

PLACKBAND
VISIONS
Like many progheads I have been aware of the existence of an outfit in Holland called Plackband (named after the adhesive tape that used to hold their gear together), and that they had started life in the Seventies. But I had never heard any of their music until I watched this DVD – something tells me that I am going to be buying some CDs soon. Imagine IQ crossed with Gentle Giant with a guitarist who often thinks that he is Steve Howe (but not always) and you will have the band nailed. They even set up like IQ, with drummer on stage left, keyboards on stage right, bass in front of drums and guitar in front of keyboards while the singer has two mikes, one at the back of the stage and one at the front and he is even wearing some makeup. It makes an old proggers heart warm just to see that. This is top class prog with harmony vocals and a band that are extremely tight who produce melodies and complexity but manage to make it all so damn accessible all at the same time. As well as the DVD, there is a separate CD containing an audio mix of the concert as well as bonus features including one song with their new singer and one with their original, plus a 'Making Of' etc. I was not sure what to expect from this DVD but now that I have seen it, I know that I have been missing out and I urge all progheads to at least check them out.
#88, Jun 2006

QUIKION + LITHUMA QNOMBUS
LIVE
Quikion are one of my favourite Japanese bands, just because I feel that they are so very different to everything else that I have heard and are very strong musically. Here they

have been joined by Lithuma Qnombus to provide them with a rhythm section so there are two bands onstage, but that still only makes five of them. The bassist Kajiyama Shu is a real star as not only is he an incredible musician with a great touch on his fretless bass, but also, he is the only person standing and he is really into the music. He may be stuck in the corner, but he is moving around and provides the only action to be seen. Everyone else is seated, and lead singer Totki Yukiko accompanies herself on either concertina or harmonium or provides percussion, while Sasaki Emi provides accordion, glockenspiel and percussion whilst Oguma Eiji provides both guitar and bouzouki. The line-up for this show is completed by percussionist Kudoh Genta. The gig appears to have taken place in a small club and the audience are sat very close to the stage, but they are appreciative – clapping nicely at the end of the song and being perfectly quiet during each performance. It is hard to describe their music, which is folky and ethnic and very different to what we would normally hear in the west, but I know that I like it. Excellent camerawork and good sound production make this a good introduction to the band and their music.
#86, Feb 2006

SAGA
ALL AREAS

Having long been a fan of the Canadian prog rockers it was with eager anticipation that I put this DVD into the player. Filmed in Bonn in 2002, it was recorded to celebrate their twenty-fifth anniversary. My copy is a promo, and I hope that the final version hasn't been released in this format. The reason being is that the menus are quite hard to read, and when selecting the concert, it is not possible to select the gig, but rather the first track. I could not believe it when after the superb "Careful Where You Step" the picture faded to black, then back in again for "Compromise". This was a pattern that was to be repeated throughout the disc and spoilt the viewing. Maybe it has been done to assist in the separation of songs, but if this is on the final version then this is a big mistake as it just is not possible to let the concert flow through and over you. And that is a real shame, as these guys know what they are doing. The show starts with three keyboard players, but somewhat surprisingly it is the guitar that makes the biggest impact. They may have keyboards in abundance, but Saga are a rock band, and it is this combination of rock guitar and powering keyboards with the outstanding vocals of Michael Sadler that has made the band one of Canada's top acts for so long. The music is great of course, with songs such as "Take It Or Leave It" and "You're Not Alone" being of particular interest. Good camerawork and sound are let down by the fading, and there is little in the way of extras on the DVD, with just a discography, gear and too short voiceover saying about the problems they faced in putting the gig together. Apparently, the DVD is available with a bonus DVD of the 2003 world tour – let's hope that this is of better quality. An opportunity not totally missed, but

certainly not as good as it could have been.
#79, May 2004

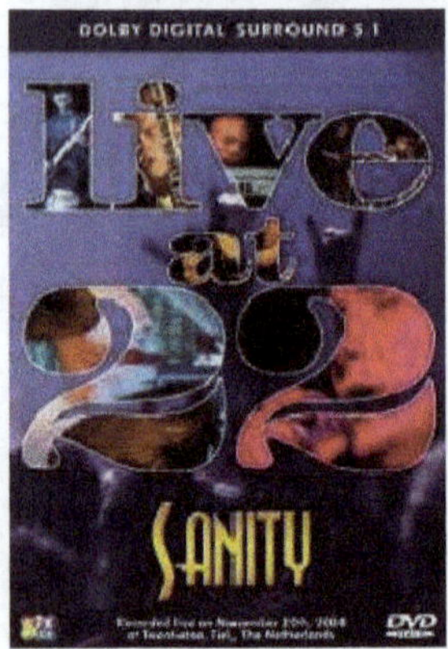

SANITY
LIVE AT 22

One must admire these guys. Sanity are a Dutch prog metal band who have been influenced by Queensrÿche, Dream Theater and Savatage for the heaviness, along with Marillion and IQ for the progginess and so far, have released two demo CDs and a mini-CD. Of course, the next step had to be to release an in-concert DVD! This is a concert from the end of last year in their home country, recorded using five cameras for the visuals and a 24-track mobile studio for the sound. They are proud of the fact that there are no overdubs, and this DVD been released with a bonus CD so that it can be played in the car etc. The sound is great; the band are into it and musically they have a lot to offer while in frontman Kees van Huelen they have a great singer. I came away very impressed indeed, as they have the music and presence to make an impact (I would have thought that Inside Out or SPV would want these guys) and they have the enthusiasm to make this work
#84, July 2005

SHADOWLAND
BLOWING THE WHISTLE

This video was recorded on the 'Lurve Ambassadors' tour with Jadis last year, at Tilburg in Holland. It was recorded on two cameras, and the gig is interspersed with Clive answering questions he is taking from a teapot! I was very much looking forward to this video, as Shadowland are one of my favourite bands, and I must admit to being a little disappointed. The people operating the cameras are quite a distance from the stage, and like following Karl around. On a personal level, I want to see who is singing, unless there is some dynamic fretwork. The lighting could also be better, and the sound is not perfect. However, I must admit that since receiving the tape it has been played as much as I have had the opportunity to do so. The set is the same as the one that Shadowland played in the UK, namely the CD plus "I, Judas", which appeared on the SI compilation. The actual performance is spot on and got a great reception from the Dutch crowd. My five-year-old daughter was well impressed as it contains her all-time favourite track "Scared Of The Dark" (thinking about it, she plays the video as much as I do). The gig ends with assorted members of Jadis joining the band onstage for the 'Lurve Dance' which accompanies "Ring of Roses". By the end of the tape you have forgotten all the faults that are apparent at the beginning and are just deep into the music. Possibly this is for fans only, and I would recommend purchasing the CD before the video. Still, it is an accurate portrayal of one of the UK's top prog bands.
#18, May 1993

SPACED OUT
LIVE IN 2000

As you may have guessed this was recorded six years ago and it has only just now been released on DVD. I am not sure for the reason for this, it may be because it features original guitarist Mathieu Bouchard who left that year, or maybe due to the camerawork itself. It does not appear to be lit very well, and there are some annoying effects, such as everything suddenly going black and white or being solarised. There is also the additional problem that there was only one camera used in the original recording, so to provide some flow this has been edited so that what you are seeing may not be what is playing musically. That to one side, this does capture a very impressive prog fusion band and I am sure that it is why it has now eventually seen the light of day. All the guys are consummate musicians, and often the person who is doing the least amount of work is keyboards player Eric St-Jean! Martin Maheux obviously knows his way around his kit and goes from frenetic to controlled back to over the top at the drop of the proverbial, he is incredible, and manages to put a lot more rock feel into what is a band often moving into jazz. Then add to that the wonderfully warm and inventive bass playing of band leader Antoine Fafard and you have a band that know what they are doing. I enjoyed the DVD, but I could have done without the gaps between songs and the only extras are a few pages of text biographies.

#86, Feb 2006

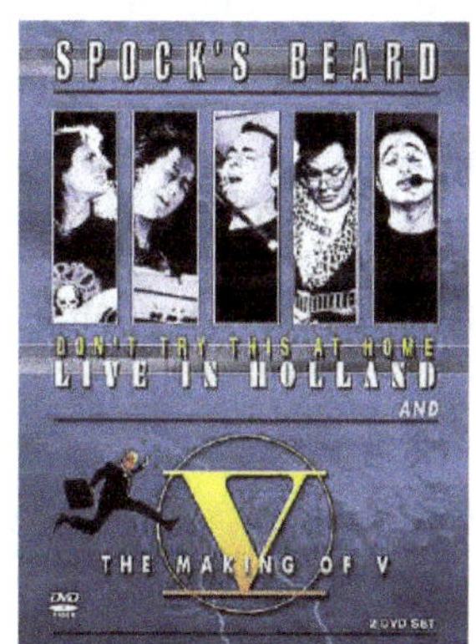

SPOCK'S BEARD
DON'T TRY THIS AT HOME/MAKING OF V

This double disc must be one of the best value for money DVDs that I have come across. Firstly, it contains the 'Don't Try This At Home' concert that was recorded in Holland: given that Neal has now left the band, this may well be the only opportunity to catch the original line-up. Having seen them in concert three times, I can say that this does do them justice. The band is on a large stage with good lighting and plenty of cameras and it brings home the spectacle of the Beard at play. There are too many highlights to mention, but I must confess to being somewhat disappointed not to have on film the Morse brothers playing the same guitar at the same time. However, when I turned to the bonus material what did I find? There is some footage of SB in the studio, then a live rendition of "Space Trucking" with Nick on lead vocals, and then the Morse brothers in action. I still find that bit hard to comprehend even though I have had chance to watch it just a few times now. As if that was not enough, there is another disc 'The Making Of V', which surprisingly enough is a camcorder documentary of the band recording 'V'. This gets up close and personal, and for the Beardfan it is a fascinating insight into the way that their music is put together. Add to that yet more bonus footage such as live clips and the promo video for "All On A Sunday", and here is a DVD set that is more than five hours long! Superb value for money, and easily available through

Amazon – this is essential!
#74, Jun 2003

THRESHOLD
CRITICAL ENERGY

Threshold have been the UK's premier prog metal band for quite some time now – their debut album came out as long ago as 1993 – and at last their live show has been captured on DVD. New bassist Steve Anderson has slotted right in, linking in with drummer Johanne James to provide the backbone for the rest of the guys to strut their stuff. Mac is a perfect frontman, one who has obviously been studying Ian Gillan, and keeps the crowd going, while Karl and Nick riff hard and Richard provides the melodic overtones that manage to move Threshold out of the pure heavy metal arena. But be in no doubt, Threshold are a hard rock band first and foremost. There may be room for some widdly-widdly, but these guys play using Marshall amps for one good reason – they like to play loud! The concert (which is approx. two hours long) covers the depth of the band's career, and even has room for some acoustic numbers in the middle. This allows everyone time to have a rest, but not for long. This is a rock band that is out to grab you by the balls and shows that even though 'prog' is in the title of the genre, 'metal' is the other one. With songs as powerful as "Sanity's End" (which has long been my personal favourite) or "Phenomenon" who could ask for more? Great production (mind you, you wouldn't expect anything else) and strong use of cameras and lighting means that this is a joy to play, time and again. But it does not stop there, as Karl and Richard have gone into the studio and added a commentary to the gig which goes some way to showing what a good time they have in the band. There are also some songs from the gig they played in the States at ProgPower 2002, as well as a feature of them on tour. Lastly there is a photo gallery care of Sy 'Wooks' Seddon and the menu and design are of the highest quality. This DVD is also available as a set with the double CD of the same name, but no matter how you get this DVD it is a definite purchase for all lovers of prog metal/melodic hard rock.
#78, Apr 2004

TRACTOR
BEYOND DEEPLY VALE

Tractor is not only a band, but also an important part of the musical history of the North. If it hadn't been for them, their studio and their PA, and most importantly their festival Deeply Vale, then quite a few bands may not have got off the ground. As well as established bands, newcomers to the stage were Mark E Smith, The Ruts (who formed at the festival), Mick Hucknall and members of OMD. Tractor started life as a two-piece, and when they got back together after many years apart it was again the duo of Jim Milne (guitar, vocals) and drummer Steve Clayton. This DVD contains two sets performed in 2003, plus a host of extras concerning Deeply Vale. For those who have yet to come across the reissues of their debut album, shame on you, this is a great introduction to the

band. All these years later and Jim has lost none of the touch that inspired John Peel to say about him "the man responsible for some of the most urgent, flowing and logical guitar playing I've ever heard", which is some statement. In many ways Tractor have become something of a forgotten band, but this DVD shows just how powerful they are in concert. Jim sometimes is on acoustic, sometimes electric, but his playing is always full of passion whatever the instrument while Steve is much more than just a sidekick with a real understanding and intuition and of what Jim is doing. The extras concerning Deeply Vale are fascinating, including footage and interviews at the time (including some clips of the band in the 'studio') plus loads of photos then a return to Deeply Vale by Steve and Jim as they chat to Chris Hewitt then perform some music. There is a feeling of wanting this to be as complete a picture of the time and the people who were involved, which is brought home by the three small pieces of film of people who have since died. This DVD shows a great band in concert, plus some interesting musical history. There is also a 24-page booklet.
#80, Jul 2004

TWELFTH NIGHT
LIVE FROM LONDON

What can one say about this DVD? It is one that many of us have been waiting for, for a long time. Originally broadcast as part of the 'Live In London' TV series it was released commercially as a video (called 'Creepshow') many years ago but has long been deleted (although I do have a copy). This is the only 'proper' film in existence of TN doing what they did so very well, taking The Marquee by storm. Filmed in March 1984 this was prior to the band recording any material with new singer Andy Sears but he was doing a commendable job of taking on Geoff's legacy. The DVD starts with the very naff intro that was part of the TV programme, but that gives way to Andy Revell and Clive both playing electric guitars as they crunch into "The Ceiling Speaks". TN were a prog band, but they were also very much a rock band as well as this more than demonstrates. This DVD is only 59 minutes long but even so we manage to get gems such as "Human Being", "We Are Sane", "Fact and Fiction", "Art And Illusion" and "Creepshow". The final song, as if it could be anything else, is "Love Song" which is faded out!! Unfortunately, the only video that exists appears to be what was broadcast, but at least the band managed to get hold of the soundtrack and they have remixed it and made it available as a CD. If you purchased this DVD direct from Brian then you got the CD free, and although it only contains the same songs it is great to be able to play it in the car as this is a very energised performance from the band and from Andy Sears in particular. If you call yourself a prog fan, then this is a DVD that you must have.
#85, Nov 2005

URIAH HEEP
MAGIC NIGHT

The band that the critics and record labels love to hate refuse to die, and anyone who has ever seen this band on the road (I saw them in Eastbourne of all places) will testify that they are as relevant now as they have ever been. When Trevor Bolder takes over the mike during opener "Easy Livin'" then images of The Darkness definitely spring to mind. But these guys are no copyists, thirty years ago they were one of the hardest working bands in the business and here they are still pounding away today. This gig was recorded at The Astoria in 2003, eighteen songs showing why the band have managed to stay around for so long. Remember, when the first 'International Encyclopaedia Of Hard Rock and Heavy Metal' was published, the cover was a photo of Mick Box. Maybe this DVD will go some way to getting people interested again; as it shows a band at home. They can provide hard rock with an American tinge if required ("Too Scared To Run") or classic after classic. Okay, "Gypsy" is missing, but "Lady In Black", "July Morning" and "Stealin'" are here among many others. Lee Kerslake makes it out from behind his kit to duet on "Firefly" when Mick goes all acoustic. The band probably should sit down about then as they are not as young as they used to be. There are four acoustic numbers, with the section finishing with a subtle take on "The Wizard". But there is nothing subtle about "Been Away Too Long" when ex-frontman John Lawton joins the band. Bernie Shaw enjoys the competition and it is good to be able to compare the two (Bernie slightly higher, John with more emotion and breadth). John sticks around for "Cry Freedom", where six hardened rockers can be heard singing "ooo-oooh"! It is the sort of song that made Heep, loads of pomp and power and a refusal to take themselves too seriously. Heather Findlay from Mostly Autumn joins the band for an emotional take on "Love In Silence", before the band blasts back with the penultimate number "The Other Side Of Midnight". Great production, both on sound and audio, along with multi-camera angles make this a DVD to enjoy. There may not be many extras, just some interspersed rehearsal shots and the rear projection footage, but this is a DVD that any Heep fan must get.

#79, May 2004

URIAH HEEP
BETWEEN TWO WORLDS

Recorded at The Magician's Birthday Party in 2004, it is interesting to contrast the thirteen songs on this DVD from the eighteen songs available on 'Magic Night' which is a DVD of the same show in 2003. There are only two songs that appear on both, "Cry Freedom" and "July Morning", but the new DVD does feature two classics that are inexplicably missing from the former in "Look At Yourself" and "Gypsy". It is certainly hard to imagine Heep ever playing a gig without performing the latter. The guys may be getting older, but they certainly show no sign of slowing down or changing their attack. This is melodic hard

rock with strong use of keyboards – they have always been far more rock than prog, in a similar vein to Deep Purple, and critics may always have hated them but they have been going for the best part of forty years now and with this loyal fanbase will probably keep going until Mick Box has to be wheeled onstage. The first edition of the 'International Encyclopaedia Of Hard Rock and Heavy Metal' featured Mick as the cover photo, and to be honest the face may be a bit older, but he still looks as happy playing as he ever has. The band are joined onstage by Osibisa who reproduce their drumming attack on "Look At Yourself" which they did in the studio all those years before. This is one of the highlights, along with the wonderful "July Morning" and "Words in the Morning". They are happy in what they are playing – knowing that they will never be fashionable but who cares? Not them, and not the fans. Plenty of camera angles and strong sound makes this essential.
#83, Mar 2005

RICK WAKEMAN
LIVE FROM BUENOS AIRES

This DVD captures Rick in front of a large audience and shows that those who are not aware of how powerful keyboards can be in a rock environment need to hear him with the English Rock Ensemble. This is the line-up that performed on his last album, although they have here been filled out even more by the addition of Rick's son Adam. Damian is in fine voice, and it is a real shame that for some reason he did not make it to the recent tour. The sound is very good, and this captures Rick in his element as he takes a trip through his musical career. There is plenty of old material, yet it still manages to sound fresh and invigorating. There is just the one Yes number, "Starship Trooper", but here Rick proves that Yes need him much more than the other way around. He not only is a great musician but also a showman and he revels in playing both the fool and the maestro. There is bonus material available in an interesting (but far too short) interview, but the main extra is a CD. This captures the band with Chrissie Hammond on vocals, which give the music very much a different feel. It is called 'The Official Bootleg' and certainly the quality is not brilliant, but it is well worth hearing and very interesting.
#74, Jun 2003

RICK WAKEMAN
JOURNEY TO THE CENTRE OF THE EARTH

RICK WAKEMAN
LIVE IN CONCERT 2000

'Journey To The Centre Of The Earth' was recorded on February 4th, 1975, and in true Seventies overblown style Rick was accompanied not only by his band but also by the Melbourne Philharmonic Orchestra and the Melbourne Chamber Choir. Not only did he treat the audience to songs from both 'Six Wives' and 'King Arthur', but also to a

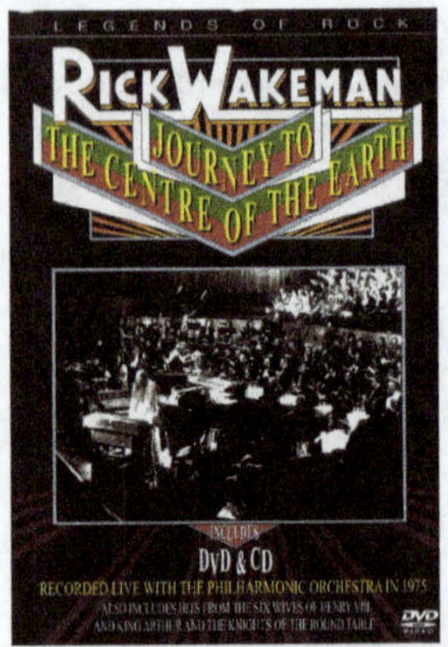

complete rendition of 'Journey', along with narration by Terry Taplin (who performs reading from his book, sat on a large chair). This is 95 minutes of a musician at the pinnacle of his solo career, and he was out to give it everything. Musically the highlight is from seeing two of the UK's greatest vocalists attempting to outdo each other and thriving on the energy. Ashley Holt and Gary Pickford-Hopkins are superb singers, and to be able to see them when they were both a little younger is wonderful. Having seen Ashley with Rick recently and hearing Gary's new solo album, it is a little surreal to see them together on stage looking just ever so slightly different. This is progressive, pompous, classical, totally over the top, yet quite majestic. And to cap it all there is also a CD included that contains all the songs as well.

The 'Live In Concert 2000' DVD is the third Wakeman DVD that I have reviewed recently and is very different to the other two. In this one there is Rick Wakeman, lots of keyboards, a microphone, and little else. There is no band to hide behind, as if he ever needed one, and this give him the opportunity to talk to the audience and share some anecdotes (his story about performing drunk must be one of the funniest I've heard), as well as performing some songs in a fashion that he may not normally attempt. The menu has also been set up so that it is possible to go from one story to another. One of the most interesting performances is "The Nursery Rhyme Concerto" where he plays nursery rhymes performed in the manner of famous composers, including Les Dawson. The piano features much more on this DVD than on the others, as this is a more delicate and reflective side of Rick. Of course, he can still be overblown when he wants to, and he performs some of his classics with a real passion. As well as the 12 songs from the concert he has also gone into the studio to revisit some songs, and there are six bonus numbers including new versions of "Morning Has Broken" and "Merlin The Magician" among others. Again, there is a CD that contains the concert.

Which of the two DVDs do I prefer? Hard to say, as they are so very different to each other, so it depends on the mood. But if that mood is quiet and gentle then it should be the latter.
#76, Oct 2003

RICK WAKEMAN
OUT THERE
Rick's album, 'Out There', was one of my Top Five albums for 2003, and I was looking forward to seeing him in concert with the New English Rock Ensemble. It is well-documented that two days before the tour singer Damian Wilson decided not to take part, which left Rick with having to find a new singer at short notice. The fact that he managed

to convince Ashley Holt, who had toured with him in the Seventies, meant that the tour could go ahead but that there was more of an emphasis on older material instead of the new album. We were given some glimpses of the new DVD as back projection, but it is only now that it has been made available. Play the whole film, and you will also listen to the complete album at the same time, the concept finally given life. With a combination of high-quality computer graphics, NASA film and performances from the band the result is a film that probably has 'Fantasia' as the mother, and the power of Rick combined with a rock band as the father. Since I have had the DVD, I have found myself playing this more than the album, which has now been relegated to 'car only' status as the visual seems to add to the overall effect in a real bonding of the senses. Added to that is an interview with Rick where he tells the story behind the album and the ensuing tour, along with all the associated difficulties. There is footage from the tour, both behind the scenes and onstage. The result is a DVD that any fan of Rick Wakeman will want to have – it is superb.

#79, May 2004

YES

SPECIAL EDITION

This is an intriguing but quite strange release. Firstly, there are three songs taken from German TV ("No Opportunity Necessary, No Experience Needed", "All Good People", "Yours Is No Disgrace"), which are then repeated as 'Pop Up' versions. That the songs are of great interest is not disputed, but to have them repeated? Then there are twelve minutes of previews, which is basically a long advertising section (which is again interesting), followed by four selections while are available on other DVDs. The best of these to my ears is an in-concert performance of BJH and "Mockingbird". Quite a weird concept for a DVD, but it is available at a reduced price, so why not visit the site for more details

#74, Jun 2003

YES

ACOUSTIC

On January 26th, 2004 there was a live satellite broadcast of the film 'Yesspeak' to cinemas across the States. Following the broadcast, fans in the cinemas could watch a live performance from Jon Anderson, Chris Squire, Alan White, Steve Howe and Rick Wakeman where they played acoustically for the first time. Somehow I get the impression that it is the last two members of the band who enjoyed this, and Chris Squire looks as if he has returned to the late Sixties (the years, not his age), but this is a light-hearted approach to some of their more well-known songs. There is an audience at the

TV studio where they are playing but it is obvious that somehow it feels all a little artificial. But get the opener "Tiger Rag" out of the way and we are into the serious stuff. First up is "Long Distance Runaround" which seems a little strange without the heavy bass line that is so important, but that is what makes it so interesting. Chris is playing an acoustic bass, which obviously does not have anything like the extremely heavy bottom end which is such an important facet of Yes. "South Side Of The Sky" and "Roundabout" are two of the songs to benefit from this but my favourite is "I've Seen All Good People" which of course always had a strong acoustic element. However, this song is transformed without the normal electric instruments, which blast into the second part. There are also some special features with all of the trailers for 'Yesspeak' that were shown in America, but the best bit is the rehearsal and behind the scene footage which is interesting in its' own right but is definitely made by the commentary from Rick Wakeman who yet again shows his wicked sense of humour. Any fan will want to have this because it is so unusual.
#83, Mar 2005

Interviews

All the photos in this section were sent to me by the bands at the time for promotional purposes (yes, I kept every single one), so I don't have photographer details, sorry.

Nick Barrett (Pendragon), # 12, Feb 1992

Most of the bands that used to be in the UK prog scene with you have fallen by the wayside. What do you put your longevity down to?

It's ironic, but the fact that we did not get a major record deal! It forced us to start our own label for our album releases, which has built up a very strong base and obviously has the policy of pushing Pendragon as much as is humanly possible; if we'd had a major deal there could have been problems such as pressure for a silly image. They do not always promote their bands properly, and they can drop you from the label as soon as they get bored with you. A lot of bands put too much faith in a record company when they get signed, and often pay the price.

Do you see Toff records as being the vehicle for all future Pendragon releases, or would you prefer to sign for a major label for extra support?

It all depends, if we felt we could manoeuvre Toff to have some clout then I would rather stay as we are; if there was a major who believed in what we did then we'd consider signing for them.

Clive is working with both Tracy Hitchings and Shadowland. How does he see this progressing (sic) with Pendragon?

Clive in fact sessions for Pendragon and is not a partner in Toff Records either. He does not write Pendragon material, so he has enough time to write his own stuff.

'The World' is a superb album, but how do you personally rate it alongside 'Kowtow'?

Very difficult to say; you tend to have your personal favourite tracks with each album, and I really like "Walk The Rope", "Kowtow" and "Total Recall". Obviously, we did not have the budget to spend on 'Kowtow', so I've always felt that it could have been better, both presentation wise and production wise. With 'The World' it was all brand-new material (not played live) and with the cover artwork and general structure of the music was a fantastic challenge, so perhaps more satisfying to make than 'Kowtow'. In fact, 'Kowtow' was bloody hard work: we did not have a wiz producer then like we did for 'The World'.

Having just released one album, when is 'The Window of Life' due out?

Well, I've got to write it first. Umm, I'm getting lots of new ideas for a new album and I'd like to think that it'll be out this time next year. but it depends, sometimes the writing just does not happen fast, and other times the ideas just flood out.

What have been your greatest musical influences?

There are thousands of influences; from the start of when I was really getting into music, when I was about twelve, I was listening to 'Dark Side Of The Moon' and 'Ziggy Stardust And The Spiders From Mars', T. Rex, Slade etc. Then I got into Genesis, 'Lamb Lies Down', and worked back to get all the other Genesis albums. Also, bands like Camel, Jeff Beck, a band called Split Enz, Mountain. I had a really big Queen phase, Supertramp's 'Crime Of The Century' was a big influence too. I listen to quite a lot of "mellow" stuff at the moment, like Pat Metheny, Gary Burton's 'reunion' album, Ennio Morricone who did stuff for films like 'Once Upon A Time In America' and "The Good, The Bad & The Ugly'. I really love that music. I like quite a lot of classical as well, Elgar, Beethoven, just about all of 'em in fact! At the moment, I've been listening to a lot of Ozric Tentacles, and the rest of the band like the same kind of music. Fudge likes Sting and a lot of 'clever' jazz stuff, Peter likes more or less the same as me, and Clive likes Queen, Daniel Lanois and used to love Kate Bush. All this is music we listen to, and somewhere along the line it influences your writing.

What bands in the current scene do you tip for the top?

Phew, do you mean the current progressive scene? It's very difficult to say, because sadly I do not think it's down to the quality of the bands so much as getting some backing from record companies and the music press. Without some kind of support, a lot of the new bands will struggle. But current popular prog bands are Galahad, Final Conflict and Grace from the UK. There are thousands playing this music in Europe, but who could be tipped for the top is impossible to say.

The tour and the new recording are going to take up a lot of time soon, but what are your plans after that?

Well, this year we're going to try to get more gigs both in the UK and Europe; we're trying to get a release in Japan and USA too. Mainly though, because 'The World' has gone so well we want to try and write a new album as soon as possible.

How can you get the music of Pendragon across to a wider audience who tend to dismiss music because it is labelled "prog" without realising that this term covers a multitude of sins?

With great difficulty! It's hard to get radio airplay with singles by bands like us, and therefore we have to rely on reputation and word of mouth and any kind of promotion we can get! The only way it'll really become accepted by the masses is if they get to hear it, and this means that radio policy has to change: tastes in music are so dictated by the media. There is a massive potential audience out there who generally like 'melodic music', but it must get some coverage to find that audience.

Pendragon are arguably the biggest prog band of the 'underground' scene, but how do you see yourselves getting the foothold of Marillion et al?

Well, the basic difference between Marillion and ourselves is that they had EMI behind them, and we have Toff Records, so to get that heavyweight promotional machine going for us is very difficult, but it's slowly building. We are doing more comprehensive tours and building a massive following in Europe. The media are taking more interest in us now, so the floodgates could open. We've laid down a very solid base over the last few years: Pendragon have a strong foundation, we have an outlet for our albums, and with the strength of the label increasing, the band will move forward too.

Brian Devoil (Twelfth Night), #12, Feb 1992

Twelfth Night were undoubtedly the top UK progressive rock bands of the Eighties, but never manged to break through on the scale of Marillion. What do you think were the reasons for this?

I think the main reasons were the market for prog rock was not considered a particularly large profitable or global one by the record companies, and that the large investment required in that kind of band was not worthwhile. Hence the recent (last ten years) trend towards singles, dance artists, and the consequent lack of development of album artists (of longevity), lack of songs, etc.

Marillion had in Fish the best frontman at the time, and EMI decided to take the gamble – no other label decided to follow suit at that time. Without a major record deal no other band could compete with Marillion, so they were unchallenged except possibly in the hearts and minds of the fans who had heard of other bands such as Twelfth Night, Pallas, Pendragon etc.

What was your relationship with Virgin Records?

However, we did eventually get a major deal with Virgin some three or four years later (our deal with Music For Nations was a licensing deal, i.e. more a distribution deal). Our relationship with Virgin was because our management company, Hit & Run, already had two major artists (Genesis and Phil Collins) signed to Virgin. Whether we were signed to keep that company "sweet" is a matter for debate, but we never felt that Virgin understood the band or were particularly interested in us. When neither of the first two singles made any impact, I feel their initial enthusiasm finally disappeared. To understand you need to know how record companies work and what makes things happen the way they do. Basically, there was not anybody at Virgin that cared about the band – hence when the first year was up, they decided not to carry on "investing" in us – despite that fact that we had a new singer (in Martyn Watson) and a great batch of new songs. They have never yet, to this day, written to any member of the band to let us know that our "services were no longer required".

What finally caused Twelfth Night to break up?

The reasons we finally broke up had a lot to do with the events detailed above. We felt very disillusioned after the experiences of the previous two years (1985,1986), and that starting all over again was something we did not want to do. We were not enjoying it as much as we were before, and after all we were not getting any younger. On top of that we were not earning any money at all, just running up more debts (we ended up probably owing over £250,000!). We did enjoy working with Martyn once Andy Sears and Clive had left, and have good memories of that time and of the songs we wrote together (as yet unreleased).

Geoff Mann has been recording and touring with different bands, but what have the other band members been doing?

The rest of us have not been involved with music full time like Geoff
Clive ran his own recording studio for a couple of years before deciding to go back to university to study ancient languages.
Andy S went into sales, whilst continuing to write songs, and works occasionally with Davy Jones (ex-Monkees) who is an old friend of his. He too is going to university (for the first time), to study psychology.
Rick is no longer playing and works as a mortgage person but has also become a Cordon

Bleu chef and wine-making expert.

Andy R now works for the Wellcome Foundation as a PR man, spokesperson for AZT (their anti-AIDS drug). He travels the world for conferences and is our Yuppie member.

Me (Brian). I've been running my own business for a few years whilst training as a management accountant (I should qualify later this year). I've kept the Twelfth Night banner flying by running the fan club, putting together 'Collector's Item' and generally managing all the business affairs (e.g. putting together the deals for 'Collector's and the release of 'Fact and Fiction' on CD).

Are there any plans for a possible Twelfth Night reunion after the success of both 'Collector's Item' and the new booming UK prog scene?

Not at present, although who knows in the future? It would only be to play some gigs (i.e. not a permanent reunion). Is the prog scene really booming again in the UK?

Are there any plans to re-release the albums currently not available, or material that was recorded but never used?

Yes, I am hoping to release most of our albums on CD eventually, although this depends on the continued success of the songs released so far. As for previously unleased material, there are plenty of songs but I'm not sure whether it would be viable to put them out. I think that at least one volume of "new" material may see the light of day, probably on cassette.

What is your happiest memory of Twelfth Night?

Let me think... Our first performance at the Reading Festival in 1981, and the post gig backstage party: a very proud moment for me in particular. The earlier times were perhaps the happiest because we were still doing it "for love", i.e. it hadn't yet become our career. My happiest times would centre around the sense of common purpose we had when working together – band, crew, girlfriends, fans etc. Typified by some of the Marquee gigs and Geoff's farewell gigs for example. In a personal note, playing the Dominion theatre in London on my birthday and seeing a forty foot "Happy Birthday" banner held up by the front row.

In Kerrang!'s feature on the UK prog scene in the early Eighties, Malcolm Dome stated that "their excellent musicianship and lyrical content seem likely to seem them gain final recognition". There were also two photos of the band. How was your relationship with the press?

Generally, our relationship with the music press was quite good. We had a full-time press officer (who also worked for Marillion, Pallas, Pendragon and several others). When the press showed interest, we did some good interviews, and I became quite well known in the Sounds/Kerrang! offices. I met up with Malcolm last year and we reminisced about old times. I was also quite friendly with Chris Welch and various other journalists. By and large though, it was a bit of a struggle for coverage because prog rock was not then (and I suspect never will be) TRENDY!

What are your views on the bands currently around, and what are your tips for the top?

I must admit that I do not know much about the current scene, although I have seen Casual Affair and Galahad, who I wish well as I think it's probably difficult to get a deal in the Nineties. I think the only route for a band to make it now would be playing some kind of new hybrid music, say prog dance or prog metal funk? Record companies need a new fix from time to time you see.

What are your plans and what do you see yourself doing in five years' time?

My plans… get a new job, get married, move to a new house, go on holidays, have children etc., and hopefully most of them within the next five years. Musically I'd like to play drums again, although not professionally, and I'd like to get all the Twelfth Night stuff out on CD.

Stu Nicholson (Galahad), #14, July 1992

During one of our conversations I suggested to Stu that it was about time that he was interviewed for Feedback, and he kindly agreed. I think you will all find the following very interesting and I would like to thank Stu for his time. Read on.

How did you and Roy first meet, and how did Galahad come about?

In June 1985, I answered an advert in a local paper advertising for a singer, for a band that was influenced by Twelfth Night, Sky, Yes, Genesis etc. I rang the number, but Roy said that they had a singer, who had already gone for the job, but he said that he would like to meet me anyway. I was quite worried because I fancied doing this as I had been in a NWOBHM band for the previous three years called Sidewinder which was going nowhere, and I was very bored and had lots of very sore throats from trying to do Ronnie James Dio impersonations all the time. We met in a pub car park in Christchurch and went back to Roy's house where he told me all about it. Luckily, the singer, who was the first guy to go for the audition, completely freaked out when he saw the band playing and decided that he could not do it, he just froze: he could not believe the level of musicianship, which he thought was great, but looking back was not that wonderful; but it was good. I then went for the audition, and my audition piece was around at Mike Hooker's house who was our original keyboard player, along with Nick Hodgson, our other original keyboard player. We had two because Mike was the first to apply but Nick had a Mellotron, so Roy thought we had to have him as well. Our first audition song was "Afterglow" because I knew all the words and they knew all the music. They loved it and we've never looked back since, basically. Well, me and Roy haven't, although several other members of the band have.

What are your biggest influences?

I can only speak for myself, but initially I was not into Prog when I first started listening to music, but more into Sixties stuff as well as Queen and the Beatles, which were my first big bands. I was also into a lot of beat groups such as The Troggs, The Dave Clark Five, The Tremeloes and even The Monkees, who I used to adore for some strange reason, and The Banana Splits. Then, in the late Seventies, I started getting into all the progressive bands such as Genesis, Yes, Rush, Pink Floyd, ELP, Barclay James Harvest, Jethro Tull et al. I also liked a lot of the heavier groups like Purple, Zeppelin, Jimi Hendrix and Black Sabbath. I thought at the time that Sabbath were very proggy, especially their earlier stuff with lots of Mellotrons and things, "Changes" is a brilliant song. Towards the later Seventies I got into some punk bands as well, I did not see the problem with that kind of music. It was all getting a bit insipid at the time with all the first disco wave and everything. I quite liked The Stranglers and some of the Sex Pistols stuff, and Poly Styrene and X-Ray Spex were quite a laugh, and The Damned were funny as well. Roy hates all that lot and I must admit that I do not like all of it in retrospect, but I like a lot of it. I listened to Marillion in the early Eighties, but contrary to what people might think, they were not an obvious influence because I was in bands at about the same time that Marillion started, albeit local bands. I was in Sidewinder, whose biggest gig was supporting Dumpy's Rusty Nuts at Bournemouth Town Hall in front of 700 screaming long-haired grebo-types with lots of denim and leather. To be honest I was scared shitless when I walked onstage and saw them all. Of the later bands, I've been listening to quite a lot of Dream Theater lately, and Queensrÿche I admire, and Faith No More who I feel are quite innovative. I'm also looking forward to the new ELP album and Asia as well. I've also always admired singer-songwriters such as Peter Gabriel solo, Kate Bush, Carole King, Joni Mitchell and Barbra Dickson. Roy is very into the European style of prog thing, especially the earlier bands such as PFM, Focus, Anyone's Daughter. Karl is more into the prog thing plus a load of American rock: his last band was an American rock band, Espirit, the sort of band our last keyboard player Mark Andrews would probably have liked to have been in.

What has the reaction in Europe been to 'Nothing Is Written'?

Bloody marvellous, better than over here. People seem less prejudiced in Europe about the sort of music they listen to. They seem to listen to Motörhead and Diana Ross in the same evening, although preferably not at the same time. No, it's been great. We've sold several thousand CDs in Europe: the distribution outlets have done a good job. They've

advertised it, promoted it and it's sold, hence the dates that are coming up later. In a way, it's the Europeans and Japanese that keep us going. They write the letters and they're great, they are complete fanatics. They are more fanatical about our music than I would be about anyone else. Genesis were probably my all-time favourite band, but I've never been particularly fanatical about them. I get off my ass sometimes and go and see them if they are playing in London, but that's about it – I just love listening to the music. Reaction has been very positive and hopefully we can keep it going with the next album.

Is there anything on the CD you would like to change?

In retrospect, you will always look back and think "That's not quite right" or whatever, but I think we realise we should let things lie, it's a learning process. We did it all ourselves, and it was the first time that we had any substantial time in the studio, trying to get things right and I think we did a very good job. It's also a very subjective thing. Personally, I think the guitar could have been a crunchier, a bit meatier, a bit heavier in places, and maybe a rawer live sound. I think that possibly we sanitised it a bit too much, it does sound a little contrived in places, but I think I'm being over-critical as there are many people who probably do not like the heavier side of things and prefer it as it is. Overall, we're very happy with it and we wouldn't change a thing.

Many of the songs on the 'Crimes and Misdemeanours' tape justify re-recording and releasing. Have you any plans for this?

The short answer is "no", and the long answer could take me years. Me and Roy, being the nucleus of the band, have always loved all the old material that we wrote and have a great deal of affection for it. I personally, and I think Roy as well, both feel that it would be great in the future at some point to get some of the old songs and re-arrange then with modern instrumentation and production. A lot of the material on 'Misdemeanours' has archaic instrumentation and dodgy live recording. Although some of them are in the studio, they are live outtakes. At the moment, we do not have the time to record any of the old stuff, you are always looking forward to the new material, striving to write the perfect song that keeps you going and keep on doing what is now and not what was then.

Again, Genesis are a prime example as they probably felt that 'Invisible Touch' was one of their best, solely because the songs are fresh and they were new and has a vitality which some of the old songs hadn't, especially if you had been playing "The Knife" for twenty years or so. We would like to one day, when we've got time, it might even be with different musicians, I don't know. It is always difficult in a band when people join later because they are not always keen on doing the old stuff. But Roy and I feel that we could do justice to some of these songs, so it may be a possibility at some point in the future. It could be a year from now, or it could be ten years from now, we must wait and see.

Will you at any time put 'A Moment of Madness' on CD?

Again, we would love to, it's all a question for money and finance. We have just signed up to Canyon International who have licenced 'Nothing is Written' and possibly the next one as well in Japan and South East Asia, release date 17th July. It would be nice if they could put some money into us to do that, it's something we might have to negotiate. The only thing with 'Madness' is that it's only thirty minutes long, so we really ought to record some additional tracks to go with it and maybe put that on CD as well. Then maybe we can justify selling it at a normal retail price. I have often thought about it, and it would be nice to release it on CD with some better packaging and one or two extra tracks. Again, it is something for the future, it depends on when we have time really.

What plans do you have for the next six months?

In the immediate future, all we want to do is write songs and record as many of them as possible, so we can choose the best tracks for the next CD, which will hopefully be released towards the end of the year. Providing again that we have financial backing, and of course that nothing goes wrong. We start recording on 1st July and we will spend the next few weeks recording the album, laying down the backing tracks and doing any embellishments afterwards. We are trying to get a more live punchier, more spontaneous feel to the album, and I think we'll achieve this as we are using Tony Arnold, who has extensive experience and has worked with Robert Fripp, King Crimson, Bill Bruford etc. We are looking forward to it, so that is part of it. After that we will still try to get interest from the major record companies, but if we don't, we don't mind too much as have enough going on abroad as it is. To tie in with the Japanese and South East Asia release we are hoping to possibly do some promotional dates over there as well, whether it be concerts or just interviews I do not know. I've recently done interviews for eight Japanese radio stations, which was quite interesting. We should have the first copies of the Japanese version through shortly. They do include an extra song, ("There Must Be A Way"), so they will be limited edition items only. They have lyrics in both Japanese and English, so all of you who can speak Japanese will find it all very interesting. In a way, we are looking forward to it, but the best thing is that they are import albums, but we are still getting royalties for them. So, it is writing, recording, and we have a few gigs coming up. There is the Red House in Whitchurch on 19th July, we are supporting The Enid at a warm-up gig at The Royal Standard on 18th July, billed as "Galahad plus Aerie Faerie Nonsense". We are headlining a festival at Tramonti do Sotto, Italy, on 30th August as well as playing at the Marillion German Fan Club Convention on 25th September, and the Amsterdam Paradiso on 26th September. There is the Classic Rock Society gig on 17th

October at Rotherham Arts Centre and the Royal Standard on 9th October with Loermel. We thought it would quite nice to try and get some newer bands down when we play in London and give them a chance on the London circuit. I do not mean to sound patronising, but I think it would be good if lots of other bands did that as well. Loermel have never played in London before, so it will be good for them. I think they have had a bit of feedback from record companies as well following on from their slot on the Friday Rock Show. You never know, there may be a few execs down at the Standard.

You have just started on the follow-up to 'NIW'. When do you hope to have it available, and have you a provisional title for it?

We have not got a title for it, but Karl came up with the idea of calling it 'Pantomime'. There are various connotations you can draw from it, i.e. the literal translation of pantomime, or "life's a pantomime" or whatever. Very deep and meaningful, very progressive, probably very pretentious as well but that's what we are so that's' fine. We hope it will be available towards the end of the year, but if not then next Spring. It depends on if we get tied in with record companies and if we can sort out distribution deals which hopefully we can. As things have been going well for us lately, we have been making a name for ourselves. Whether it's good or bad, at least we are getting there.

Galahad appear to have had a very fluid line-up, how has Neil settled in?

"Fluid" is not the word for it, it's quite incredible really. Thing just keep cropping up, either people are not pulling their weight, or they've other projects on, or they can't commit themselves or something like that. I do not think that some of the people who have been in Galahad realise what it means to me and Roy. I know it sounds awfully serious, but Galahad are like one big family and a lot of ex-members we do still see. It would be nice to get a gig together one day and we could all go onstage together and play different songs and have fun and all get drunk. Neil is settling in very well. He's quite a technical bass player, and one of the great things about him is that he does not have that many progressive influences. He was going on about us lending him all our Genesis albums, Dream Theater albums, Yes and Marillion albums etc., but we said "no, not really" because it means that by not listening to it he is not influenced by it so he can come up with his own ideas and will help Galahad to gain more of its own identity. It means that the bass player will not pretend that he is Geddy Lee, which Tim used to do just a touch, I think. Neil's actually a songwriter as well, and he's very up on technology which is a real bonus for us. Me, Roy and Spencer have not a clue about technology, while Karl and Neil have, so hopefully it will help when it comes to resequencing songs, which we must do in the studio for some reason, to ensure that we get the songs all in time. It's probably because we're completely incompetent musicians, I do not know. He's got a good attitude, very level-headed, so I do not think that there will be an ego problem, unlike some people we've had in the band, me in particular.

What does the Japanese deal mean to the band?

It means a lot: we're really pleased that it came about. We know that there are a lot of progressive bands that have sold CDs in Japan, and there is quite a large market for this kind of music over there. What happened was the A&R guy from Canyon International went into a shop in Tokyo and found the Galahad CD. He listened to it, liked it, and asked the shopkeeper if they had been selling many, and he replied that it had been selling in quite large numbers. He wrote me a letter, told me and offered us a deal; it was as simple as that. We then spent a few months sorting out a deal, taking it to our solicitor, and thrashing things out really. It was quite strange because I dealt with a lot of it from our office in Fordingbridge, which is right in the middle of deepest Hampshire, and I was faxing Tokyo and London. It means that the album will be available in huge quantities, and hopefully it will sell in huge quantities. There will of course be the import CD, which initially will be very rare but if it sells well, then the English version may become the rare version. They are very behind the band and what also is nice is that in Japan they are not necessarily going to promote us a progressive rock band, but as good modern creative rock band. Obviously, we have progressive overtones and progressive influences, but we do not want to get too bogged down by constricting ourselves with labels, which is something that we've done in this country. If you are an up and coming band and you label yourselves "prog" then you have an instant audience, but as you get bigger it gets to be a bit of a noose around your neck, the more people you reach, the noose gradually tightens and in a way, it's not shaking it off but proving to people that you are not an archetypal hoary old progressive rock band that just stands around on stage playing endless keyboard and guitar solos. I think that especially with our gigs we tend to jump around and have a good time and be a bit rock 'n' roll. I think ELP were all good performers and at the end of the day it was just another rock 'n' roll show. That was without a lead guitarist, but with Keith Emerson who needed it?

Clive Nolan, #16, Dec 1992

Clive willingly (and exceedingly quickly) replied to a request for an interview, and on writing to André Ruaud of Acid Dragon I discovered that Clive had completed one for him as well. Although some of the questions were similar, overall the two interviews combined well together so what follows is a joint interview that will also appear in Acid Dragon.

Where and when did you start playing music?

My parents are music teachers, so I was in a classical music environment right from the beginning. I know that I started learning piano when I was four, and my parents were always teaching me musical appreciation. My main instruments were violin and cello as because my parents taught piano, I tended to rebel against this instrument. Nevertheless, although for a long time I was not officially learning the piano, I was always playing it!

Did you go to any kind of music school?

I made music my main study from quite an early age! I took all the exams in the violin, cello and in the theory of music; I then took the necessary exams and was ready to go to university or music college. While I was at school, I took a diploma in composition (I was the youngest person in the country, at the time, to get an "A. Mus L.C.M." - Associate of Music from the London College of Music). I then went to London University to do a B. Mus degree, and later I did an M. Mus degree where I specialised in composition and conducting.

What was Sleepwalker?

Basically, Sleepwalker started off as a school band, after I suggested to a few friends that we form one. I was only just beginning to listen to rock music of any kind, as up to the age of sixteen I only listened to classical music, then I decided to open my interests. I went to a record shop with £12 and chose a record just because of its cover (I did not know anything about any rock or pop music!). The album I chose was 'Seconds Out' by Genesis, which I loved, and that was the beginning of my involvement with prog rock. Sleepwalker carried on as a band while I was at university, the line-up changed a bit but the main five guys were: me on keyboards and backing vocals (this seemed to be the obvious instrument to play but I learned to play each of the other instruments just in case), Paul Allison on vocals (he was good, but a rather mad character – he went on to sing with another prog band called Gothique), Cliff Orsi on bass (he went on to play in a band with guitarist Pete for a while. Recently he has set up Cleopatra's Needle who may be recording an album with us next year for SI), Pete Wyer on guitar (he played with me in The Cast after Sleepwalker ceased to exist) and Rich Jones on drums (boy he was weird. I do not know what he is doing now – he actually left and re-joined about five times. The only problem was that he could not drum!).

How did you get involved with Pendragon?

I have known Nick from the age of five, when we went to school together, so it always seemed possible that we end up playing together. After Rick (Carter, original keyboard player) left they used a session keyboard player for a few months, then asked me to take the job. "Join Pendragon" said Nick, "It'll be fun" – I did, and it has!

All of Pendragon's material is written by Nick, but do you choose your own sounds?

What happens at the moment is that Nick will prepare a song, with the main features on tape. He will have perhaps chosen some keyboard sounds that he wants to hear on the tracks and at this point we sit together and look at the keyboard parts. I will then, obviously, suggest sounds and alternatives. In "The Voyager" for example, Nick told me that he wanted a harmonica sound in one of the leads so I found him what I thought would work best.

Do you ever have any problems with the music of Nick, because 'The World' is very different to 'Ring of Roses'?

That's precisely why there are two bands, and not one! Nick has his own way and style of working and so do I. When I first joined Pendragon, we agreed that I would not work in the band as a writer, therefore I would concentrate on writing for other projects, and this has worked well for both of us. I think 'The World' is a great album, I have no trouble

playing it in Pendragon – obviously, my own style of writing is not the same, but there is never a clash. My role in Pendragon is as an interpreter of Nick's music. That's the challenge of Pendragon, while the challenge of Shadowland is as a writer and creator.

On a personal level, you play in two bands and produce others. How do you find the time?

I enjoy the variety of bands and music that I'm involved with, and personally I need these different elements to keep me challenged. Also, I love working with different musicians who all have their own brand of individuality towards their performances: this keeps the whole thing fresh and interesting. When you want to do something strongly enough you can always find the time. I admit that things are pretty busy but that's great – I'm still looking for other things to do as well! If anyone needs a session keyboard player for anything, then let me know!

You write for a lot of different bands. Is not there a danger of the whole music scene becoming the same?

Firstly, the challenge I enjoy most is writing in many and varied styles, even within the one overall area of music. I believe that each of the bands I have written for have their own musical identity. This is because I am writing in a specific direction for the album in question: each band is different in their demands and expectation and therefore they each provide an individual challenge. Naturally there are stylistic compositional elements which people may recognise as "Nolan"; in fact, I hope there are! You must remember that the identity of sound comes from the musicians as it does from the writer. I think that there are obvious "separate identities" to all the albums we have made.

How do you know so many different musicians and can use their talents? Do you contact them, do they contact you, or do you bump into them at gigs?

I have always believed that what killed off the so called "Prog Rock Revival" of the Eighties was the ridiculously insular and defensive attitudes of the various bands. This rather overprotective aloofness prevented the "prog movement" from growing outwards and it just caved in on itself! My interest has always been in working with different people so that the results are always fresh, different and a new challenge. Basically, I'm always watching out for musicians who might be good to work with. I meet them in all the ways you mentioned and hope to continue doing so.

Is there anyone you would like to work with?

Yes. Peter Gabriel and Rick Wakeman. Peter Gabriel once expressed an interest in producing The Cast (one of my old bands) but sadly he was just about to start writing his own new solo album so it could not happen, but I have not given up on the idea!

We still call "Progressive Rock" the kind of music we love, but in fact it does not seem to be really "progressive" anymore. Where is the progress in modern Prog Rock, where some of the bands use influences of Rush, Genesis, Pendragon, IQ etc.? Is there a problem with the identity of modern Prog Rock?

Could it be that the problem here is the expectation of the fans? It can be difficult to "progress" when there is a rather obvious leaning towards "playing safe". Perhaps people feel safer with the unchanging world of "early Genesis" and "vintage Floyd", in which case they should listen to those bands and leave the new ones free to develop! One question I am asked all the time is the one about "going commercial" or "becoming too poppy". Firstly, "going commercial" basically means something that is selling well, which is the obvious aim of all artists and bands. Pop music also need not be some kind of artistic leprosy, more often than not it is merely a question of production. I believe in "progress" in Prog Rock, but it would seem to be a difficult area. Genesis, for example, have progressed but I'm not sure that progressive fans like what they have done. It is inevitable that there will be stylistic similarities between bands such as the ones you have mentioned, but personally I have no interest in just churning out songs that these bands did first! I can't see the point in being a Genesis (old Genesis of course) or Floyd or Marillion clone – they have already done it and done it far better! We now have new bands, new facilities and new musicians – these musicians are excellent and can offer a great deal – new approaches, new styles and new sounds. I think we should allow this to happen, because then it will be "Progressive Rock" again. Prog Rock fans, in my opinion, are some of the most dedicated and appreciative in the world of music and it is their encouragement and belief that will guide the progress of this genre of music.

One of the big dreams of the progressive musicians of the Seventies was to play with a full orchestra. Do you have such a dream?

I was lucky at university, because I had plenty of experience playing in, writing for and conducting orchestras: I have a great love for this medium. When Sleepwalker was around, I wrote a piece for "rock band and orchestra", but it never got properly performed. My big ambition is to write for film and television music, and this could give back the opportunity to write and arrange for an orchestra again. In the meantime, we have performed the "Thin Ice Orchestra", which will be an in the studio recording for the new Strangers On A Train album. Believe me, it's not easy getting eighty musicians in our studio.

What bands in the current scene do you rate for the future?

Apart from us maybe? Well, my money might go on Jadis (I think they're a great band). Also, I think that Galahad have developed a great deal over the last few years. There are many promising new musicians and bands, but they need to be allowed the freedom to "progress" and not just find themselves replaying the music of old Prog bands.

What is Thin Ice? What is The Secret World?

Thin Ice is the name of our studio. After the making of the first Strangers album, 'The Key', Karl Groom (guitars for Strangers, Shadowland, Threshold etc.) and I decided to merge our equipment and become partners in putting together a studio. We have developed the studio as we have received recording budgets from SI. We call it Thin Ice because we always seem to be close to various disasters! The Secret World has been set up to put people in touch with what we do at Thin Ice. We are a direct communication with the artists, which gives a slightly new angle on the fan club thing because although primarily The Secret World is a kind of Shadowland fan club, it also covers the activities of acts such as Casino, Geoff Mann, Twelfth Night, Landmarq, Strangers and Tracy Hitchings, whilst also covering bands who are associated in some way such as the guys from Pallas, Jadis, Final Conflict, Galahad, Winter etc. The great thing is that much of the news happens here!

What is your relationship with SI Music?

SI is basically our record company. I've known Willebrord Elsing for some years now, and the record company idea was sitting around for a while. Then it seemed like the right time, with the Strangers album. That was my first opportunity to have my music on CD and SI's first opportunity to try selling albums – luckily it worked out for both of us. It has been a developing experience for both parties, but it's great to have a label that believes in this style of music, and it's great that they believe in what I'm doing.

Do you think that there will be a possibility of any of the prog bands getting big label support? If this happens do you think that there could finally be recognition for all the great bands in the UK?

To be honest I think it's highly unlikely. The big companies consider this style of music to be too much of a risk for them. They are not ready to pile money into nurturing a prog band in the way they do with other kinds of music. Success and recognition must come from the "do it yourself" approach that we are all adopting. This gives us greater artistic control, and maybe one day no prog band will even want the dubious support of a major company, who can often cause more harm than good. They are not qualified to deal with this area of music – they are too out of practice!

The fanzines really like 'Ring of Roses', but what have the sales been like in the UK and Europe?

It has been terrific to receive so many good reviews from people, and I pray that they will continue. The album has become the best-selling album on the SI label, which I'm very proud of. Sadly, I doubt if we have sold anything very much over here in the UK as most of our sales are in Holland, Germany, France and Japan.

How did the Casino project happen?

SI suggested that it may be interesting for myself and Geoff Mann to work together on something. We spoke on the phone, and then he came down to the studio for the day and by then we were sure we could do something good, I decided that it would add a new dimension if we included a lot of different players on the album. Originally, I was trying to get the musicians from Twelfth Night to appear but that became impossible except, of course, for Geoff and Brian Devoil.

What does the immediate future hold both for yourself and for Shadowland?

Now, we are preparing for the Shadowland tour with Jadis, which will take about a month. Then I'm out with Pendragon for some Christmas dates, then must complete the writing of the new Strangers album 'The Prophecy', which we will record in January. Next year we should be recording the next Shadowland album, as well as the next Casino and Tracy Hitchings album, then there will be the production of the new Landmarq album as well as a new band (Grey Lady Down). Also, we are doing a new Pendragon album. I also hope to be involved in various dates and tours as well to promote some of these things. So, a pretty busy year, I think!

Geoff Mann, #17, Mar 1993

This is not an interview with Geoff, but rather my tribute to him after he passed. It includes comment from some of those from the prog scene at the time.

As I am aware many of you are already aware, with pieces in Kerrang! and Raw, Geoff Mann died at home recently. He had been ill for several months and was diagnosed as suffering from cancer of the colon. He will always be remembered for his time with Twelfth Night, possibly the most important and influential British progressive rock band never to make the big time. The band were formed by friends at Reading University, and although Geoff guested as vocalist at a gig there in 1979, he decided to become a painter in his hometown of Manchester. Twelfth Night persevered as an instrumental outfit, and then in 1980 recruited American singer Electra Macleod. She did not last long, and Twelfth Night recorded the instrumental album 'Live At The Target' and promoted it with a tour in 1981, supported by Geoff's new band God Stars. By the summer Geoff became a full-time member and with him they opened Reading Festival in front of 25,000 people. A tape, 'Smiling At Grief' was recorded, and in 1982 all efforts went into 'Fact and Fiction'. Now available on CD, it was voted by Kerrang! as one of the ten best progressive rock albums of the 80's. With Geoff, Twelfth Night appeared on the David Essex Showcase (performing "East of Eden"), and completed a full tour supporting the album. After two sell-out gigs at The Marquee in November 1983, which were recorded for the album 'Live and Let Live' (now available on CD at long last) Geoff quit the band,

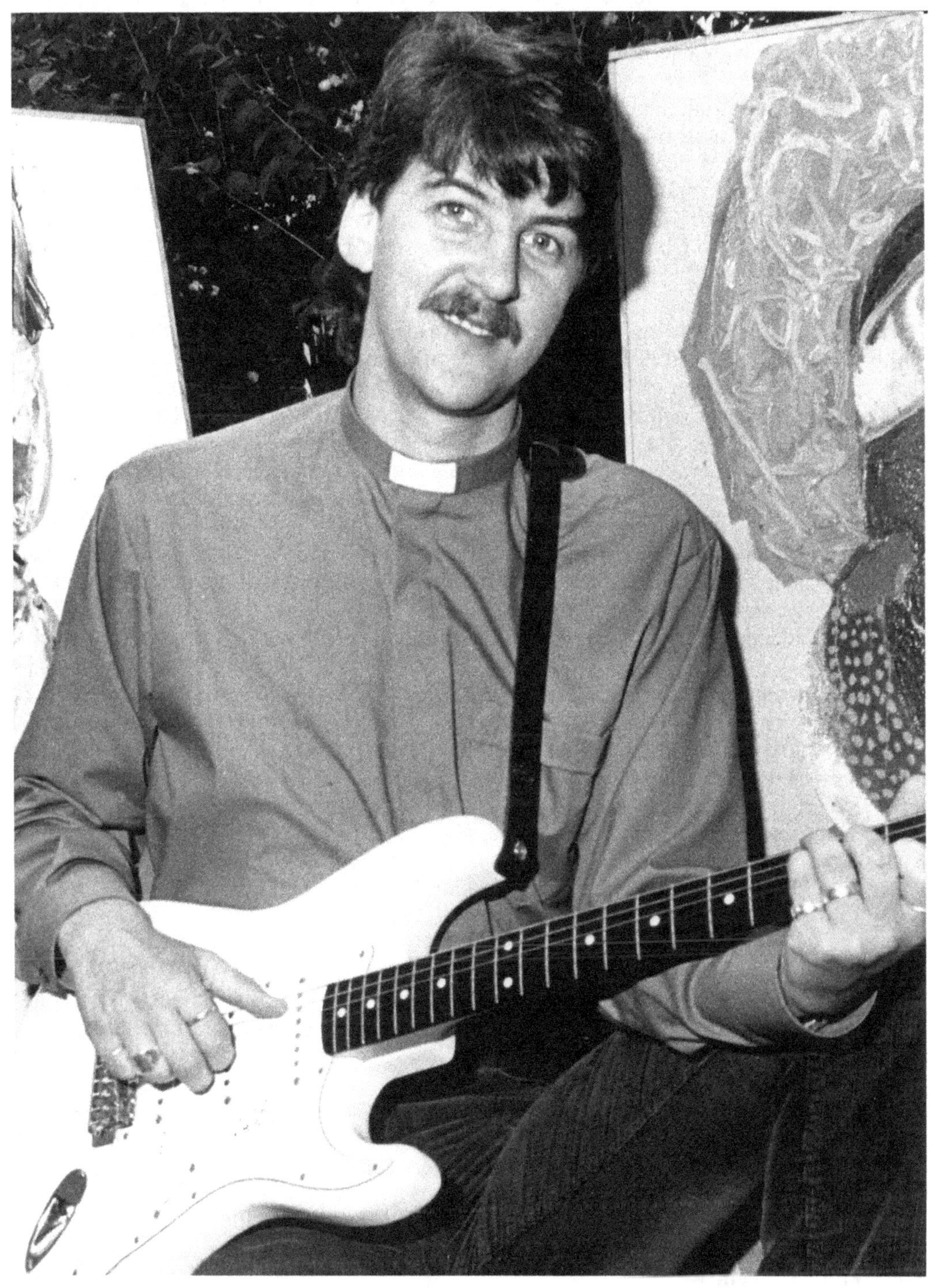

leaving behind a wealth of material including "Art and Illusion" which was recorded with new singer Andy Sears. After leaving Twelfth Night Geoff recorded four solo albums, plus two albums with The Bond, two with Marc Catley, and two with his last outfit, Eh! Geoff Mann Band. These incorporated many different musical styles, including straight four-piece rock, instrumental, solo acoustic, and some strange things with a lawnmower. On the Twelfth Night front, in 1988 the original line-up reformed to record "The Collector", which had been performed live but never recorded, and re-recorded Geoff's most famous work, "Love Song". These were included on the masterpiece of a compilation, 'Collector's Item'. More recently the two albums he has been involved with on SI, namely 'Second Chants' and the 'Casino' project, has seen him very much back in the public eye.

Aside from his music he spent three years as a curate of Christ's Church, Harwood in Bolton, and was ordained last year as vicar of St. Luke's, Deepish, in Rochdale. He was married for fourteen years to Jane, and leaves behind three children, Thomas, James and Bethany. On the day Geoff died, he sold his doctor two CDs. This was typical of a man who was loved by all, and who had a wicked sense of humour. He was at peace with himself and was concerned only for other people. Ten minutes before he died, he said that he kept hearing music. When told that there was no music playing, he asked if the music had stopped. When told by Jane that it had, he replied, "So that's it then" and died. Geoff was loved and missed by many people. I contacted musicians within the UK prog scene and asked them for their thoughts. What follows is Feedback's tribute to a man who has left behind some wonderful recordings and some magical memories, and whose death personally saddened me more than anyone could imagine.

Geoff was an exceptional man, ordinary yet extra-ordinary. His love of life was exceeded only by his love for his family and God. His music had a powerful effect on many people, and his direct lyrics could be alarming yet moving. He lived his life with the enjoyment knob at 10 and we certainly had a difficult time keeping up. Heaven will undoubtedly gain from our loss. The last three years with Geoff have been tremendous fun. His musicianship is irreplaceable and will be sadly missed by all members of Eh! Geoff Mann Band. Our thanks to all the people who have supported the band over the last three years, without you it would have been impossible.
Andy Labrow, John Maycraft, Gary Mitchell, Paul Keeble (Eh! Geoff Mann Band)

It's a sad loss, not just for prog but for music in general, for someone who had the courage and of their convictions and was articulate, generous and honest. It's such a shame that it had to happen to someone like that, one of the nicest guys you could meet.
Stu Nicholson (Galahad)

It's strange how certain songs wither pick you up or seem relevant at a certain part of your life. "Love Song" said it all, and although Geoff's music never reached the number of people it should have, it touched many who were certainly richer for it.
Mark Colton (Freewill)

Geoff was one of the prog scene's truly unique characters, who will be sorely missed.
Steve Paine (Legend)

It's difficult to "brush over sadness" and think clearly about all this now: it just does not seem fair. Geoff was an idealist and his ideals carried real conviction. In this world, this is a rare and wonderful thing.
Greg Spawton (Big Big Train)

Geoff was easily the nicest person in progressive rock, and it was a pleasure to know and work with him.
Martin Orford (IQ, Jadis)

It's very hard to know what to say when someone you know, particularly from "our musical era", goes to the other side. The main thing is that Geoff's faith was obviously very strong: you can't help feeling that he's OK wherever he may be, and perhaps his faith has helped his family and friends with the pain.
Nick Barrett (Pendragon)

He struck me as a gentle man, friendly, polite and so very enthusiastic on the subject of good music (I will not call it progressive rock or whatever – that would be too restrictive for his tastes). He told me he could not stand the term "prog rock" and when I told him that we billed our music as being "English Rock" he said he fancied adopting the term himself. He was a superb singer, good guitarist, and excellent writer – never afraid of trying new things. We had a great time that night at The Wheatsheaf and we had planned on doing more events – obviously, that was never meant to be. We would just like to say that whatever it is termed – "Prog", "English" or "Classic" – the world is suddenly emptier. He will be missed by many hundreds of fans and colleagues. Our feelings go out to his family and may he rest in peace.
Dave Rushton (Grace)

I'm grateful for all the help he gave us, and I wish I had known him better as he was a great bloke.
Gary Chandler (Jadis)

Geoff was a very good friend, and probably the most generous person I have met in prog rock or in the music business. His love and concern for everyone he met spoke volumes for his strong Christian faith. We will miss you very much Geoff.
Peter Gee (Pendragon)

I'm proud to have worked with Geoff, he was an inspiring man. I value what we did together both as a friend, and as a fan. I do not believe in the finality of death, so I hope we will share such moments of connection again.
Clive Nolan (Pendragon, Shadowland)

I still can't believe that it's happened. I can't begin to understand why such a courageous and compassionate person as Geoff should be taken from us, I can't make any sense of it at all. Anyone who knew Geoff, whether it was for five minutes or five years, was touched by him, by his creative energy, by his humanity, his zest for life. It was impossible not to be swept along by his boundless enthusiasm: he put people instantly at

ease with his honestly and approachability. Whatever the gift is, Geoff had it. I never heard anyone say a bad thing about him, everyone who knew him liked him, and that in itself is quite an achievement. I miss hearing Geoff's laugh, I miss his warmth, his friendship, I miss him popping around for a cup of tea, I miss his smile and his sense of humour, I miss his voice, I miss seeing him play live, I miss him being dotty over a new CD. There's so much I miss about him and I'm not alone because he really did touch so many people's lives. He was a rare and special man, an inspiration to us all. My thoughts go to Jane, Thomas, James and Bethany. God bless, Geoff.
Peter Nicholls (IQ)

There are talks of at least one tribute gig being held later in the year, more details as they arrive. Also, it looks like a tribute to Geoff will be available on CD towards the end of the year. the man behind it is Willebrord Elsing of SI, but the finished product will probably not come out on the SI label. The album will be comprised of songs performed by other artists, in recognition of the debt owed by many to him. Although full details have yet to be discussed, I understand that groups such as Shadowland, Galahad and IQ among others will be recording sometime in the summer with the release date set for the end of the year. "The Ceiling Speaks" and "Love Song" both look set for inclusion but other tracks (and who is recording what) are still to be finalised.

Finally, I have been asked to pass on Jane's thanks for all the encouragement and support she has received.

Tracy Hitchings, #19, Aug 1993

How did you first get involved with rock music?

In my native village of St. Mawes in Cornwall, when I was fourteen, there was a family of musicians and we put together a band and called it Purple Haze. There were three other guys and a girl drummer from surrounding villages who would sit in depending on who was arguing and who was not. We recorded two tracks, one of which was played on Radio Cornwall and we were very excited at the time as I am sure you can imagine. That was my first real experience of being in a unit, something happening and writing the lyrics, which in retrospect are quite funny when I listen to them now. It was a start and was very important. Then I was taken under the wings of a great called Jeff Jefferson, no prizes for guessing the type of music. His four-track gave me some great basic grounding for recording which in fact has proved to be invaluable.

Do you play any musical instruments?

Clive says no. Well, I suppose I strum a pretty bad guitar and some appalling keyboards. My first experience of playing live with Clive was at The Paradiso, Amsterdam, and it was Strangers On A Train first concert over there. It went brilliantly, but I was participating on keyboards on "Crossing The Wasteland" and I swear it was the patches that did not change that made it sound funny, it was not my playing, honest! But Clive

says I mustn't play live again, which is a bit mean.

In an earlier Feedback, I reviewed 'The Lorelei'. How did you get involved with Quasar, what did you think of the album, and why did you leave?

Basically, through an ad in Melody Maker. I had just finished with an HM band called Panic. I just felt there was no room to be expressive, it was just screaming all over the place and there was no control at all. I felt I was not getting anywhere, and it was all crumbling anyway. Through the ad I walked into the studio and listened to what they were doing live, and it just sounded brilliant. The ad also said "drama" and I could see what they meant. That made it for me, there was so much room to be expressive. Straightaway it just gelled and felt good. There was a brilliant rapport with the blokes, they were very mature and obviously knew what they were doing. Then I got introduced to all the other so-called 'prog' bands (I hate the word).

I think it's a great album, but it's appallingly recorded, and the lyrics are a bit, well, a lot, dated, but I came in on a band which was ready to record. Most of the stuff was all written and ready to go, it had already been done once with somebody else. I wanted to make my own changes and I did what I could. Being totally new to this area I was not really in a position to completely rewrite everything. I just did not know this type of music and I had to learn, but we changed a lot of it to suit my style of singing. Yes, it's a great album. I preferred it live and this happened on a few occasions, brilliantly. The album has the most appalling production, we know that, and you can pick on a thousand things, but the songs stand alone. There are some beautiful melodies in there. Take "The Lorelei" for instance, I think it's great and is probably one of the best tracks on there just to listen to. The awful production is down to the fact that we did not have the finances to do it, but we did the best we could. A lot of blood sweat and tears went into that and if we could have afforded a great producer, we would have got one, but we could not, but we still got the album out there and I'm very proud of it, regardless what anyone says. Bandwise Quasar are the best band I have worked in; it was a unit and there was a real working relationship there. I enjoyed working with them so much, and we did a lot of rehearsing, and we had great fun and I enjoyed working with Keith (Turner). I miss that and feel quite sad I'm not there anymore.

I did not, and I swear I did not leave Quasar. I was not told to leave, I just started doing other projects and the band did not go anymore. Things were souring for various personal reasons, but that's between the band members. I still have a good relationship with Keith and feel sad that I do not work with him anymore. I enjoyed the time; I did not leave Quasar it just stopped happening. I never announced that I left as I was hoping that at some point things would mend but we moved on. Obviously, it has given me the opportunity to branch out in other areas and do other things, but although I would still like to be in Quasar, I can't see it happening now.

How did you first meet Clive, and how did you get involved with the SOAT project?

That was down to playing a double bill in Holland when I was in Quasar, with Pendragon. Clive approached me afterwards and of course I jumped at the chance, with no intention of leaving Quasar, just doing another project. Within 3-6 months we had the project recorded. That was how we met.

On your solo album Clive wrote all the material; yet you were co-credited with many of the songs on 'The Lorelei'. Are you a frustrated songwriter?

Of course I am! Who isn't? My solo album came quickly after the first SOAT album as Clive was just coming up with ideas to put it together. He knocks everything out quickly and the lyrics were virtually there so there was almost no need for me although I had growing pains to intervene and do my own thing. What we did I think proves it for itself and was great anyway. As regarding involvement on that album, I had the right to veto on everything, I did not do anything I did not want to. I chose all the songs, the direction. He came up with the title track and I thought "Wow this is brilliant", and then he came up with "Caamora" and "Hide and Seek" and I thought "This is great, and he knows what he is doing". So, there was no need, but now a couple of years later we've got a great rapport going and we know each other well enough, so I feel that I can do something with him on the writing front, lyrics wise, and we've been talking about doing that anyway. There are future possibilities there. The deal basically is that Clive is the songwriter and lyricist, and we are just developing very well at the moment. I think 'The Labyrinth', the latest SOAT album, has proved a point for me that there is a maturity there now. For instance, when I was recording, I just knew how to appreciate the mood he wanted: we have a good working relationship and not much has to be said. I come up with an idea and they like it, I'm pleased with the way that the album has worked out. There is a lot more trust now, there's lot more respect. That's how a relationship works, one must prove oneself. I am doing other projects of course, for which I am writing, commercial ones. As for being co-credited on 'The Lorelei' that was the deal when I walked into it, the new singer replacing the male singer, and it was obvious that a lot would change. I've got a totally different style to the guy who was in before me. I did what I could do best, but it was a totally different area for me. What I find a pity is that Keith and I, and the rest of the guys but mainly I worked with Keith, had started on a third album. We had a couple of great songs coming together and it was Quasar progressing, not just prog, not just back in the Skylab days of Quasar, but really progressing. Obviously with everybody else doing their bit, but I felt part of it, and I feel sad that as it stands now it will never be heard.

As well as the latest SOAT album you have been in Europe working with Gandalf. How did this come about?

Actually, I first worked with him back in '92 when myself and Steve Hackett were offered the session on the album 'Gallery of Dreams'. I sang the title track and that came about as he saw the first SOAT concert at The Paradiso and he approached Willebrord Elsing of SI (my record company, the one I work under sometimes) and put a concert together a few months later of SOAT and Gandalf at the Nordelicht. He asked me if I would sing a song he had written so SOAT went on first, then Gandalf, then we came back on afterwards and I did the song "Gallery of Dreams" then he did our song "Looking From Outside In". We were all on together and it was a great ending. After the show, down in the dressing room, he asked how I would like to record it on his next album. He already had Steve Hackett and he would like me as well, so that's how it started. I recorded that, and I have just come back from Vienna having done another album with him which I believe is going to be called 'To Our Children's Children' or 'Aquarius'. I did five tracks on there, it's a concept album, and it probably will not be released until the year is out.

What was it like working with Alan Reed?

I don't know; I was in Vienna! I was recording with Gandalf when Alan was recording with Clive and Karl. I've not actually sung live with him, so I'm looking forward to it when we do some SOAT concerts. I was determined to try and get Alan for this album because I know we would have the perfect voice for it. He's got so much control, it's just perfect. He's added a new dimension to the album which was needed. It makes it.

Do you intend doing more live gigs with Clive, or do you envisage having a permanent backing band?

To be honest there's no hard and fast rules. I will probably do a lot more gigs with Clive because it's great fun and a very simple package to put together and cost effective. We're out there gigging and enjoying it. As to envisaging having a permanent backing band, no, at the moment it just is not realistic. I would like it, and it's not impossible, but it's just not realistic financially. To have a permanent backing band, to have good musicians, you must be prepared to pay good money. I'm not on a great retainer, in fact, I'm not on a retainer! When I was going on tour in Holland and was going to be playing a couple of gigs with IQ, I went begging to Landmarq and they agreed because I thought it would be great fun. It was before they became established and before they got their first album out, and they thought it would be alright for a laugh. We were rehearsing and it was sounding great. They got all the songs from the 'Ignorance' album superb and they were so easy to work with. I had worked with most of them in Quasar, and it was a pity when I fell very ill and had to pull out of the gigs. As to a permanent backing band, there must be something in it for them, either they get paid a session fee or they are part of the team, and as things stand now Clive is the writer, lyrically and musically. There are not the number of gigs to warrant a permanent band but when the next gigs come up, I'll round up a band and we'll have a great time. It'll be wonderful.

On your next album, do you expect Clive to write all the material again, or will there be a different set-up?

No, I wouldn't expect Clive to write all the material again but it's just the way it happens, because that's the working relationship we have. He seems to be able to come up with something that suits me so well. As for me writing with him in the future, yes, we have discussed that and hopefully on the next album, regarding what project we decide to take,

I'll be doing a couple of the songs with him lyrically and melody-wise. I do something because I'm happy with the situation.

What are your biggest musical influences?

One of them that always remains the same is Barbra Streisand. I know you hear many women singers say this, but she is a fantastic singer and sets an enormous height for anyone to try and reach, which is almost impossible. It is impossible, and makes you work so there is a great influence. A more recent one is Kate Bush. When I first heard her, I loved "Wuthering Heights" but felt a lack of power, which obviously was a great insult on my part because I was just tapped into this powerful way of singing. But Kate Bush is just something else, something so special and different from anybody else. Going on from that I've got so many influences. Obviously, Heart, who are the greatest band for me. Ann Wilson is the greatest female rock singer and her delivery as a rock singer is outrageously sexual with sincerity and is just so natural. She performs as easily as the best ballet dancer, just great, just athletic in her vocal cords. And again, Nancy Wilson is superb, I'm bowled over by her vocals,

What does the immediate future hold for you, and when can we expect to see a follow-up to 'Ignorance'?

Who knows? Only fate, so I can't answer that.

Clive and I have been discussing two different projects and we have yet to take a course on either one. We have been discussing it with Mr Elsing, but nothing decided yet.

Again, my grateful thanks to Tracy for this lengthy interview. If you have yet to hear any of her recordings, then you are missing out on some great singing. I've been fortunate enough to see her perform live twice recently, and she's as good in concert as she is in the studio.

Clive Nolan (Shadowland), #21, Jan 1994

One day in October I received a call from Mark Colton, telling me that Credo had just been offered a gig at the Phoenix in Staines. As I was supposed to be seeing Shadowland there on the same date, I felt that a phone call to Clive might well be in order. It transpired that they had had to blow the gig as they were behind the deadline for recording the new album. Still, not all was lost as Clive invited me over to Maidenhead for the afternoon. Having been there for almost five hours, and with talk switching from one topic to another, instead of trying to put down word for word what was said, I've tried rather to convey what it was that we talked about.

I made it to the famous home of Thin Ice and was greeted by a very sorry sounding Clive. He was suffering with a cold, and as he was yet to lay down the vocals this could be quite a bit of a problem. Karl was in, as was evident from the sounds of guitar that were coming from the studio as he was trying to complete his parts that afternoon. Clive and I settled down in the front room, and I was introduced to Chekhov and Sulu (two of the cats you will find credited in the back of Thin Ice recordings. Yes, Clive is very much a Star Trek fan, even having a poster in the studio) and started talking about many things musical. Because of his cold, Clive was not being as effective as he would have liked to have been. He was still writing lyrics for the album (his chair was surrounded by many reference books), and these lyrics then had to be recorded (and his voice was not all that it should be). Although they were working to a tight self-imposed deadline, Clive was still confident that the recording would be finished on time.

He explained that initially they had had problems recording the drums. For the previous Shadowland recordings Nick had played drum pads, thereby triggering drum samples, but for this recording the decision was taken to use "live" drums. It took them two days to set up the drums, which meant that Nick only had three days to record the entire album. Still, Clive was very pleased with the overall results. It also did not help that half of the Thin Ice studio was set up over at Nick Barrett's to record the new Pendragon album, and there were also keyboards over there as well. Obviously, as Karl was co-producing that album, he was over at Nick's even more than Clive, which all added to the time spent that could have been utilised on the Shads own project. All the bass parts had to be recorded in the evening due to Ian's work commitments, but one big advantage of having their own studio meant that Clive and Karl were not working to any time constraints. I mentioned to Clive how effective the use of fretless bass had been on the first album, and apparently, Ian and Clive were discussing the use of fretless bass so Ian went home, removed the frets from one of his basses, filled in the holes, and taught himself a new instrument! An offshoot of this is that he has now appeared on other albums, specifically to play fretless bass. Karl appeared at this stage, having problems with one of the guitar parts. Clive suggested that he groove it along, and Karl responded with the very quotable "It's quite hard to groove in 7/8!"

Richard West is no longer a member of the band, as he was unable to give enough of his time. Clive decided to get someone else in straightaway, and put an advert in a music shop, to which Mike Varty responded immediately and so joined. At the time of our discussion, Clive was still to hear Mike play, but he seemed okay so that was enough for Clive. I mentioned to him that he always seems to have something on the go, if not many things at once. It transpired that by the end of the year he and Karl would have worked on something like ten albums between them. On top of that, there was the live work, with gigs in Holland with Final Conflict in November and a European tour lined up with Red Jasper for February, and there will also be a big Pendragon tour following on from that in April and May. Already lined up is the new album by Tracy Hitchings, a re-mix of the first Strangers On A Train album "The Key", the third album, as well as all the tracks they were working on for the Geoff Mann tribute album, while there is also the possibility of a new Casino-style album, with Rog Patterson on vocals. Add onto that a possible contemporary classical music album that Clive may record for the new label being set up by Mick Pointer (the label is called Verglas Music and Mick will be releasing an album later in 1994), so he does have his hands full. It is little wonder that Clive does not know when he is likely to have a holiday.

He is also working on some dance music with someone signed to RCA Italy who he describes as being a sort of laid-back male version of Sade. Clive does not listen to prog for pleasure very much, although he does confess to liking the new IQ album (and who doesn't?), but normally listens to groups like Queen and enjoys compilations, best of etc. HM does not appeal at all, and he's not into bands like Queensrÿche either. He initially sang because he could not be bothered to teach someone else to sing in the way that he writes. He feels that the singer carries the personality of the band and the first time he got a positive reaction was in Holland with SOAT playing with Egdon Heath. It was the first time that an audience were responding to his music and singing. He confesses that he is not necessarily a good singer, but feels he is right for his own songs and that he feels lucky in that audiences have always given a friendly reaction to this (this must be true of CD buyers as well, as Shadowland's 'Ring of Roses' is still SI's biggest seller).

Gigs are on the whole strategically chosen, with small gigs only used to try out new material or personnel, or to warm up for high profile events. His favourite instrument is the piano as it has a specific relationship. He tends to look at recording on three levels, piano, synths and keyboards (arranging etc.). For this recording, lots of material was put to one side, with as much being discarded as being unsuitable for Shadowland as was used; Clive found it very difficult to write the follow-up. They have also been recording a video as they have gone along, using a "fly on the wall" approach. There are plans to record the gig with Red Jasper and use these for a live CD and full-scale video release with good sound quality, which will also include documentary footage.

Having adjourned to the pub, talk turned to the new album, which will be called 'Through The Looking Glass', after the Lewis Carroll book of the same name. It is a concept album about dreams, the subconscious and the inner person, examining the darker side of the human mind. The songs look at different parts of the darker side and continue the personal themes of the debut. There are eight songs, although the first is a short acoustic and voice version of the closer.

"A Matter of Perspective" acts as opener to the album.

"The Hunger" is the title of a vampire film with strong atmosphere, but this is about more than just a lust for blood, social vampirism.

"Dreams of the Ferryman" is about a series of murders with a sense of something evil. The murderer always wears a mask, and Clive is always present.

"Half Moon Street" is a link with "Scared Of The Dark" from the debut, and continues the theme present in that song.

"**When The World Turns To White"** is about how snow cleanses the world, but although it becomes far more pleasant the darkness is still there.

"The Waking Hour" is about when you are awake, feeling slightly disoriented, and you are no sure if you are present in reality, or if you are dreaming. The songs go further than simple analogue; they are about interaction with people: it is the hidden side of what people may feel or do.

"Through The Looking Glass" is the umbrella for all the songs, and at more than twelve minutes in length, it looks at the power of imagination and the crossover of that and reality, where it is and where you want it to be.

"Mindgames" sums up the whole thing. Lot of memories and specific anecdotes flavour this song that may not mean anything to anyone else. It's like a Floyd ballad with the lyrics far more sinister than the music suggests. The chords are very simple, and clichés are used as a vehicle.

Repetition is important in music for people to equate with the musical ideas. All the great composers believe in careful repetition, as without it, music will not last long. Clive tries to write songs that will last a hundred years, going across fashion phases, pigeonholes and styles. After leaving college, Clive decided he wanted to make his career as a full-time musician, and that he would live or die solely by his own efforts. He has never signed on or drawn dole but stuck by his ideals. Three years ago, he was on the verge of giving up when the deal for 'The Key' came through. Thanks to that, he could stick at music full-time and I for one am extremely glad that he did so. My thanks go to Clive for an extremely enjoyable afternoon and having seen the studio I am amazed that so much great music can come out of one little room.

Nick Barrett (Pendragon), #21, Jan 1994

What would you personally say are the major differences between 'Window of Life' and 'The World'? How much are these due to you now having your own studio to record in?

I do not know why, but I find it almost impossible to list differences between our albums; perhaps it's because to me it's all music, and I've heard it so many times when recording I do not get the "initial impression" thing. That's the arty answer, and now the real answer... um... well, having our own studio has made it possible to home in on more details. With the guitar, I spent ages getting the right kind of feel and tone, previously I've just closed my eyes and gone for broke! I think the vocals are much better on 'The Window' as I've found a microphone I'm happy with now. On the guitar on this album I used more slide and the wah wah pedal too, which is new! The drumming's a lot better because Fudge had longer to get into it.

Can you briefly go through the tracks on 'WOL' and say what you wanted to achieve for each one?

"Walls of Babylon". I wanted to open with an atmosphere, everyone expects an album to start 1234 BANG! but I felt this was more absorbing and different. Then I wanted the track to be quite rocky with power melody slabs.

"Ghosts". Here I wanted something with a lot of drama in short bursts, thus the amount of changes, again ending with a strong rocky feel.

"Breaking The Spell". This I wanted to have a very bare emotion, but with a sense of majesty about it.

"Last Man On Earth". I aimed for a combination of musical ideas with a good flow, and good melodies all the way through with a rousing end section.

"Nostradamus". This comes in three sections. For the first I wanted a Jeff Beck style atmosphere, for the second a good vocal melody, and for the third I wanted the Pendragon bounce.

"Am I Really Losing You?" Again, the bare emotion was the thing, and, in some ways, this is the most striking because of the vocals.

Although it is unusual for prog bands to release singles, have you considered doing this to gain airplay? Which track would you choose?

"Nostradamus". We did some special radio edits CDs and sent them to radio stations, but so far not a lot of plays! We'll probably continue to have a bash at singles occasionally, but I wouldn't pin all my hopes on this expensive and rather silly practice. Nowadays there's total emphasis on singles and radio play, it seems so shallow, to judge the worth of a band that's been around for twelve years in three and a half minutes. I'd rather go against the grain a bit and filter through to people with the much wider statement of an album. I've an idea we'll see the music business shift importance to albums, but by then most record companies will not know what to do with them, as they've been totally absorbed into the 'singles making machinery'. Our records take what used to be termed "a good listen": I'd like to see the value return to music.

To someone who has never heard Pendragon, how would you describe your music?

Odd. It's funny, because most people who have not a clue about the prog thing first listen to us and think... mmm? But after a load of plays they become fanatical; they are jumping in cold and do not listen with tainted ears. I would say that if you want music that touches your soul, and you're prepared to give it lots of listen, you'll like. That's how I got into Genesis, and I still love them today!

Since the release of 'The World', both Peter and Clive have become more active on the CD releasing front. How has this affected Pendragon?

It hasn't affected anything, we go on! I've a deep feeling that it's dangerous to be involved in too many projects but Clive seems to manage this okay although it's not something I would embrace as I feel putting everything into Pendragon gives the band a very strong focus.

At times, there are some very rocky passages on 'WOL'. Did you find yourself being influenced by having Karl at the controls as his style of guitar playing is usually heavier than yours?

No, not really, it's just the way the music went; we wanted a bit more guts to the guitar sound and I guess this makes it a bit heavier. Karl's the sort of bloke who would adjust to the intrinsic sound of a band, and not really push his musical influence on you, although his production and engineering influence has undoubtedly given a gutsier sound to the guitar. In places, we did want the album to rock, so arranged and recorded in that fashion.

Pendragon is very much the vehicle for your song writing, while Shadowland is the vehicle for Clive. Can you see yourselves working together on a project?

For Pendragon material, it's probably unlikely. We both have very different objectives when we write material, we both have a 'vision' with our music, and I think they are quite different. It's strange both being in the same musical area, but our backgrounds are very different. Clive comes from classical, and I come from a blues/soul (not soul as in Soul!), and it's quite tough to marry the two.

As on the cover of 'The World', 'WOL' has a lot of symbolism. Do you tell Simon Williams what you want included, or do you just give him a set of lyrics? Can you explain some of the themes?

I give Simon a list of the concepts, he drafts the picture out of a pencil sketch, and then we make any alterations before the finished thing. The bloke turning into swallows symbolises the spirit leaving the body, the swallows represent a free spirit. The old geezer in the bottom left of the picture is Nostradamus considering the future in the bowl of water and seeing warplanes, which he did see in the 14th century (I think!). The main characters, the Toff dancing with the girl are not specifically from any one song, but they cover the whole concept; they are ghosts and are alive and well and having a jolly good time on 'the other side'. The chimps were also nothing specific, but I thought they were a good idea as they are completely unserious.

It has been a long time since Pendragon were first formed, how has the music industry changed since then and how has this affected the UK underground prog scene?

Well, I do not think the industry had changed all that much, but our way of getting benefits from it has; it's still as difficult today (harder even) as it was ten years ago for a new band to break through. The prog network hasn't changed at all, so it means there is always some kind of outlet for new prog bands. There are always a lot of fanzines and people into this music if you can get to them! Prog is so disconnected from fashion and 'the social scene', which means that people like it for the music, which is a very powerful thing: it's like jazz, once you get into it you never turn your back on it. So many other forms of music today have short-lived appeal because they are shrouded in everything else but the music, and that fascination has a habit of losing its interest. Bros, Aha, Kylie etc. have all had something today, but not much of it was about music. Their fans have gone onto other bands, and the whole industry machine grinds on. It's only those who have something to offer in terms of music who can last. They might be less famous, but they can sleep at night happy. Nik Kershaw, the pop icon of the eighties, just disappeared and then popped up working with Tony Banks as he is in fact an extremely good musician on keyboards, vocals and guitar. Duran Duran made a good album recently, not as commercially big as their earlier records, but with a sense of musicality about it. Many prog bands have that musicality and integrity, just lack a bit in the fame department, which is just fine!

What are the immediate fans for the future? Looking more to the long term, what do you see happening to Pendragon over the next five years?

No idea! There's no master plan, which is what makes it still interesting and exciting to do.

Rog Patterson, #22, March 1994

Rog tells it like it is. Sort of...

1961 I was born on Midsummer's Day (which, as nobody at all seems to know, is 24th June) in Birmingham, England. My father, an electrical designer, was 59 at the time so I feel rather fortunate to be here at all... An only child, apparently, I was very quiet and well-behaved, which just goes to show how things change as you grow up! My mother used to listen to Radio 2 before I went to school in the mornings, so I had no exposure to music whatsoever until Terry Wogan accidentally played T. Rex's "Jeepster". I discovered that we owned a record player (well, Gerrard Radiogram actually) and I decided that it was the time the 10-year-old Patterson joined the rock 'n' roll circus.

1971 Persistent whingeing produced a guitar for Christmas, a classical (made in Czechoslovakia) with a neck so wide I could not reach half the strings. Hours of patient miming to Slade records yielded the ability to play perhaps as many as five chords, randomly mixed with several hundred appalling dischords.

1975 Eureka! The discovery that I was holding the guitar the wrong way up revolutionised the Patterson technique, as reversing the strings enabled me to play five entirely different chords, and an even more exotic range of dischords which the acquisition of a twelve-string enhanced beyond belief, and beyond the tolerance of any mother less patient than my own! Having so far been self-taught (I was always catching myself gazing out of the window or skiving off altogether), I decided that my en passant left-handedness would forever prevent me from learning to play "properly", so I'd bypass the scales-and-exercises thing, avoid formal lessons and just go straight for the miming on Top of the Pops and being immensely famous. Sadly, things did not quite work out in this direction; I spent several years sitting around writing songs about nothing in particular, while everyone else at school was messing about with pubs, discos, and each other's girlfriends. I never really got the hang of being a school kid, I did not mind the lessons so much, but the being perpetually irritating was something I did not master until later.

1979 Eventually all this self-denial and comparative sobriety paid off, in an extremely small way, when by some quirk of mistaken identity, I was asked to join Trident, a Thin Lizzy meets UFO band with their very own roadie! How could I refuse, even though what they actually wanted was a bass player? No problem I thought, fewer strings, fewer cockups. So, I bought a dangerously cheap bass, and played my first gigs on the Birmingham rock circuit. I learned a lot from that band; mostly about pointless rehearsals and the evil powers of the "band girlfriend" (pardon the sexism, but all the band were male, despite haircuts to the contrary). In the same year, I met for the first time someone who I wanted to write songs about, for purely personal reasons; this permanently changed the way I approach music, and even now flavours my attitude to what I do. Like it or not, I just can't write about anything that I do not personally believe in: if I do not mean it, I do not say it. Leaving school with no real wish to continue the process of education any further than the impasse it has now reached, I found myself brow-beaten into getting a job with Post Office Telephones as it then was (these were the days of Trimfones, Buzby, and payphones that worked). As a sales officer, I offset the effect of dealing with the general public by developing my somewhat ludicrous sense of humour and found myself appointed custodian of the office Silly File, easily my most interesting duty.

1980 My old office drinking partner showed an interest in my semi-musical pursuits, and I persuaded him to help with Trident's laboured proceedings; in due course, we conned him into referring to himself as a manager and told him that it would lead to great things! Of course, when Trident split, we expected him to forget all about music altogether, and sure enough he did; he's now tour manager for Metallica...! Apart from brief silly projects such as the Booze Bland, my musical dabblings returned to the bedroom, until I could finally take no more of the hectic excitement of sitting behind a desk five days a week; a colleague persuaded me to apply for a university place, and much to my amazement I slipped through the net to get into Nottingham University, to read Philosophy.

1982 Which is probably the best move I ever made. Despite telling myself <u>not</u> to spend all my time with a guitar in my hands, I soon made the acquaintance of a large hairy person by the name of Greg Smith, a fellow 12-string player and Ant Phillips fan. Soon the nocturnal corridors of his hall of residence echoed to the sounds of obscure D minor chords and tortuous tuning difficulties.

1983 In due course, Greg's neighbours suggested that we go and play some gigs, presumably so that they could get some kip (did you know "kip" is Dutch for chicken? You can't say I never tell you anything). Taking the name TWICE BITTEN from an incident involving a pharmacologist and a friend's dog, we made our live debut in a church hall in Billericay. The ensuing sequence of preposterously lucky breaks saw us playing our fourth gig in front of a thousand people, supporting Roy Harper; and our fifth, seventh and eighth at the Marquee in London. We somehow found ourselves accepted into the then-thriving progressive rock scene, supporting Twelfth Night, Solstice, Pendragon and others.

1984 Back in Nottingham, our professor was surprisingly well-disposed to our being out on tour instead of at lectures, presumably because without Greg there was a lot more room at the departmental coffee bar. At around this time we met a band even sillier than we were, in the form of Haze; we were to tour together, as if bound by some vengeful Olympian edict, until their eventual demise in 1989. We released a couple of cassettes, 'Dialogue' and 'Third Man'; the first with the help of Robin Prior of Twelfth Night, and the second under the auspices of Jennifer Moore (Single Bass).

1985 On graduating from Nottingham we decided to keep the TB thing going for a while, and continued to play extensive and increasingly pointless tours, which were fun up to a point, but in reality, little more than ever-decreasing circles.

1986 In due course Greg decided that more than enough was enough and threw in the towel. We played a thoroughly memorable farewell show at the old Mardi Gras in Nottingham, which may or may not have been the musical highpoint of our career, but which certainly taught us what a powerful unifying force music can be. Ever the glutton for punishment, I resolved to carry on making twangy noises and yelling, and released 'M 25', a cassette of songs I'd written as TB was winding down. Much to my surprise I found myself taken reasonably seriously as a solo performer, and I carried on playing within the prog rock circuit and beyond, supporting Harper again and John Martyn, The Strawbs and many more. By way of a diversion, around this time I was also back on bass guitar in a rather different idiom; I found myself playing in Stop The Bus, a local funk-rock band. That was great fun, certainly more of a hobby than a serious part of my career, but I learned a great deal from it. It's always a good idea to tinker about with as many styles as possible, especially if your own style is as, er, idiosyncratic as mine!

1987 The Haze connection was still there, of course, and in the Autumn of 1987 Haze, me and Single Bass toured Holland; this was the first foreign tour for any of us, and probably the least comfortable tour undertaken by anybody since Captain Scott. It was tremendous fun, and again we learned a lot, especially about Dutch beer! I released another cassette, 'Talking To The Weather', which was recorded at home using the 8-track studio which was nominally providing my income. I did quite a lot of recording for other people during this period, but most of the musicians involved had a very well-developed ability to not bother paying for the privilege, so my subsistence money had to come from the music. At this point I'd like to mention a BIG problem with being a professional musician. If you want to eat, and to be able to keep making music, you have to write and play what people will pay for. But this may not be what you want to play, not what makes you want to be a musician in the first place. Unless you can persuade people that they want exactly what you play, you have to compromise, and compromise is the death of creativity. That explains why I now spend much of my time sound engineering; if I earn enough to keep myself alive, I can then concentrate on the content of my own music, without having to worry about whether it's too interesting to be saleable. It's the only way I can see to preserve my aesthetic integrity, without starting out rich in the first place! Sorry – brief digression on behalf of the Art For Art's Sake Party. What was I? Oh,

yes, 1987. Not content with just churning out my own brand of Heavy Wood, I joined with the studio band Coltsfoot and we recorded the 'Action At A Distance' cassette, a process which at no time involved all of us actually being in the same place!

1988 Now it all starts to get really silly. I was asked to join Pendragon's crew, as a favour, for one gig. So, what happens? I somehow end up becoming their tour manager and sound engineer. Just what I needed, something else to do. My own gigs were starting to take me further afield, so I thought it was about time I got a vinyl album out. Having written the bulk of the material I wanted to include, I tried to find time to get into the studio to record it. And tried, and tried, and eventually found the time in late November; but I also found I had the flu! So, with the help of my engineer Dave "Wedge" Hadley (the LARGE roadie), I went in and recorded "The Unexpected EP' (so called because everyone was expecting an LP) which includes "It Always Rains On Christmas Morning", the world's first realistic Christmas song; an obviously, nose-blocked "Pagan Man" (known to us all as Bagad Bad); and two instrumentals recorded at home for friends which presented themselves as a readymade B -side.

1989 Following the fiasco of trying to get the EP pressed in time for Christmas, the last thing I wanted to do in the new year was make another record. But, the nagging of the Wedge prevailed, and so began a series of sessions which would have made a great Channel 4 sitcom, except they were not sufficiently believable. Half the intended tracks never made it onto tape at all; the title tracks, having taken over a year to write, was re-recorded in a total of about 24 hours (spread over two weeks); "An Englishman's Home" was written and recorded in about half an hour, when I took out the 12-string to play something else entirely and started playing the wrong chord pattern; "Speak For Yourself" was recorded twice because the first version had bus noises all over it; Dave and myself were reduced to gibbering caffeine addicts, as most of the actual work was done overnight; the final mix was done in a control room containing Dave, myself, Chris and Dave (the producers), and four people from next door playing bridge..; half an hour before doing the final edit we still had four versions of the running order to choose from; the cut had to be done twice due to an expensive error by the cutting engineer; consequently the records arrived two weeks late; the sleeves were on time, but the colours were the wrong way around, etc. etc. As you can see, this making records lark can be rather, er, entertaining! The upshot was that 'Flightless' was released in March 1989, and

I'm surprised to find that I'm actually quite pleased with it. I usually hate everything I do within thirty seconds of having done it, but on this occasion the record says pretty much what I wanted it to say. With the album complete I was soon on the road again, in Britain, Holland, France and Germany supporting Pendragon. I've always been impressed with the attitude of European audiences; their English is usually better than mine and it's always a pleasure to play to such an attentive lot. British musicians are always very looked after on the continent, especially in the free beer department! This business has its little perks you know...

1990 Since the bout of manic touring which followed the release of 'Flightless', I came back to Nottingham and concentrated on writing new material, as well as finding myself involved in various other musical projects. Most of 1990 was spent on the road, engineering and tour managing various bands in Britain and Europe. I worked with a lot of thrash metal bands, which is not as terrifying as it sounds; a lot of these chaps are remarkably good musicians and lyricists. I even found myself playing keyboards on the debut album by Skyclad, a sort of Pagan thrash folk-metal band…?! In December, I found myself thrust back in the fray (oo-er) of standing up and yelling by an invitation to play a show in Rome, as guest of the Italian progressive rock band Leviathan. Not being one to turn down the chance to go somewhere foreign instead of working for a living, off I went, and as well as having a jolly good time thanks to Alex and the others I decided to get on with being a musician (-ish) again when I got home.

1991 I did genuinely intend to release a new album in 1991, but then I say that every year. I did a lot of writing, but fewer and fewer live shows, because I found myself getting involved with ever more interesting bands in my dual role of sound engineer and tour manager. Rather than try to keep too many balls in the air at once, I decided that it would make more sense to put my own musical career (such as it is) on hold while I pottered around the word helping others get their music and words into the ears of the public.

1992 And so it carried on with me sitting at the back of the tour bus writing music to the bafflement of various bands including Murder Inc., L7, Lawnmower Deth, L7, Mordred, L7, L7 and then…

1993 Rage Against The Machine. This was the band I'd been waiting for, in many respects; they try to do with their music what I try to do with mine, although in a very different idiom. Their work is highly political and totally sincere, and as their tour manager and sound engineer, I feel that I'm making the political contribution that I always hoped music would enable me to make. Their success has been very sudden, and very widespread; we've been on the road almost constantly for a year. Now I'm back home, I at last feel ready to turn my full attention to my own music; I find that the last few year's writing has produced a set of new material which is sitting there waiting for me to do something about it. I'm currently exploring various options with a view of making the new album a rather more high-profile project than it was with 'Flightless'; and I'm looking forward to touring as a musician again, now that I have a whole new perspective on the process.

1994 Of course, it's never quite that simple: I've still not quite finished the new Coltsfoot album, and I've been working on Anthony Phillips' new album, so that I still have not actually recorded anything myself. Oh, bugger. But, at last, I have started playing live again, with shows in England and Norway; I am getting on with it, honestly. I do things which are not directly related to music, albeit not very often: my main hobby is cricket and Ant Phillips and I both play for a couple of London-based wandering (well staggering) clubs, the Send Occasionals and the Non-Conformists. Apart from that I sometimes manage to get down to Trent Bridge to watch Nottinghamshire beat everybody else, and I play pool with the enthusiasm you'd expect from a man whose life appears to take place entirely on licensed premises. I'm also a keen member of the Nottingham University Society for Philosophical Aesthetics (honestly) – we have really good parties!

Well, there's a brief (?) summary of Pattersonism as we know it, from 1961 to date. There's a method in the madness, but it's quite heavily disguised…

Steve Paine (Legend), #22, March 1994

Steve Paine is keyboard player with Legend, as well as being a director of Pagan media, which is home to both Legend and Incubus Succubus. He is also in demand as a producer and engineer.

So, where and when did Legend first form?

I suppose the real start to the story was in about 1985. Having been out of a regular band for some time I decided to form one to play the plethora of material I had written, and we formed a band called Nightshade. The name came from a band I was previously associated with which was also a prog band, but more along the lines of early Grace, who were a big influence at the time. It did not come to fruition until we moved from Reading to Runcorn, and I formed the first basis of Legend in 1988, on August 18th to be exact. The original Legend line-up consisted of Chris Haskayne on drums, Sean Gallagher on bass, Neil Gallagher on guitar, myself on keyboards and we had a dual vocalist arrangement with Kerry Paine (my ex-wife) and Debbie. They split leads and harmonies between them, although it must be said that Kerry was the main vocalist, though that did change during the years. Sean and Neil did not last very long, with Neil being replaced at the eleventh hour from our first gig by Paul. I turned up on Paul's doorstep about nine o'clock one evening with him completely unaware that I was calling, and me not knowing him at all, just working on a friend's recommendation that he was a good guitarist. I knocked on his door and asked him to stand in, to which he agreed, and he is still standing in to this day.

The first gig was on September 23rd, a little bit hurried to my liking, but the local bike club were desperate for a band. Not a particularly successful event as you can imagine, as the sort of sound Legend produces does not go together in a few weeks, but we played it and it's all gone from there. The Legend we know and love today probably did not come into effect until 1989 when I split up with Kerry, and Debbie moved onto lead vocals. We had quite a bit of fruitless time with various bass players until we got Ian Lees in at the beginning of 1991. We've not been terribly lucky with our rhythm section, but things seem to be stabilising, so fingers crossed.

Legend are very different, both musically and lyrically, from all the other 'prog' bands around. Please cite your influences.

Well, influences are quite a difficult one because there is no real main influence that's common throughout the band, all of us have a very wide taste of music. The writing core of the band, which is essentially Paul, Debbie and me (Debbie being responsible for mostly lyrics) has a main common influence of folk-rock. We all like Fairport Convention and Steeleye Span and those are a few of the gigs we go to together. Paul's major influences are heavily rock guitarists, and his big hero at one time was Gary Moore although currently I believe he favours more technical US guitarists such as Tony MacAlpine, Joe Satriani and Steve Vai. One thing I will say is that Paul is an extremely versatile guitarist who also plays bass and trumpet, and his other interest is big band music. In his case, quite diverse, anything from Glenn Miller to the mass bands of the RAF. As for Debbie, she is a little more complicated. Her father was funnily enough leader of one of the mass RAF bands, and she was brought up on a wide range of music. Her father was particularly keen on jazz, and she studied piano and clarinet as a teenager, so her base is in classical music. She listens to quite a lot of folk music and tends rather than being into bands, more into particular albums. Her record collection is as diverse as from Yes to Saxon, though I think her classical singing obviously has a strong base as to where she comes from, but her tastes are extremely catholic. Current favourite albums are 'Midsummer Night's Dream' by Red Jasper, 'A Tab In The Ocean' by Nektar and 'The Best of Joan Sutherland'.

As for myself, I listen to quite a lot of medieval music, which does show up in Legend I know. I'm also a great classical buff, although mainly from the Baroque period although I do move into the early romanticism with people like Mozart, Brahms and Beethoven. Again, the folk influence is quite heavy, I'm particularly fond of The Strawbs, but I'm the one who is a real prog freak. I think if I had to admit to having a hero it must be Richard Harvey from Gryphon. The guy's a brilliant keyboard player and multi-instrumentalist and he's just far too talented for his own good. No, that's not true, he's a very helpful guy. As for John, the drummer, his influences are much more modern that then rest of us in some respects because of being a lot younger. When he joined the band, he was only eighteen, and I think it's been quite an eye opener for him, he was brought up on a diet of bands like Aha, Wham, Duran Duran, though he's now moved onto bands more like Queen and Marillion. Rush is a favourite now since joining the band as Martin our previous bass player was a big Rush fan, as am I, so that's rubbed off on John whose tastes are evolving, as are his contributions to the band. Our new bass player, Mike, comes from a hard rock background, anything from Thrash through to Death to the more commercial AOR sounds. It's hard to place bands who were an influence on him, I do not know him well enough to delve into his record collection as it were, and it must be said in some respects he does keep himself to himself in terms of influences so it's a bit early days yet, but we will no doubt find out in the fullness of time.

Have any of you been involved in other projects. If so, what?

I suppose the most noticeable one is our new bass player Mike Thomas who used to be in Demon, and played on their last recording, 'Blow Out'. He also toured Germany quite extensively with a band called Chapel Of Rest, latterly shortened to Chapel which is a sort of Thrash Death crossover, and whilst I'm not into that genre I must admit that I find this one not only extremely tight but extremely interesting; it was because of the Chapel tape that we were so keen on having Mike. Paul's been involved in quite a lot of local/ regional heavy rock bands that have all made their mark in the area, the most significant of which was FTW. Whilst they had no major success, they did have a very strong following and gigged regularly. As for Debbie and John, Legend is the first band for both. As for myself, working as an engineer since 1981 I've depped on quite a few things, principally Nightshade, which as I mentioned before had two versions. In the first one I played flute and keyboards and odd bits of guitar and even sang, much to the detriment of the audience. In the later Nightshade, I moved over to purely keyboards, though there was the odd bit of guitar on slight occasions. I think the most amusing band I've was worked in was one called Pinky Pinky Slap Slap, who were a nudist jazz funk fusion band whose major stage performance was playing without the benefit of clothing. They lost their keyboard player, not surprising I suppose, and I stood in for him, but history does not recall whether I kept my jockstrap. Also, I've drummed in a band called Deadlock, who were a local band in the Reading area and I currently drum in a Pink Floyd Hawkwind crossover band called Syd's Spirit.

Did you feel that the criticism of the first album was justified?

Definitely a yes and no question. On the yes point, I think the way the drums had to be recorded due to equipment limitations, and possibly as a producer I was not firm enough with Chris over the way he did his rolls, or the amount of embellishment, and that has put quite a lot of people off. On reflection, it does not sound as good as it could have done, and I think these criticisms are reasonably fair. What I do feel was mostly unfair was the way that the mainstream press such as Melody Maker, Kerrang! and NME were unnecessarily personally critical of Debbie. For example, the Kerrang! review started with the statement of how in a previous incarnation Debbie Chapman was a dinner lady and now she sings for Legend. Melody Maker said that she had the appearance of a battered wife while the Reading Evening Post described her as a bi-spectacled typing pool type. I feel this direct personal criticism of her appearance, perhaps on reflection the photo was not as flattering as it could have been, was a little unnecessary and directly personal. As for the other criticisms, especially those levelled by Melody Maker, I must admit we had a good laugh over. One of the reviews that I will always remember is that Acid Dragon described the overall effect of listening to Legend like a nightingale soaring over a tribe of rioting gorillas, or was this prejudice against gorillas? If nothing else, I was extremely entertained. What impact it had on album sales I cannot say, but I feel that possibly if the production had been slightly better than it might have sold more but having said that it exceeded my wildest expectations anyway.

How would you describe your music to someone who had never heard you play?

I'm going to have to think about this one. A friend of ours did recently describe us as being flash gits who were too clever for our own good! I do not think that is necessarily totally true. The key to Legend's sound is that every song has a strong melody, a well-defined structure, and should be clear lyrical eloquence and plenty of emotion. The technical bits that we put in, we put in simply to enhance the mood of the song rather than throw them in simply because we can, though I must admit we do thoroughly enjoy playing the more complex sections. The music is built and quite critically edited around getting the point of the song across, rather than just throwing it together for the sake of it. For reference of bands, I think if you sort of boil up a strange alchemical brew of Renaissance, Magnum, All About Eve and throw in a touch of Camel for good measure, I think you have about the size of it. Somebody recently criticised 'Second Sight' for a couple of the songs being a bit long, but I think we make our pieces as long as they turn out, rather than deliberately intending to write one that's over ten minutes. It is very difficult to describe the sound of the band, because it is a combination of all the people who come to it. With our influences being very diverse, it gives an opportunity for every band member to put their own standpoint on it, which gives us a refreshing sound. Whether it's modern or trapped in a time-warp no doubt journalists will be arguing about until the end of time, but as long as they are arguing about it that's the main thing.

Legend are very strong live, yet you have not played as many gigs as you could have. What is the reason for this, and will it change in the future?

No, we do not gig very often, and there are two reasons behind this. One, we do find difficulty getting into venues as promoters particularly do not seem to like Debbie's voice. Paul and I have lost count of the number of times we've been told that the band is great, but the vocalist can't sing, which is a bit ironic considering that she's a classically trained soprano. There is a lot of prejudice because the sound is unique, so we do not get many bookings, and subsequently we stage an awful lot of gigs ourselves. Also, the second reason is that when we do play, we like to put on a show which means not just standing up and playing: it means a full PA, full lighting rig, special effects, costumes, anything we can deploy at the time. Obviously, it varies from venue to venue, as if you get a small venue you can't put in a huge lighting rig, well not if you want an audience or if you want the fuse box to stay intact. But when we gig, we like to make it as spectacular as possible, and given that this costs large amounts of money we tend to do it relatively seldom. Things are on the up because as the pagan scene is growing, and to a certain extent the Prog scene as well, we are getting more opportunity to play things like pagan festivals and we seem to be getting many bookings through those circles now. Also, strangely enough, we're touring for the first time since 1991 at the end of March. We're in support mode for this, and you may well see Legend out and about quite a lot supporting over the next year or so. Though we've sold a lot of records, our following is very widely spread which means that it's difficult for us to gather a large live crowd to justify the expense of staging it. That's the main reason we did the 'Playing With Fire' video, because there were so many people from all over the world writing to us. We decided we would stage a spectacular show, and video it to the best possible standard we could afford, which was not a lot quite frankly. The budget turned out to be less than six thousand pounds. That sounds a massive amount, but you do not get 30 seconds of a promo video for that, let alone sixty-six minutes of explosive live action. We did 'Playing With Fire' principally to enable audiences and people who would like to see us to get an impression of what the band was like under as ideal as possible circumstances, I think in that respect its' succeeded quite well, as it's representative of the band. We pulled out all the stops and it's possibly slightly more spectacular than a normal gig. '94 and '95 may well see us out on the road a lot more than we have been, as things are looking promising for prog and pagan alike.

Has being a pagan band been a help or hindrance so far?

On average, it's actually been a help, although there have been small areas of hindrance such as when we dipped out on the opportunity of supporting Runrig. Jon Moreau, our manager, was quite friendly with Marlene Ross, their manager, and they met up when Runrig played in Manchester recently. It's obvious that she's a devout Christian and she was not at all keen on the band being on a label called Pagan and being pagan in nature. It has been a help because paganism is on a significant upsurge now as it is starting to be more widely recognised than it used to be. I've been a pagan for over ten years now, and it was a very hush hush thing when I first came to it, but now things are a lot more open. There's a whole range of magazines and fanzines and events, which are good as it gives us the opportunity to play and express ourselves, and a whole wide range of people we can reach out to. In things like promoting 'Second Sight' the pagan angle adds extra interest for journalists and interviewers alike, because little is known about it comparatively. It gives something else to talk about rather than just another bunch of musicians playing their instruments.

Do you see yourselves playing more with other pagan outfits or prog outfits, or are you going out to get a whole new audience?

I think ultimately, we will reach a unique audience because some of the pagans who listen to us are not into prog, may not necessarily know what prog was, and be very surprised to discover that Legend was an example of it. The prog audiences tend to ignore the pagan angle so I think we will generate a completely unique audience. There are many people of a distinctly gothic persuasion who are keen on the band and playing with Incubus Succubus has meant we've reached a whole audience we would not have reached previously. I think the people who listen to us will be neither necessarily prog nor pagan, but people with just good taste in music. That's what we aim to do, rather than specifically aim to one sort of genre or another. We're also finding that a lot of people who wouldn't call themselves fans of rock music of any type, find Legend good listening. If we can get people to listen to Legend, then most of them take to us, which is extremely satisfying from our point of view.

Why and when did you form Pagan Media? Do you see yourselves signing more bands or are you just going to concentrate on Legend and the Inkies?

The when is very easy. Pagan Media was formed with Mike Turner on June 1st, 1985, originally as Pagan Music Ltd, though we changed to Media in 1988 when we diversified the company slightly to take in photo and video activities. This was because the studio was closed in 1987 by the council, who decided to revoke our planning permission under somewhat suspicious circumstances. The why, was I had been freelancing on and off for about four years, at that point with an eight-track studio in Reading, and they decided to relocate. We set up Pagan as an eight-track studio to fill the gap, as there was a demand for low cost eight track recording in the area at that time. We also diversified into things like public address lighting rigs and rehearsal rooms, which are always popular anywhere there is a strong musical community. Come 1986 the obvious conclusion to promote bands came into the picture, and initially we were going to bring Nightshade up to scratch and record what would have been 'Light In Extension', but the band was not strong enough or together enough at the time. We decided to work with a band from Bracknell who were doing well on the local/regional scene, The Magic Mushroom band, and we produced and released their first album for them, 'Politics and Ecstasy'. I was inexperienced as a producer and in controlling a band, and there were quite a lot of internal factions within the band at the time, and the album was not anything like as successful in terms of the technical recording elements as it could have been. Also, we were extremely naïve and so despite all efforts at promotion it never took off, although it is now retailing for £70 to collectors. As an album, I must say that I'm truly not proud of it, and I feel I could have done it better.

With the studio shut down in 1987 due to the council, the hunt was on then to find a new location. It was obvious we could not stay in the same area as we just did not have the money to afford a suitable property, and the council were going to be extremely awkward over planning permission, so we started to look further afield. We looked in many places, including Exeter, Taunton, Cheltenham and South Wales. Due to a phone call from an old friend who had moved back to Runcorn, we ended up here. The main reason for this was the building was right, we could afford it, and we could get planning permission for a recording studio. As for the second part of the question, the plan now is that we intend to make other signings in the fullness of time We will probably take a maximum of four or five bands and aim to work with them long term and in detail.

We obviously have a very close relationship with Legend and Incubus Succubus, and the main aim of the company is to be able to support and develop the bands through a period of their career, rather than just doing lots of albums by lots of bands, releasing them and seeing which one's stick. We like to work very hard in producing the album, and then promoting it to the hilt directly ourselves on a one person one project basis. There are possibilities we will sign another band this year, The Rattlers, who are a folk-rock band.

We would like to try and have bands that are distinctly different from each other, rather than a whole clutch of bands who sound very similar. They must be the right people because we must work so closely together. I do not think we would have any more than four or five, because I do not think we could give them the backing they deserve.

How many units have you sold to date?

The quick answer to that is lots! I think probably the total is something over 13,000 which boils down to roughly 11,000 units of 'LIE', about 2000 units of 'Second Sight' and the rest are made up of video. About half of the 'LIE' total was sold in Japan, and the other half was spread throughout the rest of the world, although principally in Europe. We seem to have been quite popular in Italy, which is nice as that's always been a popular bastion of prog. One of the nice things about it is that all the people we've had contact with we would never have reached otherwise. It's a great thrill to receive letters from people from all over the world who our music has touched sufficiently to make them put pen to paper. We would never ever have encountered them by any other means, and I think that is for me the ultimate in job satisfaction.

On a more personal basis, are you happy playing keyboards in a rock band, or would you rather spend more time engineering and producing?

I like the balance as it is, I can't imagine not doing one thing or the other. Sometimes it's a bit of a juggling act, and sometimes one must suffer for the other. I've played piano since my fifth birthday, and I do not see me stopping in the future. I drum as well and enjoy the playing of musical instruments. I enjoy all aspects of writing and arranging music, and it seems a logical progression to go onto engineering and producing. I have a keen interest in matters technical, and the engineering and production is just a progression of that, so I think I would like to continue the balancing act. This year will certainly see a lot more production for me, but also hopefully a lot more playing live.

What is the plan for yourself, Legend, and Pagan Media for the next five years?

Our projections for Legend are not that long term. In five years' time, I would like to see us as a name band, but whether that will happen or not is hard to say. I must admit I personally have a theory that Legend will either be a very underground band or a very big band, there's no middle ground. It's going to be purely luck of the draw as to which of these happens. We released 'LIE' for the sheer pleasure of it, and to see whether we could possibly make it work. We expected to sell a few of them locally, but as it happens, we sold very few of them locally and a helluva lot around the world, which is still a continual source of surprise. We will continue to do Legend regardless, as we all get so much pleasure out of playing with each other and writing music and performing it. As for the more practical plans, after we've toured the intent then is to concentrate on writing material for the new album, which should be out around the beginning of November. The provisional working title for this is 'The Triple Aspect'. After that we hope because of us playing more live this year, we may be able to undertake a short tour in our own right. I would like to see something quite theatrical, possibly in art centre staging, but that's very dependent on a lot of other factors. I think we will probably do a live album with some additional material as we always have quite a lot left over in one way or another. It would give us an opportunity to do renderings of tracks from 'LIE' in a slightly more relevant and sympathetic manner.

As for plans for Pagan, these are going to be very much dependent on Legend and Incubus Succubus. Aside from the new Incubus Succubus album, 'The Wytches' (due for release mid-March), we intend to do another Inky's album and another Legend album this year and see what comes in on the signings front. You may see a Rattlers album before the end of the year, depending on how negotiations and things go with them, but it's very early days with that so anything could happen. In terms of long term, I think we have gone away for now from acting as a technical services company, and we do very little in the way of commercial studio or PA work.

We still do odd bits for friends, but principally we're concentrating on being a record label and using the technical facilities to support our bands both in the studio and in the field. Jon is currently finding that it's a full-time job promoting two bands, and if we get any more it's going to be a distinctly full-time job but quite thrilling. It's more fulfilling than seeing lots of young hopefuls come in and record their demos and then go away to a somewhat jaundiced world. We're working on projects we can get our teeth into, and I think we will continue to do that. Whether Pagan will ever become a major label I doubt, because we would lose our integrity, which is one of the things we strongly wish to keep. We believe in what we're doing and believe in giving our bands a very fair deal. I think it will always be a company behind a few bands rather than a major sprawling multinational.

As for me, it looks like quite a full year ahead. I work closely with Incubus Succubus in terms of production and arrangements, so what with the new Legend album to write and record and the new Inky's album to drag kicking and screaming onto tape that's going to keep me off the streets. I've also been asked to produce the Mr So & So album for Cyclops, which I believe is going to be recorded in the summer, and I've even been asked to produce a few tracks for some friends in a local band who have some backing from MCA. So, on a production front I'm going to be very busy. I have also been approached with a view to doing a solo album, though that is going to be unrealistic for the next twelve months, but before the end of the five years is up, we may well see a solo work from me. I have several items of material I do not feel are suitable for Legend, and I would like to experiment in one or two other areas. There are a few folk musicians I would like to work with, and see where that goes, overall we would like to concentrate on keeping doing what we are doing, because it sure as hell beats working for a living and if we achieve nothing else Jon and I will have a lot of stories to tell our grandchildren about many good times.

My thanks go not only to Steve who spent a lot of time completing the interview, but also to my wife Sara who took on the unenviable task of transcribing it from tape.

John Dexter Jones (Jump), #23, May 1994

I recently met up with John prior to a Credo gig, after he kindly agreed to come down and have a chat. With the tape running we just sat and talked…

How did Jump form?

Jump was formed by Peter Davies in the High Wycombe area in 1990. He was very disillusioned with the band he was playing with at the time, Big Rain. He poached a couple of members of bands that he knew from the area, i.e. Steve and Mo, who then introduced him to Andy and Hugh through separate contacts, although I think Peter played with Hugh in years gone by. They were all from that area, and I came down last of all. I answered an ad in Melody Maker, because it sounded like the sort of thing I was looking for. They did not cite it as progressive rock, they did not cite it as heavy metal, they were talking about producing a quality band. They listed very diverse influences which straightaway struck me. I moved up in 1990 and auditioned for them, the audition taking the form of me singing into a cassette in Steve Hayes' front room. It was quite the most embarrassing audition I had ever done, but probably the best way of doing it as well. They gave me a tape to take away and come back and sing to. They did a second audition in a rehearsal room and it worked well, it's like one of those clichés when we all talk about chemistry, because we did not have to work hard at that or at the material.

You used to be a band called Thief?

I was in Thief for about three years, and prior to that I worked with Francis Lickerish who was the guitar player from The Enid, for about eighteen months. It was one of the great things that never got out, a terrific band put together internationally. We did some gigs in Welsh castles and summer festivals and then disappeared as Francis decided that things were not turning out as he wanted it to. One of the tie-ups with Jump that appealed to me was that they were talking about using two guitars, not necessarily in a Wishbone Ash mode, but two very strongly linked guitars doing chords and rhythm parts. After that band had folded, I went with Thief which was the complete antithesis to the pompous rock band as it was a three piece, very sort of hard rock, but with a drum machine so nobody liked us. It was like the end of the world because we could only play in heavy metal clubs up North. They liked the music we were sending them on tape and demos, but as soon as we put the kit up on stage that was it. I suppose Thief were an education for me as I played hundreds and hundreds of gigs in the Northern and North Western rock circuit and it was desperate, but I learned from it. I find playing in the South and South Eastern England a relative luxury, especially with a drummer and two guitars. I suppose that's the background, that's the story, Pete got it together and I was the last one in.

How would you describe the music now to someone who hasn't heard the band?

Let's just start with the obvious ones and then get less obvious. It is not a progressive rock band in the mould of a traditional progressive rock band. It is a rock band but is a progressive outfit in that we are not trying to stylise one form of music, which I think some prog bands around are trying to do. It's not quite progressive, but there are elements of that and in the true sense of the word I would say that it is a progressive band. We are widely influenced, and the sound is unique, probably more so now than when we started. I think the new album has sort of tied the thing up with an identifiable Jump sound. There are elements of hard rock, elements of folk, we are putting something across that draws on very wide collective influences and puts them onto something that is identifiable as one thing. I describe the music as "it's a rock band with very diverse influences".

I was playing 'All The King's Men' on the way here, and it reminds of Marillion although it does not sound like Marillion at all. Does that make any sort of sense?

It does. The Marillion tag is one that you and a lot of the other fanzines were not too quick to pick up on, although the nationals were. They always have to pin themselves onto something extremely quickly. You and fanzines like Blindsight and lately The Organ did not make too much of that. Marillion are a popular band with half of Jump, I will not say which half, and then you must consider that they are terribly influential on musical style. I enjoy Marillion, I saw them back in the early Eighties when Mick Pointer was still drumming with them, and I think that if you detect that sense from 'All The King's Men' it was a sense that I detected with Marillion and Genesis. At the time this was the nearest band that anyone could compare some of the sounds we were putting together. But it is very much a sense of Marillion, and I think that it is what it is with us. The Classic Rock Society's magazine mentioned the Marillion thing for that track as well, but I think it's much heavier than the Marillion they're talking about would do. Certainly, where it gets away from it, I suppose it is a little more acerbic? A little darker and angst-stricken perhaps? I do not know, perhaps a fall back to my Thief days. You have got the piano with the strings on it, and I think that has become synonymous with Marillion but the rest of it, like the syncopated beat, and the guitar solo and stuff could not be further. I listened to an album that Malcolm Parker from GFT gave me, Grey Lady Down's 'The Crime' and while I appreciate the music, I found them to be derivative of Marillion, I couldn't see two further poles really. When you hear the production on an album like Lorien's, which I found a little derivative for my tastes, and then put on 'The Crime' I think hang on a minute, these are the same sounds, the same actual keyboard sounds that Mark Kelly was using in the early Eighties. While anyone who plays a Les Paul will sound a bit like Jimmy Page or whatever, I think the arrangements and attack, and everything are like that. Whenever anyone mentions Marillion I point to GLD. At the same time, I got that one, I also got the new Grace album which is not trying to be anything other than Grace. I told Malcolm that there is no comparison in terms of production or ideas; I think it's one of the best albums around presently, and one we play a lot. It was produced by the guy from Epilogue, who are going to be supporting us sometime in the summer. When we gig, we gig hard and play something like four nights a week. As a small independent set-up, which is what it amounts to, you have to, we sell most of our CDs on the road. In fact, the total sales by the end of this month will be between 1500 and 2000 which without a distribution deal is a lot.

How has the new album gone down?

The established Jump fans to a man, and woman, all say that it is the best thing we have ever done, the strongest thing we've done. The muso people who have heard it say the

same, particularly pointing at the recording being a great improvement. I will agree with that as recording is now 24 tracks as opposed to 16 tracks. This one's digital which has helped with the production and engineering no end. Everybody I've spoken to so far likes it better than the other two. I've been sent an advance copy of the review that is going to appear in Kerrang! that bastion of British rock opinion, and once again they have given us a 3K rating. We think that's marvellous because anything prog they get their hands on they absolutely pan. More importantly the content of the review is very up. I've been sent the unexpurgated version which may get cut down, but there is nothing negative in the review at all, so that's very encouraging. The other reviews we've had so far are from Blindsight and Wondrous Stories, and they have given it very positive reviews, so all in all we're on a bit of a roll now. In terms of radio coverage, we got some here and there with 'World of Wonder' and the reaction to this one is that they have could select tracks from it quite easily. It appears to be quite radio friendly and it's been getting intensive airplay on Radio Russia, just a shame that we can't get out there and support it. I did an interview on the phone with them last week for over an hour, I do not know how much it cost them, but they were very interested and have been playing the album a lot. We are taking steps to see what we can do, but I suppose the response to all of it has just been very positive.

I think this is more complete than the other two with no fillers at all. Why is that?

I think we spent more time and more money from the sale of the last one, having 24 tracks helped and we could expand a bit more. We left some off it as well, which I think is a good thing. Using football parlance, if you have a strong enough squad you should be able to leave things out. We left a few things off so that it did not get too long, and we feel we left the strongest on. There is a better sense of continuity, while perhaps the others were a bit spikier. I've been the closest to it since we started recording it, been in on every session. Sometimes when you get that close to it you get the feeling that you never want to hear any of it again. The difference is listening to it back now it does not feel any longer than 'World of Wonder' when in fact it's about fifteen minutes longer.

How did Chrissie Hammond get involved?

Chrissie is a mate of mine. When I first moved down to the South-East, I was introduced to a bloke called Les Paine who's played over five thousand gigs; he's had deals that have fallen through and is one of the unluckiest guys in the business. Anyway, he sorts out gigs at The Pegasus down in Marlow Bottom, and through his contacts he managed to get a lot of good musicians down there, people like Jeff Beck, and Chrissie was one of his regulars who came up and did songs. I used to do that as well to get my face about, just get up with the house band. I established a good rapport with Chrissie, getting her to do backing vocals and the other way around, I've always stayed in touch with her. There are a couple of out-takes from the 'World Of Wonder' album with Chrissie on, but we felt they did not fit in with the nature of the album, so we did not use them. She just did it as a favour. I left an answer on her messaging machine, asking her to contact me when she was back in the country. She had flown back from Europe somewhere, and was on her way to South America, so phoned Jo up who told her that we were in the studio that day. She said that she only had half an hour as she was on her way to Heathrow, but Jo asked her to come and see us. When she got there, she said that she could not do anything because she only had half an hour, so I told her to get in the booth and gave the words to "Share The Shame" and told Martin to run it by her a few times. She had twenty-five minutes' blind, she had never heard the song before, and it came out like it did. The other two songs she sang on she did in an afternoon, all of them blind, she did not even have rough demo. That was the other thing about this album, we hadn't even performed any of this stuff live. That was a remarkable session as that track has been played on the radio by our local station quite a lot. I go back and listen to it and just feel that she is a tremendously talented lady and should be fronting a band in her own right.

What's next for Jump?

We need to start all over again now that we've got three CDs to sell, we've a catalogue if you like. We need to play as many gigs as we can, wherever they are. Things are looking up with this gig in Rotherham with IQ, and we're doing this festival at Whitchurch and there should be a spin off from these within the prog side of things. I would like to see the next album out within about eighteen months, maybe by someone else. What we would like is some sort of benefactor who believes in the band to put money up and not want too much input in the creative side of it. There are people like that around who have paid for certain sessions and have been glad to help us out because they like the music so much. We know pretty well what we can turn an album in at; we run our own rehearsal studio which used to be a recording studio in the bowels if High Wycombe. This means that we can do a lot of pre-production that does not cost us a lot. What we are looking for is someone who has confidence in the band to shift a certain number of units. I think the next album may well be in the hands of someone prepared to play benefactor without getting involved in the creative side, certainly get involved in the business side. We have a proven track record in looking after that side of things. I do not think the albums we've made have cost a large amount of money, and we have recouped the money within six months of putting them together.

My thanks to John who completed the interview under trying circumstances. Credo were setting up and sound checking which meant that we changed location three times in all. A really friendly guy, I wish him and Jump every success with the wonderful new CD 'All The King's Men'.

Clive Nolan and Mick Pointer (Arena), #27, Feb 1995

Early in January I had the pleasure of spending the afternoon with Mick Pointer and Clive Nolan of Arena. After meeting at Thin Ice Studios, we departed to the nearest public house, and the following in no way conveys what a very enjoyable time we had – laughter is so difficult to transcribe. My grateful thanks to both.

After leaving Marillion why did it take so long for you to return to the music business and what have you been doing for the last ten years?

MP: It felt like a divorce to me. I did not want to be involved with Marillion and music again. I'm sure that people who have been though divorces and split up relationships know that the last thing you want to do is to go through another bad one. You eventually go back to it, but I did not want to be involved in anything musical for some considerable time. I was asked on a few occasions to get back into a band, but I only wanted to do it my way. I formed Marillion, the people that joined that band joined me, not so much like a hand-picked thing but you generally pick people for their personality, their ability, and whether you get on with them okay. It's all very well getting on with someone for a couple of hours, but in a band, it's very much like being in a relationship with somebody. You share so much, not only music, but also being in the same room as somebody for half a day. Also, I could not bear the thought of going back into playing pubs after headlining everywhere. As soon as we started doing this album, I said that I was not going into the back of a van and playing pubs! It's out of the question; I will not do it, because I've done so much of it. As you get older you want little comforts in life like a shower and a bed. I've had the fighting to get into the single bed to see who sleeps in a bed and who sleeps on the floor. I'm beyond that and do not want to go back to it.

I'm a carpenter by trade, a kitchen designer. I formed my own business and have been quite successful. Most people have a day job and I used to do that and then pack the gear up and go off and play at night, get home at 3 am and go to work the next day and do the same thing. We gigged so much, Marillion, more than most bands. The bands that work hard get somewhere if they're good enough. Generally, they get to a stage where they pick up a few fans every time they play, those fans then travel to a gig that might be a bit further away and before you know it you are starting to play in front of two or three hundred people. Then the new people who arrive at a gig think that there is a bit of a buzz going on and enjoy it. I do not want to have to go through that process of going through little gigs and working at that. It seems to me that the way it is done these days is the opposite of the way that we used to do it. In those days, you had an audience and made an album, whereas these days it seems that everyone makes an album before they get an audience. Maybe it is because going to gigs is so expensive and people can't be bothered to leave the comfort of their armchair or because they want to hear what someone is like before they go and see them.

How did you and Clive meet?

MP: The guitarist in Revelation, a couple of years ago, asked me if I knew that there were magazines around with me on the front of it, all dressed up as Father Christmas. I thought, somebody's taking the piss, I'll sue! Three months later the guy that writes the magazine (Silhobbit), Richard Jordan, phoned and I told him that if I did not like it, I would sue, and he got a bit worried about it. I met up with him, and he told me what was happening in this sort of music, and how a lot of people did not like Marillion anymore because they had changed direction, and there was room for other bands playing that old sort of Marillion music. He told me about Clive and the people he is involved with, and the music they do. A couple of months passed by and we met up, then another couple of months passed by and we talked about doing a Mick Pointer solo project, and then after another couple of months we said let's do the album but as a proper band.

CN: We met in a pub and were introduced to each other and the idea was to make an album. A few weeks after that we got together and spent an afternoon writing which was going to be the deciding factor – if we could not work together or the music sounded a bit limp then forget it. It did not, it worked very quickly, and we had a couple of tracks in the bag by the end of the first session. It was a very good writing partnership that felt good, so we thought let's do it. Because of that, ideas developed straight away to the band concept and then after that we thought maybe we should bring this album out ourselves because we were putting all the effort into it. If that first day Mick had come down here and it was not working out, then we wouldn't be here now. The whole thing was very secret. We had written half of the album before anyone knew, even anyone in the house. We thought that we would keep it quiet until we knew what we were going to do with it.

MP: It was November '93 before we got something happening to each other. We had spent a lot of time thinking about what we wanted to do on the album, getting a load of material together for it. Because we worked together so well, we just hit it off immediately.

CN: This is because he was willing to buy the drinks, and I am always willing to give time to someone who does that.

MP: Starting in the middle of November '93 we virtually had the album written by Christmas. It went over a little bit into January, but every time we wrote something, we spent time thinking about it, making sure that we felt that the material was strong enough. There were no lyrics at this stage; it was just getting it musically strong. I wanted to approach it from that direction, the way that Marillion used to write material. A lot of stuff was written before Fish joined the band, there were lyrics, but then he put his own to music such as "Grendel", "The Web", "He Knows You Know" and "Garden Party".

CN: We redeveloped the music with the lyrics. They were not an afterthought; they became the new direction.

MP: We thought let's take a chunk here, split it here, and put a little bit in here. Every time we did that, we took time making sure that it would work, rather than thinking that's it, let's move on. We made sure that we listened to everything after we had done it and the pre-production on the album was enormous, six months at least.

CN: We probably threw away as much material as we used. The easiest thing about the making of the album was the writing and that was great. Things came together easily. It was a very positive thing and people passing through the studio started saying that it sounds good. I thought that this was interesting, what was different about this from everything else I had done? There was a definite vibe about it, and we sensed that quite early on. I think that this is probably what gave us the encouragement to go and do it ourselves. Perhaps it was time to get something back from all that we have put in.

How did you settle on the line-up for Arena? Was it a conscious decision not to involve Karl Groom?

CN: The conscious decision not to involve Karl was more down to the fact that Karl has his own line of things that he does. Obviously for the majority we work together, and it is good occasionally just to separate. He does Threshold and I am not involved in it, it's not my kind of music: I do Pendragon and although he is now involved with the recording side of it, it is more me than him. In a way, we wanted to put together a line-up that was completely fresh: if it had been just me and Karl then everyone would have said it was just another Thin Ice production and they might have enjoyed it, they might not. The idea was to create a line-up that was very special to the band, instead of it being just another combination of the same people, so that was a conscious decision. Also, the general plan was to record our album while he was intending to record Threshold.

MP: We had the drummer and keyboard player already sorted out. The hardest thing in any band is probably the vocalist, because he is the person who gives the identity. That's not putting down the other musicians in the band, but the vocalist is the one who is instantly recognisable for that style of music. Clive was not sure about my enthusiasm for finding the vocalist. Years ago, you used to put an ad in the paper and about 400 vocalists arrived and you sifted your way through it. I put an ad in Melody Maker, which Clive did not think was a good idea, but musicians even these days look in there, that tradition has always continued. There were some good guys, but the one that stood out more than any was John Carson. I got it down to two tapes and I sent them to Clive to have a listen to, but especially John. He sent me a tape that was about ninety minutes long, it was him just singing into a karaoke machine doing twenty-four track stuff. You generally get a tape and you listen to the first thirty seconds, then wind it on for five minutes, but I said to Clive to listen to all of it because parts of it are not very good but parts of it are excellent.

There were certain bits he was doing that could be developed.

CN: There was a song called "Black Sheep Of The Family", and I had put it in and there was something else at the same time it was playing and there was something about the way he sang it, there were elements in it that I thought would appeal to Mick and I listened to it carefully and started to find all sorts of things. First, he had good range, good tuning and sense of rhythm, all the basic things, but there was also a definite character in the voice. We thought this sounds like the man for the job, so we rang him up and told him that the auditions were on such and such a day so he came down thinking that he was simply on day one of a series of auditions but all we wanted to establish was that he was the same man who was on the tape. He was very confused because he spent one hour in the studio and four hours down the pub – the real audition took place there because we knew he could sing but we wanted to find out if we could get on with him. Cliff the bassist I have known for years. He has always been on the scene and it has just been a case of finding the right job for his way of playing and this seemed to be the one. He did a tape for Mick just to prove he could play and that was that.

The guitarists did cause us a problem though. We had Jeff Ward, who is a very good guitarist, at the beginning and I contacted him as he is also a drummer and is very good at getting recorded drum sounds. By the time we had done the recording and started on the guitar parts he was not comfortable with it: it was not his thing and we were trying to force him down a route. We agreed after trying it for several days that he was not going to be the man for the job, and he had also moved to Ireland which made the practicalities a little difficult. I was running out of inspiration so I rang up Mike Stobbie and asked if we could come to his studio for a week and ended up staying for two months. We got another guy which did not work out, and Mike put us onto Keith More who originally came over as a session, but he loved it so much that he joined the band. He is probably the finest guitarist for years, having done Asia and Tina Turner and God knows what else, so he is obviously a very good player and that worked.

Why was the album not completed at Thin Ice, and why was Mike Stobbie involved?

CN: The easiest part was the writing, but the problems began when we tried to turn the dream into a reality. We recorded the drums near where Mick lives, a friend of ours has a studio which was equipped to do drums so we thought we would start there as it was close to home. We chose the hottest two weeks in the summer and all the equipment was breaking down and we ended up recording the drums three times! The multi-track was destroying the tape; the tapes were just melting and all sorts. Once we had got the drums, we came down to Thin Ice and recorded the vocals and bass, but the problem was that Threshold were due in a couple of weeks after that, so we had a deadline. The plan was to stop, let Threshold record, and then come back in and finish which was kind of okay. But we wanted to get the guitars finished before Threshold came in and it was not working with Jeff. I rang Mike up as I was running low on productional inspiration and said how about coming over to his studio for a week. The intention was for him to help us to get the guitars down, and then he got into the album and said how about if we finished the whole damn thing. Mike was good and thoroughly got into it: he cancelled all his advertising work and took over production.

MP: Mike Stobbie's contribution to this is immense.

CN: Everyone involved in this has put in 150%, and that has been the best thing about it. You can tell the difference, and I think that this comes across in the album as well. Keith was originally phoned up and told three days' tops to do the guitar parts, and he was there for two weeks. He started off as a session and left as a member of the band and has already put aside his time to go on tour. While he was there, Asia were ringing him up and asking him to re-join and he stayed with Arena. I recorded all the keyboard parts there as well. I brought some of my stuff, but Mike's got some Moogs and Mellotrons and it was a real opportunity to have a bash at some of them. Once Keith had done his guitar parts I thought "Hey I sound a bit boring now" so we beefed it up. That was the thing, we just kept upping the stakes. First, we started thinking let's just make an album and then it kept getting better.

MP: We intended to bring the album out at the end of September, beginning of October, but as time drew on it became clear that there was no way we were going to meet that.

CN: I had barely finished before I went straight out on tour with Shadowland, and then straight after that there were dates with Pendragon. The mix was finished after I had to go, and I was there for two months so it was probably longer.

MP: The album from start to finish took about four months.

CN: And we brought a new guy in at the end, Teo, who did the mixing. Again, he has had a lot of experience with a lot of different bands, not so much with this area of music. We had Pinnacle up there before the final mixes and Ian Roe said that they would sign it, no problems. Then we went out and celebrated and Cliff set fire to himself. You know Sambuca, the drink they serve at the end of a meal at an Indian restaurant with a little blue flame on top – the trick is to stick your finger straight in and out and your fingers on fire. Cliff waited and looked for a while, then had a go, panicked and the whole thing went over his hand, trousers and the tablecloth, and the whole thing went up in flames. It was on the point of not being funny, but luckily it was funny and not dangerous.

MP: It's strange how everything takes a lot longer than you think it's going to. First, we thought it would take a month, then we changed it to six months.

CN: It has been the longest period I have ever been involved in making an album. We usually expect to record an album in four weeks, five tops. Mick said that he wanted to spend six weeks and I said what do you want to be doing?

MP: A year ago we had all the music in place and here we are, and the album still is not out yet, it's ridiculous how long it takes.

How did you decide on the musical direction?

MP: There was no definite "Let's write this album or that album". I had a lot of musical ideas, either singing or humming into a tape machine, and Clive had lots of ideas about material that he likes. I am sure that some of the stuff that Clive writes is commercial, and some more to the prog end, and at the end we pooled our material, and this is what came out. With me doing it and Clive doing it there was an even chance about what we were going to come up: we were not going to be too far away from early Marillion.

CN: Our original idea was to make the second album that Marillion never made. Mick walked out of the studio from 'Script' and the next time he walked into a studio was now. So, forget the ten years, this was the next stage.

MP: I do not think you can say to yourself let's make a Marillion, Def Leppard or Bon Jovi album because you end up sounding like shit. You must do what comes naturally, and it's inevitable that it is going to sound like early Marillion because of my influence on that and what I was doing then, and what I'm doing now. As far as I'm concerned it is my next album after 'Script'.

CN: I had never co-written when it comes to music, with Geoff he did the lyrics and I did the music. That was great as well, and he was very inspiring, but there was a kind of line between what he was doing and what I was doing whereas here we developed everything together from square one.

What was the idea behind the four-part "Crying For Help"?

CN: Musical mouthwashes. We were building the big songs and we were aware that the overall album had to be a certain size, a certain length. Instead of working on certain songs we thought what we should do is have interludes between the five main pillars of the album, themes and variations. Each of these songs is a development of one very simple thematic motif. It is picked up on the guitar, then on the harpsichord, the next is an atmospheric Pink Floyd sort of thing and then the last one is the fullest version of it. That's all it was, musical interludes to give a chance to breath before the next track.

MP: It's a build-up to the long track at the end.

CN: We could have done these four in a row but doing it this way is nice and interesting and gives the album a symmetry as well. We were thinking a lot of the time about structure, not only to the songs but also to the album. We worked very hard at finding the right pace for the album, we spent time seriously considering what order the songs should be in terms of pace, key and everything. To us the album is structured in such a way as to be a whole.

MP: Once you get to the end of the album you feel that you would like to listen to the whole piece again, rather than just a few bits, but it is not actually a concept album. It was not written with a solid theme throughout it lyrically or anything like that.

Are there any plans for a single?

CN: I think the problem with a single is the investment necessary to make it a practical option. There are a couple of bits on the album that could be made into a single, but the reality is that without some substantial backing it would be very hard to do anything with it. It is not impossible. We are toying with the idea of making a video because there are options to get onto MTV and TV in Poland and a few other places. If you like, that would be the single, but the chances of releasing a single are less likely.

How did Steve Rothery get involved?

MP: About a year ago, when I first started writing the album with Clive, I told John Arnisson, Marillion's manager, that I was doing an album. He told the other guys in the band and after a month or so Steve phoned up and asked if we would like him to play on it. Obviously, it must be good for us if he is involved with it, but the logistics of getting us together and getting it done is something completely different.

CN: It was nice in a way because after all this time, it was almost like getting a stamp of approval from Marillion, getting their official support. It's good for them, good for us, and was a nice move. What's been done on the album is good as well. There are some nice moments a bit different to the rest of the album: it has a flavour of its own, its Steve Rothery.

MP: March last year Clive and I met Steve to discuss how to do it. He wanted to do some production work on the album, but they were about to start the 'Brave' tour and the practicalities of getting together proved impossible. It was decided that he would do a solo and we put together a demo track that we would like him to play on. He wanted a choice, so we gave him a choice of one! He put down about twenty solos, decided on two himself and then left the choice to us.

Why have you started your own label and not signed to any record company?

MP: Because we are fully in control and no-one is telling us what to do and when to do it, and we can call the shots.

CN: We can only blame ourselves if it does not work. We had the faith in the whole idea when it started, and it just seemed the right thing to do. In a way, I think a lot of people did not necessarily think that anything would come of it, they thought that it was just another Silhobbit idea, and we latched onto the potential magic a long time before anyone else. It seemed a logical step to take the experience I have had, together with Mick's business acumen from what he has been doing and just do it ourselves. The beauty of this is that we are our own A & R men, if we are satisfied, we do not have to look up to anybody else. Also, SI Music do a lot of things I'm on, and I did not want to dilute what they are already doing.

MP: We were approached by EMI to take the album either as a distribution or licensing deal and we humoured them for a while to see what they could come up with. There is not such a great gap between what we can do and what they can do as you would initially think. There are only x number of routes that you can go down and people that you can get in contact with.

CN: With EMI, we would have been at the end of a very long catalogue.

MP: I am sure that with EMI we may well have sold more albums, certainly initially, but whether they would have been good for us at the end of the day, we will never know.

CN: The band is our responsibility. Ultimately Verglas was ready to put a lot of effort and time into pushing it which might be a small-scale thing, but ultimately the results might be larger.

Is Verglas just a vehicle for Arena, or are there going to be other bands on it?

MP: Obviously, the future of Verglas will be based around what this album does. If this album does not do anything then we should rethink the future of Verglas.

CN: Verglas will always be a record label; it will not just be for prog music, but it will always have an element with good songs. We have an artist for our theoretical second release called Kimberley. She is very young, about 17, and is very talented with a great voice like Tori Amos and Kate Bush and should have great crossover appeal. It's not just a clone and has a great flavour. We should be recording her album in the summer with a release later this year.

MP: Of course, not every release on Verglas must have Clive Nolan on it, there is room for others.

How is Arena going to break out of the underground prog circuit?

MP: Our first marketing ploy must be to promote me. You must use every conceivable angle that you have got. I desperately tried to avoid using the term "Prog Rock", I do not want to put a label on it.

CN: If you accept that prog is an attitude and not a sound then you could possibly call what we are doing as prog. If prog has got to be a particular type of sound then how are you going to establish what that is, considering the wide variation. What we are doing here is melodic rock, it's rock, it's songs. You could say that it is prog, but it is more than that, a lot of bands are. They appeal to prog rock fans but that does not mean that it is the end of their appeal. We are not aiming to sell songs to a couple of thousand people throughout the world who buy fanzines that write about this type of music. We tried to write and produce an album that will appeal to heavy metal fans, to pop fans, to indie fans. We come from a prog rock background, but that is a starting point and not a finishing point.

MP: Marillion fan clubs have been brilliant: they've been doing articles about me and have written about the album. That alone takes us out of the underground prog rock scene. I do not think that just Marillion fans are going to like this album.

CN: It is an album music much more than single music: it is for the CD buying market.

When are we likely to see Arena gigging?

November. There are a lot of practicalities. Firstly, we must sell the album – we've put up quite a lot of money, plus a tour costs money, so not only have we got to break even we have to make some money so we can put it into the tour. Also, we have five high profile musicians who had other commitments even before Arena was thought of. If we are going out, we want to make this a good show, one that is going to knock a lot of people's socks off. That means rehearsal time, and making the whole thing more of a production, not just standing up on stage. We want to do reasonably sized gigs, and we want them to have an impact. Obviously if we could end up doing a couple of supports with Marillion that would be great.

The tour is designed to be a vehicle where Arena will promote Arena, we do not actually think of ourselves as an underground band. We are going to try and do everything as can to make the show a show and are talking about all sorts of possibilities from make-up to backdrops. The beauty of having Mick in the band is that we cannot be called Marillion rip offs. We are going to go in to create something that to the best of our abilities is special to this band. Already we are starting to plan the tour and it will take us at least six months before we have set dates.

MP: Where could we possibly play if we bring the album out and go on tour? We must make everybody Arena aware and it is going to take six or seven months to do that.

What's happening to Shadowland?

CN: The next Shadowland album is due to be recorded straight after the Kimberley album. Mike Varty will be playing keyboards on the album along with me. With Strangers On A Train we are expecting to record a new album at the beginning of 1996. Then we are planning to do one big gig in Holland with loads of musicians where we will be performing songs from all three albums.

Have you any tracks you have not used?

CN: No, but we have just got back on the horse and started writing again Hopefully we will start writing the next album in the next couple of months and this time it will be a bigger job because not only are we going to write it, but it will be a band thing. All the band are invited to be writers and they all have ideas, so we should draw all these different lines together, and it will come to us and we will act as a kind of filter. It is very much our band. We hope to have the album written by the end of 1995 and recorded in the summer next year.

My thanks to Clive and Mick for a wonderful afternoon. The Arena album is brilliant, and anyone who remotely likes good melodic rock will fall in love with it on first hearing.

Fish, #29, Jun 1995

This year has seen Fish in the recording studio working on two albums, set for release in the autumn. They cover songs from all areas of his career both as a solo artist and as a member of Marillion. Now seemed to be a good time to catch up with him and find out what was happening.

How is the recording for 'Yin' and Yang' going?

We finished in March. The album was originally scheduled to go out in June, but there was a problem with a big management restructure in the German distribution company and if we had put the album out when that hadn't been completed we could have lost a lot of impetus, a lot of sales. We also had a load of stuff to do in Japan so rather than rush the album out we put the release back to September. The first single is going to be "Lucky" which is coming out on 7th August in the UK, and the albums are coming out in the UK on September 14th.

They're both coming out on the same date?

Yes, the masters are just coming back from America now where they've been mastered by Bob Ludwig so it's a serious piece of work. We've gone into it and have recorded a lot of tracks; there are 14 re-recordings out of the 26 tracks across the two albums. I think each album is 72 or 73 minutes long, so it's a humongous collection. We've got special guests like Steve Howe who spent hours on "Time and a Word", Capercaillie are playing on a couple and Alan Dean's on one of the ones we've resurrected from the EMI sessions back in 1989. Then we've got people like Sam Brown, who has done a duet on "Just Good Friends" and backing vocals on a track, "Favourite Stranger", It's a devastating collection.

How far have you gone back with the selection?

We went back. I did not do the 'Script' era material because I felt it was kind of awkward to do; I think the simplicity of it did not warrant any re-recording. Also, I did not want any original recordings from the Marillion era. My band has been together for nearly four years now, apart from a change in drummer, and there is a tightness, an energy, a style to the band and in concert we play a lot of Marillion songs as well as from throughout the years. Rather than just send out the Marillion songs as yet another reissue of EMI material, we re-recorded them and put a different energy into them. I used the studio experience I have accumulated over the last fourteen years, and the technology we've got available, but at the same time kept it stripped down and did not wander into the realms of over-production. It has ended up as a very lean album and the life and spark of energy that is in some of the stuff like "Incubus" has meant that we are very, very pleasantly surprised at what we have managed to achieve.

A "best of" collection was overdue from myself; Marillion had put theirs out in '92 and it was basically just a couple of remixes and one new track. Instead of putting out the same old numbers I wanted to show a lot of the solo period at the same time. With not having

played a lot of territories, not having had a lot of exposure outside of Europe, I felt that 'Yin' and 'Yang' would provide a passport to those areas. We wanted to provide the existing fans in Europe with a package that was interesting, which was the cue for the re-recordings. This meant that it was a very good value for money package for the fan who has been with me for a long time and also for those who stopped buying it because of the confusion with my move to Polydor and integration. I wouldn't say that it was a relaunch, but it is a big introduction of Fish into Europe and a passport to take me into new territories. In the last week, we've done Singapore and Hong Kong and sold out a 5,000-seat capacity in Istanbul, so the Dick Brothers label is moving all over the world. 'Yin' and 'Yang' are a perfect vehicle for what we are doing right now.

You mention the band, is Micky Simmonds back with you now?

No, although Micky came up to play on "Incubus" with Kevin. We've a good relationship with all the past band members and Micky's contribution to "Incubus" back in 1991 and 1992 was phenomenal so I wanted to get him back. He's a great prog rock keyboard player and he was just perfect for it. Micky hasn't been in the band since he left in March 1992.

He played with you at the recent London dates, didn't he?

That's right – Foss and David Paton were called up to play at a Hogmanay show, so we got a bass player from up here and Micky Simmonds came along without any hassles and did a spectacular job in London. We've a good vibe with family past and present and people can walk in and play the material to a high standard. We have a lot of fun as a travelling unit.

When can we expect the brand-new material to come out?

The next one is called 'Sunsets On Empire' and we're starting to write that this summer. Currently, we have some dates booked from the end of August when we are doing some charity gigs in the UK and then from there we are go into Europe and South Africa, where "Lady Lies" is a Top 40 hit at present, and then we've a month in SE Asia. We're pretty much booked until the end of December and then into January where we've some festivals booked in Vietnam. We do not envisage going into the studio to record and finish off writing until February, March, April which would probably mean it being scheduled for a September release next year.

How do you go about writing the material?

Usual painful process. There are a lot of little hook lines that start flying around, little melodies and rhythmic ideas and it all crystallizes over quite a long period. There's no fixed formula or format to work to. A lot of the sets we do now are more acoustic based, and I would like to do a more acoustic based album focussing very much on the melodies and grooves. As you rightly pointed out, the next album should follow-up reasonably quickly on 'Yin' and 'Yang' and if we can get it out within a year then that would be perfect.

How is 'Suits' doing?

Very well, it's still selling 500 copies every month, particularly in places like France. In Britain, it probably does 100 copies a month as people are still discovering it. We can sense the positive reaction just through the growth of the fan club, The Company, which is going from strength to strength. I think that the patience I've had is paying off now and 'Yin' and 'Yang' is definitely going to get my career back up to the level it should be in the UK.

How do you view media in the UK?

It's sad, even if you pick up Music Week, you'll find a huge thing on dance music which is alright for singles charts but apart from Various Artists, album acts are being ignored. There again, Portishead's album was platinum pretty much before the single came out as it came up through the underground and grew over a long period. It is reassuring to find that there are opportunities for albums to grow, but it is nice to get a healthy wedge in the door first.

What sort of packaging is going to be with 'Yin' and 'Yang'?

We got permission from EMI to do all the re-recording and stuff, but I did not want to go too much into nostalgia corner. The cover artwork is basically two trout with the 'Yang' album being two white trout and the 'Yin' album being two black trout and there is a 16-page booklet. Fin Costello came up with a lot of black and white shots in keeping with the spirituality of the album, it's all very much up to date material. Also, it reflects the fact that the album is built around re-recordings more than me just pulling all the old tracks off and putting them on an album, which I think from a production perspective would have been a bit of a mish mash. The sleeves reflect that in the way that there is a lot of energy, a new soul about, so to speak.

If you came across someone who had never heard your music, how would you describe it to them?

It's rather good!! It's a bit like asking someone to describe their face, when you use it every day in the mirror it's rather hard to find perspective on it. I find that is the same with music. It blends a lot of stuff, what you would call the traditional progressive rock ethic, into dance grooves like “Mr 1470”. I went through a period where I hated the term ‘progressive rock’, but now I feel that there is probably a lot more progression in it. We are very much open to modern sounds, modern influences, and rather than let them work us we work them in conjunction with the traditional Fish style, to try and keep it with a modern edge. It’s more like movies for your ears than the Chinese style of rock music that you get nowadays.

Why did you start Dick Brothers?

Dissatisfaction with the major record companies, realising that we were not selling enough albums to keep a major totally interested, we were more in a holding pattern than anything else. What we have done here is shape a mean little guerrilla outfit that is very highly mobile, very highly flexible, and we are maximising our earnings now. It makes a lot more sense to have the control. We manage ourselves; we are our own record company; we are our own publishing company and we have the studio. It’s a lot like an elaborate cottage outfit, and it has helped me creatively and given me a percentage of freedom. With ‘Yin’ and ‘Yang’ if we can go out and get a gold album in the UK then I am going to be absolutely over the moon. It’s going to mean a degree of consolidation after a period of five or six years of a lot of doubt and a lot of negativity going around. It’s important to me to have an outlet like that just to work with. With a major, if you do a bad album, then the recovery is far more difficult, so many questions are drawn about your creativity and bankability. With Dick Brothers if I were to put out a bum album, I mean one that is not received well, then it’s not such a desperate situation. It is nice to take that sort of pressure off, which means that I can be more flamboyant with my style.

What plans are there for Dick Brothers, apart from Fish?

We have a band called The Dream Disciples who are on the road in June. They are a young live band working in a very hard area of the market, in the rock mould with a hint of The Mission, The Doors and early progressive stuff. We are about to sign another act called Tam White who is a Scottish blues singer who has been around for an awful long time and has been deserving a break. I have no plans to become some big sprawling monstrosity and want to keep it clean and pristine. That is the magic of it: I have no interest in becoming a mini-major or anything like that.

How is the studio going?

It’s going great! Then Jericho are in now, finishing their album, then Iona are coming in for two weeks, Kit Clarke will be in for the summer, and then we’ve Tam White’s album as well. Del Amitri recorded some of their last album there as well.

If you were to be remembered for one song which one would it be, and why?

Probably “Kayleigh”, as it is the most successful song I have ever had, but I think when people hear “Just Good Friends”, the duet I’ve done with Sam Brown, and it may well overtake that as it is such a brilliant song. Also, there are a lot of my songs that have just gone missing, stuff like "A Gentleman's Excuse Me", but on a personal level I think that the song which is closest to me is "Raw Meat". I'm proud of that lyric, I got a lot out of my system with that lyric.

How do you deal with the grind of touring, as you show in "Raw Meat"?

I love gigs and hate touring. It's been nice for the last couple of weeks to do Singapore, with a few days off before, then have a few days off before Hong Kong, then a few days off before we did Luxembourg, and the same with Istanbul. It was great, but financially it was a nightmare. It's nice to be able to go out with your voice at full throttle. I always get depressed when are on tour with the wear and tear on the voice. I'm going through a non-smoking phase this year, and I've been seeing a speech therapist as well. I've found out that I've been breathing completely wrong, which has put an extra strain on my voice, but over the last month or so that training has made my performances a lot easier and put a lot of life into my voice. We are touring for four months this year, but agents have already been told that we want breaks, not just one big slog. A) We've got families and B) we've our physical and mental health to consider. Someone is paying a fixed price to see you perform and they do not want to see someone croaking away. My lifestyle on tour has completely changed since the days of 1987.

Seven years down the road how do you now view the Marillion split? You seem a lot happier and settled than you did a few years ago.

Yes, I am. Marillion became a big stumbling awkward monster and it was going to trip up and fall, and I am very glad that I left when I did. I left at the top, I did not leave it when it began to spiral out of control, which I felt it was about to do. Creatively the chemistry between the five members at that time has changed, and what was coming out of that chemistry was not very palatable. If I had left the band after a bum album people would have said that I was a rat leaving a sinking ship, but I left fans with good memories of a certain period. I rather that people talk about the album that could have been, rather than the album that was shit that was. They could do their own thing; they are happier doing the technical stuff and I'm more interested in doing the soul stuff. I have no regrets.

We went to Istanbul with 5000 people who had their lighters in the air, and the production manager said that it was like Lorelei. Yes, it was, but it did not have the hassle and unpleasantness that surrounded the band in a business sense. The only thing I regret about leaving Marillion is the fact that we did not manage to salvage the friendship. The water is still passing under that bridge for them. For me it is a long time ago and I just do not give a damn, I'm too long in the tooth to be holding a grudge for seven years. I'm just looking forward to the next couple of months, which could prove very interesting. One of the songs on this album is "Institution Waltz", which was never recorded by Marillion and has been lying about for years. Everybody hated it apart from me, but I loved it, loved the lyric on it. It's been interesting taking a song like that, then all the way up to re-recording "Somebody Special" for this album. It's been very interesting, and I'm looking forward to the reviews.

John Dexter Jones (Jump), #30, Aug 1995

September 25th sees the release of Jump's fourth album. 'The Myth of Independence'. After the success of their three earlier albums on Salad, 'Winds Of Change', 'World Of Wonder' and 'All The King's Men', they have now signed to Cyclops and Mr. Mark Kelly of Marillion has produced the album.

So, how did Mark Kelly get involved?

Mark first saw us play last year, in 1995 at the Marillion fan club convention.

How did you get that gig?

We got that in the first place because we had played the venue where it was, about a month before. There was a DJ there called Steve Wheeler who enjoyed the band and at the time he was helping The Web with their database. They were looking for a band and he said that he had seen a good one and that they ought to check us out. We got that gig, and the only member of Marillion who was there, was Mark who was with John Wesley who was playing as well. We went down well and had a chat with Mark outside who said that he enjoyed it. He put his name down on our mailing list and became a subscriber to the newsletter. Then in September last year he phoned me up and asked if a gig was still on, I told him that it was, so he came down to it. After that things moved swiftly. He had obviously considered it all and had taken away a copy of the last album and had liked it. He asked us what we were doing, and we told him that we were planning to record again, and he said that he would like to get involved in that side of things. He had produced the John Wesley album and we liked that, the production, and then we were shown around the Racket Club and it was suggested that we move our recording base to there, which sealed it. He came down to our rehearsals, all the pre-production and stuff. It was not a case of him fiddling about and letting us get on with what we were doing; he was involved from the basic skeletons of the writing, right through the arranging.

Did he have much to do with the music?

He did a lot of steering, a lot of what we hoped a producer would do. We had written the stuff and we presented arrangements to him, and he suggested other ways of trying it.

From that you got the Marillion convention gig again

That's right, it was the equivalent gig. It was the Web Convention, which coincided with the release of the new album. We played at the album preview party and we got that along with Jadis. The Marillion acoustic set was reviewed in Kerrang! and in that issue was a letter from someone saying that it was the best six pounds that he had ever spent.

When you play live you are a very dramatic band, there is a lot going on. There is real interplay between the whole band, and I feel that an apt description would be of a Sensational Alex Harvey Band for the Nineties. Is that fair?

The first time the name Alex Harvey came up was in Blindsight some time ago, and he had never seen the band, this was just from the music. It has also come up a few times after gigs and a friend of mine gave me a video of Alex Harvey on the Old Grey Whistle Test, and after seeing that I can live with the description, as they were such a dramatic band. They were theatrical, but also a bit tongue in cheek, a bit of self-parody but not too much and that sits quite easily with me. I do not get worried with any comparison with any good band, whatever it is. Some people fight shy of comparisons, but I think that to be compared with a band as good as them, that can't be bad. I think I've got a lot more in common with Alex Harvey than with things a bit more regular, things that we are normally compared with. Maybe not so much Alex Harvey in a Seventies sense, but SAHB in a Nineties sense, could be.

How would you describe Jump to someone?

Probably badly. It's a rock band, I do not know what type of rock band, but it is definitely a rock band. It's rock music because there are guitars, electric guitars, and the music is dominated by these and then spiced up with Mo's keyboards. Mo's keyboards are to me the crucial elements, if they were not there then it would be a hard rock band, but the fact that they are there colours the music. Whatever kind of thing she is playing flavours what is effectively two guitars, which for a lot of the time are giving it some stick. We are a rock band with different styles drawing from many different influences. We are not afraid if there is a little bit of dub in there, or a bit of 3/4 like Alex Harvey. It draws from a lot of things like folk: I'm very into folk and folk festivals and probably go to more folk gigs than rock gigs now. Huey, the bass player, is into Cardiacs now, and we are both big Talking Heads fans, and the guitar players are big rock fans.

We are a rock band that draws from lots of different influences that sounds like itself, not many bands do. One of the things we are trying to be is musical! We analyse everything. If we write something and we are there in the studio we can be blowing away for ten minutes and think it's fantastic, but when you hear the tape a week later you may ask why are we doing it for so long? It's all honing, keeping it musical and keeping it fluid instead of bashing away on the same thing, even if the same thing is good. We try to not to do things to excess, perhaps. The idea is to keep it as musically good as we can, that's how it comes across, and to be entertaining as well.

This is your fourth album, so why now sign to Cyclops?

In the UK, it does not make a lot of difference. Malcolm has distribution with Pinnacle in the UK, and we had distribution when we were with Salad. Salad was something we were involved with the guy where we were recording, who ran the label. Malcolm will agree that what he can do in the UK is very much the same, it is down to us, we must get out there and play and people have to come to gigs. Obviously, we hope that Mark's involvement, and the fact that Malcolm has become more established, will help. When Sony signed Echolyn to him in Europe it showed just how far he has come with Cyclops. In the UK, it is down to us selling at gigs, and on the basis that we are never going to get a great deal of airplay. We got one or two plays on GLR, and one allegedly on Virgin, for the last album and that is not a lot. We are not expecting a great deal more. We are expecting to expand our market in the UK just the same as if we had stayed with Salad, but crucially it is Europe where Malcolm and Cyclops can hopefully help us. I would be lying if I said that we had a toehold in Europe, and we want to develop that. We play gigs in North Wales and it would be nearer for us to play gigs in Holland. But we need to get profile over there before we do it. Malcolm has a good distribution network out there in Holland, Germany and new fields opening like Italy, and Salad just could not do that. To be able to play places like Germany, and thus develop further, we needed somebody who already had the machinery in place, because it is hellish difficult to start up. Malcolm knows the pitfalls; he knows the things not to do. It would have been like going back to square one, back to 'Winds Of Change' days in the UK and we did not want to do that.

What's the next step?

The next step is to get out there in September and do a bunch of gigs here there and everywhere, there is no doubt about that. I rather suspect your question is what after that. In the short term, it's to get out and do some gigs to promote the album in the UK and maintaining our profile as we do. We are opening at The Forum for Marillion on the first date of their UK tour and that must be the most prestigious date on the tour. We will do that and hope again that it generates a little more profile and we finish that around about the end of November and then we have a well-earned break. January, we will spend probably rehearsing and writing again. I think that if you ever stop that process and stand still, in fact you are not just standing still but moving backwards. There will be new material with plans to record, but over what timescale I do not know. This is a one album deal with Cyclops so we are not over pressurised particularly, if we feel that it will be mutually beneficial to sit down with Malcolm after 'Myth of Independence' has been gigged then we will. We already know that we are going to be gigging hard throughout February, March and April, and then next summer we are going to try and get ourselves some festival slots. We have reached the stage now that we have played so many gigs, approaching 500 together with an unchanged line-up, that we would like to play some of the bigger audiences that we do not have to drag to the place. We will try to leave some space over the middle period of next year to sort out some events in Europe.

Has having Mark Kelly producing changed the sound?

Yes, it has improved it once again. I think that the steps we took through the first three albums, all improved right from the first one, which was recorded pretty much all live in under forty-eight hours. For the second one we had a little bit more time and a few more ideas so we tried them out but did not go over the top. On 'All The King's Men' we had a little bit more time again, because we had that much more money to spend in the studio. That was better, but as a self-produced thing 'All The King's Men', if not the apex, I think we were in danger on this one, even though we feel that the material is stronger, of doing the same album again. We needed that much more experience. To be producing you need to have a wealth of resources we do not claim to have and when Mark came it to do it, we accepted that if he was going to change the sound radically then that was what was going to happen. After all, he is the producer of the album, and there you go. What happened was that he opened our eyes to a lot of things about ourselves. In a sense, he was quite ruthless about what we dropped after we recorded them. To me it is the tightest thing we've ever done, it's a tight bitey sort of sound. The vocals are very much up front, but there are less of them. There are not nearly as any multi-tracked vocals as there have been before, so although they are more in your face there is still plenty of room around them.

The other thing is how we recorded the backing tracks. Instead of Andy being in a room and me counting him through bars, which is very difficult, like playing in a vacuum and possibly being sterile, the Racket Club is a big room and we all got in there and all had live monitors and we all played at the same time. The drum tracks that were recorded were recorded while the band were playing and blowing away through the songs. The drumming to me is sparkier, and that helps. Although we did not tape much of the stuff we did while we were doing the back tracks, the odd thing does appear. That gave us a stronger basis for going in and doing our stuff and there is more space throughout the material on this album than there was on the last one. The production is different, good and sharp. We wanted to try and put some of that Jump live feel onto an album and I do not think that we succeeded in the past. This one has more on it in common with our live act.

The issues dealt with on the material are not quite the same as on 'All The King's Men', where perhaps there was a theme of songs dealing with global issues and how they affected people e.g. "Shed No Tears" was about Yugoslavia and "Share The Shame" was about the Gulf.

That's right, these are more personal, people stories. They are the other way around now, looking at individuals. "Tower of Babel" for instance, is about confusion of languages. I was pulled up after a gig for swearing, and at first I apologised for offending anyone and then I got to thinking that this a bit hypocritical as the person having a go at me had said that we all swear but there is a time and a place. What time, what place? I'll decide that. Princess Di, and her complaining that she felt that the press had raped her inspired "Princess of the People". I just wish that I could get the same amount of coverage that she does, there are little personal ironies on this one, "Drivetime" is about being sold independence by having cars, cruising free along the highway but we all sit on the North Circular going along at two miles an hour. We're independent you know, all ten thousand of us in a line. Whereas the last one was a global thing, this is a little more personal observation that anyone might make about things that are a little closer to their lives.

After 'All The King's Men' I wanted to say what I felt but did not want to be thought of as a pompous git preaching it all: they are little snapshots of people.

Chrissie Hammond was involved again?

This time she had rough monitor mixes that I sent from the studio on cassette. We picked her up and brought her to the studio and although there is not much on there, what there is we spent more time on. It is probably subtler than the last one, and as a singer listening to her every time is like a revelation. I just sit there thinking how did she do that? Mark was very impressed with her and it gives us a little sprinkling of magic dust with that quality. She's got more talent in her little finger than I will ever possess in my whole life. It's just fortunate to be able to call on mates like that and obviously, it gives a little bit more interest to Rick Wakeman fans.

I hope that this interview will give you a small insight into the wonderful new album by Jump, which could well be the breakthrough that they deserve.

Stu Nicholson (Galahad), #32, Dec 1995

I've just caught up with Stu Nicholson, vocalist with Galahad, to reflect on a very busy year for the band, and to discover their plans for 1996.

How has 'Sleepers' been received so far?

As far as the fanbase of the band are concerned then the reaction has been positive. There has been a sigh of relief that most people are pleased with the product at the end of the day. There have been one or two detractors, who think that it is not as good as what we have done before and that certain things are not right, but to be honest this time we have had a lot of hassles and at times our hearts were not in it because we have been bogged down in other things that shouldn't have affected the music. We are very happy with the way it turned out, and the production is the best we have done, although there are things that I would have done in different ways. But I am sure that everyone in the band has his own idea about the way things should be done – we are pleased with the overall outcome. We have been getting some positive press from the progressive rock arena but as far as the wider press are concerned, we have had very little because it is difficult trying to get publicity and exposure. Even Kerrang! have not done anything this time.

1991 saw you as BBC Radio 1 Rock War winners. Do you think that the progressive rock scene has changed in those four years?

Yes, it has changed; there is no doubt about it. There are probably more progressive rock acts about these days then there were then. Until we had recorded 'Nothing Is Written' we only really knew the older progressive bands and also obviously, Pendragon, IQ and Twelfth Night because they were around while we were coming up. Then suddenly we have had a mushrooming of other bands coming into the arena, which I feel is quite

helpful for the genre, as it were. It shows that younger people and musicians are still interested in playing that kind of music, whatever that type of music is. I think "progressive rock" as a label has been left behind in terms of the mainstream press, even though there are minority organisations promoting it. It is doing quite well abroad, in Japan and the Eastern Bloc countries such as Poland it is doing well and even in America as well. I do not think that progressive music is any worse off than another music really. Even Heavy Rock is suffering a bit now, and I think live music in general has suffered over the last few years because young people seem to have so many other things to occupy themselves.

What plans do you have for Galahad to re-promote themselves?

We have been working on this. We went to Europe to promote the album, and did a tour over there, which was great fun. The gigs themselves were great, with the reaction in Holland much better than you would ever get over here, except for one or two places. Unfortunately, our tour bus broke down and our driver has a stammer and we had a very bad experience trying to get hold of the RAC, which had provided cover for the tour bus. We were stranded in Austria and could not get to the gig in Italy. We had to ring the venue to say that we could not make it and apparently, there were over 350 people waiting. We have got a lot of goodwill to rebuild over there now, and all in all it has been a bit of a nightmare and has cost us quite a lot of money in lost revenue and caused us a lot of fuss and frustration at the time. Now, we are trying to sort it all out.

The Galahad Acoustic Quintet CD came out earlier this year, what was the reasoning behind that?

This was my idea. I was getting so frustrated with 'Sleepers' taking so long, and I was not doing anything musical or creative, which is the whole idea of being in a band in the first place. I was feeling stifled by what was going on, as we never knew from one week to the next whether we would be able to go in and mix the record and it is very difficult to concentrate on doing anything else. The initial idea was to do a four-track piano/vocal EP with Mark Andrews, our old keyboard player, who was also interested in the old songs that we knew Galahad would never record. We went to Rob at Voiceprint and he said that he would be prepared to finance it and suggested recording an album. We wrote a few new songs and it was exciting to rehash and rebuild old Galahad material. I got a friend of mine from school, Sarah Quilter, who is a sax and flute player, to add a different dimension to it and although I did not think Roy would be interested, he was, so he played guitar. I wanted it to be all acoustic guitar because we had never done anything like it before, and it gave the band a different angle. It was just something to do at the time and it alleviate a lot of the frustrations we were having.

Are you going to do a follow-up or is it just a one-off project?

Basically, we have left it open. I know that Sarah wants to record again, but she has just had a baby so hasn't got a lot of time now. I still see Mark quite a lot and the others are keen, so there is a possibility of doing something in the future, but it probably wouldn't be so folky. I would like to branch out and so some other stuff, maybe some blues or something.

There was quite a lot of controversy over the cover of 'Sleepers', what was the reasoning behind it?

We just thought that it was a beautiful picture of a beautiful girl, a wonderful image. Her eyes are closed, which ties in quite well with 'Sleepers'. The "Julie-Ann" connotations are nice and even "Pictures of Bliss" goes quite well with it. It is not a concept album, but the imagery tied in and it was not until later that we were told about the controversy of the cover. The guy who took the photo was a very good friend of Karl's who worked for a large advertising agency in London, and we were gobsmacked when he told us that she was not of this earth, as it were. It is a beautiful image and we wanted to get away from the prog rock imagery simply because we wanted something a little modern, and a little up to date, so that someone looking at it in a record shop wouldn't necessarily look at it and think "Oh no, progressive rock". We did not want a Roger Dean or Mark Wilkinson type of cover and did not want to be lumped in with other bands and accused of plagiarising their covers. We wanted to be different.

What are you working on now?

As you are speaking to me, I am in a farmhouse that is on a flat piece of land up in Nottinghamshire in the middle of nowhere, snow has just fallen, and it is quite bleak now. We are currently working on a gig that we recorded at the Classic Rock Society in April this year, we have mixed two tracks so far and we are going to start on the third in about ten minutes. This will hopefully come out as a live album in the New Year as we are very pleased with the way that it has turned out and the live material is good as it shows the band in its' true spirit, its' true light. Hopefully it will capture the rockiness of the band because amongst some of the detractors we have had people saying that it sounds too clean, which is just the way that the albums have been produced. We are a rock band, not just a progressive rock band, and feel that we can rock out as good as anybody. Also, the 'Other Crimes and Misdemeanours II' (a fan club only tape) is going to be mastered and we are going to put that out on CD in the New Year.

What about the first 'Crimes'?

The problem with that tape is just the quality of the recording is terrible. I do not think we can justify that on CD, also some of the tracks are on 'Other Crimes II' anyway as better-quality recordings. If someone was to bootleg it and it was treated as a bootleg CD, we wouldn't mind so much, but people buying a CD expect a certain quality and we want to make sure that people do not think we are duping them or something. Even with 'Other Crimes II' it is going to be difficult, but there are things on there which people keep asking for on CD, and we would like to put it out as it contains the bits between the bits, as it were. Most of the songs on there are much shorter and show a more commercial element to the band, almost a rockier edge to the band. I do not think that much of it could be classed as progressive rock really, apart from the last song, which you do not know about. We are going to put "The Chamber of 32 Doors" on there as well (a track Galahad recorded for a Genesis tribute album). Not a lot of people are going to hear 'The River of Constant Change', and we are very happy with our version of that song. At the moment, we are making sure that it is airtight with Hit & Run Music and other bodies.

Is there a working title for the live album?

Yes, it's a bit of a pun and is not to be taken seriously at all. It is called 'Classic Rock Live'.

Nick Barrett (Pendragon), #34, Apr 1996

With the new album 'The Masquerade Overture' just about to hit the shops, it seemed like a good time to catch up with Nick for a chat

So, what is 'The Masquerade Overture'?

The whole thing is about the influences of good and evil. The idea started out just before Max (*his son*) was born, and it starts off from when someone is born right the way through until they die. It is about the influences of good and bad spirits, which I think are around us all the time: that's why the characters on the front cover represent good and bad, and all the others around are involved in that. The masquerade bit is that it is all an illusion, an illusion over what is good and what is bad.

On the cover, why is the Toff carrying a violin?

The idea behind that was we were going to have a swordfight, but the power of music and communication, along with that attitude, is mightier than the sword. Again, it is an illusion thing.

Do you discuss with Simon Williams, the artist, exactly what you want, or does he throw ideas at you?

I usually pretty much give him a list, saying things like "Toff character with violin, bow pointing at baddy" and he does a few sketches. The first one he came up with was the same background, but the main Toff character look a little bit tame and I told him that we wanted him to look a lot more aggressive. It's difficult to explain your ideas to someone, but I told him that I wanted the Toff to look as if he was saying “I'm going to knock your flipping block off” and that's what he got with it. He does an incredible amount of research, even with the frog, to make sure that he got the right kind of frog. For the violin, he went out and borrowed a violin. All the characters are based on people he knows, and he uses their facial expressions.

The scene is set in Venice isn't it?

Yes, it is. I went to Venice with my wife and I thought the magic of the place was amazing, stunning. Masks seem to be a big thing over there, and it fitted in quite well with what I wanted to do with this album.

How do you feel that the music has moved on from 'The Window Of Life'?

With each album, we tend to get more and more deeply into it, and I suppose on this album spent a lot longer getting what we actually thought was good, there was higher quality control and I kicked out a lot of stuff we thought was not really up to scratch. We were aiming for a certain kind of direction, sound and style, and that comes over. It sounds a bit deeper than 'Window', which probably sounds a bit deeper than 'The World'. Each time there is more concentration on trying to achieve the correct result, and it gets harder as well as these days if I do not think a certain lyrical line says what I want then out it goes, whereas before if it was pretty much okay then it would stay. With the performances, this time we kept with it until we got exactly what we wanted.

Your own studio has been set up for a couple of years now, which must have helped, as the last time you were still working on it when you were recording.

Yes, that was tough because last time we had just finished it but did not have all the gear in, but now we have been there a couple of years and we know what it sounds like and have adjusted a few things such as speakers. We've also got some better equipment such as new microphones and things for the drum kit while last time we begged and borrowed anything we could get. It was all very very rushed and Gavin, who mixed it, only had five days to do the whole thing so there was not any time for judgement, which I hate. I can't stand doing things that quickly; I like to do a mix and then go away and listen to it. Listen to it the next day; listen to it on a Walkman, in the car, on someone else's system etc. just to get a good idea of where it is going. Quite often, a few months after the album is released, if it is done quickly then you can think that certain parts are far too loud while others are too quiet. This time we have made sure that have it pretty much as right as we can. To anyone else it will sound like a normal Pendragon sound, but we feel more satisfied with it because we have achieved more of what we aimed for.

Pendragon has an extremely settled line-up

Yes, this line-up has been going since the tail end of '86. Many bands in their infancy find it tough: it's difficult as you are finding out about each other's characters and there is always a lot of antagonism over certain things. Our early days were hell, even up to 'The Jewel' ('85) as there was always someone who clashed with someone else but now nobody can be bothered so that has made life a lot easier. Everybody knows their position, knows what it is all about, knows what they are going to get and what is required of them. It works very well, but there is nothing to say that tomorrow someone may phone up and say, "I don't want to do it anymore".

As it stands, it seems to be a good way of working and a lot of the tension has gone. With many new bands, someone often feels that they are being hard done by, or they are not being given the same amount of time to record their part as somebody else and it is this sort of thing that makes a difference. I do not see the point in changing it if everybody is happy to keep doing it. Even this line-up, in the early days probably had a few difficult times, and when Fudge first joined we did not really see eye to eye. We did initially, but when it came down to touring and recording, we had a few arguments but now so much has changed. Since we have our own studio everyone can have as much time as they like to record, whereas before it was, "I only have ten days to do my bit". My attitude has changed a lot and I have learned a lot about dealing with people, and that has also made a difference.

You're also settled with Karl as a producer.

Yes, we like to groove in Groomaphonic! Karl is a very rare breed. A lot of engineers we have worked with before have done maybe one or two albums, but it has always been quite tense. Sometimes in the studio it can be quite nasty, nothing is ever said, it is just the way it is. Towards the end of the day, if you are working long hours, everyone is getting a bit tired and there is this inter-band tension because someone earlier in the day did not like your lead guitar riff, so there is all of that. You always feel with producers that you must be a bit wary when you ask for a bit more treble, or the snare drum higher up, but with Karl it is easy to say what you feel. He takes it very well and is good to work with – very easy, very professional, very efficient, and very silly.

How did ProgFest go? (Pendragon recently headlined the American festival)

Frogpest! It was great! Being the first gig we had done for a long time we were probably a little bit shaky. We looked at a lot of the material we thought people would want to hear and played it. We played a lot of stuff from 'Window Of Life' as that has been quite available, and we played some of 'The World' as that had also been released there. It was quite strange as people over here have known us from "Black Knight" and have gone on from there, but in America it was "Great, you played "Breaking The Spell" but it was also nice to hear some old classics dipped into like "Alaska" or "Black Knight". They did not realise that we do not play those songs very much. Many people thought that it was the ideal set as it covered right across the spectrum. We only played "The Voyager" and "Shame" from 'The World', and some very old stuff like the "Excalibur" medley but we were a bit rusty. We had a week's rehearsal, but you can rehearse for three or four weeks and still not be tight onstage, it is gigs that tighten us up. If we do lots of gigs then the band starts to play well and there is a fluid sense to the whole set, and we start cooking.

We did not play any gigs over here at all in '95 as nowadays there is so much concentration on the album. It's a strange setup I suppose, because people wonder how long does it take to write an album, how long does it take to walk on stage? Those are two end results and the things they do not see is that we do not have a record company, agent, or a promotions company – those are all things I do. To do it properly takes up a lot of time. For example, stuff like the folder promoting the new album must be put together manually, and I always feel with each new release that we want to do better things and make a bigger splash. I do not see the point in going out and playing loads of gigs as we did that in the early days and it just got everyone down. It's fun to get into the back of a transit van and tour around, but you do get to a point when you think are we getting anywhere doing this? This is quite prevalent in many bands, and it is this that affects people. They all take it personally as they want to become successful as bands and want to make money and a living as a professional musician. They want to write music in the way that they want to write it and be appreciated for doing that. Playing anywhere and everywhere is not the answer. We did that up until the 'Jewel' tour, which was '85 and '86 when we felt that it was ridiculous and that we would be better off sitting down and thinking where we trying to take the band, as opposed to just breaking our necks to get gigs in places where nobody was coming to see us. True, some of the gigs were great, and some of our best gigs are from that period, even at places like Inverness Ice Rink where ten people turned up. While we were there somebody came up to Peter and said, "You're Freddy Mercury, aren't you?" – this guy really thought Peter was him.

Are you going to be doing more live work this year?

Towards the end of the year we will be doing a tour. Providing everything comes off in the way that we hope, then we will be touring in November and December, but if it all gets a bit delayed it may push into the New Year. It's good fun to a do a big tour: the last one was great! At this sort of age, you just can't get into the back of a transit and sleep on floors. I mean, Fudge wants luxury and it does not come cheap! The whole thing is a spiral upwards and this is the reason that people stick because it is enjoyable with a nice hotel and a good gig. The whole thing is packaged well, and it makes everyone feel great about the band.

The Mob (Pendragon's fan club) is going from strength to strength with the release last year of the 'Live From Utrecht' CD

The Mob has become more and more important. In the early days, we used to sit around and write out the envelopes by hand and then send them out whenever we did gigs and things and keeping the grass roots of things alive. Since then it has been a development of that. We have always believed that the people who come and the band, buy the record and get the T-shirts are a very important thing - I can't see it any other way, it must be. I know a lot of fan clubs are shit where you pay a lot of money and do not get anything, but CDs are not that expensive to make although 'Utrecht' was as there was a lot of stuff like a great booklet. We have always felt that getting more people into The Mob was a good objective, and we hope that we provide value for money.

There is a big difference between 'Utrecht' and 'Very, Very Bootleg'.

The very very horror! Initially that was recorded in a two track DAT at Lilles in France on that tour, and it sounded okay. Obviously, we could not remix it or do much with it, but we thought that as it was digitally recorded, we might as well make it into a CD. Originally it was only going to be for The Mob, but it branched out from there. Hopefully this sort of thing will continue although we have got to a point this year that doing another CD for The Mob is probably not a very good idea. To be honest I do not want too many albums out, particularly live albums. 'Masquerade' will be our tenth album and three out of the ten are live, and that is quite a lot. I think that with any more people just wouldn't bother with it. They want new material, which is the name of the game.

What was the reasoning behind the initial double CD which is coming out this time?

On the last album, four months after it came out, we decided to release "Nostradamus" as a single because it was picking up quite a bit of airplay in Germany. We did this CD for radio stations to play, with shortened versions of the song and was a good promotional idea. We thought of doing the same thing this this album as a promotion and maybe release it as a single, singles are not the thing we're after but they're a bit of a laugh now and again. We want people to think that we make good albums and that is that. We decided that if we were going to release a single, why not put it out with the album? A lot of people who buy our stuff will not go into a record shop and buy a CD single, so we thought we may as well put the extra CD in there. So, then we thought, if we were putting the edit CD in why not put on some extra tracks and do something with it? That's what happened and we decided to do that with the first lot of CDs. On these extra tracks "King Of The Castle" has the same chorus as the end chorus as "The Shadow" but the rest of the song is completely different. We did call it "The Shadow Part Two" as the end chorus is the same, but I structured the lyrics so that it has a double meaning. The initial pressing is fifteen thousand, but we are going to be getting on with some more very very soon. 'Windows Of Life' sold thirty-five thousand.

Are we likely to see a Nick Barrett solo album?

I don't think so, as I don't see the point. The only other thing I would like to do is work with other people now and then, and one idea is to work with Tracy Hitchings on an album. I would like to do one where I wouldn't have to write within a certain format, but it will probably sound like Pendragon to be honest, it's bound to, but I've no real desperate need to do a solo album. People tend to do solo albums when they are discontented with their band set up and it seems to be a bit of an answer, escapism from their main stuff. My escapism from Pendragon is that I have done this style of music for a very long time and it has got to the point where now it has got harder and harder to write. It has become more squared into a certain kind of area. It would be nice to write music over which people had not expectations. With this album people will immediately compare it with the last, and the album before that, so each time you just make like harder for yourself. It would be nice to do an album where there would be no pre-conceived ideas about what it might be, and just release it and see what happens with it. It would take a lot of pressure off. This album has been bloody torture as it has been two and a half years since the last one and it feels like I have not had any time off. People think that I've just been sunning myself on a beach, but I put in the hours on Pendragon and there is a lot of stuff going on behind the scenes.

Clive Nolan & Ian Salmon (Shadowland), #34, Apr 1996

With Shadowland just about to start recording their third album, the time seemed right to meet with Clive and Ian to discuss it.

So, what is the idea behind the new Shadowland album?

Clive: As per usual there is a thematic idea. This album is called 'Mad As A Hatter', and a lot of it is to do with the subject of insanity, which sounds fairly dark and brooding, but hey, it is!

Ian: That's Shadowland, and that's the way we like it.

Clive: We've had some close examples of this experience recently, so that helped me to get the idea for lyrics and it just took shape. The whole album addresses the idea of madness and sanity from a few different angles.

Ian: To some extent it seems to be developing into what is insanity, and the way that it goes into normal life. Everybody is on the edge at some point.

Is this more of a band project?

Clive: I know what you mean. It is more bandular this time than ever before, in as much as there is more than just me writing on the album, which is a first. We've got a track basically from Mike (Varty, live keyboard player) and one basically from Ian as well.

Ian: We've all worked on the material and the overall concept as well.

Clive: It has given the band a fresh angle and I think the material is the strongest we have done. We've got more a of a vibe about this one than we had about the second one, more like the first one where there was a real sense of occasion, I was a bit pissed off for the second as you may remember, it was not a very good time: it was hard to get people motivated, there was not a lot to work for. We had done quite a few albums of different natures and knew that we were not going to sell that many. It seemed a lot of work to put in, when we were not getting the results we needed.

Ian: I'm not sure what, but it was just like doing a job during the second album, but now it seems as if we are doing what we want to do.

Is Mike playing on the album?

Clive: Yes, we are sharing keyboard duties. From the way it's worked, when I am writing, I tend to put a lot of keyboards down because it is the foundation from which we build, Mike's been working on his track and he has worked with Ian as well. We will get Mike in to do some leads on some of the other tracks because as the keyboard player who is going to play them, they may well come from him. A lot of more traditional piano stuff will come from me, so it is a joint effort.

Has he brought in different keyboard sounds?

Clive: Not so much sounds, but style. It fits in very well, not a million miles from where I am, but obviously his choice of notes will be different from mine and it gives a fresh approach again.

Ian: He can bring in different sounds if he wants to, as he becomes more and more involved with it. His involvement comes in at the beginning and right through to the end.

What timespan have you set yourselves for the recording?

Clive: Six weeks. The release is set for May 21st, but the tour is a little open ended now as it must fit in with a host of other things. We will probably do a strategic tour where we will play a couple of reasonable profile gigs, one each in Holland, Germany, France and England. We'll build up some reaction and then see what to do next. That will take us up to the summer, and then we will work out a tour for the end of the year, or maybe the beginning of 1997. I am going to keep the whole thing ticking over this time. Shadowland has been out of the public eye for about one and a half years and the last gig was probably the last time the whole band were in the same room together.

Are you going to record any of the gigs for a live album?

Clive: The plan is to record a couple of gigs and to bring out a live album if it is a decent enough performance. We have a record company that will back the idea, and if the band are prepared to go out and do the gigs the record company will put up the cash to do the recordings. I would like Shadowland to do a live album as we will have three albums out, and it will be a good time to do one.

Recording the drums effectively should make a big difference

Clive: Yes, it's the first big change really. On the last album we recorded real drums, but we had to go somewhere else to do it, then we had to farm it back across to us afterwards. This time we are all here and it should make a big difference.

Do you find it hard to swap musical hats?

Clive: No, not really, I find that different times of the year seems right for doing different things. Usually when I start writing I just write something and then look at it and say that is Shadowland, or that is Strangers. Often, I know that there is going to be some activity with one of the bands and therefore write with that hat on. It is as simple as picking the hat up and putting it on, I've never thought about it and do not have any difficulty doing it. I enjoy writing and that is what matters most to me – I could do without every other aspect of the business. With Arena, it is easier again because I am working with someone else. Mick sets a stylistic attitude and I fit in with him. The one that I am doing with Oliver Wakeman is again two people working together so the style will take on a different shape.

I was going to ask you about that, because the last time we spoke you said about having Rick do a voiceover.

Clive: That was an idea, but we have pulled back a bit from it. We are trying to find an actor, somebody interesting with a good voice; I'd rather get Rick to play. We are wondering whether to get Eric Idle, and if he comes back and says he'd love to do it then all he will have to do is speak into a DAT in America and send it to us. We will sample it and move it around; all we are trying to do at present is to track down some suitable people.

How is Verglas going?

Clive: Verglas is very very happy because we have signed a new band, Shadowland. They are a fabulous band and such wonderful people to work with, a jazz funk beat combo! We wanted another band and it seemed to be a logical decision. With that and the Project series, that is probably it for Verglas as a record label as we do not want to sign hundreds of bands: I am completely opposed to that. I would rather put a lot of money and effort into promoting Shadowland, Arena and the project series. For us to have more acts we would have to hire extra staff, and if we do have to do that at some stage then it will be fabulous but until then we do not want to start bringing out an album a month. Two or three albums a year is what we have in mind, and record company support for the bands. I want to give Shadowland a proper crack of the whip – I'm not saying that anyone else hasn't done that, but the people involved in the whole operation have a personal reason for wanting it to work which I think is going to give us an edge. It is expensive. It costs a lot more money than we thought it would, but we are learning as we go. We have the Shadowland album coming out in May, there should be the second Arena album coming out in September, and then in the following year there will be a bag of live albums from both bands and a special album from Arena which is kind of an offshoot from the first two albums, a collector's thing. That will take quite a long time to record and it will not be started until next year. In fact, it may not be until the end of 1997 or even the year after that.

Are you going to be cutting back on other projects because of your work with Shadowland and Arena?

Clive: Well, I have never thought that I have been doing a lot of other projects although everyone else says that I do. If you run a studio, and are a keyboard player, then the chances are that you will be asked to slap down some keyboards at some stage. Usually when I do something like that, I become a member of the project or band; I enjoyed Medicine Man for example. But Strangers are the only other thing that will happen, which depends on what is happening with SI. We can't release it now so it is on the back burner for a year or so and we will wait until someone is ready to cut us a deal. I do not expect that it will come out on Verglas unless we had the first two albums as well.

Ian: All of us tend to do one or two other things as well, whether it is playing or engineering.

Clive: Often it is the case that someone else is not available for Shadowland, not just me.

This will be the first time Shadowland will be available in the shops?

Clive: It will be the first time that it will be readily available in England. Pinnacle Distribution are very excited about the Shadowland album, which is great as they did not do a deal with SI. Pony Canyon in Japan are excited as well but are scared about legalities as far as back catalogue is concerned. They want to release it in September, which is good, as it will give us some more money. There is more interest and we will be able to utilise it. It is quite a coup for us to reach some areas and fans which we previously have not been able to do, which hopefully will mean that we will sell more albums.

Ian, will you be using fretless bass again?

Ian: Yes, I've managed to borrow a decent one from the God of Bass, the person who gets the John Jowitt award every year at Classic Rock. It's a lovely bass.

Has he let you touch it?

Ian: On no, no, he's just let me have the case! It sounds gorgeous, but there are quite a few tracks where the aggression of a good fretted bass is needed so I'm using that as well. There are a variety of sounds coming from the bass end.

Clive: Fretless bass and acoustic guitar, I'd like to see some more work on that. It's been some time since we damaged Jon's guitar so we should see if we can get away with it again.

What's that about?

Clive: Jon Jeary has this acoustic guitar that we borrowed. It is his life, and somehow it got very slightly scratched, the sort of scratch that you wouldn't even see. I still do not know how it happened, but we have not had the heart to ask him for it since. Still, by now the wounds should have healed.

Ian: It sounded gorgeous in "Kruhulick's".

Clive: We have got another "Kruhulick's" style piece called "A Curious Tale". The opening section is very lush with strings and a vocal, and then it goes into a rhythmic instrumental section for the second half. It is a tricky instrumental and comes out at the end in a big tune and march time. There is a lot more instrumental work on this album: it is good to have a break from the voice. I have the kind of voice that wears you down after a while, I know my limitations. I am not a great singer; I just feel a lot for the songs. People will enjoy me singing a lot more if I am singing a lot less. As well as the instrumental song, there are quite a few songs where there are much less vocals but quite a lot of action going on around them. It feels right, it is instinctive. I feel that the material is the best that Shadowland has ever had, that is from everybody. There is a real vibe about it, and I have felt more team spirit on the three days of working on this one than there was for the whole of the making of the last one.

Ian: "Vibe" is not very proggy, but there is a definite vibe about this album.

What about the environment now?

Clive: It is strange, but three fifths (Clive, Karl and Ian) of Shadowland now live in the same house. I am not a big advocate of living together, but it works. Having the new studio is a big inspiration, and it makes it easier. Also, it is a proper studio and not a dining room and this is what Thin Ice has always dreamt of being. Because the studio hasn't been active until a few days ago, and the fact that we have been living in the house for six months, has meant that I have had a break from being in the studio, which is weird. I have just been writing my guts out and have written more in the last six months than I have ever written in a solid mass. I have written the Strangers album, a lot of the Shadowland album, I've started writing the Wakeman album and have an hour's worth of Arena material.

Can you take me through the album?

Clive" It starts with "Koyabashi", then "The Burning", "Flatline", "USI (United States of Insanity"), "A Curious Tale", "Mad As A Hatter", then the un-hidden track "The Gift". "Koyabashi" is an aggressive and no-nonsense song and comes from Star Trek. It is the no-win scenario at the Academy that Kirk beat by reprogramming it and is a song about no-win situations – life is full of them. "Flatline" is Ian's song, which came from the film "Flatliners". Also, one song I forgot to mention is "Mephisto Bridge" which is about the gateway to insanity: whichever side appears to be the mad side depends on where you are stood.

"Mad As A Hatter" is the last official track on the album and dissolves into harmonic anarchy. There will be a sound effect that will give a knotty feeling in the stomach and will go on for five, ten, fifteen minutes. Usually with a hidden track there is silence until in the distance there is something but with this one you are going to have to wade through this annoying sound until you come to "The Gift" which is almost gospel, more like "Mindgames" from the second album. Martin Orford is going to do some backing vocals and Damian Wilson, Gary Chandler, we're going to get them all in. I want to get this massive choir sound. Every Shadowland album has a song that is out of place, if you like, not strictly in sync with the others, and this will be that on the third.

My thanks to Clive and Ian for not only taking the time to do the interview, but also for letting me take along Elizabeth, my eight-year-old daughter, who is Shadowland's greatest fan.

Fish, #51, Jan 1999

With twelve albums being released on the same day, it seemed like an opportune time to catch up with the man himself. Unfortunately, Fish was not at his best, suffering not only from a cold but also from the launch party of 'The Young Person's Guide To Becoming A Rock Star' that had been held the night before. However, fortified by a large pot of tea we got down to business, and after such a long period running his own label, I wondered just why had he signed to Roadrunner?

It had got to the stage with the 'Sunsets On Empire' album that I realised we had made a great album and trying to promote it as a small independent we financially could not invest as much as we would have liked. At the same time, with the tour promoting the album, and the recording of the album, we got into a heavy overdraft at the bank. I realised that we could not compete with the majors with buying power. I decided to go for a huge tour, 120 dates, 22 countries, and at the end of it we came back and not only had it had a negative impact, but I lost a lot of money on the tour. In equivalent terms, it was about seven hundred quid a gig, which comes down to if you had just sold another hundred t-shirts, or another fifty or seventy-five tickets a show, then would have broken even. When you put that all together over a long period it puts you into financial chaos. I had a couple of choices. I could either keep furrowing the same path and try and get an album together but realised even then that we were going to have difficulties funding the album, and the promotion of it would be nonsensical. Also, I was getting disillusioned with the practice of running my own label. It was becoming very time consuming and my energies were being channelled into the wrong areas. On top of that my wife had been very ill last year and everything else. With my daughter only being seven years old as well, it was a long time away, eight months of the year. I could have spent the money going down to the Caribbean renting a nice house, written two albums and got a good scuba diving card

In January, the bank manager asked what had happened to all the money and the first thing we decided to do was cut right back on touring. The second thing was to shut down the studio, because we had this huge asset and a huge overdraft with a lot of interest payments. We were making those payments, but we were not biting into the debt. The problem was that with the financing over the next year it was unlikely that we were going to get through it. I was gambling every time we went on tour and every time I made an album, gambling the entire house on it. I'm not the sort of person who can afford to throw a couple of hundred grand, which is what it costs to get an album done. The next step was to put the studio up for sale, then phone my theatrical agent and tell him that although in the past he had been working second to me he now had full scope. The thing after that was to find a label to take over. I had been negotiating with Polydor to get the two albums back, and by the summer of last year I had all my solo albums in my own name.

I knew that the majors were never going to be a goer for me. I just could not see myself going back, they have an air of an insurance company about them now. What I needed was someone with a lot of ambition, and the name of Roadrunner kept coming up. I got talking to them and realised that they were an ambitious company, and although they had

a certain name of being heavy metal that did not disturb me as from Day One with Marillion we were always user friendly as far as the Metal Hammer's and Kerrang! There are a lot of heavy metal guys who have always been into the sort of stuff I'm doing. Another aspect that I liked was that they have global distribution, good sound financial backing with bands like Sepultura, Type O Negative, Biohazard and Fear Factory and I thought that this could work. By having the full catalogue there, as well as the 'Kettle of Fish' thing, it was attractive to them and it was attractive to me. It made a lot of sense to put out a re-mastered catalogue on the one label. Financially they have helped us but as a career move it is more important than that.

'Kettle of Fish' represents ten years of songwriting, during which time most people will not even have heard of us, so that is where it stands now. In the summer, we put the new album in the can, so it's not as if we are sat down somewhere thinking we've got to go and write an album. It's written, and you will be very, very pleased with it. I took your words to heart (*my earlier review of 'Sunsets' – Kev*) and it is better than 'Sunsets'. A lot of people who have heard it have already said that.

What was it like going back over the old albums to write the sleeve notes and digging out extra tracks, reliving the past as it were?

It was not reliving as such, as most of the extra tracks that are on there were original 'B' sides so it was not as if I had to go into any dusty vaults or anything; they were on singles that had long since been deleted. The sleeve notes were interesting as lots of people do not know what has happened in my career: most people were unaware of what was going on behind the scenes as my solo career was unravelling. Quite a few people have read all the sleeve notes and have said "but you're still here!". I'm quite proud of it. Some people have told me that it is too down, too dark and that I ought to concentrate on more positive things such as being #33 on the Albanian charts last week, but I wanted to be more truthful and explain the environment in which the albums were created.

Why were there no sleeve notes on the reissue of 'Sunsets'? I found that a bit strange.

To be honest I was really happy with the packaging of 'Sunsets' and I did not really feel that it needed to be broken into. I think it would have been too big a job to rip the original artwork apart and go in and do it. One thing is that my lyrics tend to be quite lengthy and everybody was saying "well we've got to have the lyrics", and then to put the sleeve notes in on top of it would have made a booklet that even Roadrunner was going to be concerned about.

'Kettle of Fish' is the new compilation. What has happened to 'Yin' and Yang'?

'Yin' and 'Yang' will be released sometime next year, probably as a double CD. And as some of the tracks double on 'Kettle of Fish' maybe we will take some off and put some on.

It would be a good time to do a studio version of "Faith Healer".

At this point Fish leaned back, laughing, and I wondered what I had done to provoke such a reaction.

Funny you should mention that, because it is on 'Raingods With Zippos'. What happened was that on the 'Songs From The Mirror' album we decided to do a couple of extra tracks and recorded "This Town Ain't Big Enough For The Both Of Us" and "Faith Healer". We started to put it together when we became aware of this American publishing thing that basically means that if you have more than ten tracks on an album you must pay for it! If I had put twelve tracks on 'Songs From The Mirror' and it came out in America then I would have ended up paying publishing royalties for my songs, which was ludicrous. It is daft to put out an album and everybody else is making money from it, but you are paying for it for putting songs on it. So, we said that we would just stick to ten songs. I did not like the version of "Jeepster", it was the weakest song on the album, but at the same time we did "Time And A Word" and "The Seeker" which were very relevant. "Time And A Word" would have got quite a lot of airplay in America so it made sense to have that on the album and "The Seeker" by The Who which is another band relevant over there. I'm saying that because on the last tour, and the last album, there was a lot of very positive reaction from America, and with this whole catalogue coming out it will be the very first time that all my albums have been available in the States as of January next year.

It was like, what do we do with "Faith Healer"? We started work on it and we decided to go for a real heavy vibe, like a Nine Inch Nails sort of thing. As it started to come together it was far too good for 'Songs From The Mirror'. It was very different from the other songs, which are kind of faithful to the originals, not drastically different although obviously, the performances are different they are not huge re-workings. "Faith Healer" was very dark and fitted in more with the whole shade of 'Raingods With Zippos'.

What about some of the other releases such as 'Fish Head Curry' and the acoustic set?

There were enough live albums being released now anyway, and these were originally limited editions and we are down to the last four or five hundred of a five thousand run, so we kept these on the label. That is only available through mail order, so it only comes through the web site. The site has been well hit this year, something like 160,000 hits, which is good for a band site. The mail order is directly fan oriented through the internet and there will be others as well. There is a compilation of video clips that is only available through mail order; there will probably be a live video from the German Fan Club Convention this year that again will be limited, and possibly a live album from the Haddington Fan Club Convention this year. It keeps the fans happy with this stuff, but we are not overdosing retail.

The new album is called 'Raingods With Zippos', Why Zippos?

Zippos have been turning up for years in my life; they are even on 'Clutching At Straws'. I've always loved the sound of a zippo; it was a name that came up on a list. Another thing that happened this year was that Miles Copeland asked me to come down to Castle Manoir in France. Twice a year he brings in loads of songwriters, and when I was there, there were 24 songwriters from all different genres. Every day we were put into three member-writing teams and were only introduced to each other at that point. The duty was to write a song that day and then demo it. That is a tough order for me, as coming up with songs is like pulling them out of concrete. At least that was always the impression I had; I just do not write songs quickly. It was a fascinating experience and I came back with six songs. Being away from faxes, mobiles, all the noise I have back up in Scotland I came back rejuvenated and feeling very positive and very excited.

Tony Turrell and Mark Daghorn, who sometimes go under the name of Positive Light, and ironically had done that work on the Marillion remixes album, came up to do a remix of "What Colour Is God?", and although I was not overly happy with what they did, they had a track and asked me to do some vocal samples. Then I heard the track and I thought that it was good, and I suggested turning it into more of a co-writing thing and splitting the song up and changing it around a bit. That has become a 27-minute piece called "Plague of Ghosts" and with that the album was virtually there. Then Mickey Simmonds came up and I wrote two tracks with him and together with "Faith Healer" we had the album. That was all done in the summer, so the two tracks "Chasing Miss Pretty" and "Mr Buttons" which came from the Castle sessions ended up on 'Kettle of Fish'. The others we recorded all the way through the summer up at the Farm before we shut the studio down.

What was it like doing epic pieces?

I felt that it was a challenge and because my confidence was at a high I felt I could approach it and I have been involved in writing long pieces all the way back to 'Misplaced Childhood' and even the first side of 'Clutching At Straws', all of that "Hotel Hobbies" kind of thing. If it has got light and shade, dynamics, is interesting and has a flow and feel to it, which was one of the problems I had in '88 when we were writing this stuff but I never thought that it had a good soul to it. "Plague of Ghosts" was originally called "All These Christs" and when I first heard it, I thought that it had a good curve. I was playing about with a couple of ideas and the conceptual sort of feel of it, then one day it just clicked, and I could see it. If you look at it on paper, then it cannot exist. It has beat poetry, drum & bass, classical piano, severe funk, huge atmospherics and layer after layer of different things from French horns and strings to the sound of rainfall to recordings of Vietnamese radio broadcasters from the Sixties. It's wild, it shouldn't exist, it shouldn't have happened. But it does, and it's brilliant.

The production is very Nineties, more of the styles used in drum & bass: the end section has a Mancunian groove to it. That's what progressive is all about. I get sick of progressive music because everybody who calls himself or herself progressive is just incredibly boring. I felt it was just going back to the same thing instead of exploring. There was an interesting article in Mojo, where they were reviewing Family's 'Music From A Doll's House' and they said that it was a shame that we did not have albums like that anymore where there is folk mixed with rock mixed with quasi-classical. I took that in and tried to do that, and that is where 'Raingods With Zippos' is. It has got a very heavy version of "Faith Healer", it has got a 27-minute track which also has a folk element in that, there is one song which is a great pop song called "Incomplete", which was written down at the castle. There are so many different styles but at the same time it is still a Fish album. It is 'Sunsets On Empire' another hundred miles down the road. It has got great melodies, great production, great song structures, but so many different styles it is interesting.

Elliot Ness produced the album. He was the engineer/producer on the 'Sunsets' album with Steve Wilson and when I asked Steve if he was interested in producing this, he said that he did not have the time, but luckily enough Elliot did. Calum Malcolm mastered it, again the same team as 'Sunsets'. I did not want to do a complete change from 'Sunsets', as I wanted to use that as the foundation for the next move: sonically I wanted to keep some of the same approaches and that has happened. For example, the use of strings on 'Sunsets' has carried through to 'Raingods' and we were very lucky that Steve suddenly found time in the summer to come up and do most of the lead guitarwork for it.

Going back to the 'Sunsets' album, who was Mawgojzeta on "Goldfish Clowns"?

She was a girl I knew in Poland who was working for the promoter. When we were introduced to each other I asked her name and she told me that it was Margaret. I said that was not a Polish name and I asked her for her real name, which was Mawgojzeta. I just thought that it was a beautiful name and as soon as she said it, I knew that I had to use it in a song somewhere.

What about the concept behind "What Colour Is God?"

In the Spike Lee film 'Malcolm X', there is a great scene where Malcolm says that we live in world where God is a white man, and considering that Jesus came from Sumeria he asks what colour is God? It rattled me and I came back and my daughter was being taught Religious Education at school and she had been going on about God and I asked her what he looked like and she told me that he was a white man. I told her that he was not, and that God could be any colour and I told her that the next time the teacher said anything like that she should stick her hand up and ask what colour is God? It came from there, and then I went down to the Caribbean for three weeks and got involved with some local guys, kicking about in the scene in St. Lucia. I suddenly became the minority and not the majority and saw racism from the other side. There has always been a religious element in my songs, from "Credo" all the way back to "Forgotten Sons". It has been something that has always fascinated me and repelled me at the same time. It was natural that there would be one song on there which was heavily focussed on religion.

How did playing the character Derek Trout come about?

Well, the writer Bryan Elsley came up to the house in '91 to do research. He was at the same school as me, although different years, and he wanted to do research on a programme on music. We sat and talked for three hours or so and then years later, when I had made a conscious move to do more acting, my agent phoned up and told me about this project. He went for it, and Bryan had written this part for me, with the character being called Derek Trout, and Derek Dick being Fish, and the guy lives in Harrington and has a German personal assistant and runs a studio that the band can use. I walked into the audition and said, "Unless I get this job, I'm going to sue you" and then had to explain it to them. I was at the launch party last night and saw the first two episodes. There are a couple of things in there that I told Bryan, such as the guy working in the social security office trying to use the phone to book gigs. I had told Bryan that was what I had done in the early days as I worked in an employment office in Aylesbury and I used to sign on the band and the crewmembers and go into the back office and book gigs. I had two options. I could have become pissed off with it or decide to roll with it and basically take the piss out of myself. That's what I decided to do. It was the first chance I ever had to do comedy, and I've always thought that I could go into that. Some people view me as a po-faced individual writing serious songs, who lives under his own dark cloud. But I enjoy comedy and have a good sense of humour, and I thought that this would be a good opportunity for me to show that I can do comedy and being able to laugh at myself, as well as showing that I am an actor.

So, a new phase in the career of the large Scotsman. With all his solo albums re-mastered and readily available in record stores, now could not be a better or easier time to discover his music.

Steve Howe, #54, July 1999

So, how are things?

Good right now, we just got back from Vancouver about two weeks ago where we had been finishing the Yes album

Let's talk about the solo album first. Why Dylan, and why now?

When you say "Now", I started thinking about this some years ago, and basically I tried "The Lonesome Death of Hattie Carroll", and when I got the arrangement on it that I liked, the Spanish guitar style I brought to it, then I got the confidence to take Bob Dylan songs that I liked and do some arrangements. There's so much talk about who's great, and let's give him an award, but when I look at the music (and I see a lot of music) I see that Dylan is a unique and special entity in the fact that I can't compare him to anybody, apart from possibly Joni Mitchell. Perhaps even she would say that the length and breadth of his writing leaves a lot of music to choose from, if you know his songs and feel them in body like I do. Not only did I grow up with his music but even took the arm off the 45 player so that it kept playing "Positively 4th Street" for about four hours and driving the rest of my family through the roof. The songs are very deep, mysterious and poetical, and when people mention how great people are Bob does not get a mention, or at least not mentioned enough. I just thought, "Why not do something different?" The more I do things different then the more I learn about myself and hopefully surprise people, but the worst thing about being a musician is not being surprising.

How did you come to choose the tracks? Were they personal favourites, ones that you thought you could work with, or a combination?

A combination really. There were two basic areas, firstly I had to get a guitar arrangement that I could conceive that I wanted to take on and I tried some of the songs to see what came to me. One message that drew these songs together was a growth in learning in your relationship in your love for somebody and Bob talked a lot about this from "Tangled Up Blue" to "Sad Eyed Lady of the Lowlands" and some of that just seemed to hang together for me. I have always liked his romantic songs and yet he never seems to sing "Baby I love you" songs. Love is a different kind of animal to Bob; he talks about it in terms of lots of interactions in a very classy way.

How did you choose the guest vocalists and why did not you sing more of the songs yourself?

If I had sung the whole album then I would be basing the accessibility, not the commerciality, for other people to hear. I think that the principle singers do something like I do with my guitar playing. I do a little bit with my voice, but I did not want to take on the whole album because I felt that was not my job. My job was to develop the record and as it developed Annie Haslam came in and sang "It's All Over Now, Baby Blue" and when I heard it I thought "Wow!" and knew that I needed more female singers and I hadn't even thought about that until I heard Annie. Things did springboard as we went along. I told Jon that I was doing this project and that I had backing tracks for all the songs and told him that he could pick from them and Jon said that they were all very nice songs but that he had always wanted to do "Sad Eyed Lady of the Lowlands". In fact, Jon got on board very powerfully by suggesting doing another song, a song that I thought would be almost impossible to do, one of the hardest Bob Dylan songs to do, and Jon was going for it. Once Jon had said that it set me off and the idea for singers became much warranted in my mind. When "Well, Well, Well" came along which I sang originally, as I did with all my songs, and I heard PP Arnold singing it I enjoyed that sense of collaboration. Also, as it was under my control I could invite people to come although some could not as they were too busy, some did not like Bob Dylan enough, or know the songs enough while others we just could not get in the right place at the right time. I think the album is a special album due to the guest vocalists I invited.

There are lead vocalists from bands that you have been involved with such as Jon Anderson, Max Bacon and Keith West. Did you consider inviting John Wetton?

I wish communication between us was good enough to make any idea work from any of our past encounters. I like to think that music feeds us knowledge that makes up harmonies together. I have been out of touch for quite a few years, but that does not mean that we could not work together again. One of the parameters of this was that it had to be with people I was in touch with in some way or another, so not being in touch with John might have made me think. It was much more like a Steve Howe & Friends album, and although I would call John Wetton a friend, we have not been in touch for many, many years.

I was interested by the silhouette in the booklet which has a very Sixties feel. Was that deliberate?

I wanted to use a picture of Dylan there, Dylan by Andy Warhol, but while we kicked the idea around, we came up with some potential problems with it. My friends the Gottlieb Brothers, who have done many sleeves with me, used my silhouette on the sleeve with their own rainbows. We took a bit from Dylan really, in the way of Dylan design.

What is your own favourite song on the album?

I like "Going, Going, Gone" very much, a song that I did want to sing myself, but I felt that Max did it better than me, so I went with Max. He took that song on very well, and that got me at it, it is great. I am very happy with the whole collection; it is something that I have created and is very satisfying for me.

Did this album give you new life going into the new Yes album?

It must be said that releasing something can give you great enthusiasm, and my approach to this Yes album has been fuelled by some of the things that I have done which are very different to Yes, which is what I like. One or two members of Yes do not manage to find the time to take that idea out and come back to Yes having tried something else out. We all do it a little bit, although I think that Jon and I do it the most, but I think that is quite a healthy thing. It certainly is evidence of my productivity and I like that side of me. I do not put albums out every year, but a pattern has come about for artists to release all the albums that they want to, and I am pleased that Eagle signed me up for this project and for future projects. I am looking for that kind of home where they can make it work for me much better.

I saw you on the 'Night of the Guitars' tour where you really seemed to be enjoying yourself.

Yes, it was not too dissimilar to my solo tour. It gives me a lot of satisfaction to be able to pull music from my career and just play it. That was a good time for me and one of the nice things was that everybody thought that we would get on badly, but we all got on really well. It was a very nice feeling to do that tour, but my spot was exciting for me as I used to go out and play "Sketches in the Sun" on my own and then play "The Clap" and stuff with the band. The fact that I have taken the opportunities that I have been offered has put me where I want to be, which is quite often on stage. I have done a few shows that England probably does not know about. In New York, for instance, I played three years running at a big guitar show while I have also played down in Devon in a church hall for a fete for three years, so I quite like going out on my own.

How has the new Yes album come out?

Immediately before we started rehearsing, we decided that this album had to be a collaborative album, and if anyone brought a finished song then we were not going to listen to it. If anyone had done that then there wouldn't have been anything that anyone else could have done to it, which pins it down too much. We all brought in these confusing little pieces of music, which were not put together on purpose, which were kept apart, as well as lots of ideas and lots of bits and pieces. When someone played something, if we did not like a bit of it then we would say "I do not like this bit, but that bit's great" and as soon as someone did not like it then that bit is history. Then we met the late Bruce Fairbairn and he decided that he would produce us. We rehearsed for a month last year but went back in January and he spent two weeks with us in the rehearsal room, deciding what songs he thought were right for the album. Then we rehearsed them with him and at the beginning of February we went into his studio and recorded the whole album in just under four months, with a couple of weeks off here and there. It was a long slog of work, but it was all done in the right way until we heard one Monday that he had died, and we just did not understand it. He passed us a little bit of work to do on the mixing, and Jon and I stayed with the engineer Mike to finish it. Mike deserves a lot of credit as he could go on after the loss of a nine-year companion. It was mastered yesterday, is coming out in September and I can only say that I like the whole thing. It is called 'The Ladder', 63 minutes of music. We expect to be playing the whole album on tour in October in Europe so hope to see you all then!

Neal Morse & Nick D'Virgilio (Spock's Beard), #63, July 2001

Having been singing their praises for so long, I was extremely happy to be given the opportunity of speaking with the band when they visited London recently. I looked around the foyer of the hotel, but did not see anyone I recognised, so rang Neal in his room. When he came downstairs, he spoke to someone with extremely short hair, and asked if he wanted to join in the interview. It was only then that I realised that it was Nick, who I later found out had just been scalped by his three-year-old daughter. We found a table, and the conversation just flowed...

How did the band start? I noticed you in '96 when the Synphonic release came out and there was a real buzz in the scene but did not know anything before then.

Neal: Well, I wrote some stuff, "The Light", "Go The Way You Go" and "The Water" and demoed the stuff at home using a drum machine, which was funny. I would get up to certain points playing along with the drum machine but there were parts which just were not in time. Then Al got excited about it and it was funny, the whole idea of getting a band together at that time. Al and I had been in millions of bands and they were always so much work, all those rehearsals and something for nothing, all those band meetings.

Trust us on this; you do not want to get involved in band meetings. If someone calls a band meeting, get out of it!

Were you sessioning at the time?

Neal: I was playing covers for a living, with full hair and a beard too. Al and I felt that putting a band together was out of the box, and Al wanted us to go to jam nights and look for players. Who are we going to get that a) can play this stuff and b) who would want to? There's no money in it, there's not going to be any money in it, probably. So, we went to a jam night and I consider it a definite act of God. It was one of those places where you put your name in the hat and they pull out five people and those people then get up and play. They called out Neal Morse, Alan Morse, Nick D'Virgilio and two other people, and I think we played 12-bar, right? I can't believe that Nick would even speak to me after that because I played so badly. Me, Al and someone else had gone out into the parking lot and smoked a joint and I do not usually smoke pot and then they called our name! I think I played in the wrong key. We were talking afterwards, and Nick said that he was a big fan of early Genesis, and I told him about the stuff we were working on and he came over and picked up a tape the next day. Underneath those mild manners, Nick is quite a go-getter. That was how we started to put the band together, which was in '92. We did some LA gigs, as a four piece.

Nick: We did not have Ryo and we had another bass player, not Dave. Then Al got Ryo in the band, who he knew from someplace else.

Neal: We were talking to Magna Carta about signing us, but it was a very long negotiation with a 63-page contract. People ask us why if were together in '91 or '92, why did it take so long to record an album. However, we spent a lot of time waiting for them to call us back, which could take months at a time. I am so glad that we did not do a deal with them. They offered us a couple of ADAT's and a microphone for the exclusive worldwide and publishing rights on 'The Light'.

Nick: And they wanted him to change all his lyrics!

Neal: They wanted me to change lyrics, although they deny it to this day, but they did! They gave me a list, like they wanted me to change "reaching across the water for a drink of wine" as they felt that I shouldn't mention alcohol!

They must have loved "The Water" then

Neal: Yeah, that was the first thing. It started off with that, and I understood that, and I tried to change it to other things like "Screw You".

Nick: "Hate You"

Neal: "Go Away"! But I was not comfortable with any of it.

Jumping on a couple of years, what made you pick a George Harrison song as a cover,

because it was totally deconstructed?

Neal: There is a Leon Russell version on the 'And The Shelter People' album, which is an album I grew up listening to a lot. He does lots of little piano solos and stuff and I took some of these and put them into the instrumental parts of that song. It literally came to me in the shower one day. I was singing the song to myself in the shower and started to think about all the different things we could do with it, then went downstairs and demoed it up. Kevin Gilbert said that we shouldn't have started the album with that as it was not that strong, but I like it.

When you are composing, do you use keyboards or guitar?

Neal: Evenly mixed. You can probably guess. Most of the happy stuff, like "All On A Sunday", was written on guitar. Whatever is closest to hand, or whatever vibe I want or mood I'm in.

What is the story behind "June" because every time I play it, I get the impression that it is based on something that happened?

Neal: I think that song is a testament to my pessimistic nature. That song is about something that hasn't happened, such as getting our own private hotel rooms and stuff. One day, we reach the pinnacle! That song is about the idea that you have one good season then it comes to pass, and you have the feeling that you know that it has passed.

The video for "All On A Sunday" is a bit strange and hard to watch.

Neal: With the split screen? Yes, and with all the double imaging and moving in and out.

Was it the band's idea?

Neal: It was completely the director's idea; it was all a matter of budget. They firstly had these treatments, and ideas such as me in a spacesuit but the cost was $2500 a day, so that was that. Everything they came up with was too expensive to do, and then the director came up with the split screen deal. We essentially just did what they said, pretending that we were rocking out in the middle of a field.

You have released a couple of live albums, but 'Do Not Try This At Home' seemed very short, why was that?

Neal: Yes, fifty minutes is now short.

But the Transatlantic live album which you played on is a double live CD, and this seemed short, especially having seen you on that tour.

Nick: The recording of that gig was nothing short of a huge pain in the ass. We recorded it and filmed it, and the levels on the ADAT were shite. Everything was messed up. We recorded it on multi-track so that we could fix it, as everybody does, but we could not even mix it and make it sound good. We picked the best ones and made the record.

Neal: There were other things that we could have used on it, but we felt that another live version of "Go The Way You Go" seemed redundant. That is why it mostly only has stuff that is not on the others.

The albums you have released on Radiant, your own label in the States, are they going to be licensed over here?

Neal: I do not think so; they are more fun, lower quality albums. They are much more for the real hardcore fan. The concern is that you do not want the new listener who has read about us somewhere to walk into a store and buy something that is not our best work. You do not want to take the chance they might be put off by something that is maybe a little bit less. The hardcore fans can get it at the shows or through the web site.

What song are you most proud of, as I got the impression on the last tour that it was "The Great Nothing"?

Nick: Well, I think we have recorded some pretty great things and that is one of our best. It's all down to Neal though, he has written some great songs.

Neal: That one, and "At The End Of The Day" are two of my personal favourites. I am as proud of the short ones as I am of the long ones really. Anything that kicks ass.

Nick: One of my favourite things that we have ever done is "Strange World" off 'The Kindness Of Strangers' album. I just love that song, the way it rocks so hard. It is just short, but it was fun to do. I'm proud of that one.

Neal: I'm proud of all of them. Really. It is such a moot thing, to be proud. To feel like you have accomplished something, to have written the whole thing from the ground up. It is a great feeling. This band is all the same guys, who have stuck it out. There have been some hard times, tough tours but no one complains much as they are all into it. It is just amazing. When Nick tours with Roland (*Nick drums for Tears for Fears*) he stays in the nicest hotels and is recorded in the best places.

Nick: It is different when you are in your own band, in an up and coming band, especially when playing this genre of music, which is not so mainstream. You will not be given much money to go off and do things so you just kind of put up with what you are given because you love the music. Hopefully one day it will get better and we will stay in nice hotels.

Neal: We've been hoping that for a long time!

What are your own favourite bands and what has influenced you?

Neal: Things that influence us are bands like Genesis, Yes, ELP, Gentle Giant, King Crimson, The Beatles, Steely Dan, CS&N. But I listen to a lot of more mellow things, or if I am cooking with my kids on a Sunday morning, I'll put on some jazz, or some Mozart.

Nick: When I was growing up it was bands like Led Zeppelin and early Genesis; they are the big ones for me. Also, Stevie Wonder, anything Motown, was a big influence on me. Mostly from the drumming side of thing. I had a fusion thing for a while, Jean Luc Ponty was one of my favourite guys, but I was also into Judas Priest at the same time. I even managed to see both in the same week one time, which was weird.

When I've watched you play, and I do not want this to sound the wrong way, but you are one of the laziest drummers I have seen. Your style is so languid and laid back. If you just look at the body and the head there is not much going on, but if you listen to what is being played……?

Nick: Phil Collins!!!!!! He was my favourite; he was my idol. Anything he played drums on I had it and memorised it note for note. I got a lot of my style from that.

How is the solo album coming?

Nick: It's done. It will be released in August sometime.

Neal: Mine as well.

You have got another one?

Neal: Yeah. There was going to be another Transatlantic in August, but it has been delayed, and I can't go for too many months without putting a record out. I just freak out!

With that, the guys had to leave as the bus was coming to take them to the venue. The above does not do justice to all the laughter that came with the interview. They were very easy to talk to, and Nick and I chatted very easily while waiting for them to leave. Nice guys, and a great band.

Brian Devoil (Twelfth Night), #75, Aug 2003

With the recent reissue of 'Fact and Fiction' I thought the timing was good to speak to Brian and ask him about that period of Twelfth Night.

Looking back at the heady days of 1982, what are your fondest memories of the recording and writing process of 'Fact & Fiction'?

We had some great times when Geoff came down to Reading (he was married with children and living in Manchester after all) particularly at weekends when the girlfriends arrived and spoilt us rotten. I also remember the sense of fun and adventure staying in the Mann's house in Salford - and going off to record late at night in leafy Cheadle Hulme.

The whole period was characterised by the sense of the unknown, a bit like the nervousness and excitement of a new love affair. I particularly enjoyed the responsibility of managing the band, which included negotiating the record/ publishing deals, getting gigs, organising the finances, press and publicity etc. The others were less interested in the business side of things and allowed me a large degree of control, which has become my favoured way of working ever since!!! Naturally this did cause some problems, but overall there was the sense that we were working together to achieve something, and although we did not enjoy significant commercial success, the fact that I am writing this now - over 20 years later - does show that the pride and care that we took in creating and promoting our music was well spent.

Why did Rick leave before the recording only to re-join again afterwards?

In 1981 the four of us (Andy, Clive, Rick and myself) were living together in Rick's house in Reading. Although it was a 3-bedroomed property - we were a bit cramped - what with all our gear, using the smallest room for rehearsing, and I think having numerous people staying over all the time - including my personal roadie, Tony, who slept in the lounge for at least six months!!! One of the consequences of this was that Rick understandably felt a bit uncomfortable in his own house, so when he decided to sell it and move to a smaller flat, Andy, Clive and myself moved across Reading and rented another house together. It was here that 'Fact & Fiction' was written, using the large lounge as a writing and rehearsal area.

Once we were back on the road it soon became apparent that we needed a separate keyboard player and as Rick was still a good friend, and had finished his own project (I think though I've never heard it to this day!!!!) he was the obvious choice. He did however cause us some consternation when, within hours of his first gig back with us, he ran off with our sound engineer's girlfriend!!

When MSI released the original CD, was the cover reversal deliberate or accidental?

Accidental, I think. We had only recently contacted them (as they had previously released the 'Live at the Target' CD - without our prior knowledge or permission!!!) - and hadn't yet developed an effective working relationship. Hence the mistake with the cover - and the lack of any input from us in the release.

What is your favourite song on the album and why?

Probably 'Creepshow' - because it contains several interesting musical themes, has great lyrics, and was fun to play. It also worked well live - both with Andy & Geoff.

In my review, I state that the album is one of the most important in the prog scene and is still relevant and powerful today. Are there are things on the album that you wish you had done differently?

At the time, yes - however listening to it now the only thing that stands out is the production, which leaves a lot to be desired. The engineering (basic recording) was not good enough and the circumstances that prevailed did not allow us to finish it off the way we'd have liked. We eventually 'bought' the album from the studio's owner - because we were not happy with their focus on "Eleanor Rigby" and "East of Eden". I seem to remember that we only had a day to mix all the other tracks - after the studio owner had spent about 4 days on the singles tracks. So, spending more time here would have helped. As for the final track selection, I think I marginally prefer the original version of "Human Being" - though there are great bits in both versions.

You have just been working on 'Art & Illusion'. When will this be released and what extras have been included this time around?

My copies have just arrived so if anyone wants one, they can order it directly from me, though it will not be in the shops until late September. Again, there are several extra tracks, primarily the 'MCA demos' ("Blue Powder Monkey", "Blondon Fair" and "Take A Look") which sort of re-creates the originally intended album, plus studio demos of "Counterpoint", "Kings & Queens", "Blondon Fair" & an edited version of "Take A Look". We've spent a lot of time on the artwork, photos and sleeve notes too - to make it a good package. I'm very pleased with the way it's come out. ....'Big up to the GFT massive', and all that!!!

Are all the albums eventually going to be reissued through Cyclops or are there any difficulties that may prevent this?

Hopefully, although the re-issue programme is dependent to some extent on the success of each new release. 'Live at the Target' is the next one due - again with a whole load of wonderful extra tracks. I'm starting work on it this week!!!! .... Sadly, we do not have the rights to the 'Virgin' album, and they seem reluctant to release it themselves - despite the best efforts of a 'TN' supporter who works for Virgin-Sweden - so we may have to release our own version of that one at some later date. (Same tracks - different recordings, to get around the copyright issues).

Are there any plans to have 'Live In London' available on CD or DVD? Are there are any plans to make any other live recordings more fully available?

As we do not own the rights to the pictures - turning 'Live From London' into a DVD would be problematic - however the soundtrack may well be issued as part of a series of CD-Rs that we are planning now. I'm hoping that our friend Mark Hughes will be masterminding this, with help from Jerry (the web-site man) - with me overseeing the process. My problem is simply finding the time to do all the things I'd like to do, in addition to all the things I should do!

I know that Andy Sears is now living abroad, but do you ever see any of the others and do any of you still perform?

I speak to Andy Sears quite often, and he has written some fascinating sleeve notes for the 'Art & Illusion' album too. Unfortunately, I do not speak to the other guys very often, and no-one is currently performing as far as I know, though Andy Sears would always be happy to sing you a song!! .... I'd like to think that one of these days some of us might get back together to play through a few tunes .... we'll keep you posted.

Who would you like to cover a TN song, which song would that be, and why?

I expect there's some clever answers to this question (though I'm not able to think of any at the moment) which is not one I've ever been asked before, so let me think .... For financial reasons ....how about Eminem doing "Creepshow"!!! .... or Pink Floyd to cover "Sequences"!!!!

Alan Morse (Spock's Beard), #75, Aug 2003

Of all the tracks on 'Feel Euphoria', the first few minutes of "Onomatopoeia" are the most unlike the old Spock's Beard. Was this set as the opener to prove that the band had changed and moved on?

Oh, I don't know...I think it was just a good hard rockin' tune to start off with. I don't think we needed to tell anyone that we've changed and moved on. We also wanted to use it as an English spelling test.

The whole album is very different indeed to 'Snow', how would you describe it to a newcomer to the band?

It's probably our hardest rocking record, so if you like that, you'll probably like FE. It's got a lot of changes, some longer songs, cool vintage keyboards, everything but the kitchen sink, as we say here in the US.

For me this album took a surprising amount of time to get inside, but now feel that it is one of my favourites, but that it is far removed from what I expect from SB. Do you feel that there has been a logical progression to this point through all your albums or has this been more of a leap?

It's funny, because I do not hear it as being all that different; I guess I'm too close to it. I did not set out to make it different, except maybe a little harder. I approached it like all our other records: we want it to be different enough that it's new and not a rehash of our previous records, but the same enough that it still sounds like the same band. There's less of the "singer/songwriter" stuff that Neal was particularly fond of. I guess you could say there is an "illogical progression" to this point!

Hard rock, ballads, but just enough complexity to remind the listener that this is still SB. You used to be a firm favourite of the prog crowd; do you think that 'Feel Euphoria' still fits within that label?

I hope the prog guys will like it. I think in some ways it is "proggier" than our previous records. There are more odd times & such; long songs and Mellotrons - it must be prog!

The whole writing and recording process must have been very different this time. What impact has it had on you personally, on the band and ultimately on the music?

It was totally different for me. I have more on the line with this record, more at stake personally. I think having everyone writing opened things up stylistically, we got a lot of different stuff, which is cool. It was fun writing the stuff. I mostly just went and hung out with friends and noodled around in my studio, so it was fun.

There was a time after Neal's departure when you were working with another multi-instrumentalist, John Boegehold. Some of his contributions have appeared on the album, but was he ever mooted as the next member of SB. If so, what happened?

John's a great guy and talented, but not up to playing the stuff live. We asked him if he would be interested in joining the band ages ago, before we found Ryo. He said he'd love to, but he was not that good a keyboard player. He's more of a writer and producer.

There has never been any doubt that Nick is a great lead singer, and he has more than proved it with many different styles on the album, but was it always the choice after Neal that he would take on the vocals?

We were not sure at first. We thought about getting another singer, but Nick wanted to go for it. Once we started recording vocals, there was no question he was the cat for the gig. He rules!

How are you going to play live, and have you given any decision as to who you may draft in?

We're going to play REALLY LOUD! (ha ha). But seriously, we plan to bring in another drummer to cover most of that so Nick can be out front most of the time. He'll probably play guitar a lot of the time. We do not know who the other drummer is going to be yet; I think Nick has some ideas. Guess we better find somebody soon!

Was there ever a time that Neal's departure was going to herald the end of SB?

No, we all wanted to keep going. This is, like, the most fun you can have! It was just a question of how to do it, and whether we could pull it off. It looks like we have pulled it off so far; I'm keeping my fingers crossed...

Genesis recorded a much-heralded concept album, lost their singer and replaced him with the drummer. If that comparison holds true to form, then you will be the next one to leave. Is it hard to be in SB without Neal, or has this in some way revitalised the way that you feel about the band?

I'm not going anywhere! Being in SB is a gas, great players, great music, everybody's cool. What's not to like? I do not want to sound like I'm dissing Neal, I'm not. He wrote a lot of great stuff, is amazingly talented, made this band what it is. But it's fun to get a shot at writing and doing some different things. It's an incredible opportunity, especially now that it looks like we'll be able to keep going.

What are the next steps for the band, and most importantly when are you next going to be playing any gigs in the UK?

We're getting ready to tour in October. We're doing one date in England this time, in London (surprise!) at the Mean Fiddler on the 22nd, so mark your calendars. Check our website though, things have a habit of changing sometimes. Hope to see you all there!

Karl Groom (Threshold), #78, Apr 2004

Although I have known Karl for years and have reviewed many albums he has been involved with, I had never conducted an interview with him. As Threshold are shortly releasing a new DVD and CD the time seemed right to correct that anomaly.

How would you describe your music to someone who has never heard it before; what do you think of the term prog metal?

Our intention when we started the band was to mix the styles of music we liked at the time. Nick and I liked the hard rock and metal bands, such as Testament and Metallica and others were into progressive bands like Genesis, Rush and Pink Floyd. The heavy side conveys the power and excitement in our music and the progressive influences allow a freedom of composition and strong sense of melody. When we started writing there was no genre called prog metal and we thought our strange hybrid of music would stop us getting any record company interest. I guess the title prog metal sums it up quite well. The only problem is that this usually makes people think of an American style of production and song writing. I always feel that we have a very British band sound though. Most bands in the genre are either US or German in my experience and this has helped us keep our own individual identity.

Is there one song that you think pinpoints the band, and why.

From the earlier albums "Into The Light" gives a good idea of what the band is about.

Typically, Threshold songs would combine melody and passion with a heavy backing which puts across the power of the music. Also, the lyrics have always played an important part of the composition. All too often in metal the lyrical side seemed like an afterthought, but we wanted look at more in depth subjects. The other side of Threshold, which is probably demonstrated better in the later albums, are the shorter arrangements. They also often involve technical aspects with time signature changes, but never at the cost of the song. Songs like "Light And Space" barely ever go into standard 4/4 metering, but the beat flows and this is what we are trying to get across.

Can you provide a quick thumbnail sketch of the other members of Threshold?

This type of question usually gets me into trouble. You can't please everyone!

Mac – Energetic, disorganized, a great communicator on stage, likes red wine

Nick – His equipment is always the first to breakdown, comes alive when we go on tour, likes beer

Rich - Competitive (watch out on the computer games!), organized (all keyboard players are), addicted to fresh coffee

Johanne – Phlegmatic, reserved off stage but flamboyant on stage, many hidden talents but never announces them, will only drink water and soft drinks

Steve – played the last tour and will play the new album, Nick and I have known him for a long time, very easy going and talented, drinks everything going!

Is there a band that you aspire to, or do you all have different musical influences? What musically gets you excited and is there anyone new we should be looking out for?

I'm not sure we would aspire to be another band. I could not try and write songs in the style of other musicians. In fact, we hope that the band has a distinctive style of its own. Most of the new music I hear is that of bands which I am producing in the studio. Also, I get a good collection of free stuff from Inside Out, our current label. Of the bands in the studio, there are a couple of good new power metal acts. I have just finished new albums for DragonForce (Sanctuary) and Power Quest (Now and Then). Both albums are released soon and are a big improvement on their debuts. The term power metal can put some people off, but there is a lot of melodic content and some great musicianship. Of the Inside Out releases I quite like the new Symphony X. Also, a favourite of mine is Testament – 'First Strike Still Deadly' – a new recording of some of their best songs.

I never expected to see Threshold without Jon Jeary, what is his reason for leaving the band and is Steve a permanent replacement?

Jon left the band at the end of 2002 after I persuaded him to play the ProgPower USA show in Atlanta. Three songs from this show are in the bonus section of the forthcoming DVD 'Critical Energy'. He had had enough of touring with the band and did not enjoy

the travelling anymore. Also, he wanted to find more time for his young family. Along with frequent touring commitments there is also the question of writing and recording which takes up a lot of time and effort. If you do not enjoy the whole process the quality of your performances will not be good enough. I think the reason the band have lasted so long is that we have always put in everything in the cause of composition and performance. Nick and I have known Steve for a long time and have played in bands together before. He comes from a different kind of musical background but enjoyed playing the dates last June and has the technical ability required for this kind of music. Last month we agreed he would record the new studio album and will join the band for the next live dates.

How did it feel not having Jon there to provide some of the backing vocals – did you and Richard have to change how you performed? Why don't you sing high anymore?

After so many years with Jon in the band it did feel a bit strange at first. We have always worked together in the band and in writing music. Rich and I did not have to change our performance – we are just a bit lazy when it comes to BVs and would gladly get someone else to do them. Before going out on tour we work quite hard on vocal harmonies as they are integral to our music. I do not find it difficult – just not fun to learn and rehearse. We briefly threatened Nick with some vocal duties, but he pretended not to hear! As it happens, Johanne is a very good singer and probably better than Richard and me, but I never like a drummer to sing as most of the noise going through the vocal mic would be drums which compromises the sound. With the high vocals, there are a couple of reasons. I did not like singing that way and I do not think it sounded very good; it is outside of my range. Also, the very high parts were usually as a result of Damian's recordings and we play less of those songs now.

There is an acoustic section within the concert on the DVD. Is this something you now put in regularly, and what benefits do you think that it gives both band and audience.

Last year we made an acoustic album called 'Wireless' which is available through the website. Thus, we wanted to play something from it on tour. The songs have drums and bass as well, so it fitted well with the live set. We also had a few songs from the past albums which were acoustic. I do not think we can do it all time, but in longer sets it adds some extra dynamics which make the following songs have more impact. Much like an album it is hard to have everything on one level and things need to build.

Regarding the DVD, what gave you the idea for providing a commentary on the concert? And why it is just you and Richard?

We just thought it would be quite unusual for a music DVD release. Director's commentary is usually part of a feature film DVD. Rich and I were the only two in the studio for this project and it was a bit of light relief from the production of the soundtracks. The work involved on this production for sound was a large undertaking. Our aim was to make the thing sound even better than previous studio albums and capture the excitement of a live recording. For a start the gig is over two hours long, which roughly doubles the length of a studio album. Secondly, you must make several mixes: stereo sound on the DVD, 5.1 surround mix for the DVD, which is time consuming, but a lot of fun, stereo mix for the commentary on DVD, stereo mix with edits for the CD release Also, there are a lot of problems to deal with on a live performance, mainly being that there is a lot of spill on microphones. You can hear at least some of the rest of the band on all mics. This means editing out the noise on each track before mixing to get good separation. In the end, it took as long to do as it would take to record and mix a studio album, but we were very happy with the result.

You have been more successful on the continent than the UK, why do you feel this is?

There are more venues to play and more people turn up to live shows and buy CDs. Also, I think rock music in general is more popular in the rest of Europe and America. Manufactured pop music in the UK has long been the most exposed and promoted style of music over here. If that is all people hear it will naturally be the type of music which is most successful. Having said that, with the advent of the Bloodstock festival in Derby, it shows there is quite a large support for prog metal and power metal. There are still relatively few good venues to play compared to the rest of Europe though.

It has been a long road since 'Wounded Land' in 1993. Apart from the new DVD what musical highlights have there been for you both inside and outside of Threshold.

It is a joy to still be making albums with Threshold now we're on our seventh studio album. I think things have lasted and we are still fresh because we have a great time doing it. I also have a lot of fun producing other bands in many different styles.

What will 2004 mean for Threshold?

We are finishing writing for a new studio album now and will start recording early in February. The release of the live DVD and double CD set of 'Critical Energy' will also be February. In addition to that the 1997 Threshold title 'Extinct Instinct' will now be released on Inside Out. The album has been re-mastered, the artwork has been reworked with a new booklet and three extra tracks have been added. Two of them are radio mixes of "Exposed" and "Virtual Isolation" and the other is the track "Mansion", previously only available on the Japanese version. Also, there should be another Bloodstock appearance with some other UK shows, followed by a European tour.

Kerry Livgren, # 80, Jul 2004

Your first band was the Gimlets, formed some forty years ago now, what inspired you to pick up the guitar? What sort of music were you listening to and playing at the time?

I grew up listening to a mixture of Jazz, Classical, Movie Soundtracks, and of course American Rock and Pop, and later British Pop. The Gimlets did some original music which was patterned after bands like Paul Revere & the Raiders, The Outsiders, Beau Brummels, etc. I was a huge fan of The Yardbirds and the Kinks, and later of Procol Harum. Hearing the first Procol album was a turning point for me.

In 1969 you formed The Mellotones with Don Montre, how did you first meet him? Were Reasons Why and Saratoga formed after this group had folded or did they run concurrently?

I met Don when he invited me to do a "pick up gig" with the Mellotones. There was a brief period where I was immersed in playing Black R&B - The Temptations, O' Jays, etc. Don and I became fast friends and knew we would be playing together from then on. The mixture of his R&B feel, and my leaning toward progressive rock made for an interesting mix. The Reasons Why was an R&B club band doing all covers and was where I met Lynn Meredith and Zeke Low. I talked them into doing something more serious and we formed Saratoga and started doing our own music. It sounded like a cross between Spirit, Chicago Transit Authority, and early Santana, with a bit of Procol Harum thrown in for seasoning.

Saratoga then became Kansas, including later famous players Phil Ehart and Dave Hope. How did this line-up compare musically with Kansas II, and are there are any recordings from this period?

Oh, how I wish there were some decent recordings of the first Kansas. It was quite a bizarre band - difficult to describe. It was truly prog rock before we had ever heard of that term, but a distinctly American version of the genre. It was a bit heavier with more of a hard rock feel than the second Kansas.

Were Phil and Dave both still in White Clover at this time?

Phil Ehart and Dave Hope, along with Rich Williams were in White Clover in 1970, which merged with Saratoga to form the first Kansas. It was a 7-piece band.

What sort of places were you playing, and were you performing totally original material? Did any of this resurface in later Kansas songs?

We played anywhere we could - schools, clubs, festivals, etc. It was an ever-diminishing list. Wc did almost all original music, with a few heavily altered cover songs. I do not believe any of the first Kansas songs resurfaced later, until "Myriad" on the "Somewhere to Elsewhere" album.

How did you meet John Bolton, and what impact did his joining have on the sound of the band?

When the first Kansas split up, I was used to having a woodwind player in the band, so we searched for a replacement for Larry Baker. Lynn Meredith, our vocalist, knew John from Manhattan, Kansas. We tried him out and knew immediately he was the guy. John came from a real jazz background, plus he had a penchant for using his instrument in unorthodox ways.

Why did you join White Clover, and why then was the name changed to Kansas?

The second version of Kansas (now Proto-Kaw) struggled for several years before I finally gave it up, reluctantly, to join White Clover. Kansas II was dogmatic about our originality, and the band was just in the wrong time and place, perhaps ahead of our time. No one knew quite what to do with us, and we grew weary of trying to get a record deal and having things fall through. It was a heartbreak leaving my friends, but something had to change. When I went with White Clover, I told them the name had to go, and since Kansas II disbanded after I left, we took the name.

What are your favourite memories of the Seventies with Kansas?

Well, I suppose my favourite memory was just those days when we were first seeing the long struggle finally pay off. It was very exciting to have albums out on an international label and to be on tour with some of the very bands that we used to idolize.

Why did you originally leave Kansas?

Steve Walsh and Robby Steinhardt were gone, and it just was not the same. I had been with the group for 13 years at that point and I needed a change. I had formed A.D. during my second solo album, 'Timeline', and it was fresh and exciting, and we had like goals and motives.

What were you doing between leaving Kansas and re-joining? Why is it that you did not have greater commercial success during this period?

That covers quite a few years. There were the A.D. years, (1983-1986), there were several solo projects, video soundtracks, writing for Kansas, etc., but there were also a few years of sabbatical where I went after other goals such as theology, aviation and agriculture. (I realize that sounds like a strange mix). I was not pursuing commercial success in a big way during those years.

What brought about the reformation of the 'classic' line-up for the superb album 'Somewhere To Elsewhere'?

I was on a writing binge, and much of the material sounded to me to be quite well suited for Kansas. Phil Ehart agreed and out of those sessions came 'Somewhere To Elsewhere' and my CD entitled 'Collector's Sedition Vol. I'.

Is there going to be a new Kansas studio album, and will you be involved?

With Kansas, I have learned to "never say never". There are no present firm plans, but one never knows.

Were you asked to be involved in the DVD recording?

There was a bit of confusion surrounding that process when it took place. I would have liked to have been a part of it, but for whatever reason it did not happen.

What was it like reforming the old line-up of Kansas? Had you kept in touch in the intervening years?

No one, in their wildest dreams, ever thought this band would re-form. We had pretty much drifted apart. I knew Dan Wright's whereabouts but that was about it. It took some detective work just to find everyone, and of course I knew that Don was deceased.

Were you surprised that there was so much interest in the original recordings?

Quite surprised. In retrospect, I realize those early recordings are a historical footnote which chronicles some (very rare) early American Progressive Rock.

Had the other guys been totally out of the scene or had they stayed involved?

For the most part, they were out of music altogether. In some cases, they no longer owned musical instruments.

Which of the songs on the new album are from the old days?

"Axolotl", "Heavenly Man", and "Theophany" were performed by the band back in the 70's, although these versions are a bit different. Most of 'Before Became After' is totally new.

What did the current Kansas line-up say when they heard that the original band was reforming?

I'm not sure they were aware that it was happening. I talked with Phil a bit and he thought it was great that these musicians were "finally getting their shot".

Will Proto-Kaw and Kansas ever gig together?

That would make for quite an interesting show. It would certainly be a busy night for me! We'll have to wait and see on that one…

How did you get involved with Neal Morse?

I was certainly aware of Neal's work with Spock's Beard, but we were not previously acquainted. We began to talk a bit about other things, and Neal was asking me for some advice. Later, he came out to Kansas and asked if I would play a bit on his project – of course I said yes.

Was it ever mooted that you would tour with him?

No, we never discussed that, although there has been some talk about Proto-Kaw doing shows with Neal.

What is the rationale behind Numavox?

Numavox is an artist-run label which exists primarily for my solo projects. It gives me total artistic flexibility and freedom, but it is a bit of a trade-off, as I certainly do not have the distribution I would otherwise have, but the financial side of it is good too since "I'm where the buck stops" and there are no legal hassles.

Is there going to be another album from Proto-Kaw and are we ever likely to see you in Europe!

In answer to both – we certainly hope so!

Martin Orford (IQ), # 80, Jul 2004

Martin has been one of the UK's most important progressive keyboard players for many years and with the release of the IQ's new album, 'Dark Matter', the time seemed right for a chat.

The music for 'Dark Matter' seems to have shifted away from previous IQ albums, bringing in older influences yet also maintaining certain IQ traits. Was this a conscious decision?

We never make conscious decisions about what direction to take - the music just evolves its own identity in the writing process. However, there was definitely an intention to use some classic "retro" sounds on the album simply because there are so many good products on the market at the moment.

Keyboards seem to be playing a more important part in this album with lots more sounds and styles. Have you used different keyboards to those on 'Seventh House'?

Yes, and the most significant one for me was the Korg CX-3 organ. It's basically a grungy old Hammond sound-alike, but it does not weigh a ton and take up half the house like the original. As soon as I borrowed the CX-3 from a friend who works for Korg, I just started to write music that had a much harder direction, and before I knew it I had quite a large chunk of the album done. This fitted in very well with what the others were writing too, and I soon gave the borrowed CX-3 back and forked out for one of my own.

At about the same time we came across a software module called Sampletank which runs on the Apple Mac within Pro Tools, and it just had the most superb Church Organ and Mellotron sounds. I used to have a Mellotron, but it was a terrible old thing that was terribly abused on the road and ended up hardly working at all. The Sampletank sounds are like a brand new Mellotron just out of the factory, and as such were a far cry from what I've been used to. With such a rich assortment of retro sounds available (and no-one is doing anything with startling new sounds in the synth market presently) the album took shape around those sounds, and we make no apologies for that. Retro keyboard sounds are bang in fashion now, so we seized the moment. Old is the new New.

Who would you say is the biggest musical influence on your own writing and why?

Classical Music. Always has been and always will be for me. However, I did dig out a couple of ELP and Deep Purple albums this time for some handy hints on rock organ playing as my skills in that department were a bit rusty.

What is the writing process for IQ?

A great big fight with lots of bloodshed and ill-feeling all round. It works, but it's not pretty to watch.

Do any of you influence Peter with his lyrics, and does he ever explain what they mean?

No, the lyrics are Pete's thing and he does it very well. I was happy to record most of the vocals for the album with Pete, and occasionally I will suggest ways of making some lines sound more natural by adding or dropping a syllable here and there, but that's only details really. Haven't a clue what any of it means of course, but it all sounds fabulous.

It is now twenty years since 'Tales...', and the line-up today is four fifths of the line-up then. What has kept you together for so long (although Peter did have some time off for good behaviour), and what has been the highlights of that time?

Don't know - answers on a postcard please...! There is no logical reason at all for the longevity of IQ. We are certainly not always the best of friends, and we rarely share a common ideology, so it's a complete mystery. Except of course that when IQ is in full flow it's as good if not better than any prog band in the world.

You keep yourself busy with other bands as well, but is NO ever going to be resurrected for a whole album instead of just one song?

I don't know - if Clive ever pays me any royalties for the one song that NO did, I might consider it!

When are you going to be releasing your follow-up solo album?

At the moment, I am very busy with all the promotion and admin work for the 'Dark Matter' release so I will not have any time to work on music for weeks. However, I will try to dust down what I have already for the next solo album later this summer and start getting it into shape, hopefully with a view to having an album out some time in 2005.

What albums or artists excited you recently?

Nothing much really - I try to avoid listening to music altogether when I am working on a project as big as an IQ album. I find it terribly distracting to hear other stuff during a work period, and I'm not a great music listener even when I have a bit of leisure time - I'd generally rather watch the telly. I am fascinated by the construction process of music, but as a leisure activity it just does not do it for me. I suppose familiarity breeds disinterest, and in just the same way I could understand how a gynaecologist wouldn't be interested in pornography or a carpenter wouldn't go out at weekends looking at timber. If you know exactly how it all works, somehow most things lose their fascination.

What can we expect from IQ and yourself personally over the next year?

IQ have some gigs coming up in the autumn, but in the meantime, I have a good album to sell and when that's done, I'm going fishing.

Lastly, why is the label called Giant Electric Pea???

After a mythical instrument that Mike Holmes is alleged to have played on the 'Are You Sitting Comfortably?' album. If you check the credits, the label narrowly escaped being called "Flying Tart" or "Gas Driven Sea Biscuit"!

Woolly Wolstenholme, #81, Dec 2004

Following on from the release of Woolly's new solo album, I caught up with him to ask about the album and some matters** relating **to Barclay James Harvest.

Why did you leave BJH in 1979?

My body left in 1979 - my mind went two or three years earlier. The issues that prompted me to take the leap had been lying around for a while and included a changing dynamic within the band. Certainly, the music was going in a direction that was not to my taste, and I had to decide whether it was in my interest to try and hold the musical direction and send it along my preferred route, or to bail out. Sometimes things are done not on the spur of the moment, but arrive progressively and, rather like any other relationship, you know when your number is up.

Things appeared to go well with 'Maestoso', so why did you not initially complete 'Black Box'?

Funds! There was a catch to Polydor carrying on with the second album and that was that one other territory had to "join in" with the project, and no-one did.

Not many musicians have given up the business to become a farmer. What inspired you to take this course of action and what do you think that you gained out of it personally?

I did not know what to do, so I went down the road that was offered, rather than by choice. I think I gained some muscles (which I have now lost).

Did you keep in touch with Mel, John or Les when you were farming?

Nope.

Were you doing anything musically at all during this period?

Yes, I would sing "Two Little Boys" at barbecues. Very popular ...

When did you meet with John and what brought you back into playing again?

Two people organised a clandestine meeting at The Bull's Head in Delph, then we went to an Art School reunion and finally John's sister said, "Just bloody do something!", so we did.

What has been the response of fans to the fact that there are two versions of BJH playing and what are your own feelings about it?

Dazed and confused.

Do you think that you will ever play with Les again?

Nope.

What one memory would you like to share of Mel?

In the very early days, we used to do a cover of "She's Funny That Way", and Mel spent the best part of the song warming up a trombone for the centre solo, but when the appointed moment arrived, he did not use the trombone, but made the sound with his mouth - he was funny that way!

Why record another solo album after all this time? What drove you to this and did you enjoy the experience enough to contemplate another in a slightly shorter timeframe?

I prefer not to be too pedantic about labelling my output. Since I returned from the wilderness, 'Nexus', 'Revival', 'Black Box Recovered' and now 'One Drop' ... are all part of my musical renaissance and I like to think of them being a continuum. The next album is already written, and when we sell enough of this one there'll be another.

There are many different styles on the album - what music do you listen to for pleasure and what inspires you?

I chiefly listen to classical music. Current playlist is Hans Rott's one and only symphony - he went mad, and Cecil Cole's "Fra Giacomo" - he died in the first one. And as usual, Salome and Die Frau Ohne Schatten by Dicky Strauss. On the pop/rock front (usually other people's houses) King Crimson, Procol Harum and Madonna!

How would you describe the album to someone who hasn't heard it?

It would be easy to view my writing as being limited to one "big one" per BJH album, but the truth is that I have written in many styles over the years. On the first three EMI albums, I batted my end with a variety of songs, but by the time of 'Baby James Harvest' I went for the orchestral approach with "Moonwater", and that set the scene for the future. As my arrangements became more set in stone, whilst it might have been easier to offer ten songs played on guitar or piano, I usually provided one large-canvas piece and only a couple of others. By 'XII' I'd managed to get two songs through, but some of the stuff on 'Maestoso' had previously been offered to BJH for inclusion ("American Excess", "Gates Of Heaven" and "Maestoso (A Hymn In The Roof Of The World)" etc.), but by then the die was well and truly cast.; John 5, Les 5, me 2 (or 1). Stylistically, the songs on 'One Drop In A Dry World' are indeed broad-based, but a song dictates its own direction. The first twang or plonk gives you the mood and it's hard to change style once you have set out on a road.

Why did you credit it to Maestoso instead of Woolly?

When I work with John, there is a vehicle that uses the BJH banner plus a by-line of Through The Eyes Of John Lees. If I do not work with John, it must be solo, although since 'Black Box' I preferred to call it a band, and that's why it's Mæstoso (occasionally it's credited as Woolly Wolstenholme's Mæstoso, but that is only an advertising masterstroke).

"Souk" is a strong favourite, but I must ask, is "Carpet" directed at anyone?

You, the listener.

What is next, both for you and for Maestoso?

Currently working on a limited-edition live album of the Mean Fiddler gig, a Christmas single (!) and hopefully lots more live work after the November concert at the Bloomsbury Theatre in London (tickets 35p from the man outside!).

Peter Nicholls (IQ), # 82, Jan 2005

2004 saw not only the release of 'Dark Matter', but also the DVD of the Twentieth Anniversary gig from 2001 so, this seemed like an opportune time to look at what has been happening with all this prog nonsense.

The DVD shows the wonderful band that was such an inspiration to IQ, The Lens. Did you ever see them play, and how did you initially get involved with Martin and Mike?

Mike and I met on July 10th, 1976 at Bingley Hall in Stafford when Genesis were playing there on the 'Trick Of The Tail' tour. It was that hot summer that everyone remembers and there were hundreds of us sitting outside the hall in the afternoon, waiting for the doors to open. I forget now exactly how we contacted each other but I do remember he was holding a copy of 'The Lamb' which, at a distance, I thought he'd been scribbling on. Closer inspection revealed he'd got it signed by the band. I was massively impressed by this and I got talking to him and his friend Niall. We exchanged addresses with the intention of swapping bootlegs and during our letter writing he revealed that he was a guitarist and Niall was a drummer. I'd spent many long hours miming with a hairbrush in front of the mirror so somehow I announced in one letter that I was a singer (never having sung a note in public!) and we decided we should get a band together. With them living in Southampton and me in Manchester, this was not going to be easy but two months later I was down in Southampton and the three of us were jamming about together.

At this point, we were calling ourselves The Giln and that name changed to The Lens about a year later, I think. As the band developed and other members joined, they tended to rehearse without me because I lived so far away, because of which pretty much all the material they wrote was instrumental. I appeared with The Lens at one concert, in the grounds of Netley Abbey in Southampton, in 1978. I introduced the songs but did not sing at all (although I seem to recall a ramshackle attempt at 'Afterglow' by Genesis as an encore, but I could not say for sure now if I sang on that). After that gig, I kind of faded away from the band, and the bassist and keyboardist left to be replaced by Les 'Ledge' Marshall and a certain Martin Orford respectively.

Had you been in any bands prior to that?

No, this was my first experience of being in a band though I must admit I was very intimidated by the musicians, especially Mike who, even at the age of 17, was already an amazing player and quite a charismatic character. On the rare occasions, I did manage to haul myself down to Southampton for a rehearsal I was too scared to sing, and I had no confidence whatsoever at that time, it was just something I wanted to be able to do. I thought as soon as I opened my mouth to sing it would be blindingly obvious to everyone how lousy I was, so I made the wise decision to keep quiet if possible.

What are your fondest memories of those early days?

It was a whole new world to me, and I was happy to be swept along by it all. I just wish I'd had the courage to sing at those early rehearsals. If I'm honest with myself, I was pretending to be a singer in a band, but I had to start somewhere. They were very rich formative years and the perimeters of my life opened after meeting Mike and Niall. The chances of us meeting at Stafford in the first place were probably thousands to one. If any of us had arrived half an hour earlier or later that day, we would have been sitting too far apart to ever have met and there would have been no IQ as we know it. A scary thought!

Right from the beginning you were producing lyrics that were of an extremely thoughtful nature - what inspires you, and have you ever considered writing a novel or collection of short stories?

I went through the teenage phase of writing angst-ridden poems, which I think all angst-ridden teenagers go through, and some fragments of these were recycled as early IQ lyrics. I was also into writing short stories and plays for two or three years and was quite prolific, looking back. I had a play called 'Pedestrians' performed by the Contact Theatre in Manchester. I suppose I was exploring different formats, different ways of using words.

Writing lyrics is probably the biggest challenge because they must fit the metre and the mood of the music, of course. There's less room for waste, each line should count, I've always written from an emotional point of view. In the early days, lazy journalists would slag off progressive rock for its 'wizards and elves' imagery so I made a point of avoiding that, to take away some of their ammunition when they took a swipe at us. Songs like "The Enemy Smacks" and "The Last Human Gateway" approach the subject matter from the perspective of a central character's experience. Some of my attempts at tackling slightly more controversial topics like domestic violence in "Just Changing Hands" were clumsy in retrospect and they did not always work but all the way through my lyrics you'll find an emotional core which I hope the listener connects with.

Do you explain the concept of the lyrics to the guys, and which comes first, lyrics or music?

It's pretty much always the music first, although when I'm working on a melody of my own it always has lyrics in some form or other at the same time. "Born Brilliant" from the latest album was my tune which came at the same time as the lyric. There was one time when we decided to try working from the lyrics first and that was "The Sense In Sanity" on 'Subterranea'. I wrote the lyrics for the whole track and sent them off to Martin to see what he could come up with musically. He found that he could not make the lyrics fit the tune he had in mind so I amended them to make them fit his tune and in fact re-wrote most of them in the process so we ended up doing it the way we always do!

I'm very rarely asked to explain the lyrics to the band. One thing we've learned to do over the years is to give each other the space to make our own contributions to the albums. Martin and Mike will make the occasional request when I'm recording the vocals, they'll suggest that a line should be a couple of syllables longer or shorter, but generally the band are happy to leave me to my own devices with the lyrics and I think they know by now that what I write will be appropriate for the music…and hopefully good. Similarly, Martin arranges the music with much more skill and flair than I could ever hope to, and Mike handles the production duties brilliantly, so we all have our roles to play within the band. I tend to avoid explaining the lyrics if possible, I'm much happier for people to make their own interpretations.

'The Wake' was/is an amazing album, so why did you leave after it?

By the time we started recording 'The Wake' in 1985, we'd been living in each other's pockets constantly for a couple of years. Originally, Martin, Mike, Tim and I shared a small two-bedroomed flat in north London and, although I'd moved out into my own luxurious bedsit, we were still spending loads of time together, with no money to speak of and playing gigs anywhere that would have us. It was not a very healthy lifestyle for any of us and the internal relationships were put under a lot of pressure. I finally moved back to Manchester, travelling to London and back for rehearsals and gigs, and to be honest it was a very dark time for me, I was unhappy. I was also having personal problems outside of the band and in the end, I just had to let something go. We were not the kind of people to talk about our feelings with each other, so I had nowhere to turn. I agonised over making the decision for months and eventually, even though I was very proud of the music we were making, and it felt like we were on the brink of something happening, I decided I had to get out. Martin has since said that if I hadn't gone someone else probably would have done, so I guess that shows that other people were feeling the strain too.

My leaving was not handled at all well and for a long time there was not any friendly contact between the band and me, but I do think we had to go through that bleak experience to be where we are today. Sure, there are still conflicts within the band, we disagree a lot when we're writing new material, but the situation now is vastly improved from what it was then. We're very different individuals in many ways but I have a lot of respect for the other guys.

How did Niadem's Ghost come about and why only the one album?

When I left IQ in 1985, I knew I still wanted to be active musically. Dave Bennett and I had been in a band together and had written songs together before I joined IQ, and he was working with Brian Grantham (ex-Slaughter and the Dogs!) and Dave Tompkins as We Happy Few. I needed a band, so we joined forces, ditched all their material, and obviously, all my material with IQ, adopted the name Niadem's Ghost and started afresh. It was a good challenge for me to be working without keyboards. By necessity, our more stripped-down sound meant that the writing had to be very strong. I enjoyed working that way, I felt I had more of a say musically than I'd had in IQ and initially I was happy to explore a more 'indie' direction.

Although we progressed quite rapidly in the two years we were together, and we produced some music which I felt was quite original, we had lots of obstacles to overcome. I found it hard starting over again and there was a certain resistance within the band to expanding our sound and introducing keyboards which, after a while, I thought we needed to do. We never had any money, and, in the end, that was probably what killed the band. Besides which, I do not think the name did us any favours because no-one could spell it or pronounce it properly. We should have gone for something simple and memorable. But it's easy to say these things in hindsight, of course.

Having left the fold, you were warmly welcomed back, how did that come about and were you surprised at the reaction that 'Ever' created eight years after your last studio album with IQ?

In January 1990, after Tim and Paul had left the band, IQ played at The Marquee as a four-piece, with Les 'Ledge' Marshall on bass and Martin handling the lead vocals and keyboards. By this time, we were on good terms with each other again and Mike phoned me one night to ask if I'd like to appear with them for the encores. I paced up and down backstage for the whole of their set and then we did 'The Enemy Smacks' and 'Awake and Nervous' together. There was an incredible atmosphere that night. I wore the old greasepaint because I wanted to recreate those early days for the sake of the people in the audience who hadn't seen me with the band.

At the same time, a promoter in Paris was organising a Magma concert at Le Cigale and when he heard about this show at The Marquee, he contacted us to offer IQ the support slot, but on the understanding that I was in the line-up. The Marquee was only intended as a one-off because the band felt (and I could see their viewpoint) that my re-joining permanently might seem like a backward step so initially they were reluctant to agree to the promoter's terms. Eventually, though, we decided it could not do any harm in the long run so we went ahead with it and I must say, my memories of that night are really good, though it seems Magma's fans have very partisan tastes and they did not take to us at all. Luckily, there was a sizeable contingent in the audience who were there to see us and they were very enthusiastic indeed.

Later that year, Ledge died unexpectedly, and we were all knocked for six. His death came as a massive shock to all of us who knew and loved him. It sounds like a cliché but

that experience did make us grow up and realise that our friendships were far more important than our petty squabbles and differences in the past, so when the band eventually regrouped we decided that the four of us should stay together and genuinely we all believe it's what Ledge would have wanted. For us my re-joining was not a big decision, it felt natural and it happened for good reasons. We came together as a group of friends who happen to have this special bond of being able to make music together.

In some ways, 'Ever' was quite a safe album, I suppose. It was very IQ, going back to the more atmospheric, dramatic area of music we'd done earlier, but we had to re-establish ourselves after quite a long absence and with some significant internal changes. It was the first studio album for four years, the first with me back in the band and the first with John replacing Ledge. We all knew it was a strong album, but it certainly came as a great confidence booster when it was so well received.

How long had you been working on the concept for 'Subterranea' prior to presenting it to the band?

I was at art college in the late '70s when I saw Werner Herzog's film 'The Enigma Of Kaspar Hauser' which was the story of an enigmatic young man who appeared in Nuremberg in 1828. He was about 16 years old and he'd been held captive in a dungeon all his life and had had no contact with other people. Then one day, without explanation, he was released and left to wander about on his own. No-one knew who he was or could explain why he'd been a prisoner for so long but he was subsequently killed and so his secret died with him. The story made quite an impact on me, I was intrigued by it and it stayed with me over the years. When we were writing 'Subterranea', we knew we wanted to try presenting ourselves differently on stage, more theatrically, so the idea developed that the album should be a double, which would give us enough material to support a completely new show. I thought it could be good to update and expand on the original Kaspar Hauser story. Isolation has cropped up from time to time as a theme in my lyrics and this would take it to its logical extreme.

I used elements of the original story (Kaspar said his father had been a 'gallant rider' which I used in the lyrics) but shifted it to a modern city setting. Usually we write the music first, then I lock myself away and work on the lyrics on my own. With 'Subterranea', the whole creative process was more integrated. I still wrote all the lyrics, but we would talk about the story while we were working on the music, as well as thinking about how it could be presented visually. It was a great collaborative experience and one that I personally really got a lot from.

What was it like touring with that show?

Great, I loved every minute of it. It was like performing a film live on stage. I liked the fact that the visual presentation moved it away from being a rock gig and into a new theatrical area. Without having to speak to the audience between tracks, I could stay tuned into the story for the whole 100 minutes or so. We dived in at the start of the show and did not come up for air until it was all over. Very atmospheric on stage and some of our very best music is on that album. Getting the gauze screen to cover the front of the stage was an enormous achievement for us. We approached several theatre companies to ask their advice on how we could construct a roller so that the screen could rise and fall, and they all said it could not be done. Fortunately, with people like Martin 'Oggie' Ogden and Andy McEvoy on our side we found a way. All the projections were done using VHS tapes and poor old Andy had a suitcase with all these tapes cued up to the right point. Nowadays he and Dene use DVDs so if we were to stage the show again now it would be much more impressive, I think.

Setting everything up and taking it down at the end of the night was very demanding and time-consuming, an enormous amount of work especially when combined with all the travelling we had to do on tour but for us the production drew a line in the sand and showed us what we're able to achieve with the right amount of determination and an amazing group of people who wanted to see it work as much as we did. It led to us using the three screens which we now have.

How did the concept for the cover artwork on 'Dark Matter' come about - do you influence the design?

Not really. Tony Lythgoe, who designs all our packaging, has always been into IQ so he's very sympathetic to what we're doing musically. Mike and I made the odd suggestion here and there, but the finished art is very much Tony's brainchild. We knew from the outset that this would be a dark and brooding album so that was Tony's brief – to come up with something almost gothic in approach. I'd keep him supplied with discs of the music as it was developing which he used for inspiration and finally he came up with this very striking image which everyone liked immediately and, I think, captures the atmosphere of this album.

What is the story behind "Harvest Of Souls"?

In March of last year, while we were recording 'Dark Matter', we played at Baja Prog in Mexicali. A week later I was due to start recording the vocals, so I was under a stupid amount of pressure while we were there to get the lyrics finished in time. Consequently, I spent most of my time on that trip stuck in my hotel room trying to get these damn words written. It was a very weird time because I kept falling asleep in the evening and then waking up at 3.00 the next morning, not knowing where on earth I was. I felt very detached from the rest of the band.

Most of the time I concentrated on "Harvest Of Souls" so that feeling of being in unfamiliar surroundings and out of my normal routine seeped into the lyrics. Loosely it's kind of about judgment day, the final day of reckoning when all the souls are brought together. Cheerful stuff, as usual. The 'America' section is the most contentious part of that track because it sees us stepping into the real world lyrically, which we do not normally do. That came about purely because we had the tune for that section and the word 'America' fitted nicely as a hook. So, then I thought, "Well OK, if I'm going to refer to America, what do I want to say about America?" While I wouldn't want to make overt political statements through the lyrics, because I do not think it's the place to do it, it's hard as a parent not to wonder about the future of the planet. What kind of world my daughter will grow up in? I'm making a comment on the mistaken assumption that military strength gives you the right to do what you want. I kept it quite vague because I can't hope to represent the views of all the members of the band but it's probably obvious that I'm expressing a satirical view. But the 'America' section is only a small part of a 24 -minute track.

Who comes up with the idea for the encores, and what is your favourite, or has that yet to appear?

They're all band choices, usually determined by what everyone likes and what we have the time to rehearse. "Jet" was good at the 20th anniversary gig in London (on the DVD) and we did a great version of Björk's 'It's Oh So Quiet' a few years ago (though it took us ages to get right!). Back in the early days we sometimes ran "Intelligence Quotient" into a Genesis medley which included "The Cinema Show", "Robbery, Assault and Battery" and "The Musical Box". That was good fun to do. I always enjoyed doing "Suffragette City" and "Relax". "Sweet Transvestite" with all the costume accessories was a memorable one, too. I'd like to do Talking Heads' "Psycho Killer". Maybe we should do an album of covers.

Of all prog bands that I have seen you are probably the one that enjoys themselves most onstage. Are you ever concerned as to what Mike and John might get up to?

Well, John certainly likes to bound about all over the stage and I have to have eyes in the back of my head sometimes. I think he found some aspects of the 'Subterranea' show quite difficult because it was more choreographed than a normal gig and he was forced to stay rooted to the spot more than he perhaps would have liked. The hardest thing for me during a gig is if I happen to glance over at Mike and he pulls a funny face, it just cracks me up. Also, the minute I forget a lyric (which I often do); he always notices and lets me know he's noticed.

IQ are a very theatrical band with a strong visual image, do you miss the make up?

In some ways, I do. I wore it again for the 20th anniversary tour. It seemed an appropriate time to do it and I must admit when I was putting it on in the dressing room it did help me to focus my mind on the gig ahead. I also felt very different with it slapped all over my face; it made me behave in a different way. There's no denying that it was something for me to hide behind when we started out, as well as being a device for trying to draw attention to us. For a lot of our early gigs, we used to set up in the corner of a pub somewhere and half the battle was to get the audience, such as it was, to notice us so the make-up helped a little in that respect, I think. At the time, I preferred people to think I looked ridiculous (which I frequently did!) than not even notice we were there and I'm not the kind of person who can amble onstage and trot out a couple of songs without some kind of thought given to how it all looks. I can't see myself wearing all that greasepaint again soon because it's a real pain to get off at the end of the night.

23 years down the road - what has been the highlight of your time with IQ?

Well, it's been a succession of highs and lows, to be honest, though the highs outweigh the lows these days, I'm happy to say. The early days were quite tough - we built up our following slowly, with constant gigging, thundering up and down the motorways of Britain in a van that kept breaking down. It was the only way we knew how to do it. Progress was painfully slow sometimes and we often felt like we were not getting anywhere but we developed the ability to play good gigs which has always stood us in good stead. Without doubt, the lowest point was when Ledge died in 1990.

For me the highpoint, apart from the fact that the band still exists after all this time, is that we're still doing our best work. Since 'Ever' in 1993, the first album with this line-up, we've maintained an upward curve creatively. 'Dark Matter' received some fantastic reviews and is our best-selling album to date, which is a great achievement. I'd feel bad if I thought people were only coming to see us live in the hope of hearing us play some of the early songs but the truth is they want to hear the new material just as much as the old stuff and in fact songs like "The Seventh House", "Born Brilliant" and "Harvest Of Souls" are among our strongest and most effective live numbers. It will not be long before we're playing our 25th anniversary shows! If you'd told me when I joined the band in 1982 that we'd reach our 25th anniversary, I would never have believed it possible but here we are, defying all expectations.

Neal Morse, #82, Jan 2005

Neal has a new album out, 'One', but I hadn't spoken to him for a while so firstly I asked him about his leaving of Spock's Beard and 'Testimony'.

Looking back at your decision to leave Spock's Beard when you did, do you now regret not touring 'Snow' and why did you have to leave as soon as it was completed?

Well that's what I felt the Lord wanted me to do. That was the hardest thing I've done in my life so far. And doing that without touring…I worked and prayed about that one for a long time. It kind of did not feel right not to tour…for the fans. But I also felt in my spirit it would ultimately be a bad decision. I can't explain it. I have no explanation to provide other than I felt it in my spirit…that it would not be wise.

Did you consider staying in Spock's Beard and writing Christian songs within that framework to possibly reach a wider audience, as Geoff Mann did with Twelfth Night?

I did not consider it because it did not seem like the right thing to do. I was already feeling a little awkward just knowing what I was singing about in 'Snow'…in songs like "Open Wide the Floodgates," "Love Beyond Words" and "Wind At My Back." And the

band...having people who did not believe what we were singing about...that would be strange. I would have done whatever the Lord asked me to take on, though. But I was just trying to be obedient. I still am today.

Were you surprised at the reaction to 'Testimony' from the prog magazines?

I did not know what to expect. I hoped that people would be open to it...would like it. I hoped that my traditional audience would embrace it, but that's not something you ultimately have control over. Some people, I felt, might find the lyrics challenging. For the most part, though, people were very positive, and the prog media was generally very supportive, for which I am grateful. When I was creating it, I had no idea what people would say. At that point, I was just trying to follow where I felt led in prayer...so ultimately, the [media's] reaction was not important.

I was at the London gig and there seemed to be a real understanding within the audience, an embracing of your personal story. What reaction was there to your music within both the Christian music field, and the churches themselves?

Well it has been good in the churches...as far as the music industry; I'm still working on that. It's been slow going there, and that's OK. But man, that London gig...that was a powerful spiritual experience for me. When I felt the Lord pierce my heart to talk about Jayda's healing...I had no idea how that audience, in that dark place was going to respond. But I felt the power of God to do it, and when the audience burst into applause, it was touching.

What was Kerry Livgren's contribution, and why did you ask him to become involved?

I heard Kerry made a great cup of latte; and I love latte. That was pretty much it (laughs). I spoke to Kerry through a mutual friend. Around this time, I was saying, "Man, I wish there was someone I could get counsel from about this (*leaving Spock's Beard and Transatlantic*). But who's been down this road before?" And my friend said, "Well, I've got Kerry Livgren's number." And I was like, "Really?" So, I dialled the number and called Kerry...and he answered right away. It must have been the Lord, really...he's hard to get on the phone! And immediately, we had a Bible study. He told me his testimony... how he became a Christian. He was quoting Roman's I...it's marked in my bible now. So, we developed a real relationship there. And later, I was praying, "Who do you want me work with on 'Testimony'?" And I felt it was Kerry. For the tracks, we could have just done it over email. But I felt the Lord wanted me to go be with him…and I happened to be in the Topeka area around then, so I stopped by. When I showed up, I found out he'd already completed his tracks! So, we just talked all day.

'One' is your third consecutive progressive rock concept album. Are you going to keep developing within this field or are you going to release another album along the lines of 'It's Too Late'?

I'm currently putting vocals on a song-oriented Christian album for future release. Also, I'm considering making a children's album with my kids. And I may do some dates and touring…there are a few possibilities. But ultimately, I do not know what's ahead. It's not in my hands. And that's OK!

What is the story behind 'One', and what inspired it?

'One' is the biblical story of God and man. It begins with Creation and continues with fall of man in the Garden of Eden. Man is then portrayed trying to make it on his own…the separated man. Then, God sends Jesus. And God and man are reunited; they become one, again. It's a celebration; a homecoming, really. Throughout 'One', as with 'Testimony', I examine feelings, and emotions. But whereas 'Testimony' tells my spiritual journey, 'One' tells mankind's spiritual journey.

Was the writing process for 'One' different to 'Testimony'?

'Testimony' was a solo effort…especially from a writing perspective. With 'One', though, there was collaboration. Early in the writing phase, I felt I should work with other people on it…though I did not know who. But I felt the hand of God moving. Randy George was out in Nashville to do a gig with me, and he was around while I was cutting some scratch vocals. He offered some ideas at the time…they were great! So, we started collaborating. He understood what I was going after and could offer some great lyrics… some of my favourite on the album. And then Mike Portnoy came on board. He was great at looking at what I had in my demos…at helping choose which parts worked best. Everything just came together.

The introduction to the album is wonderful. Was this all layered in separately or did you manage to work with an orchestra?

I started with MIDI synthesizers, and then replaced the synths with samples. Finally, I replaced most of those tracks with real strings. Mainly what you are hearing is two violins, one cello, and a double bass; tracked over three or four times, and then layered with some samples.

Who played with you on this album, and what was their input to the overall process?

As I mentioned, mostly Mike Portnoy and Randy George. I played the keyboards and most of the guitars. Randy played bass, and of course, Mike played drums. That was the core, and we collaborated on the material, as well. Many other wonderful folks played additional instruments…horn players, string players, and other singers, of course. Phil Keaggy played some guitars and sang with me; that was very special.

When is this going to be toured in the UK, and will you have a similarly eclectic line-up as with the last tour? How did that line-up come about?

A tour, of some sort, is something I'm considering for next year. But it's just a possibility right now. As to who might play on it, I'm not sure, either. But I would love to tour…to come back to the UK. The story of the 'Testimony' band is amazing. It just kind of happened. I had prayed about it, and I felt that God helped put it all together. The players were wonderful; many of them I hadn't played with before. One of them, John Coroza…I never even met him until he arrived at final rehearsals! Eric Brenton had recommended him…it all worked out really well.

Lastly, and some would say the most important question of all (he says totally tongue in cheek): When are we going to see Yellow Matter Custard, and why hasn't that been released in Europe?

Well, that's Mike's project, really…there's not much I can say about it. I think that's going to remain a one night only thing. It was great fun, and I feel it came out great.

Nick D'Virgilio (Spock's Beard), # 82, Jan 2005

Nick rang me recently to talk about the new Spock's Beard album 'Octane', and the interview below does not do justice to the very warm and friendly chat that took place.

What was different about the recording and writing process?

Well, we took a lot more time and we recorded a lot more material than in the past. For 'Feel Euphoria' we felt that we needed to get a record out quickly after Neal left to keep the momentum going and ensure that people did not forget about us. I had "A Guy Named Sid" already written so this time we wrote about eighteen pieces and took a lot more time. There was a lot more influence from Dave on this record, so I think that the amount of time that we spent and the way that everybody put in a lot more ideas and so on than in the past made a difference. Everybody participated in the writing process.

As for the recording side, there were a couple of things that we did do differently. We did not record at our normal studios, Lawnmower Studios, because it is no longer there but our engineer Rich, who has been with us forever, has a brand-new studio just up the road from Lawnmower so we recorded everything at his place. It is the first time that we have recorded everything with Rich in his studio. In the past, something would be done at everyone's house. Al would do his guitar parts at his house; Neal would do all the overdubs at his place and go to Ryo's to do the keyboards there. This time we did everything with Rich in the studio, so we got the opportunity to tweak the sound and to make sure that it was recorded correctly and all that kind of stuff, so it all sounds great in that respect.

How do you think straightforward prog fans are going to view this; do you think it might alienate those looking for another 'The Light' or something from 'Snow'?

I hope it does not. I personally feel that there a lot of good prog moments on this record. I think that it is a lot more rock but there are a load of prog things happening. "The Planet's Hum" is by far a prog song, and there are lots of bits and pieces in the epic "A Flash Before My Eyes" and "She Is Everything" is straightforward as far as time signature goes but it is proggy. I do not think that it will alienate some fans – they may not like the rock angle that we are taking these days but to be honest I think that it is a natural progression of where we are going. We are not going to write albums like 'The Light' or 'Snow' because Neal wrote those and that is his forte, his thing, and even though we are going to try to keep the prog thing going we just have a different way of doing it. Hopefully they will love it, the reason we are here is because of those fans and we do not want to alienate them. We are still trying to move on and to find our footing as a band and I think that this record is a big step in that direction for us.

Can you explain the concept behind "A Flash Before My Eyes"?

That started between Dave and our song writing friend flash webmaster John Boegehold, they were writing songs together via email. I'm not sure how they did this, but I think that Dave would send him a bass riff and then John would add something to it and the next thing you know they are writing a big epic. Once we decided that we were going to start on the new record everybody started sharing ideas with everybody and that is where it started. We all built it up from there.

John added a lot to this record, he wrote a whole bunch of lyrics and he co-wrote a lot of stuff with us and he is a good addition to the four of, he has a lot of great ideas. We have known him forever – I know that Dave and Al have been friends with John since their early twenties, so he adds a cool flavour to things we already have. He has always been around helping us out. Back in the 'Beware Of Darkness' days he was taking pictures for us.

How have you found taking on the role of frontman for the band?

It's a killer! I love it, it's a lot of fun, it's like I'm on a new career. Usually I'm playing drums and making my living most of the time from doing that, and it's a lot of fun but getting out front, I've always been jealous of guitar players, but I can play guitar now and sing and have a blast.

Did you provide more guitar on this album as there is much more acoustic?

I only play a little bit, Al plays the majority, 95% of it is Al. But I play a lot of the guitar, all the acoustic, on "Climbing Up That Hill" and some of the electric rhythm on "NWC" but I think that is it apart from maybe one small passage on one of the bonus tracks. Al is the guitar player; I just added a couple of things.

Was it always a given that you were going to take on the frontman role?

At the beginning, there was a lot of discussion about it, but I always said, "I want the job". I think that the guys were just used to me being the drummer, and they expected me to stay there, and I took this as an opportunity. I did not want to pass up really. I think that it was a natural progression, at the very beginning there was a question but once I proved myself to everybody, I don't think that there were any more questions now.

Did you know touring drummer Jimmy Keegan before he joined?

Yes, I basically knew Jimmy from around town for a long time, playing in local covers bands, that kind of stuff. We're trying to book dates now and sure hope that Jimmy will be able to do it this year as well. He added a great vibe onstage; he has so much energy and is a great entertainer. Hopefully he will be around.

Have you been able to book the dates yet, when do you expect to be in the UK?

We are going to try and come over in March, and it is getting late now. There was a problem with the dates being booked and a lack of communication, but we want to get out soon after the record is released and then there is the opportunity for us to come out again in the fall. So hopefully we will be out for just a little while now, and again late Summer, early Autumn.

Looking back now, a couple of years on, how do you feel about not being able to tour 'Snow'?

I love 'Snow', I think that it is a fantastic record. There are only a few moments that I am not a huge fan of on that record. I think that is a little too long, but that is about the only bad thing that I can say about it. I think that is cool and I am glad that we did it. I wish we could have toured; I think that it would have been a nice concert trying to do the epic from beginning to end, make a show out of it, but I guess that it was not meant to be. I still put it on every occasionally, it's cool. There are some great moments on that record.

You have been touring recently with Tears For Fears, how did that go?

It went great. We're going to be out again in April, doing a UK tour. It's fantastic, I love playing with those guys.

So, then you have also been playing with Fates Warning which is totally different.

Yeah, I know. I can adapt to different situations. The reason I am doing the Fates thing, which is coming up, is because there is no Tears For Fears work or Spock's work at that time. I did it with them a couple of years ago, we did a short tour, and they are a great bunch of guys and fortunately for me they liked what I did to their music live. Their drummer just does not want to tour anymore, which I totally understand as it can become a hassle, so they asked me if I wanted to come and do this short ten-day trip but it's fun, and challenging music to play, that's for sure. It makes me feel good that I can adapt to different situations like that.

How would you describe Spock's Beard?

That is a hard question to answer, I'm not good at that. I do not always say that we a prog band, especially if they are not a prog fan, as I do not know what the heck that is, especially if they are not into that kind of music. I say that we are a rock and roll band and that sometimes we have long songs that tell stories and I know that it is a lame description but is hard for me to describe it, so I normally say that we are a rock band. I say that our influences are Genesis, Yes, The Beatles, Led Zeppelin and things like that and they usually say 'Oh, I like things like that'. I suck them in that way if I can.

Gary Chandler (Jadis), #83, Mar 2005

With the reissue of 'More Than Meets The Eye' being released by Inside Out, and a DVD also now available, it seemed the right time to catch up with Gary and have a chat.

You supported IQ on the 'Nomzamo' tour, then Marillion on the 'Clutching At Straws' tour as well as playing plenty of gigs in your own right, so with things going well what led to the band fallout in 1989 and you being the only member?

Well it was the first time that we decided to have a band meeting. It all started off in a very civil manner you know tea, muffins and crumpets but after twenty minutes it turned in to a bit of a shouting match. I think I had initially suggested a way of promoting the band that involved a small investment but it was turned down flat: I got the impression that some of the guys saw me as a bit of a dictator and maybe thought it might be a good opportunity to drive a wedge between the band. I remember storming off to a Pink Floyd gig down in London while I presume the others conjured up of ways of starting another band without me. I think they got as far as choosing a name for it, but it did not go any further than that. I left the place we were all staying at in Stony Stratford, Milton Keynes and came back to Southampton to rekindle a new line up of Jadis.

What gave you the idea of approaching Martin Orford?

I had known Martin for quite a long while prior to discussing the possibility of his involvement in the band; we had occasionally shared accommodation while living in London and he had mentioned that he liked a lot of the Jadis material, so as we were both back living in Southampton and drinking in the same pubs we decided it might be a good idea to write extra songs to the back catalogue that already existed, and eventually 'More

Than Meets The Eye' was completed.

How did you hear about Steve Christey?

He lived about a mile from me so his name kept getting mentioned every time the words 'new drummer' were said, so I put a cassette of a demo of 'The Beginning & The End' through his letterbox and waited for him to call ... no reply. I eventually caught up with him in a fish and chip shop and he agreed to give the band a try.

Nick May had one of the proggiest backgrounds of all, so why was he asked to leave the band in 1991?

Probably for that very reason. I did not want the band to sound too proggy, I wanted more of a guitar driven vibe to it and some of the bass lines he came up with were a bit busy for the songs being written. Also, the drummer and bassist relationship were not exactly made in heaven. Yeah, maybe that was the reason!!

John Jowitt stepped into the breach, but given that he was not on the band promotional photos of the time, was this only ever expected to be temporary?

Yes, it was going to be temporary because I knew John had a lot of other commitments, but luckily, he has always found time to play live and record with Jadis. I'm all the more thankful to him because he always finds the time to come down from Birmingham to Southampton for rehearsals

How did you feel that the band sound changed between 1989 and 1991?

It was a natural progression. I did not set out to change what we had been doing but I think I became better at writing and arranging stuff and I tried a lot harder to become a better player. We also had the added advantage that Martin can sing very well so we took every opportunity possible of creating vocal harmonies

Were you surprised at the reaction to 'More Than Meets The Eye' when it was first released?

Yes, it was a pleasant surprise and even more surprising considering the lack of internet resources back then. There was a constant stream of mail going to our PO Box and we managed to create a loyal fan base from mail shots and the occasional reviews in the

European fanzines. The fact that many people still class it as one of their favourite CDs always puts a smile on my face.

What was the 'Lurve Ambassadors' tour like?

It was a great time and all the better when looked at retrospectively. It was quite arduous in that there were about thirteen of us crammed into a minibus sitting bolt upright all the time and taking it in turn to grab a bench seat at the back so that you could sleep occasionally. It was not all bad, in fact each day we would get a hot egg and a crescent of crisps.... All in all, a lot of great memories

The shows where you perform as a duo with Martin are legendary, what gave you the idea of playing in this format?

It was mainly because to have a full band as a support act can sometimes just cause a lot of extra aggravation: it is also time consuming if you have a tight schedule to keep. The idea of stripping some Jadis songs down to a minimum, along with some of Martin's songs seemed like a great way of representing the band without the added hoo haa of transporting drums, amps, keyboards and people around

Jadis have one of the most truly distinctive sounds around, driven by your guitar. What equipment do you use and what influences your style?

Thank you for that, I do try as much as possible to sound original. I have always used a Stratocaster guitar because they are light and easy to play, but it seems that whatever different amps and effects units I use it always ends up sounding the same. This is something our sound engineer Rob has commented on many times before. My influences are Steve Hackett, Trevor Rabin, Steve Lukather and Dave Gilmour; each one of those players have their own distinctive sound. I use a Squire Strat, a Boss GT5 effect unit and a Peavey Deuce 120 amp. I like to keep a simple set up because with me also doing lead vocals I do not want to have to think about too many things at one time. I have about four or five pre-sets that I use for each song, lead sound, power chords, clean sound, crunch sound and variations of these with extra or less reverb, delay.

What was it like going back over the tapes not only for the album but also the cassettes that have been added as bonus numbers?

It was quite fun going back over the multi-track tapes to see what we had let pass back then as the original sound source. Firstly, we had to take the tapes to a specialist in London and get them 'baked'...no really!!! This had to be done to stop the oxide from the tapes crumbling off as it passed over the play heads. I also had many cassettes that I had to plough through in order to find any relevant demos from our early period. Luckily, I could find some long-lost stuff such as "Lost For Words", early versions of "This Changing Face" and an old version of "The Beginning & The End" as well as all the demos that we recorded with Steve Rothery back in '89

Why change the artwork?

Well, my brother Geoff did the original artwork for 'More Than Meets The Eye' but because it was his first project a lot of things and different techniques have been learned since then. I know he wanted a better booklet, so this was an opportunity to bring the artwork up to the higher standard that he wanted.

'Fanatic' saw the classic line-up back together again, what does 2005 hold for Jadis and when can we expect a new album and will older Jadis material also be reissued with bonus cuts?

I am still in the process of finishing the writing of the next Jadis album (I now have a Protools recording system at home so I am expecting that to 'hurry me up' a bit) but I would hope that something will be released at some point between summer and autumn this year. There are no plans to make available any other older Jadis material; the reissue of 'More Than Meets The Eye' was a great chance to finally make available all the skeletons in the cupboard.

Manfred Mann, # 84, July 2005

Manfred has recently been touring Europe but in between shows he managed to answer a few questions for Feedback.

Why call the new album '2006' when it was released in 2004?

It seemed an interesting idea, no more than that, just slightly out of time

Why is it credited to Manfred Mann '06?

Because a fair amount of it reflected my taste rather than the other guys and some of it was not connected with Earth Band, and it would stop the other guys whinging at me.

You recorded some of the backing tracks 'live' without rehearsals, why did you use this process and what do you think that you gained from it musically?

A kind of roughness, in some of the arrangements, and a freshness that is not as easy to achieve.

Noel is the singer of MMEB, and has been for quite a while, yet Chris Thompson sang lead on four of the songs. What was the reason for this and what is Chris's position within the band?

Chris and I have a very good relationship, and his voice fitted very well on a few tracks. However, he is not now a working member of the group

The theme from "Mars" has been used as a base by various artists, but yours is probably the most removed from the original that I have heard - what inspired you to treat it this way?

I did not feel that I was doing "Mars" but using it as a basis for a song.

"Frog" in some ways reminds me of "The Hare Who Lost His Spectacles" from Tull's 'A Passion Play' in the way that it is a humorous interlude, what was the purpose of this piece?

I had a good backing track: the song I had written did not sound good to me, I did not want to throw the track away, so I decided to read a joke that I often tell, and why not just be silly sometimes

If ever a song from the album demanded to be released as a single it would be "Independent Woman", which is commercial and wonderful, taking the music into new areas yet also being recognisable as belonging to Manfred Mann. Can you see this happening in any territories?

I don't know what you mean, but we are intending to make some small changes and release a single version in the UK

Overall the album brings in recognisable MMEB influences, choral singing, rap, different languages etc. yet still manages to bond together as a whole. What were you trying to achieve with this album, and do you feel that you accomplished it?

I am never trying to achieve anything other than music that can be repeatedly listened to and be OK.

It has been a while since you had a high profile in the UK, why do you think that is and what do you think of the music scene over here these days?

We have no profile over here, because we have had our day, in the view of radio and media, and regarded as old folk from a distant time. Had we been as successful as The Rolling Stones it wouldn't matter, but we never achieved that degree of success, because in truth we were not as good as that.

You have been involved in the music scene for over forty years, have sold millions of singles and albums, and this year you are 65 years old and still touring. What keeps you motivated, and can you ever see a time when you are no longer performing?

I carry on because that is what I have always done, and being a musician is part of what defines me. I shall carry on performing if people want to see us perform.

Given that this album is Manfred Mann '06 when can we expect the next MMEB album?

I have no plans to do one.

My thanks to Manfred, and to Helen Milner at the record label, and to Nigel Stanworth who run Manfred's website. Without his assistance this interview would never have taken place, and he told me that I was fortunate to get anything from Manfred as he has always been loath to provide interviews at all.

Henning Pauly, #84, July 2005

Not only has Henning released solo albums but has also worked with Chain and Frameshift and with his new album featuring Sebastian Bach now seemed a good time to ask him some questions.

What inspires you when writing music and what made you want to switch from learning piano to learning guitar?

Could be the topic. If it's about an epic battle like "Blade", I might listen to the score for Gladiator and then work off the ideas I get from that. It might be the mood (torture). Sometimes I sit down on the piano and see what happens, sometimes the acoustic guitar. I might work off a drum loop and jam around with it until I find a good riff or theme and then work with that. All these different approaches result in different kind of songs and it just depends on what kind of song I want to write. I played piano when I was 6 for about 2 years. I hated it. I did not understand that music was something you could enjoy. I wanted to play in the mud with my friends and not practice. I played Mozart and Beethoven and just did not get it. I was too young. When I was fifteen, I finally started to listen to music as something that moves me emotionally and then a whole new world opened for me. I started to play guitar and because of Jon Oliva's piano parts on Savatage's 'End of Thorns' I sat down on piano and tried to figure out the parts. So, that's how I got back to the piano, but of course I am not that good on it. I could have been a decent pianist had I not dropped the ball early on, but that's just how it goes!

How did Frameshift come about? How did you get involved with James LaBrie?

When the first Chain album was signed with ProgRock Records I was happy, but I knew it only meant selling a few hundred CDs over the internet and that was already a big success for me. I never meant to have my music sold and heard by many people, I just did not think it was anything that an audience wanted to spend time with. I saw myself more as an arranger and producer who helps the artist instead of being the artist myself. Since PRR president Shawn Gordon lives only about an hour away we decided to meet, and we had a fun time. He mentioned in that meeting that James LaBrie had mentioned in an interview with him that if Shawn had someone who could write some original stuff he'd be interested in it. He asked if I would like to take a shot at it. I knew it was a long shot, I mean a looooooong shooooot. I wrote two tracks based on the experience I had just made writing a film score for a short film and integrated a lot of those arranging techniques hoping it would generate something original. He loved them and from then on, I wrote the rest of the album and the rest is, well, you can hear it on the first album.

Why was James not on this album and how did get Sebastian get involved?

Originally, I wrote five songs with the thought in mind to present them to Geoff Tate and get him on vocals, it was Shawn's idea to get Tate. I sent the MP3s to James and started talking about it. The music turned out to be heavier than expected and it just did not seem right for Tate. I love his voice and so does James but we both thought that a voice that's cleaner like Geoff's or James' just wouldn't be right anymore. We thought it needed something rough and aggressive. James asked me who I would pick if I could have any vocalist in the world, no matter if it's realistic to get him on not, and I said: Sebastian Bach. Period, and James said: "Well, let me give him a call". So, James initiated the contact and after Sebastian heard the intro to "Blade" he was on board.

There seems to have been some fallout with him over the album, what is this and does this mean that you will not be working with him in the future?

The album was written when we started to record vocals. It was a finished work that he was hired and paid to sing. I was open to making some changes to accommodate him and even give him credit if those changes would warrant a co-write. On two songs, they did, on five others they did not. Sebastian thinks that the minor changes he did to the songs mean he co-wrote them. For anyone who wants to see what we changed they can go to my site and there is a thread in the forum where I posted the original lyrics and the final version, and you can see for yourself what this whole story is about. Bottom line is: He got a nice chunk of money and a fat percentage and for that he did an awesome job, no question about it, but it does not mean that this is his solo album or that he wrote it.

About working with him in the future I would like to, but I do not like this kind of tension and have never experienced it with anyone else. I also like to expand my writing and find new challenges. One of the fun aspects of Frameshift is to do my research and listen to everything the vocalist has done so I can write the perfect music for him, music that shows him in the best way possible. In the end these albums are not about me, they are about the vocals, that is what everyone focuses on, so it is my job to write the right music for them. Well, I know how to write for Baz now, bring on someone I don't know.

I felt that the artwork on the album was reminiscent of 'Seven'. Given that the film and this album are about violence is this deliberate or coincidence?

Deliberate. I gave the artist a few pointers and he took it from there and three things I said were: Seven, Fight Club, Twelve Monkeys. Those films have the kind of gritty atmosphere and look that I wanted, and Marko Heisig did a phenomenal job.

Are there plans to make Frameshift into a live band to be able to gig?

I am not too interested in performing my stuff live. Sometimes I think it could be a blast,

but it would mean putting together a band and this would be a lot of work. It would have to be a combination of at least five or six live musicians and some stuff from tape and several vocalists because one of the major things about this music are the vocal harmonies. It's just a lot of work and I highly doubt that it could be done and still make sense financially. Also, it would take me away from home. I have a girlfriend and three dogs, and I just like to be around them. Once I am done with an album I am right back into the next one and this year I finally must finish Babysteps, my double CD rock opera featuring James LaBrie (DT), Michael Sadler (Saga), Jody Ashworth (TSO), Al Pitrelli (TSO, Savatage), Alan Morse (Spock's Beard), Jim Gilmour and Ian Crichton (Saga), Matt Cash (Chain) and many other fun names who I will reveal later this year.

There are elements of the music that are extremely hard rock, while others fit more into a more 'traditional' prog metal style. How would you describe the album to someone who has never heard any of your music?

Loud. No, seriously. I would say its metal with a few odd measures here or there but the core of it is metal. There are two songs that have nothing to do with metal and the last one is even more of an adult contemporary thing or even Broadway, but it is a metal album which is just a little bit more complex than the average stuff. And it's loud.

What do you feel are the major differences between the two Frameshift albums?

The second one is louder. I think the first one is stylistically way more diverse and takes you on a ride through more moods than the new one. We did more with vocal arrangements on the first one. The new album is darker, heavier and the mood stays relatively heavy throughout. James and Sebastian are different singers and I hope I wrote the music bringing out the songs that each of them is best at.

Given that this album has now been released what is your next project?

I am currently working on Matt Cash's modern country album. He is an incredible writer and has written some great stuff for himself, so I am very excited to get away from metal for a few weeks and explore something totally different. After that, I am going into 100% Babysteps mode. I have over 140 minutes of music to write, over 30 songs - that should keep me busy for the rest of the year.

Mark Colton (Credo), #85, Nov 2005

There has been a fair gap between the two albums, so I thought that I had better find out why!

Eleven years. What took so bloody long?? (yes - this is a question)

Eleven years, is that all it took? The truth is we wanted to release the album on exactly the same day and date as the first one ('Field of Vision') and had to wait all that time for that to happen.

That's not quite true! There were so many things that happened over the last eleven years that I could probably fill this issue with the story of the album, the edited highlights are that we lost Mik Stovold very early after the first album and replaced him with Mike Varty. That gave the line-up fresh impetus, and we believed that it gave the songs on 'FoV' fresh legs, so we carried on supporting that as we introduced the new songs into the set. There were very early and different versions of "The Letter", "Turn the Gun" and a very complete version of "Skintrade" being played live as early as 96 or 97.

We are not pro musicians and we have to pay our mortgages so we all had day jobs, families grew, people moved, and we continued to write what would become 'Rhetoric'. We then had a run of desperate luck when Mike had an accident and fractured his skull, then Paul Clarke (drummer) left, and we could not replace him for close to 16 months. We had some very high-profile name drummers approach us, but we knew what we wanted, and we found that in Martin Meads. When we had finished writing the album, around 99/00 we/I had the most awful luck. Some of your readers will know this already, but here goes. I became seriously ill and, to date, have had three major operations, resulting in me having a large section of my colon removed, there were serious complications during the first two ops which nearly finished me off, so recording my bits against the background of that was very difficult.

Is it still possible to be an angry impassioned singer when instead of being young(ish) and single you are happily married with two children?

Well, I guess you guys will be able to tell me that. My position is that my beliefs and values have stayed the same and I am still the same guy that wrote most of "The Game" when I was sixteen and the other lyrics on the album over the last twenty-five years (Yes I am 41 now!). Yeah, I am very settled and very happily married now with two great kids, but that does not stop me remembering how unfair life can seem to have been at other times in my past! I count my blessings every day, especially considering my recent health problems, but, initial reviews of our live performances seem to say I am pretty much the same performer I ever was.

Since 'Field Of Vision' Mik Stovold and Paul Clarke have both left the band. Why was this and how did you come across their replacements? What do you think that Mike and Martin have added to the band?

Mik left so long ago now I can't remember his reasoning, on reflection it was as good a thing as could have happened to us. Mik was a tremendous lyricist, but I am sure he would agree Mike Varty is an infinitely superior musician (as I am sure his Shadowland, Landmarq, Janison Edge credentials highlight). Paul was another matter; I have remained close to Paul and Robyn and his departure was a huge blow for us musically and personally. I think he just did not enjoy the music we were playing anymore and wanted to get back to playing what he plays best. He is a phenomenal drummer, but again Martin brought a new edge, power and precision to what we do. 'Rhetoric' wouldn't be the album it is if Martin hadn't come on board.

Mike Varty has added so much to the band, we now have two musicians (along with Tim Birrell our guitarist) who can solo and make the hairs on the back of your neck stand up! Mike produced the album, and from a personal perspective coached the vocal performances out of me when I was in and out of hospital and my health was shot. His engineering and production work are phenomenal, his playing and song writing is superb, and he is a nice bloke too, so between them they have made a great difference.

'Rhetoric' is a very different album to 'FoV'. Do you see this as a continuation of where you were before, or do you instead view this as virtually a new start?

Well it is a continuation in so far that Jim, Tim and I are still there, and we are still called Credo. But it is a new start, we are a lot older now, the standard of musicianship, and my personal performance, are well above anything we could have ever dreamed of when we recorded 'FoV'. One Prog chat room has been moved to call it "The Comeback of the Year" which is very sweet, but I am a bit unsure how Dave Gilmore and Roger Waters would take that!!!

We are fiercely proud of what we achieved with 'FoV', but the album should have been called "Well this is what we spent £500 on and took ten days to produce!" 'Rhetoric' is a "proper" album. There are some strange statistics in there around cost, time spent etc., but from my perspective I recorded the vocals for 'FoV' in one afternoon, the day after a gig, when we had a gig that night, and could not afford to get stuff wrong because we were running out of money. This time the vocals were done over a three-year period, around hospitalisation etc., and if you added all the studio time up probably run close to a month of studio time.

Getting part of the album recorded at Thin Ice (I think you were there one of the days, weren't you?) and having Karl Groom undertake the final mix (which took as long as the whole 'FoV' sessions!!!) also shows. We took the decision with Dave Robinson of F2 to market the band as a new band, partially because however much people may have liked 'FoV', it was 11 years ago, 40% of the line-up is new for us in the recording studio, and there will be so many people out there who will never have heard of us in the past.

Can you give a thumbnail sketch of each of the songs on 'Rhetoric'?

"Skintrade": Inspired by a conversation with a, then, girlfriend, who announced one night she wanted to be in Porn Films! What do you say to that, it's a no-win situation! Her

view was she wouldn't be the one being exploited; it would be the people buying the magazines (to do whatever it is people do with that sort of literature!) Just got me round to thinking one day, what makes people want to do that sort of thing!!! Most of the story is editorial licence and does not reflect on her at all, but that was the seed for the song

"Turn The Gun": I was looking to write a sequel, or prequel, to "Kindness" from the first album, I would love to play the two songs together live at some point, but I ended up using the lyric originally when I was in Freewill. With Freewill's demise I still thought the lyric was valid, and let's face it, if you are going to plagiarise someone, yourself is a good (and safe) starting point! I love the power and intensity of this song, without being overly heavy it captures the insanity and claustrophobia that the cult of celebrity has bought to the modern world.

"From The Cradle…" Typical of my lyric writing I guess, bleeding heart poet time, but I think it is as good as anything I have ever written. It feels that most people of our age seem to be on second marriages, or despising the relationships they are in, and spend far too much time thinking about what might have been. Again, it is a fictional person in the song but is based on so many people who have touched my life in the last thirty years. There are some vivid images in the song relating to the feeling you get when you return to your old hometown and the places you always used to go, it does not matter how much they have changed, the ghosts of yesterday still hang heavily in the air! Listen out for the great backing vocals from Sam Collins, from Janison Edge, in the end passage; again, it's hairs on the back of your neck time!

"…To The Grave" is a continuation of the previous song and deals with the same story from the perspective of the other partner, who does not view that relationship through quite the same rose-tinted glasses!!! There are always two sides to every story, and this one details the anger and frustration of someone who gave everything they could, but was made to feel guilty that they could not fulfil the aspirations of a demanding partner, and ended up being painted as the villain of the whole affair, and can't quite believe the audacity of the other person. There is a great instrumental interlude at the end of the song, with a great rhythm which sounds simple but challenges every "air drummer" that has had a go at it! A true story? Maybe! We meet the protagonists again on the last song on the album!

"The Letter" is the oldest song on the album, we played it live at the 'FoV' launch party, again inspired by the end of an unsatisfactory relationship and as angry as it gets! A live favourite that we have now recorded three times. This is the only version that has ever captured the anger, frustration and pain that you can experience when your whole fragile world collapses due to the actions of someone else. It also contains my favourite line that I have ever written!

"Too Late…" The first part of a duo of songs that was inspired by the poems written in the trenches during the First World War. The power, emotion and majesty of those poets moved me as much as any song I have ever heard. When I first heard the music the swagger, tension and power of the chorus demanded a lyric that matched it for power and simplicity, there are any number of vocals on that track which seem to perfectly capture the chaos and fear that people would have experienced when they would have gone "Over The Top". Great violin from Mike on the second verse that blew us all away the first time we heard it. The verse allows the lyric to breathe and conjure even more poignant images before we hit the instrumental section that leads to

"…To Say Goodbye". The closing section of the song which takes us in a different direction and highlights the vocals of Jim and Mike as we take the song to the end. The end section works wonderfully well live and every time we have played the two pieces together the audience has gone mad!!!

"The Game" From my perspective is very interesting, as the main body of the lyric was written when I was sixteen or seventeen (years not stone!) whilst some of it has lyrics that were completed earlier this year! It's a lyric that deals with loves young dream going horribly wrong, and the names have been changed to protect the not so innocent! Another true story? You may think that; I could not possibly comment!!! There are some great light and shade moments on the track, the main guitar solo is amazing, and the final keyboard/vocal section is my favourite part of the whole album.

"Seems Like Yesterday" Well as I said, the couple from "Cradle to the Grave" appear in the last number again, and by this point, there is a degree of reflection and sorrow from both partners who finally get the opportunity to say all the things they really wanted to say. Feels a bit like a coffee advert following these two! But there is more to follow in the next album, which if our recent run rate is anything to go by should be out in 2016!

How do you feel that the progressive scene has changed in the UK between the release of the two albums?

Well it has and it hasn't, most of the bands still operate at the level they did eleven years ago. You have your Pink Floyd, Genesis elite, you then get down to the Marillion, Tull "Championship" level before you get to the IQ, Arena, Pendragon, Magenta, etc. level. We currently sit in the tier below that. Magenta have shown what is possible, our prog is very based in the Neo Prog movement of the 80's and 90's. That's the reason we went with F2 really, with a name like Credo and being signed to F2 people will have a good idea of what they are going to get. The latest Pendragon album is very different for them (and bloody awesome too!), Arena have moved away from their first album, and the American Prog bands seem to have changed the outlook of everyone. Our album is good, solid classic British Neo Prog, I am not sure if I thought there was anybody out there playing the kind of music I like listening to until I heard Magenta, they have shown there is still a sizeable market out there for bands like us. Dream Theater and Threshold have influenced many bands into trying to expand their fanbase by becoming more metal like in their approach. My favourite quote when we were talking with labels for 'Rhetoric' was that it was "Very Retro, 80's Prog", no s**t, most Prog is retro! But as someone once said, "I know what I like, and I like what I know…". The web chat rooms are buzzing about the album, everyone who hears it loves it. It is accessible, emotional and powerful prog, prog you can play your kids, or mum or wife!

What is being done to promote the album, where can those interested find out more information and most importantly when are you playing live?

Would you believe me if I said everything that is entirely possible? We need to raise the profile of the band, without sounding overly confident, it sounds like a "proper" album, much more so than the first album, one Prog site have been moved to call it the album of the year, something I am so proud of after the great releases so far this year! Another calls it the comeback of the year. We need to be seen to perform venues that top acts play at and behave in a manner that reflects that.

You know from your experiences with us that we can hold our own on the biggest stages with the most established bands, we need to expose ourselves to more of that. If people see us live and hear the music they will believe, we must also ensure we do not wait eleven years for the follow up! At this stage, we are happy to play anywhere where there may be an audience, so if you would like us to come to you, let us know, through Kev if that is ok with you Kev! Now, it looks like we are about to finalise dates on a major tour as support, we are talking about the possibilities of playing with The Nice too, as well as going to Ireland and Europe on two mini tours and Bulgaria (!) and Poland!

Empathy (Specimen 37), #85, Nov 2005

In the last issue, I reviewed the latest Specimen 37 album, and I was so impressed that I asked Empathy if he would mind being interviewed, so here it is.

How did Specimen 37 first get together?

It's been a long, strange, trip, as they say. Specimen 37 started as a studio project. gEE-rOj, Boone and I had all worked together for a brief period in the early 90's, and when we were finished with our respective college experiences, we decided to see where we could continue to take that collaboration. gEE-rOj, Osiol, and Boone (who, along with Ponder and Kookina, were all involved in a musical project called "Substance P") all moved up to Boston, where I had been attending school. From there we began meeting regularly to jam, and that's where some of the material from 'Adverse Reaction' began taking shape. Osiol left after a few months, as he had wanted to focus on his visual art (which we think is fantastic, and we asked him to do the cover art for Adverse). Things were going well musically with Boone, but unfortunately, he began to slip further into illness, until he finally had to be hospitalized and was diagnosed with schizophrenia. After some time, we decided to move forward, and gEE-rOj and I continued to write and record 'Adverse Reaction' as a duo. While the majority was written and recorded in home studios, we eventually decided to head into a commercial studio for overdubs. I happened to work with MojoNine at the time, and knew that he was a talented drummer, so I asked him if he would like to be involved. When the CD was done, it occurred to us that we'd like to perform this material live! So, from there, we formed a "band" per se. Our current bassist, Sketch Element, joined us in late 2001, Ponder left us in 2004 to raise a family out in California, and now we're down to the four-piece we are currently. Whew! What a ride!

Where does the name of the band come from, and why did you decide that you were all also going to use pseudonyms? Why 'Empathy'?

I'll answer the pseudonym part first. We've always had a taste for the theatrical and liked the idea of listing those involved with the music as a "cast of characters". We did this on our first release, but we moved away from it for 'The Endless Looping Game'. The fact that some of our favourite bands also use pseudonyms may have also been a factor as well. I chose Empathy because I firmly believe that it's a desirable trait to have, and something I always strive for. If humanity could truly feel the pain (or pleasure) they caused each other, I think we'd be much more enlightened as a species in general.

The band was called Substance P for some time, right up until we were finishing 'Adverse Reaction'. At that point we had discovered that there was another band using the name Substance P, and we decided it would be simpler for us to change our name. A common concept to our releases is the idea of viewing human behaviour from an "outside" perspective, as a higher intelligence might view a specimen to learn its properties and behaviours. The number 37 has haunted several members of the band (and some other friends of ours) for years now, and it's truly a fascinating number to us. The human body temperature happens to be 37 degrees Celsius, is a prime number, and seems to appear "randomly" at very specific times for us. For example, the analogue clock on my stove stopped inexplicably one day on 4:37. In the process of burning a CD once, I had inadvertently created one long track that was 70 plus minutes long. I just happened to pause it at 37:37! One of our favourite stories about the number is when gEE-rOj and I had discussed changing the band name to Specimen 37. He was not entirely convinced, and decided he needed to "sleep on it". That night he continually woke from a restless sleep at 1:37, 2:37 then 3:37. He took the hint.

Musically you are quite different to much of the prog scene. What musically inspires you and who do you view as being your major influences?

I'd have to say one of the common threads for all of us is Pink Floyd, in varying degrees. After that common ground, however, we're all over the map. I'm very influenced by a variety of prog bands, from prog metal (Dream Theater, Tool) to art rock and symphonic prog (Rush, Yes, early Genesis), to space rock (Ozric Tentacles, Porcupine Tree). gEE-rOj was very influenced by The Legendary Pink Dots, The Residents, and so forth. We're both big fans of Negativland. On the other hand, we're also big fans of certain kinds of electronic music. From various industrial groups (from Einsturzende Neubauten to the more accessible material like NIN and Celldweller), to psy and goa trance (Infected Mushroom, earlier BT, Eat Static, Hallucinogen). MojoNine comes from the metal and hard rock camp, primarily. He's a huge Zeppelin fan, but I've heard him listen to anything from Slayer to Jeff Buckley to the Marvelous Three. He turned me on to The Mars Volta, who we all think are doing some great things right now. Sketch Element has

a variety of influences as well, ranging from indie rock like Ween, Yo La Tengo, to Phish, and probably a ton more I do not even know about. He's also a very good guitarist and is currently taking classical guitar lessons.

Was there a deliberate intent to sound different, or did it evolve?

Our sound just sort of happened. We've put a lot of time into trying to describe our sound, and we feel that Psychetronic Rock is accurate. Psychetronic Rock is a contraction of "Psychedelic Electronic Rock". It's almost become a kind of sport for us to watch others try to define our sound. We've heard some off-the-wall ones. I think my favourite so far is "Rush meets the Residents". Our sound has continued to evolve, over the course of our two releases. 'Adverse Reaction' began as a two-man endeavour, and we brought in the support after much of the material was already written. ELG was much more of a band effort, with every member adding something vital to the shape of the music.

Do you fit in musically with the rest of the Boston scene or do you feel that you are out there on your own?

There are a handful of acts in Boston that are somewhat different from the norm, but not very many. It's largely a punk/indie/emo scene here. We've made some headway in Boston, but we're not where we'd like to be yet.

Are you a gigging band or just a studio project?

We started gigging back in October of 2000, but they've all been New England-area gigs. We'd love to play some different parts of the world, especially Europe, as we seem to have gotten a higher concentration of interested listeners there thus far. Within the past year, we've begun adding a visual element to the show with video projections, which is becoming an important part of the Specimen 37 "experience".

'The Endless Looping Game' only recently came to my attention but it was released last year. Does this mean that we can expect a new album sometime soon?

Well, we're not signed, so we're all holding down day jobs to pay the bills, as it were. That said, the creative juices are flowing again, and we've begun writing some new material. So, you'll hear more from us in the future. We've discussed the possibility of a DVD as well, and we'd love to see that become a reality.

Nick Barrett (Pendragon), # 85, Nov 2005

With the first new album for quite a while, it seemed to be a good time to again touch base with Nick.

'Believe' in many ways is quite different to other Pendragon albums. What do you feel influenced your writing with this album and please give a thumbnail sketch of each of the songs.

The biggest influence was what we did not do...I did not want to just repeat what we have done before...but also did not want to alienate ourselves from our sound, so I guess there are some of my other influences that came through on this album like Queen and The Who, also some more of my more Latin influences like Santana and Al Di Meola. Also, I was looking for something new and exciting in music and my son was playing these motocross videos and I heard some of the bands on the soundtracks like Lostprophets and Jurassic 5, and I loved this kind of raw youthful energy and wanted to get some of this in Pendragon.

I read some books by a guy called David Icke, who says that the history that we are taught at school is rubbish, and that we have basically been lied to. It's a deep subject about cover ups and conspiracy theories and the more you consider it the more it unfolds as possibly being the truth. It is incredible, it's too deep to say everything here, but I recommend that people check it out. This is what "No Place For The Innocent" is all about I am saying do not believe everything you read in the papers or see on TV; it might be the opposite of what we're being told!

I looked into other authors and books from different parts of the world and different times, I actually found a book called "Not Of This World" written in the 70's on this subject and found they all tell of similar findings. That the world is being manipulated into a New World Order and humanity into slavery.

"The Wisdom Of Solomon" is about one of my real hates, Political Correctness, this daft OVER compensation for someone who might be in a minority, going on and on and on about racial/sexual/age equality to the point where you almost alienate the very people you are trying to help. It's just nutty when things like the Cross, Christmas songs, the Bible, tons and tons of things have been banned in certain areas in case they offend anyone. I hate this...and I feel OFFENDED that people are driving a wedge between different cultures etc. by making such a big issue of it.

"Wishing Well" is a celebration of being human. I feel at times we are so wrapped up in Political Correctness, bureaucracy, red tape, government officialdom, Brussels!! We have just lost our humanness, you know, thank God for idiots like Robbie Williams! We almost can't say or think what we feel anymore without being sued, when you consider what the human race is capable of, Mozart, Einstein, the way we appreciate love, music, laughter, sex, friendship these are what makes the world go around, this is what we work for is not it?

"Learning Curve" is about the last few years, I have been on a search, a mission, and I wanted to find new good music, different things to put my passions into, things to believe in. I have developed stronger interests in many things like politics, economics, world history, and religion, anything spiritual, my feelings on these things are now very intense. Everyone has these times in their lives where they are put into a learning curve where they need to re-evaluate everything, it's a spiritual thing and 'part of the journey', we all need to go there, it's just that some get it easy.... like Sting for example!! The perfect life I always felt!!

"The Edge Of The World" is a song for the fans, who in many cases are more like friends. About a year ago I was thinking about what if we never get to play on stage again or make any more records, and it scared me, because this is where I feel happiest. And I remembered many of the times where fans have been very close to us, and this is something that will never go away...I hope.

It is a very intense album, and in some ways, very dark and heavy. Are you worried that it may alienate traditional Pendragon fans?

I do not think it's that dark, in fact in places I think it's a helluva lot lighter than 'Not Of'!! Like the end of "Wisdom Of Solomon" sounds quite sprightly and Summery? Nearly all the fans that have heard it like it, there are some who hate it, but I knew that would happen! Let's be honest, it's no 'Abacab' though is it? But some fans simply want the same album over again, the same sounds and the same artwork, we have challenged ourselves and them with 'Believe', most people have risen to the occasion, it's generally only the old 'formula' prog rock fundamentalists who do not like it!

Do you see this as a logical progression from 'Not Of This World' or is it more of a new start for the band?

Er... a bit of a new start really. Probably because of the things in my personal life it goes hand in hand with that! Like when we released 'The World' it was like being reborn, we had a new sound a new fresh approach and a new happiness in the band, let's not forget...there were some fans who hated 'The World'! Bands need to evolve, as long as we do not lose the heart of the band and the magic then things will stay intact. Did you know when 'Lamb' came out and 'Dark Side Of The Moon', those albums got a real panning from some of the fans!

You have also released a remastered 'The Jewel' - are all your previous albums going to be reissued in this format? And if so, what is the schedule?

I have no idea. Because of downloading, the sales of back catalogue have shrunk to virtually zero, for example when we released 'The Masquerade', we were also selling

around 500 copies of 'The Window' and 100 copies of 'The World' every week!!!!!! With the release of 'Believe' you could count the back-catalogue sales on the fingers of a mitten! We will see how things develop.

Is this going to mean a more active and visible time for Pendragon? Are you going to be gigging in the UK?

YES. Next year we will tour in May, and hopefully a lot more, I wanted to go out earlier, but so many venues are already booked up it's crazy! But we will probably do Europe and try and get to Canada, maybe South America...wherever ...whenever, we just want to do some gigs! Between now and next May, I will be working on a new Pendragon album, so I will be keeping busy.

Poland seems a very important place for Pendragon, you refer to the country in "The Edge Of The World" and you have had some material released by the Polish label Metal Mind. Why do you think that Pendragon has been welcomed so warmly over there and how do you compare their music scene with ours?

Well when you think they virtually had no western music ten years ago, they were hungry for it big time, so it just was being in the right place at the right time. Also, our kind of music found a sympathetic ear with the Poles, if you imagine a lot of their music comes from traditional Jewish or classical Russian music, it is quite progressive in a way, or at least not influenced by the US! We had some amazing gigs there, one gig in Zabrze, the audience got up on stage with us, and we started the whole gig again, it was like 900 people in your living room, unbelievable!

Do you feel that in the UK Pendragon have lost the recognition that they had in the mid Nineties and what can be done to again put you in the spotlight?

Stuff like this, interviews! We need to get back out there talk about the band and build back up, the fire is there again. I do think at times you should die to be reborn; you know what they say about familiarity breeding contempt! Well I think it's true. There was an interview with Carly Simon a few weeks ago on the radio, and she was asked what she thought was the reason for her longevity, she said "get out of people's faces now and again".

How have Pendragon managed to keep the same line-up for so many years?

I suppose because the other members of the band have their own creative outlets with Arena, Peter with his solo albums and Fudge doing whatever Fudge does (he plays with quite a few other musicians) I guess there is not the usual wrangling over 'musical differences'. We all still enjoy it too, that is a major part of it.

The scene in the UK has changed dramatically since your first studio album. Why have Pendragon managed to keep going?

We have put a lot into the actual music; I guess we have sidestepped a lot of the ill-conceived 'progressive imagery' like wearing shed loads of make-up and daft costumes. It's like Camel really, people like Pendragon for the right reasons and those reasons are solid, and we have a lot of integrity as a band, and believe in what we do, that rubs off on people.

We've had our moments where we have disappeared for a long time; I guess it's a bit like Carly Simon said.......

What's next??

Er...a lot of hard work!

Richard Sinclair, #86, Feb 2006

With all the new renewed interest in Hatfield and the North I took up the opportunity to catch up with Richard Sinclair and ask him some questions about his long career in music.

How did you first get involved in music, what made you pick up an instrument?

Father Dick Sinclair was a working musician entertaining in Canterbury and around the Kent Coast, and my Grandfather and Grandmother were also music hall entertainers around Canterbury, at the turn of the century 1900. My Dad gave me a plastic ukulele at the age of three for Christmas and by the age of five, I could play "She'll be coming 'round the Mountain...". Since then the strings have always pointed outwards and there have been mountains of music.

At Primary school, I had early attempts on violin (only lasted a painful six months, much to the relief of all) and then were my first meetings with a banjo and first attempts on acoustic guitar. As a youngster, I recall many a Sunday afternoon with Mum on the beach, because Dad played regularly at the Herne Bay Pavilion.

How did you meet the Hopper brothers, and how did The Wilde Flowers come about?

Mr and Mrs Hopper used to come out to Dick Sinclair's Dance Band gigs around Canterbury and got to talking to my Dad about their sons wanting to start a pop band and how they needed a guitarist. And so, at the age of fifteen years old, my Dad took me to their house with my new red Hofner Verithin Guitar and his own 'Selmer' portable amp and speakers combo for early band rehearsals. Robert Wyatt and Kevin Ayres joined in shortly afterwards.

It became the Wilde Flowers when we needed a name for the first gigs, starting with 'The Bear and Key' at Whitstable.

Many people even now would probably associate you mostly with Caravan, at the time were you aware of the influence that your own music was having on others?

No, we were just having fun.

As the records have continued to be made available and many young players starting out have access to the music - of Caravan and Hatfield and the North and Camel, I'm aware of the positive influence of the songs we wrote and played, especially from the 70's period - for many musicians, because they write and tell me and I'm sometimes invited to travel to them to work, usually around exam time this happens, which is a great compliment of course. So, I can now see that there are a lot of great young players around the world, learning to write and play their own music, having looked at how we did it.

Which of course leads to Hatfield & The North. How did that band get together, and what were your musical aims at the time?

Originally, Steve Miller played with Caravan on 'Waterloo Lily' and he introduced me to brothers Phil Miller and Pip Pyle, who had all been chums from primary school days. It was important for me to carry on playing music that was better and still challenging. Cousin Dave Sinclair joined in with Hatfield for a time and Virgin offered us the recording deal and a few concerts came about. Things did not work out with keyboards player 2 either and Dave Stewart then replaced Dave Sinclair.

In 2005 it 'evolved' out of The Richard Sinclair Band: me with Theo Travis, Phil Miller, Alex Maguire and Roy Dodds.

The release of 'Hatwise Choice' caused a rekindling of interest and certainly lots of email and so we asked Pip if he could do it. This time, end of January last year, Pip came along to a gig we had at nearby Whitstable, Horsebridge Arts Centre and joined in as guest. Our aims are still to play many more concerts, introducing some new songwriting and playing it the best we can.

Why did the band break up?

There was not enough money generated from that to support my family and so I had to leave the band in 75.

Were you surprised at the very positive reaction to 'Hatwise Choice' after all this time?

It's great that there has been a good response. Thanks to all you folks who bought it, you have made it possible for us to make a follow up! which is due for release this year. Well I have to say from my viewpoint, it was no surprise, I instigated the idea of a band release, back in the early 90's because of what was happening to the Caravan shows when the BBC Archives changed their name to BBC Enterprises and they started to sell the shows off.

And I also must say no surprise, because of the mail I receive. I get the other side of the picture, people badgering from many parts of the world, for what they would love to see released! And, the live music requested for me to play very often included favourite pieces from Hatfield.

What was it like going back over old material and collaborating again on the CD release?

We all did what we could, searching through dusty old boxes...and gathered up what material we could and from collector friends too. Then we signed an agreement, that we'll all agree on everything, or it does not come out. It takes time, like European politics, for everyone to have their say and reach agreement and for listening through all the ideas. Understandably time consuming, repairing the old recordings. Dave Stewart did a champion job on the recordings for 'Hatwise Choice' and coordination between us and the first batch of ideas for 'Vol. 2' have been recovered and delivered by Pip Pyle.

Do you see the band now being back together as a 'permanent' unit that will not only gig, but also record new material?

We all still have our own projects going on, Phil Millers In Cahoots, Pip Pyles Bash, Alex and myself on several different projects. And yes, there is Hatfield as well. We're picking up the familiar original tunes, adding what we did in 1990 for the Bedrock show and already playing new music, introducing it into the set and with a view to a new Hatfield CD release, yes, we're working on it. It's partly due to demand anyway, with the concert venue situation as it is. It's the concerts that bring us together and make the time for rehearsing etc.

What can we expect from Hatfield in 2006?

Release of Hatwise Choice Vol.2. (untitled as yet).

It is impossible to fully cover such a vast and lengthy career in just one interview, but looking back what do you think has been the highlights, and what drives you to keep performing and recording music?

I strive for those highlights constantly, as in the next real good concert.

Highlights are: Appreciative audiences and seeing different parts of the world.
What keeps me going, is the creative drive towards that point of satisfaction of playing with all these great musician friends, when the music goes well, and all sounds good enough to try out on an audience. Delivering the goods to those folks who have paid to

see us. At the moment, it looks like the new music with Hatfield, is being received as well as those on the two 'Virgin' albums, which is a highlight for this project from the start.

Finally, outside of Hatfield what have you been doing recently and what are your own plans for the year ahead?

Busy getting the live work in for 2006, contacting folks.

Working on my instruments now, the worn-out bass etc...in preparation for the rehearsals starting up halfway through February, (with Hatfield and Duo with Alex Maguire).

Plans are: -

Get down to South Italy and make a new Richard Sinclair CD with Angelo Losasso and Taranto friends.

Some duo work with Alex Maguire and Los Angeles Friends, after Baja Prog.

Duo work with Theo Travis.

A church concert or two with David Rees Williams on organ and Tony Coe clarinet for a new CD to follow up 'What in the World' (RSS CD 004)

Reissue the back catalogue, four Sinclair Songs titles that are still being requested by folks.

Guy Manning, #86, Feb 2006

One evening I was lucky enough to go over to Guy's studio, where we spent a very pleasant evening discussing how he got involved with music, and what follows is just a small part of the conversation that went on long into the night.

What first got you interested in music?

I started out by having the usual piano lessons but hated them. I used to hide rather than go into the piano teacher, so I went through a period of hating everything about music. I still liked the idea of music, I just did not like playing it. Then I found a beat-up classical guitar, an old Spanish thing, in my parent's wardrobe. So, I ended up twanging away on that and not getting too bad at playing "My Sweet Lord" and it developed from there. At the same time, I was just about aware of music being written and performed but there was never any music in the house when I grew up. We were not a family that stood around the piano singing songs and we did not have the radio on all day long. My parent's record collection consisted of four 78's, a couple of Frank Sinatra records and 'The Sound Of Music' soundtrack and that was it. I remember seeing The Beatles play the Variety Show;

I can remember that key moment and thinking that it sounded quite interesting, but I was still quite young. So, getting into music was a very peculiar business.

I think a lot of it is about meeting someone who acts as a catalyst for the journey. I was lucky enough to be part of a gang of kids who hung out, playing football and that sort of stuff, but one of the kids we played with had an older brother was into music. He had three plastic LP boxes in his room, and it was the most LP's I had ever seen in one place. He was one of those people who took care of his records, got them out, cleaned them with a cloth, put them on very gingerly. If you ever got invited to listen to music at their house it was a great honour, great kudos, felt important. The first things I ever listened to there was West Coast, Jefferson Airplane, Grateful Dead, Wishbone Ash, Lindisfarne, Alice Cooper, it was that period. He had a copy of 'Tarkus', but we ignored that.

I liked that stuff and was interested in that kind of music and then met a friend who was into Jethro Tull and that for me was the turning point as he played me some Tull albums and I did not know what to make of it. I thought that I did not like it much and could not work out where all the nice little tunes were that Lindisfarne used to do, but he played 'Thick As A Brick' at me and then insisted that we went to see them. He kept playing it until I submitted and said that it was not bad. From then I got addicted to it and it was a matter of finding new albums, new bands, and I was in the right place at the right time for what I do now. I saw Tull in their heyday, I saw Genesis do 'Lamb', saw Pink Floyd at that time, and all the bands that were around at that time like Hatfield and the North, Gong, Mike Oldfield, Gentle Giant. At the same time, I was looking at all this rock stuff I was also investigating singer songwriter and went to see John Martyn, Roy Harper, Al Stewart, which was a grounding of the sort of things that I like which is more narrative song structures. The perfect balance of Roy Harper's artistic poetry and Ian Anderson's sense of melody and arrangement seems about right – it is a mixture of the two. An acoustic long piece with lyrics embellished with rock is just about perfect.

So, I was twanging away on guitar, and then I formed my own band at school and co-opted a lot of the professionally trained musicians into it as I felt that they could probably play a lot better than I could. I was happy to write the songs and these people could read music so I would write it down and they would play it while I was twanging away on a 12 string. In fact, that old twelve-string (*pointing to a guitar on the wall behind me*) is donkey's years old and is still hanging on the wall. The idea that I might be able to write a tune came to me, so I started writing all these songs and it started there, and after that I was in band after band after band for years.

So how did you meet Andy?

I was in a band called King Glass, who were being paid to go into a studio to do a Radio Leeds session, so we needed a studio. We looked around town and found Lion Studios to do the session and there was this scruffy individual sat at the desk with a rolled-up cigarette in his mouth and the place looked like an ashtray with sliders. I was the keyboard player for the band, and I was setting up the sequencers etc. and he was interested and obviously knew something about keyboards, and we got chatting. He told me that he was in a band called Gold, Frankincense and Diskdrive and that was it – we

just hit it off straight away. After that he said that if I was not doing anything would I like to play guitar with GF&D so I did, and then the band disbanded as everyone was going shooting off and doing different things and it became just Andy and I, we were all that was left.

At the time, he was working as an audio technician in the Leeds College of Technology on the top floor and they were looking for equipment to set up for a course based on audio visual recording and we did a deal that if we moved all our computer and keyboard equipment up there they could use it during that day and we could use it during the night. So, students used the equipment during the day and in the evening, we were recording and setting it up and trying new things out. We ended up doing the 'No More Travelling Chess' album there, the Hammill/VDGG tribute album, and went on to record the last GF&D album which was never released but was going to be called 'It's Not The End Of The World But You Can See It From Here'. You will have heard some of it as it has come out in various disguises. For example, the song "Domicile" from 'The Cure' album was first written for there and a lot of stuff on that album has come out as part of Tangent, or Parallel Or Ninety Degrees or Manning. Some of the tracks from that he did put on the PO90 'More Exotic Ways To Die' album, on the multimedia section. There are bits of it that I wouldn't let out – I am a firm believer that you must keep some bits back. As an album, it was quite good, but we disbanded as we wanted to do other things.

Andy and Sam were writing this ambient stuff for a project called Sanctum, which was played down in Leeds Church and sounded great, but it was very Tangerine Dream sort of stuff. They were listening to a lot of Porcupine Tree and knew that they wanted to do something else and I had to go off to work in Germany and they formed Parallel Or Ninety Degrees while I was away. When I came back, they did not need me, and I had other things to do anyway and started to think about doing all my own stuff.

That was the beginning of how we started writing and collaborating and it has been going on for twenty-five years now. What a depressing thought. We still work on other projects as well as Tangent and things like that. If you look at the family tree on the website, you will see how our lives are intertwined. Sometimes we find each other a pleasure to work with and sometimes we do not, which is true of any people in a long-term relationship.

What were you trying to capture with your earlier albums as you sometimes remind me of Roy Harper?

Roy Harper is just superb. I think that he is so under rated, he is one of the best poets who puts words to music that we've got. If I can sound a bit like Roy Harper than that would be great but personally, I do not think that I can even stand in his shadow. I do not want to get too sycophantic, but he is fantastic. He is a man who puts words and phrases together like very few I have ever known. Some of my stuff will sound like Roy because I love Roy Harper and some of my stuff will sound like Tull because I love Tull and because I have a similar timbre to my voice as Ian Anderson had. When you spend your formative years listening to Tull pretty much twenty-four hours a day, then you pick up an acoustic guitar and start to play something it sort of comes out that way. Some of my phrasing is Anderson-esque and the way that I put phrases in and the way that the melody may not fit over the music, either lapping over the end or stopping short is typical Anderson technique. I use that a lot as it is just ingrained in me.

What was I trying to achieve with my early albums? Just release a record was a major milestone. I never thought that I would get a record out even though I had written these songs. In theory, the first album should be your best as you have spent ten to fifteen years practicing and getting yourself ready for the moment when you finally get asked to put some songs down. So, you have had ten or fifteen years to pick the cream of the crop and have all the best songs you have ever written all ready. Now I think I had some very good songs for 'Tall Stories', but when I came to 'The Cure' I did not have a song in my head. Now it was a green field fresh canvas and it made me work harder. 'The Cure' was quite a difficult album and I did not want it to sound like 'Tall Stories' which was vignettes of narrative strung together in a sequence of little songs which fitted together. A bit like 'Thick As A Brick' only not as fluid. I took some songs and put them into suites. How to make a progressive suite is to take five songs which shouldn't go in one song and call them parts one to five. With 'The Cure' I wanted to write longer pieces and I used a whole lot of sound effects, sound collages etc. to make it a totally different experience to the previous album, basically 'The Cure' was more of a moving thing that took you from one song to another. It was also darker, a lot darker, and it was a concept album. There were lots of things going outside of music, work etc., and I was not a happy bunny and lots of that permeated through into the album. Having come out of that I wanted to make the next album much lighter, breezy and poppy and 'Cascade' was the answer to 'The Cure'.

Each album has been a progression really. What did I do last time, what do I want to do next time, and try and move but keep a style so that people know that it is still me. If I decided next time to make a reggae album I think that it might be stretching it a little but I am hoping that I have managed to create a series of albums that at the bottom of it all it is still me but each one has its own flavour. Some of them are big and symphonic, some are more rock oriented, some are pastorals or light and acoustic. There is always a lot of variety as variety is something that I am interested in.

Because I am not a maestro on any instrument, I can hold my own on acoustic guitar or keyboard, but I am not Rick Wakeman and I am not Steve Howe, each album has been designed to highlight the arrangement skills as opposed to the virtuosity of the playing. Know your limitations. I leave the virtuosity to people like Spock's Beard or The Flower Kings who have the skills to stand on stage and jam for half an hour and it sounds superb. Me, I must arrange everything so that it all sounds very complicated and very well put together, but it is all done with the arrangement. Very simple parts put together, in the same way that Pink Floyd did 'Dark Side Of The Moon'. If you break that down into its composite parts it is very simple, but it sounds great when you put it all back together again and that is what I try to do. Keep it simple but have a bit here where the flute answers the keyboard, the keyboard answers the cello, which answers the drum and they are all talking together. There is a counterpoint parts coming together and meshing together with the impression that there are lots of things all happening and give it the complexity through arrangement as opposed to through virtuosity.

I feel that your music could be described as 'English', what do you say to that?

I do listen to a lot of American music; I love Steely Dan for example but if we are talking 'progressive' then there is something quintessentially English about it. From the moment that you start to evolve from 'Sgt Pepper' through to 'In The Court Of The Crimson King' and out into Genesis, I do not think that you can get any more English than Genesis circa 'Nursery Cryme' period. Progressive rock is essentially middle-class rock music; I do not think that it is particularly working class. I am not being snobbish about that, I'm not saying that working class do not like it, it is just that it is probably the product of a middle-class education. It implies a certain amount of literacy and education, and that is not being politically incorrect. You look at punk which came afterwards which was a call to arms from the streets and about time too, it gave a lot of force and impetus back into music, although it caused a lot of damage at the times to the bands that I liked but it was necessary.

The innovation of progressive rock came through the experimentation and crossbreeding of different art forms, artistry in terms of visual art, in terms of literature and performance arts all came together in progressive rock. To have had the opportunities to be able to do that you must have had some sort of middle-class grounded education. It was no surprise to me that Genesis came from Charterhouse. That being said, there were a lot of great progressive rock musicians who did not come from middle class backgrounds, but the clear majority tended to come from an educated background.

I write what I write because I am just a product of my generation, a product of going to a grammar school, reading a lot and the bands I admire tend to write that sort of music. If I had been born a little later then I would probably be trying to write Talking Heads' songs or XTC and basically thrashing away on the guitar, but I was born early enough to hear Genesis and Jethro Tull and Yes doing their intricate complex writing and it caught me. That is the things that I have been interested in ever since. I do think that you are a product of your time. If you were born in the late Sixties it would be totally different to being born in the early Seventies, I write what I write because I am that old, basically. You should try to be true and write what you enjoy. I love The Mahavishnu Orchestra, but I could not write it. I love Hatfield and the North and National Health, but I do not think that I could write that either. It is too musically complex for me to write. I try to write a good tune, and hopefully some good words to go with a good tune, and I leave it at that.

You have not mentioned Hammill or VDGG, is that more from Andy's side?

Yes, in the same way that I was introduced to Jethro Tull, Andy introduced me to Hammill and VDGG. My first introduction to VDGG was when I was taking a girl out in the fifth form at school and her brothers were big VDGG fans. They used to interrogate me while she was upstairs getting changed. While she was away, they put me in the armchair, play albums at me and gauge my reaction, whether I was worthy of their sister. I can remember the first thing that I heard was that they slapped 'Godbluff' on and started putting "Scorched Earth" on and they studied me to see how I would react to this guy bellowing and screaming at the top of his lungs.

I never paid much attention to Hammill and VDGG though, I missed them. When Lindisfarne, Genesis and VDGG went out on the tour I would have been much more interested in seeing the other two. When Andy introduced me to VDGG he was diddling around with "Arrow" to test the equipment out and I went 'who?', and he said that it was off the 'Godbluff' album, so I listened to that and it was quite interesting. We worked on "Arrow" and some others and then decided to work on "Ronceveaux" from 'Time Vaults' which has never been recorded properly. We decided to get in touch with Hammill and ask him for the lyrics and we went to meet him down in Bath. The actual process of going through and constructing and reconstructing these songs to put the album together gave me the love of VDGG that I have now. Basically, it opened the door, opened my eyes to this great stuff. I do not understand what he is going on about, somebody please tell me what "A Plague Of Lighthouse Keepers" is about. I think that it is something to do with isolation but who cares? I got to know each song and it just became a passion, and then of course you move onto the Hammill stuff.

Andy introduced me to VDGG, and Hammill and the dark side of the force comes from Andy, and I provided the Canterbury side of things which is more where my interests are, the Genesis sort of intricate parts. That is what I do now with The Tangent, my role is to act as co-producer on that side and to add the acoustic instruments and bits and pieces to counteract the big keyboards and the rock part of it. I try to keep the wood in there.

If someone came across your new album, how would you describe it to them?

It is tricky, as I hate pigeonholing, putting it into a box as it is only by giving people other names that they can start to recognise it. Well, it sounds a bit like Roy Harper, Al Stewart (laughs)...

The big thing on the new album is the title track which is a long thirty-one-minute piece divided into eight parts and it is basically one long acoustic song. I got so sick of not being able to play live because the band were not around, that I decided that the next time I recorded an album there would be a long piece that I could play myself if necessary. If no-one else turned up I could do this on my own. I can do 85% of "One Small Step" on my own, although it could be a bit flat, but who knows I might do it yet. I wanted to do a long linear acoustic song and this is my attempt, whereas when I have tried long pieces in the past they have been rock songs bolted together with linking sections whereas this one I wanted it to be a flowing performance of one man and his guitar, with the aid of other instruments helping and putting the icing on the cake. The basis for half this album is the acoustic guitar and the lyrics.

The other half of the album is made up of songs that I thought were interesting as complimentary to the half an hour piece which is to me the most important thing on the album, but each of the four other pieces are quite different. One is tex mex, another sounds like a Tom Paxton simple folk song type of approach and the other two are rocky songs. There is a bit of progressive rock in "No Hiding Place" where it goes completely bonkers in the middle but only because I felt like going completely bonkers in the middle. I told people to go mad and squeak and squawk and I took the best bits and made them into a collage in the middle and it works.

How do you feel you are different to the rest of the progressive scene?

How do you find that key original thing that you can do that no one else can? With me it is going back to the Harper-esque approach to song writing that I do not think that many of my progressive peers have. I think that is because I am not good enough to write long windy pieces. I could not write "Topographic Oceans", I could write some of the tunes, but you would have needed Rick Wakeman, Steve Howe, Alan White and Chris Squire in the same room to produce that result. I write by myself, so how good can it be when it is the product of just one person's brain. It is difficult. I know that Ian Anderson writes the Tull stuff, but they still knock it about in the arrangement and I have not got anybody to do that with, I write in isolation.

The thing that is so good and different about doing Tangent as opposed to what I do is that it gives me the chance to pretend that I am in a band again. I oversee just my bit of the sound, instead of virtually everything. With The Tangent, my job is going in and taking charge of the acoustic instruments and the arrangements of the pieces and the way that the songs work together and where to put light and shade. This is the interesting thing for me about Tangent even though we have never all been in the same room at one time. We met up for The Flower Kings gig in Rotherham, and we were all there apart from David Jackson and that was the nearest we have ever been to being together.

After this the tape machine was stopped, and Guy spent time showing me how he uses his Cubase recording system, playing some music, and then we went into his front room to look at his amazing collection of CDs (easily the most I have ever seen), and to see just some of the concert programmes and tickets he has kept from over the years.

Adam Wakeman, #87, Apr 2006

We all know quite a bit about Mr Wakeman senior, but with the release of the Jeronimo Road live album I had the opportunity to have a word with one of his keyboards playing sons, Adam.

Did you ever feel pressurised to learn keyboards?

No, not at all. I started playing when I was about eight (working through the classical grades until I was about sixteen) and always wanted to be a keyboard player. I saw Dad play on a Yes tour, I think it was ABWH, and thought there and then, that was what I wanted to spend my life doing. My dad and mum split up when I was very young, so I never had him breathing down my neck telling me to practice more! Not that he would anyway!

Did you follow the normal Royal College and piano route, or did you learn synths with your father?

I did all eight Classical Piano grades but went on tour instead of going to college! I felt that in the field of music I was into, it wouldn't help me going to music college. My dad would never teach me anything. As a child learning it was very frustrating – every time I asked him to show me something, he would say 'listen to it and teach yourself'. It proved to be the most helpful advice of all as it enables me to learn things quickly now, in the studio on sessions or in rehearsals.

What were you doing prior to Jeronimo Road and how did that group get together?

The group came together through meeting Fraser T-Smith. I heard his demo cassette at Tony Fernandez's house (my father's drummer) and called him up. We got on like a house on fire and remain very close friends. We had the same ideas for starting a band and started auditions to get to the band line up that's on the album 'Live At The Orange'. Before Jeronimo Road, I was mainly working on my own projects ('Soliloquy', '100 Years Overtime') and working with my father on tours and albums.

Musically what were you trying to do with the band, and do you feel that you achieved that?

We were trying to fuse all our influences into a more song-based band. There's elements of prog, rock and blues which were important to us, and in that respect, yes, I feel we achieved the sound we were looking for.

Why so few gigs and recordings?

There were only three shows, and then the band all went their separate ways. Damian decided that he wanted to concentrate on his own material at the time and the drummer Mark Heaney left to join the Seahorses, so we were left feeling a bit empty! Fraser then came on-board with my dad's band and both Fraser's and my session careers started getting much busier, so we called it a day

Do you see a point when the group could get back together?

I doubt it. Fraser is very busy with his studio in London. He writes and records with some great artists and production is his love. He's had several hit writing credits and is doing great. He still loves the rock but his heart's in the studio now I feel.

Did you introduce Damian to your father?

Yes, when Dad wanted a new singer, I put Damian forward. And Lee Pomeroy too, a bit later when he needed a new bass player.

What have been your projects since JR split up?

Since then I worked with Atomic Kitten, Tony Hadley, Annie Lennox, Travis, Ozzy Osbourne and Black Sabbath. I still play for Sabbath, Ozzy and Travis when they tour.

What sort of music do you like to listen to, and what is your favourite to play?

Now, I'm listening to heavy stuff like Pain of Salvation as that's the type of music my new band is writing and playing.

Who have been your favourite musicians to work with and why, and who would you like to play with in the future?

Favourite people would be Annie Lennox, the Sabbath guys and Travis. Touring with Annie was like going on tour with my mum! She's a wonderful, kind lady whose honesty and personality are refreshing in this industry. A truly great artist and person. Sabbath is fantastic and like working with your first band at school. I mean that in the sense of capturing the excitement of a bunch of guys playing together and reacting to what each other plays. Individually, they are all very kind, great fun to be around. I've toured the last two years with them and had an absolute ball. Travis are similar in that the interaction between them is great and I feel included in that. They're great guys and good fun to be around, on and off stage.

Can you envisage a time when you, Oliver and your father could all be recording together, and if that was the case what style of music do you think would be the result?

Who knows! We played together for the first time at two nights in Marlborough, England at Christmas, which was great. I do not know if we'll ever record anything though. We're all so busy with our own projects, I think. Maybe one day though....

What are you working on currently and what are your plans for the rest of the year?

As we speak, I'm in Frankfurt Germany playing a show for Korg. They have some new equipment and I like coming here and seeing what else is new. It's a big music trade show and great to play at. I did it about eight years ago with dad too so it's quite nostalgic being back!

The rest of the year will be spent partly in America recording and touring with Ozzy. We have fifteen or so shows in the summer and the rest of the time I will be getting my new band together. We formed Headspace last year and have been writing and, in the studio, getting our album together. It's quite heavy in places and more than the odd tip of the hat to our progressive roots. Line-up is; Damian Wilson on vocals, Lee Pomeroy on bass, Pete Rinaldi on guitar, Rich Brook on drums and me on keyboards. By the end of the year we'll be doing a few shows around the UK and Europe and showcasing the new album.

After Crying, #87, Apr 2006

After Crying are one of Hungary's leading bands so I jumped at the opportunity of having a chat with them.

As a band, what were you trying to achieve when you first formed?

Our goals were purely artistic and musical. The reason we formed this band was not to pick up girls after gigs or to be stars among our friends or among a bigger audience. The young people starting this band had several idols in classical and rock music, and we were upset by the fact that we could not hear these things together. After a thorough search in 20th Century classical and non-classical music we decided to compose our own. This was the main goal of ours and this remained ever since. Not that we would be sad to achieve more success than we did during these twenty years, but (financial) success is not an essential part of the goal, i.e. we do consider our aims to be fulfilled even if less than twenty million people know our songs by heart. Though it wouldn't hurt.

Please can you explain something of the philosophy and collective culture of After Crying as it is very different to most bands?

As a structural phenomenon, it is not democracy and not autocracy. It is a community. This means that everybody is important, and everybody has his role and vote (sometimes 'veto'), but the needs and points and goals of the individual are subordinated to the needs and points and goals of the whole community. Without these individual forces, there would be nothing there. But it has also become obvious several times that the unified force of the community is more than the sum of its' parts, even though some of these are cut during the creative process. So, there is no band leader, though for some tasks there is an executive person. For those who know how scientific anarchy works this may be familiar though we do not consider ourselves as an example of well-structured anarchy, we consider this as a community. Discipline, self-sacrifice, patience and love are important achievements of other communities (e.g. Christian ones) that we have learnt partly from examples, partly during our progress.

Our philosophy is based upon Christian thinking, mainly that of St Thomas of Aquinas and G. K. Chesterton. The latter once said something like "for an artist it is not enough to have his work taken out of him, he also has to make sure that it gets into someone else" which we take as one of the keystones of our creative thinking. But we have never wanted to be a 'Christian band' in the common sense. Rather a driving and leading force towards God, something like the 'Stalker' in Tarkovsky's film. The one who leads people into the room, but he never steps into it. This is the whole band's approach not necessarily all the individuals. Personally, everybody decides his own approach. And there are VERY different approaches among band members.

What was the rationale behind the instrumentation employed and who musically inspires you?

Peter Pejtsik says:

One of the founder members, Csaba Vedres (who left the band later) just got fed up with non-working electronic instruments, and he decided to form an acoustic band. This sounds like a joke, but it is true. And I could play the cello sounding as a distorted electric guitar. And we had been discussing (and sometimes playing together) modern classical music (the ways and traps of different approaches) for years, while going to the same music college, or secondary school, Bartok Conservatory in Budapest. He stayed together with the flute player (Gabor Egervari) from his previous, just-disbanded formation, and they invited me as a third member. This was the first line-up, piano-flute-cello, totally acoustic (not even amplified) and totally instrumental. And from then on sometimes we felt we needed an instrument and tried to find someone who played that instrument and fitted the band, or sometimes we found someone we wanted to work together with and tried to fit his/her instrument in the sound. In short there is no real 'rationale' behind the instrumental line-up of the basic ensemble; it is rather an historic-organic phenomenon. As an arranger, I can say it is not the easiest set of instruments to work for. :)

Our musical ideals are mostly taken from the history of Western music plus two giants of the 'Golden Era' of European art-rock: ELP and King Crimson. Their all-encompassing view and musical-dramatical forces were the light-towers for us. We felt that following the way the latter two started at the time when it all seemed so easy, we would get nearer to the point. We are in an easier situation than they are nowadays, since we have never been very successful and famous and so we did not have to find this success in a later period when it became less easy to be successful with free and quality music.

How would you describe your music to someone who has never heard it?

Our description is 21st Century classical music. (This has been our label even in the 80's.) We never labelled our music as 'progressive', though we are very grateful to this community for their acknowledgement. We try to unify the forces of our ancestors with the forces of our descendants. When you listen to After Crying music, you should be prepared for anything, but you can trust us that there will always be a reason and a higher aim behind the sudden changes or surprising arrangements. One thing is sure: if you tried to categorize this music while listening to it, you could be banging your head against the wall. And maybe for a while you'd think you know but then it changes again per the dramatic structure behind the actual music.

How did the concert with the symphony orchestra come about?

Though we have been featuring symphonic recordings in our albums since 1996, the first time we performed with a symphony orchestra was in Caracas, Venezuela in 2000. And even at that time it was the idea of the local promoter-organizer, Emanuel Abramovits and Alexis Lope-Bello, manager of the local band Tempano, which we shared the rock-concert next day with. We will always be grateful to them for starting us on this path. After the success of that concert we decided to do the same in Hungary. And we have done it a couple of times since, and we are planning to have more concerts of this kind. The next two gigs will be on 30th November in Budapest and in May 2007 in Miskolc, another town in Hungary.

'Show' is a very interesting and enjoyable album - what message were you trying to get across and why the need for a concept?

If the message does not come through the entertainment, then it is not worth talking about it here... The need for a concept is obvious for us, not only in music but in art in general, and in life in general. There are quite old and conservative ideas which seem to be rather radical just because people do not usually think about them in their entirety. Our concept consists of such ideas mainly. A good sample can be heard in the "News" section of "Remote Control". BTW, 'remote control' does not stand for the device you control your TV set with, rather the TV device itself that controls you... This is an example of an opinion of ours, but it should become clear in a greater context when listening to the whole album.

That album is very different to the others that I have heard of yours - was this part of a conscious decision on your part to appeal more to the western market?

Well, all the albums are different from each other. The sound of 'Show' comes from the continuation of the path started on the previous studio album, '6', i.e. to incorporate as much of the modern technical achievements as possible without moving away from our language and message. And the reason for this is to present our quite ancient ideas in the most consumable and appealing way to make it understood by the most people possible. And, to tell you the truth, after these years we did not think that the western or any market would be more interested if we did anything. And so, why not carry on doing our own stuff?

What keeps you going after all this time and when can we expect to see the next new studio album?

When we started this band all of us thought it would be a life-long adventure. Most of us still think like that. We always have ideas, even in the periods without gigs or albums (such as the period now, before the festive 20th season of the band). And when we have ideas, we always investigate them whether they are After-Crying-worthy ones. And when the time comes, they achieve their final format, and are reborn as A.C. songs or pieces. When a band is formed the members (in most cases) must give up some of their ideas to unify their approach. And they usually work very hard, and a lot, because they want to be successful in a short time, since they know that the big public's attention will not be

focused on them for long. So, they give up part of their ideas, and do not do other projects and after some years everybody starts feeling the suppressed things wanting to come out. And this is when band members start releasing solo albums, and this is when people start thinking that they are starting to disband. And sometimes they are right. With A.C. it is different.

We never thought that we shouldn't do anything besides A.C. All members do different things (they must, since this is not done as a living) so there are these safety valves and the steam does not explode the can. And when the time comes, we all come together and do what most of us like doing the most. We do not want to promise anything for a next album's release time. There are ideas in the drawer, some of them will be performed next season, but we will see when it is going to mature into a new album. We have time to kill...

How would you compare the Hungarian music scene to the rest of Europe, and can we expect to see you playing in the UK at some point?

One main difference may be that in Hungary (as in Austria) there are stronger walls between "serious" and "light/entertaining" music, where technically a divertimento by Mozart falls into the "serious" category (despite of it's entertaining intention) and e.g. King Crimson's 'Starless' falls into the "light" category, though it is sombre enough... We keep struggling against this, mostly by our hard-to-classify works. It would be cool to perform in the UK again (after some early-stage college-concerts in 1988). It may happen in the next festive season, maybe joined to our planned short European tour in spring 2007. All suggestions are welcome. Your turn. :)

Solstice Coil, #87, Apr 2006

This may be a new name to many of you, but this band are making great waves in the prog scene with their debut album 'A Prescription For Paper Cuts', and the reason that you may not have yet come across them is due to their geographical location, as these guys are from Israel! My grateful thanks to guitarist Opher Vishnia for arranging the interview, and for also telling me that this is the first UK interview they've given.

How did the band first come together?

I met up with Shir, our vocalist, through an online forum. We searched endlessly for drummers, and at some point, we were set up to meet this new drummer at the studio. When she failed to arrive, we kindly 'borrowed' Uri from the band that played before us. Things clicked and with this strange turn of events Uri's with us still today. Shai found us at an online forum as well. Later, our original bass player whom co-founded the band with Shir and me left to be replaced by Diego. Aaron played guitar in the fellow progressive-grunge band Behind The Sun, and since we had such a common musical language, it was only natural for him to join on guitar, thus allowing Shir to focus on his singing duties. The line-up is interesting, seeing as how it consists of four original Israelis, with experience in the Israeli military and all, Aaron who moved to Israel from the US and Diego who moved to Israel from Argentina.

Within your list of influences, you name many bands, but who has been the primary influence on what you are doing?

Our initial influences are Radiohead and Muse, which is quite evident from the mostly melancholic mood of the songs and the singing style. As we continued to grow as musicians, we started to explore different approaches in composition, influenced mostly by King Crimson, Porcupine Tree and Dream Theater. We infused these two approaches to come up with our own unique style. While this sounds simple, it's really hard to place your finger on where exactly everything comes from. Between the six of us, we bring in so many different musical directions, that every now and then we get a comment from someone who'll tell us we sound like we're very influenced by a band that none of us have ever even listened to.

Your music is quite different to what else is around within the scene; do you think that you being geographically remote from the normal prog area has contributed to this?

While Israel is not the first place that comes to mind when you think of progressive music, you'd be surprised at the variety of non-mainstream music Israel has to offer. We have everything from Doom metal to funk and reggae. Unfortunately, these bands do not get much attention from the local media, not to mention the global media, and it's nearly impossible for them to come through, let alone fill venues here. We do not attribute our individual music style to the location, rather than to the members of the band. While we are physically distant, we are still in touch with current music. The internet takes most of the credit in that respect, as it allows us and other local bands to expose our music globally and be exposed to new music in a way that otherwise would have been impossible.

How do you describe your music and what led Shir to sing in falsetto as well as his normal voice?

An approximate term we use is "Alternative Progressive Rock". I say "approximate", because not all our songs fit into this exact category. When we compose, we try to create what sounds good to us, but at the same time has something new in it, or we try a new approach may it be in terms of sound or arrangement. We do not like sticking to the patterns of terminology - you will not see us at rehearsal going "Well, we just have to put

this part in the song because it fits the genre". We try to convey as much as the raw emotion and energy that exists in alternative rock bands so our listeners can relate to our music, but at the same time offer the eloquence and refinement of progressive rock without succumbing to its often cold and technical nature. Asides from the fact Shir's use of falsetto is obviously derived from Thom Yorke and Matthew Bellamy's vocal styles, it is just another tool that we use to keep our edge up. It provides diversity, which is an integral part of our creation. We do not view it as something abnormal; it comes quite natural for us.

Is there a prog scene within Israel, and where do you fit within it?

Israel does indeed have a prog scene, if somewhat tiny, featuring many interesting bands such as Eatliz, Sympozion, Ahvak, Warm Fur and Eggroll, for example. At first, we were not even considered 'prog' by the scene's standards, seeing as how our music is hybrid of several genres, but they (like everyone else) came to like and accept us. The Israeli prog audience is tricky, and mostly hard to come by with. While a band like Eggroll has managed to perform before an audience of a thousand people, others are struggling to get even a hundred people to attend their shows. The market for this type of music is very limited, and unless you have got an aggressive and talented promoter at hand, it'll be difficult to reach that market.

You are one of the few bands from Israel that are getting noticed outside of your own country, how does that make you feel, and do you believe that there are other bands coming through us well?

It feels great to see how after years of hard work; it's starting to pay off! In the six months since the album was released, we received dozens of reviews from all around the world, and yet this is still just the tip of the iceberg. We now see the true potential that our music has on the international market, something that was not as clear to us before the album was released. There are other Israeli bands like Betzefer and Orphaned Land who are starting to become household names, and we're planning to follow in their footsteps.

Has there been interest from labels that want to release and promote your album?

We've been contacted by some small-time labels that were really nice to offer us a home, but being an independent artist has its appeal, and we wouldn't want to give it up unless it's worth it. We have some non-exclusive distribution deals with the likes of French label Musea, and our good friend Adam Baruch from the Jazzis online music store has managed to get our album sold on other online stores from several countries.

Do you feel that there is going to be the opportunity for you to play in Europe or the UK?

Why, certainly! Our first European tour ever is taking place this October and November. We'll be passing through Belgium, The Netherlands, Germany, Denmark, Italy and France playing with various local bands as we go. We're still in the process of scheduling the gigs, but soon enough we'll have all the details on our website. Sorry for you people in the UK, but the reasons why we will not be playing there this year are purely logistical. Given the opportunity, we'd sure like to perform there in the future! Maybe even on our next tour...

What are the next steps for the band?

Asides from our tour in Europe this fall, we still continue to play and perform here in Israel, and of course we're working on new materials for our next album, which is going to be very interesting and, in some ways, different from what we've done so far. By the way, our progress can be monitored more closely at our online band journal, which is some sort of a Solstice Coil "behind the scenes".

Jeremy Morris, # 88, Jun 2006

Having only recently got back in touch with Jeremy Morris after a gap of quite a few years, it seemed only fitting to ask him some questions.

How did you first get involved in music - what are your earliest memories?

I first got involved in music at age six when I took up the piano. I later studied guitar at the age of twelve followed later by bass, drums, mandolin, and many other instruments. I grew up around music because my Dad is a jazz musician, so there was always music and bands playing in the home. By age fifteen I had my first professional rock and roll band: I broke into the music business at a very young age. We went right out and started playing gigs. Full Moon was a great working band and we made some good money.

Were you recording and playing with bands prior to the first solo recordings?

It was 1973 when my first band Full Moon started playing gigs. We performed covers of Led Zeppelin, Black Sabbath, Jethro Tull, Mott The Hoople, Free, April Wine, Lynyrd Skynyrd, Beatles, Stones, Deep Purple, etc... And along with this we did some originals. The band recorded some of the originals that I had written in 1973. These are the earliest known recordings of any Jeremy music. The tunes were ambitious progressive pieces because I was heavy into Genesis, and Yes at the time. The tunes have remained unreleased although they will probably someday see the light of day.

At what point did you set up the record label and how would you describe the acts signed to it - do you have a particular musical or ethical policy?

The JAM record label was launched in August of 1984. Jam Records (my initials) is still going strong today. I started this label because I had been recording music for over ten years without a proper outlet for my tunes. I had tried negotiating with Capitol, Warners, Atlantic, and many other labels but it did not work out. Warners came closest to a deal, but when even that one fell through, it was clear that the independent road was the only way. So, that summer we released 'Jeremy-Alive' and pressed up 5000 LPs and 1000 singles to launch the label. Years later I signed many other bands to the label and the decision was based simply on if I liked their music. Some artists were rock, some progressive, some power pop, some instrumental. (It was certainly a love of music instead of money) Today I still stick to this slogan... "Money talks but it can't sing" so whenever I put out music on Jam, it's music that I truly love and believe in.

You have many distinct styles - how would you describe your music to the newcomer?

I release a lot of styles. Power Pop, Progressive, Rock, Electronic, Praise and Worship, Instrumental, Ambient, Modern classical. To me it's all just music. I have never felt the need to limit myself to any one certain style like the major labels do. One reviewer said, "Jeremy Morris is truly one of those rare artists who really does have something for everyone".

Were you already a recording musician prior to becoming a pastor, and have you come across issues from combining the two roles?

I was a recording musician long before I became a pastor of a church. I have not had any personal issues with wearing more than one hat. I was never into drugs, so I do not associate rock music with all that. Furthermore, I do not associate rock music with rebellion as some people do but see it as an expression of freedom. ("Freedom" is the name of the church I pastor), I have no reservations about rocking out on the guitar and worshipping God at the same time. It's all good to me!

Which of your styles gives you the most personal pleasure, and if one was coming to your music for the first time, what albums would you steer them towards and why?

I enjoy doing a lot of styles of music. It would be hard to pick a favourite because I go through phases. Sometimes I am into quiet music, other times I want to crank it up! It just depends on the mood at the time. It's all good in its proper element.

There may be some who would argue that producing so many albums is a sign of poor quality control - how would you counter that?

I have released 34 Jeremy albums. The Jam label itself has put out over 100 releases. This year a five CD Jeremy box set is scheduled for release on Bullseye Records of Canada. (Concerning quality control when putting out music, I still have around 500 unreleased recordings.) I do not release everything I record. However, it is interesting to find that some fans are requesting for me to release all this stuff. I probably will in limited edition.

What hopes do you have for your music, and have you any musical ambitions that you have yet to fulfil?

I would like as many people as possible around the world to hear and be blessed by the music I create.

Your latest album 'Faithful and True' is in your Praise and Worship series. Who are you aiming these at and what is your next project going to be?

It is aimed at those who enjoy praise and worship music. I was surprised to find a Top 40 radio station in Spain was playing this music on the air, so I am setting aside all my preconceived notions about who it is for. Right now, I am working on about five albums all at once, which has been my approach for many years. I record at home and at other people's studios as well. So far this year I have recorded an album in Atlanta, Georgia and another album in France. It's great fun recording in a variety of studios because the music comes out differently. I also record at my home studio in Michigan.

Lastly, if someone came up to you and said, "who are you?" how would you answer? How do you view yourself?

When asked "How do I view myself" I do not think too much about it. I just do what I do and hope that I bring a true blessing to others. I know one thing; I love God, people, and music. This has been my life now for all these years. I do remember there was an old song from the early 70's called "God, Love, and Rock and Roll". I think they were on to something with the lyrics!

Richard Wileman (Karda Estra), # 88, Jun 2006

I have known Richard for many years, but for some reason have never got around to interviewing him. At long last I have sought to rectify that situation.

How did you first get interested in music and who would you say were your early influences?

I liked to listen to music as a child - the pop stuff of the time like Abba and ELO. I also really liked Saint Saens' "Dance Macabre". Unfortunately, I showed no ability at playing an instrument at school. My mum plays piano and she tried to teach me keyboards on a

Bontempi organ, but it did not work. I did know I liked the sound of chords, though. Eventually, it was suggested I drop music at school in the third year because I was so bad at it and I did. When I was fourteen, like all my friends, I started listening to 70's heavy rock and NWOBHM bands. At my school, when you turned sixteen, boys either seemed to get into motorbikes or electric guitars. I choose the latter and for some strange reason, I taught myself to play - in every available spare hour! It was quite a turn around and I was pretty obsessive. I had another friend who could already play a bit, and this probably inspired me to start 'making stuff up' even when I could only fret two strings. I was also playing along with records and tapes. In the first year, I did learn a lot of Black Sabbath riffs.

Were you playing in bands at this time, and how did this lead into Lives and Times?

My family moved from Nottinghamshire to Wiltshire when I was 17. I soon formed a band, which lasted until I was 21. We were not very good unfortunately – each player was good on his own instrument, but the result was quite clichéd and amateurish - our influences were far too prominent. I decided to quit the band, which then collapsed. I bought a drum machine and synth and started writing my own instrumentals. Simon Davis, a friend I was with at art college with, played bass. This resulted in some demos being recorded. I also bumped into Lorna again who was a singer who had auditioned for my old band during its breaking up period. Those instrumentals plus some songs I wrote with Lorna during 1987 were the beginning of Lives And Times. Simon only lasted until he finished his college course. He went on to become an artist in 2000AD and for a time, you would see Lives And Times logos on posters and the tee-shirts of baddies being blown away by Judge Dredd in the strips he was drawing.

What were you trying to achieve musically with Lives and Times, do you feel that you achieved this, and what led to the decision to stop Lives and Times and start Karda Estra?

It's been a while now – I'm not sure I can remember too well... I guess it was my attempt (as I was in my 20's) to try and get a great band going and get a major record deal. It's something young musicians seem to do! In retrospect, it all seems a bit of a muddle - I think there was potential, but it was hampered by financial restrictions. I could have also used some professional guidance. As it was, I made it up as I went along. I kind of look at it now as 'a good idea at the time'. But some of it was quite good, but not where my head is at now. I started Karda Estra because I had finally got a home studio set up and could indulge my interests in classical and soundtrack music to a much greater degree because of this. And I think the whole band thing was simply passing me by.

So not only were you now working on your own, but there was now a conscious decision to change your musical direction. What inspired you to do this?

Buying a hard disc recorder. I knew I wanted to be able to spend a lot longer on recording without worrying about a commercial studio's clock ticking away. Once I got into the frame of mind that I could spend a day recording anything and not worry it was going to cost me an arm and a leg to do so, I realised that my musical horizons had expanded to, well, virtually infinity. Any sound was possible. And more importantly any mix variation.

The first pieces that eventually made up tracks one - three of 'A Winter In Summertime' were pure pieces of experimentation. I had no idea that I would give the project a name or I would release it on CD. It literally went from step to step - starting with the violin bow/guitar scrape loop on "...From A Deep Sleep". So many early discoveries during that period - that Ileesha would sound 'that' good doing the stacked choral vocal harmonies and effects. The inspiration I get from writing for and recording classical woodwind and string musicians. And trying to be permanently inventive on the instruments I play - guitars, keyboards and percussion. But on virtually every level – especially compositionally and production-wise, it was a huge leap forward from being in a band - for me anyhow.

Why the move into more classical forms - what or who inspired you to develop your music this way?

I'd always liked instrumental music - and some (mainly keyboard based) tunes had snuck their way onto the Lives And Times albums. Karda Estra was a big expansion of this. The great thing about this music is that I can attempt to convey ideas and concepts that songs are unable to - which include interests in art, film and fiction, amongst other things. I've been learning more and more about classical instrumentation and such, which adds a dimension of beauty, expression and subtlety that is unachievable with electric/ electronic instruments. However, I still must stress that I do not actually compose in a 'classical' manner. I have no tutoring in classical composition and I still think in rock and roll terms, despite what people may perceive the outcome to be. And I'm still very much interested in pushing my own electric/electronic parts and blending all the instrumentation to make something that fits well and does not sound like an awkward juxtaposition.

From where I'm at, there have been thousands of great classical composers before me and thousands of great popular musicians. Rather than attempt to be one of them in a more traditional sense, I'm more interested in trying to be a man of the times. We're in a golden era for technological possibilities in recording – it's endless and I now have a wonderful opportunity to merge styles, instrumentation and experiment and try to do something that is perhaps a little more unique and personal to me.

Your music often comes across as being very visual as if it is a film score, is this deliberate positioning on your part?

I'm very interested in art (it was my first passion before music) so when I compose, I do think in terms of light, shade and colour as well as melody, harmony and rhythm. It's why I like a wide range of instrumentation and dynamics in my recordings.

When I created Karda Estra, it seemed perhaps by accident, that I had created a vehicle where these interests could sit side by side. And since 'Constellations', I've got back to doing the CD cover art. The previous ones (and Lives And Times too) were mainly done by a friend Alan Read who I'd met when we were at art college.

And not to forget that I like some soundtrack music. Composers like Goldsmith, Morricone and Herrmann have been a huge influence on me. Sonically, you'd be hard pushed to find a wider palette than on something like Goldsmith's 'Planet Of The Apes' soundtrack. I love all that kind of stuff. 'Voivode Dracula' and 'Science And Enlightenment' does feature a 'Rastrophone' - an instrument invented by Mario Nascimbene when scoring 'One Million Years BC'. (He later admitted it was a garden rake!).

What is the inspiration behind the new album, and please can you provide a track breakdown?

The major theme of this album is Redemption.

I used several sources to convey this - some of them are also thematic links to previous albums.

The title of the album and first piece I composed was taken from 'The Werewolf Of Paris' by Guy Endore: "But there was a strange shame here that he could not overcome. Oh, the terrible disgrace, the ignominy of it - possessing a mythical monster in one's own family, in this the age of science and enlightenment!"

The "Return Of John Deth" pieces were inspired by the painting 'John Deth' by Edward Burra. My own original "John Deth" piece appeared back on the 'Thirteen From The Twenty First' album and I always knew I'd give him, like all great horror creatures deserve, some sequels.

"The Red Room" was the second piece I wrote for this album.

"Bones In The Moonlight" was the last and initially inspired by the rhythmic piano on Paul McCartney's "Single Pigeon".

"Nocturne Macabre" was a challenge to myself - could I write a quiet piece that stays quiet? (I am very fond of crescendos and generally wide dynamics). The title is my acknowledgement to Saint Saens' 'Dance Macabre' – a piece that enchanted me as a child and I'm sure its spirit still lies in the music I write.

"Talos" was inspired by one of the lifespan lengthening project names in Robert Silverberg's novel 'Shadrach In The Furnace'. Talos was the cybernetic one. I not only used this as a link to 'The Future Eve', but also because I noticed that the other two projects 'Avatar' and 'Phoenix' were also titles of pieces I had written and liked the idea of this co-incidence.

"Carmilla" was inspired by the vampire short story by Sheridan Le Fanu.

"Am I Dreaming You? Are You Dreaming Me?" was inspired by a line in Robert Silverberg's novel 'Son Of Man'. The narration (spoken by Ileesha, Helen, Caron and Zoe) are quotes from Sheridan Le Fanu's story "Green Tea".

The title for "Second Star" was inspired by a Kate Bush song "In Search Of Peter Pan", who was in turn quoting J.M. Barrie:

"When, When I am a man, I will be an astronaut, and find Peter Pan, Second Star on the right, Straight on 'till morning".

What's next?

Honestly at this moment, I have no idea. There are a few projects and ideas I would like to do, but nothing concrete has even started yet. I think it's good to take a few months 'time out' after an album is finished to get a good perspective about both what you have done and where you'd like to go next.

Mangala Vallis, #88, Jun 2006

I managed to catch up with Bernardo Lanzetti and Gig Cavalli Cocchi to ask questions about Mangala Vallis and their wonderful new album 'Lycanthrope'.

Bernardo - most prog fans in the UK will know you from your days with PFM. How did you first get involved with the band and what are your fondest memories of that time?

I saw a concert of Premiata Forneria Marconi for the first time in Bologna, they were the opening act for Deep Purple, I believe it was the spring of 1971. Later, in September, I met the band being myself their opening act: PFM were still including covers of Jethro Tull and King Crimson in their show, it was in Rivarolo del Re (CR). M. Pagani and F. Mussida in that occasion encouraged myself and other members of the band I was in, to start writing our own original songs.

A few months later Acqua Fragile was born! The band toured in Italy playing before bands such as Gentle Giant, Curved Air, Audience and more but especially for Premiata. Thanks to PFM's interest in us, our albums 'Acqua Fragile' and 'Mass Media Stars' were released soon thereafter. After PFM had been touring the US, they were under pressure because they lacked a real vocalist in their band.

At first, they contacted Eugenio Finardi, who kindly refused the offer. So, I was called to enter the most outstanding Italian band of the time, but I asked for a week's time to reflect on their proposal and this was misunderstood as lack of enthusiasm and scarce respect, thus I was refused in turn. PFM then started rehearsing with Ivan Graziani but after about 6 months, after they tried to make the new vocalist pass with the London entourage, I got newly contacted from the UK on the phone, to meet them in Milan. I went at the meeting and got auditioned at the Mussida family's, and I was kindly invited to suffocate my singing in the sofa's cushions in order not to disturb their new-born twins and the neighbours!

My fondest memories of that time? For a certain time, we began thinking that, through music and musician's attitude, one could change the world.

When you left, you became involved with Clive Bunker and John Perry among others, did you record any material during this period?

I went solo in '79 and, in the following years, was in London, at Vangelis studio, to record with British musicians like Clive Bunker (Jethro Tull), John Perry (Caravan), as well as Steve Simpson, Frank Ricotti and Ian Carr.

What were you doing musically between then and getting involved with Mangala Vallis?

After the London years, I started to develop my very personal approach to electronics. Always working around my voice and through my live performing, I have been testing and developing fine machines like the Fairlight Voice-Tracker (pitch and character-to-MIDI), ending up to invent a unique device I called 'Glovox', a glove that placed on the throat, picks up vibrations to be processed as an eclectic mono instrument.

'Christmas in the World' is a collection of classic and original Christmas songs performed by me along with Opera singers like soprano Cecila Gasdia and baritone Michele Pertusi.

'Cover Live', a live album recorded in 1997, is recorded performing with my band. Famous Rock, Blues, Soul, Progressive songs and interaction with audience are featured on a tight, no tricks, true recording. With Teatro Arsenale in Milan, in 1997 I wrote the music for a play created after Allen Ginsberg's poem 'Kaddish' and performed it on stage.

'I Sing The Voice Impossible', released in 1998, is a very special collection of studio tracks that came out after many years of dedicated writing, vocals & electronics research and experimentation. Recorded over 4 years, arranged and produced by Dario Mazzoli, this work is very innovating as my voice is featured as subject (writer), object (performer) and 'controller', affecting electronic instruments on the tracks through the help of special devices like the Glovox.

'Master Poets', released by Tring-records in spring 1999, is a tribute to the poetry of great singer-song writers. Ten compositions by major artists like Bob Dylan, Tom Waits, Joni Mitchell, Leonard. Cohen, Neil Young, Bruce Springsteen as well as Lowell George (Little Feat), Graham Nash (C.S.&N.) and Jimi Hendrix are revisited; I also wrote three originals motivated by and related to Poetry. Arranged by D. Mazzoli.

Bernardo Lanzetti 'The Best' is my latest release. It features new recordings of material dated from 1975 to 1999! P.F.M. compositions, songs taken off my solo albums, live shows and experimentation plus two brand new, original compositions comes with an 8 page-booklet with photos and official Bio.

In 2000 and 2001 I wrote and performed on stage music for 'Mr Burroughs/Mr Bladerunner' a drama by Teatro Arsenale after Mr Burroughs writings. I also acted in the role of some sort of a Virus Assistant

With the band Extra I performed in clubs and town-squares. I recently have been published Giorgio Gaslini Song Book Volume 1 and Volume 2 featuring me as one of the performing solo singer.

On the 'Prog' side, I have been recording vocals for Arti e Mestieri performing new versions of their first compositions and with Beggar's Farm have started a new series of concerts with a strictly 70's repertoire.

I am the first Italian vocalist to be mentioned in the American Rock Encyclopaedia. I successfully achieved playing twelve gigs on the same day in twelve different venues in Milan in 1982.

I had been chosen, at the time, to translate in Italian the lyrics of the album 'Nebraska' by Bruce Springsteen.

The band was initially formed in 1998, what inspired you to start making music together and how did Bernardo come on board?

Gigi - Mangala Vallis were born from a deep desire of mine to resume something that got interrupted many years before, in the middle of the 70's. At that time, I played in a few progressive rock bands, but never achieved making an album with any. In those years, I met Enzo and Mirco. I have been a professional drummer for 30 years, and what I felt that lacked was a project that allowed me to let freely go the passion for that music, prog music, that so deeply influenced the beginning of my career. So, I found in Enzo and Mirco the same will to make concrete that desire that they shared with me.

Bernardo has always been one of our favourite singers, we were great fans of Acqua Fragile and PFM, so we wanted him as special guest in our first album 'The Book Of Dreams'. Bernardo appreciated the whole thing particularly, so we met more often, and he sung in many shows of ours. A deep friendship was born, and this made us decide to have him permanently in the band, so 'Lycanthrope' is the result of this encounter of experiences and creativities.

Musically what would you say are the main differences between the two albums?

Gigi -The first MV album was basically thought and bred in studio, while the new album is also the result of years of live shows that have melt the band together better and defined a stable line-up, plus, stylistically the new album is more articulated and the fact of having one singer brought us more uniformity: the tracks are different from each other but still the Mangala Vallis trademark, sound is there.

Where did the idea for the lyrics come from?

Gigi - "Lycanthrope" at a first glance could look like an album that tells a story about werewolves, meant in the folk/movies imaginary sense. The wolf is an excuse to speak about life, of rather, about the desire for a different and renewed lifestyle. In this sense, the transformation from man to wolf is shown as an example of a changing towards one's own primitive instinct. But "Lycanthrope" does not simply tell of a need to change. It's about the "homo technologicus" that has come to his extreme halt and feels the urge to find again his simplest dimension, the one that is closer to nature. No thirst for blood then, but a hunger for finding his own true self, his natural rhythms, his true values and most important priorities.

The wolf is a great example, he's always remained unchanged through the centuries, he's in full contact with nature, unconditioned, without false objectives to struggle for. Bernardo's lyrics tell all this.

David Jackson is one of the guests on 'Lycanthrope' - how did this collaboration come about?

Gigi - A friendship was born with David years ago, I do not know if you know of his effort to allow handicapped people to express themselves through music, using the 'soundbeams', an instrument he invented himself; I took part on two stages that David held in Italy, and we met there, where I took part in a few performances of his. David is a special person, he shows an incredible positive feeling, we made friends very quickly, so I asked him to play on a couple of tracks and he accepted with joy. I have just had the chance of playing once again with him, Nic Potter, and Tony Pagliuca (ex-Orme), in Italy.

I find these crossroads of worlds and generations beautiful, because they enrich you all the time.

What are the plans for the band going forward, and can we expect to see you play in the UK?

Gigi - We have just shot a short movie based on a few tracks from 'Lycanthrope', we also have of course a lot of footage from our live shows, we'd love to release a DVD containing our films, a sort of 'Mangala Vallis Story', but this will take some time because I'd like to create a graphical package that is quite particular.

This year we're touring, also with our label, the "Tamburo a Vapore Records", we are going to release soon a rock opera that involves many different Italian bands, it will be called 'Canossa'. We are very fond of Great Britain, and we hope to have the opportunity to play there soon, it would be just great!

Live Reviews

Casual Affair, Mentaur
Brentford Red Lion

Note: This gig took place between November 1991 and January 1992, but I did not note the date at the time, and neither band leader has records from back then.

It was with glad heart that I made my way to West London to see everybody's favourite Casuals on home territory. Supping the medicinal lemonade, I had plenty of opportunity to look around the bar and was very impressed. The gigs are held in a room separate to the main bar, with a raised stage and full video and television facilities which gives up and coming bands the opportunity to see what they look like onstage and make changes where necessary. I was somewhat surprised to see Mentaur's drums set up onstage as I did not know that the Casuals were having a support act, but of all bands they could have had I was glad that it was Mentaur as I have been extremely impressed by their keyboard-dominated 'Verdict' cassette album, and have been reading some good reviews.

Mentaur made a striking visual image, as they were all wearing black T-shirts emblazoned with their logo, apart from the vocalist who was wearing a standard white shirt. It was very effective, especially considering that they had made the effort for a small pub gig. They kicked off with the very impressive "Oracles", which had a very Sabbath-esque beginning, and an interesting use of keyboards to provide light to the shade of the guitar. It was obvious from the off that Mentaur live are a different kettle of fish to being in the studio. "Towers of Silence" was followed by the excellent "Child On Trial", which had lots of heavy riffs but a commercial chorus with a catchy hook. The keyboards were strident and melodic at times, but the guitar dominated at others. Highlights of the set included "Summermoonsong" which featured only the keyboards and singer, and the set closing medley that included snippets of "Ace Of Spades", "Bohemian Rhapsody", "Crazy, Crazy Nights", Jailbreak" and "Breaking The Law" to mention only a few. For the encore, we were treated to a punk version of "I Saw her Standing There" with the drummer on bass, bassist on keyboards, and keyboard player on drums!

The stage was set, therefore, for a triumphant Casual Affair gig. They certainly had the crowd going from the off with "Playing To Lose", one of their commercial catchy ditties that turns into a crowd singalong: "Learning To Fly" was fast and furious with heavy and light patches. "Spirit Of Radio" was one of the covers that was found throughout the set, and although they were enjoyable, I would have preferred to hear more original material. The highlight was easily "Whisper In The Wind", which is my favourite from the excellent 'Well, What Did You Expect?' cassette, and live it was just as good as I could have wished for. It displays all the best points of the Casuals, with many different styles. Vocalist Mark Colton had real venom in his voice at times, but gentle and melodic at others. The set closed with the atmospheric "Too Late To Cry", which also proved to be a real winner. When they returned for the encore Mark apologised for the keyboards, which had been damaged that night (and probably explained why I thought the keyboard player was not any good). The two closers, "Wish You Were Here" and "On The Run" were both brilliant covers of the Floyd songs, but I came away feeling that all was not quite right.

This was borne out by the fact that by the time you read this the old Casual Affair will be no more as Mark is putting together a new band, keeping only the guitarist and moving to a twin guitar format. I look forward to it with great interest and know that with the quality of the songs and the great frontman they have, they will be great!
#12, Feb 1992

Galahad, Freewill
Whitchurch Parish Hall 18/07/92

I arrived at this new bastion of progressive rock in the afternoon while they were still in the throes of setting up the equipment. It was amazing what they had managed to do with the stage, in fact it was difficult to imagine that only the day before the same hall had hosted the local floral show: any person wandering in looking for plant pots was in for one helluva surprise. The time and effort that had gone into organising this gig, to make it right, was apparent. Pete Martin had hired a good PA and soundmen to ensure that it was as good as it could be and had arranged soundproofing around all windows and doors so that the music could be played as it should be, LOUD! A petition had been organised against the gig by local busybodies on the day, so it was important to make sure that there were as few complaints as possible so that the first gig here was not also the last. Galahad sound checked with two newer songs, the humorous "Dentist Song" and "Sleepers". The latter was being performed for the first time tonight and Stu was more than a little worried that he was going to forget the lyrics. After Galahad had finished, Freewill began to set their gear up, and with Louis' double bass drum kit and Karl's keyboards there was not a great deal of room left. They were playing as four-piece tonight as Jon was in Mexico, which meant that their sound was even more rocky than normal. They soundchecked with a song that was also being performed for the first time that night, "Sometimes I Cry" (also renamed by the band as "Sometimes We Get It Right, Sometimes We Don't"). That went well, so they ripped through "Learning To Fly".

It had been hot in the hall all afternoon, and as the sell-out crowd arrived, sweat started running down the walls (air was at a premium). After an introduction from yours truly, Freewill woke up Whitchurch (and probably the next village as well) with the steaming "Learning To Fly". Of all Casual songs they play, this is probably the one that benefits most from the new line-up. It stunned most of the crowd, who were not sure what they were expecting, but it certainly was not a rock band in full flow. It was followed by the classic "Whisper In The Wind", and it was obvious that the band were warming up an initially indifferent crowd. "Auf Wiedersehen" was dedicated to two particularly insular guys from Stoke who run the 'A Flower?' fanzine (in the past they have been hyper-critical of Casual, and particularly Mark). "Sometimes" and another newbie "Picking Up The Pieces" also went down well and by now Freewill were kicking up a storm and even had people dancing. The set ended with the band exhausted and Mark having given his all. The band are so tight and powerful it is strange to think that this was only their fifth gig, and only their second without keyboards.

The crowd were set for Galahad, and they opened as usual with the powerful "Nothing Is Written". Right from the off the audience were behind them, although most had not heard much of the material. They got into the groove and the hard-core gala-proggies were right there at the front. The sound was excellent, and it was obvious that the lads were revelling in headlining a sell-out event, even if it did mean performing in what was rapidly becoming a sauna. "Chamber Of Horrors" and "Aqaba" made way for "The Dentist Song", and although this has only been performed a few times it has already made itself a firm favourite, with the lyrical humour and different changes of style and mood. "Exorcising Demons" again demanded serious attention, and to my ears it is easily the best thing they have yet done. It just improves and gets stronger with each performance: this should be a killer by the time they get it laid down. Other highlights were "Automaton" (with a brilliant extended bass solo from Neil – I know it has been said in these pages before, but he is a consummate musician and has fitted in extremely well), and "Sleepers" was also well received, considering it is a song of epic proportions and that it was being played for the first time that night, although Stu lost a certain amount of street cred by having to use a crib sheet for his own lyrics. The set ended with the classic "Richelieu's Prayer", which had all the fans baying and crying out for more. By this time the band and audience were both shattered, but Galahad returned to play, to everyone's surprise, "Lady Messiah". This is one of their older songs (appearing on the tape 'In A Moment Of Madness") and was resurrected to make the gig a little bit special. Having over-run their time there was not anymore, but Pete agreed to let them come back for a second encore and somehow the totally knackered lads summoned up the energy to blast through "One For The Record".

On discussion with various others it was felt that Freewill performed brilliantly to set the

stage for the best Galahad show this year. On top of that you could hear everything, and we all lost a few extra pounds with the free heat treatment. The 150 lucky punters (which included Nick Barrett of Pendragon and Davey Dodds from Red Jasper, both of whom I managed to have long chats with) had a real experience that night. It ended with the post gig party that went on for hours....
#15, Oct 1992

Aerie Faerie Nonsense, Galahad
Walthamstow Standard 12/08/92

I was a little surprised at the low turnout, but it may have had something to do with the fact that this was a midweek gig and Ark were also playing in London that night, splitting the local prog crowd. Galahad played their normal wonderful set, a little shorter than of late as this was a joint headline gig. Standout songs were "Exorcising Demons" (that song just gets better and better), and "Parade" which segued into "Sleepers". This was performed far better than at Whitchurch, with no need for crib notes, but they seemed relieved when it was finished and launched into a rousing version of "Room 801". However, many people there tonight were waiting to see the first gig by The Enid for quite some time. The new line-up featured Nick May (bass, ex-Jadis etc.), Chris North (drums) and Neil Shepherd (guitar). RJG was on form tonight, kicking off with an excellent rendition of "Raindown" which featured synthesised backing vocals from Nick. Having not seen The Enid before, I was extremely impressed with their musical skill and the way they went from one song into another. Indeed, the only way for the unknowledgeable to realise that another song had started was when the crowd roared their approval on recognising the tunes. Other songs of real note were "Then There Were None" and "Salome", which had the vocals from Steve. Overall, the set was a lot heavier than I expected and RJG apologised for his recent forays and promised that The Enid were back, to much cheering from the crowd. Although much of the material was unfamiliar to me, I had a great time because they are all such consummate musicians playing great songs. Everyone was spellbound by the proceedings (apart from Spencer Luckman who proved the point that drummers can go to sleep absolutely anywhere at any time) and had a great time. All too soon the end came, and the band returned for an encore of "The Dambuster's March" and "Land Of Hope and Glory" which had all the crowd singing and dancing as if it were the last night of the proms. A fantastic night that has hopefully returned The Enid to where they belong, at centre stage of progressive music.
#15, Oct 1992

Winter
Brentford Red Lion 17/08/92

When on the phone to Graham Younger one night, he told me that I just had to check out this band who were new to the London scene, Winter, who he rated very highly. So, when I heard that they were playing at the Red Lion I decided to go and check them out.

When I got there, I saw no faces I recognised, in fact there were hardly any faces there to recognise at all! Still, I thought, I was there early as usual. My worries increased when I realised that Winter were not scheduled to play there at all that night, so I was glad when the music room doors opened and could get in to find out. Winter were indeed there, as a last-minute booking, but no-one seemed to have told their fans. I got talking to the guys, but as their introduction tape was running ("Tom Sawyer", followed by the winter section of Vivaldi's 'Four Seasons') I let them get ready. I was still the audience, all of it, so I was not sure what to expect. As the final note of the tape sounded the band crashed into gear and we were off. Having not heard the excellent 'Across The Circle's Edge' at the time, this was the first time I had heard any of the material, and boy was I impressed. Kicking off with "Technocracy", they ripped into the song in a way that made me think of a heavy Marillion or Twelfth Night. It was already clear that they were not going to treat this as a rehearsal, as Johnny prowled the stage using hand actions to emphasise his lyrics. As well as looking the part, with long black tailcoat, he showed that he has a wonderful melodic voice, more than well suited to the job at hand.

By the time they had worked their way through "Betrayal of Reason" and "Close Your Eyes" the audience had swollen to seven (where it stayed), but at least us few had the joy of a rock band performing at the highest level. Winter's strength is that they have honed their live act in the prog halls of Holland, and their melodic (early Eighties) sound suits well to the concert environment, Other highlights included "Scandal", which was dedicated to David Mellor, which was just a great rock song, and the epic "Toybox". On the album, this is nearly nine minutes long, and is even better live. A song of many parts, starting with an atmospheric introduction which gets into some serious riffing (très commercial). The keyboard break provided a gentle interlude while allowed the vocals to provide yet more emotion (a la Fish). As the Toybox opens the riffing begins again in the background, providing the harder edge. This just gets rougher and rougher until it reverts to keyboards again. Manic laughter heralds screaming guitars as all hell breaks loose into the guitar solo. Brilliant. They closed the set with the military sounding "Marching Out Of Time", which had a very Celtic influence, and encored with "Spirit Of Radio". At the end, I felt that had reminded me of Horslips (which is not overly surprising seeing as how they are an Irish band), and that I was honoured to have seen them that night. The crowd that stayed away will be there in force for them in the future, you can lay money on that.
#15, Oct 1992

Winter
Brentford Red Lion 17/09/92

I was determined that there would be a bigger audience than last time, so I took four and arranged to meet Mark Colton there as well, So, the audience were going to be bigger, but the band was going to be smaller. When we arrived, Tim Wilson (the drummer) was looking for their keyboard player, who had failed to arrive. Apparently, they had been rehearsing another keyboard player to replace Mario, but he had either heard about it or had decided to leave anyway. This left the band with the problem of having to play a revised set, and still put on a good show for the punters. At least it gave Tim and Mark

something in common to moan about. There was quite a good crowd here tonight and if the band had any nerves, they were not about to show them. As the tape ended and they again kicked off with "Technocracy" I found myself thinking that although keyboards do add something to their sound, they are not an integral part, in a similar fashion to Freewill. The audience were very receptive, and the band made no excuses for the lack of a keyboard player and just got on with it. The set was basically the same as before, with only "The Silver Road" showing the need for keyboards as Johnny had nothing to pitch his voice against. "Toybox" was again, for me, the highlight of the set. The album was recorded three years ago, and it has changed and improved with the many times it has been played. Considering the pressure they were under, they managed to put on a great show. Personally, I would like to see Andy move around a bit more and look like he was enjoying himself, but Richard made up for it. A great band, with or without keyboards.
#15, Oct 1992

Mentaur, Grace, Freewill
Hounslow Jolly Gardener 09/10/92

I received a phone call from Mark Colton on the evening of the gig to tell me that the Red Lion had double booked, and the gig had been re-arranged. To say that I was little surprised was an understatement, as this gig had been etched into many prog lovers' minds for quite some time. Lee Farrow, Mentaur's manager, had been told at 4:00 that afternoon that the gig was off, but Grace had already left Staffordshire, so a venue had to be found somewhere. Lee managed to book a hall, next to a pub, but it had no stage, lighting or PA. The signs were not looking good. On top of that, Lee had to hire a minibus to ferry all the fans who would be turning up at the wrong venue. It was going to be an interesting night. The PA being used was Mentaur's practice PA, so the bands all held quick soundchecks (Freewill's lasted nearly thirty seconds) and then Freewill opened proceedings by blasting into "Learning To Fly". At this time the only people in the hall were the bands and a few friends, but that did not stop the lads ripping into it with gusto. "Whisper In The Wind" and "Picking Up The Pieces" quickly followed, and the hall slowly started to fill up. The sound was holding up extremely well, possibly because there were not any keyboards. The band seemed to revel in the conditions, with only Louis having a problem. Basically, if you place a drum kit on a polished wooden floor and then play the double bass drums at full pelt, the aforementioned drums attempt to relocate themselves in opposite corners of the room: still, it gave Mark something to do when he was not singing. A new song was aired tonight, "Skin Trade", which is a blistering number that had to be heard to be believed.

I was looking forward to Grace, this being the first time I had seen them play live. They set up with Harry (flute, mime) and Mac (vocals) sharing centre stage, and I soon realised that if anyone hasn't seen Grace then you are missing a real treat. Mac and Harry vie for pole position all night; not many bands have dual frontmen. They kicked off with "Mullion Man", and it was obvious that they are as good in concert as they are on CD. They're tight, and Mac has a great voice, and by the time they got to "Success" they were cooking, and the crowd had grown to quite a size. "Holy Man" was the only time they had problems with the PA, as it just could not cope with the sheer intensity of it all. They closed with "Raindance" and I was not the only person there who wished they could have at the very least played a complete set, or preferably the whole night.

It was going to be the first time I had seen Mentaur since they had changed singer, so I was very interested in what he was going to be like. They kicked off with "The Questing Beast", and it was already obvious that the sound was degenerating, and the vocals needed to be higher in the mix. As I have said before, the band have a very striking visual image, with everyone wearing Mentaur shirts emblazoned with their logo, apart from vocalist Carlton. A new number, "Fugitive", was well received and was followed with my personal favourite, "Passive Resistance". This is a real crowd participation song, with a great chorus. By now someone was trying to alleviate the sound problem but was only succeeding in making it worse. Mentaur are a young band with plenty of musical ability and attitude, but tonight was fated not to be their night. I look forward to being able to review them again, when the gods decide not to shit all over them. By the time the set was finished they were surrounded by their hard-core fans, but unfortunately due to the sound problems many of the others had gone to the bar. After all the effort they had put into re-organising the gig at short notice, it was a real shame. They deserve better and will achieve it.
#16, Dec 1992

Jadis, Shadowland, Damian Wilson
London Marquee 06/12/92

Damian Wilson, Landmarq's singer, stepped in at short notice to open as Geoff Mann, who should have been playing but was too ill to appear. In an extremely short set (only four songs), he managed to impress. Accompanying himself on acoustic guitar he started with "Lucky To Have You". He has a wonderful clear voice, great melody, and above all a sense of enjoying himself. Up next was "Just The Way It Goes", a song about being a singer-songwriter and by this time I had been drawn into the wonderful quality of his voice. He was holding long notes with a great deal of power and was not afraid to hit high notes without any accompaniment to hide behind. The other two numbers, "She's Like A Fable" and "Nothing In This World Remains The Same" were also of the same exceedingly high quality, and I look forward to seeing him again either with Landmarq or his own Orange Band. The crowd were fairly warmed up by now and were eagerly awaiting the arrival of Shadowland. The set started with "Whistle Blower", the same as on the album. With lots of dry ice and subdued lighting, all the band were onstage while Clive waited at the rear speaking the quiet introduction. As his voice raised the band kicked in and we were off. I was tremendously impressed with Clive as a frontman, as I have only previously seen him playing keyboards onstage with Pendragon, where he is obviously more restricted in what he can do. There were lots of hand actions, and he was in his element. Karl, the guitarmeister was aloof in his attitude, and black cloaks and coats were the order of the day. To enable Clive to be a frontman they have recruited the services of Richard West of Mercy Train on keyboards. The sound was good, and the lighting superb. "I, Judas" was a new song, one that has been recorded for the new SI compilation (due out next year) and had a heavy guitar introduction (heavy prog?). It was obvious that the band were having a great time, and they all work well together. "Scared of the Dark" was wonderful, with great lighting (namecheck – Laurence) and the fretless bass coming through. On tour the song was known as "Scared of the Dog", and Clive sang that to close it with. Eight songs were played, and everyone was a masterpiece. It felt like that band had played together for years and had made many records together, instead of releasing the debut only last year. The set closed with the title track of that album, "Ring of Roses", and there was even a dance for the chorus, ably displayed by Martin Orford and others. Martin later told me that the 'Lurve Dance' had been performed throughout the European tour, sometimes onstage.

It was also my first time seeing Jadis, and I have been missing out on a real treat. "Sleepwalking" started proceedings, and again here was a very relaxed and together band. Three-part vocal harmonies added to the tight musical proceedings which included some great finger-popping and bass runs. Gary et al are musicians of the very highest order, and they are a group that do not need vocals at all. They can go from frantic rock to intricate complex melodies at the drop of a hat, and it's just wonderful. My favourite song is still the amazing "Wonderful World" from their great CD, and that guitar run straight after the vocals is just mind-blowing. For "More Than Meets" Richard ventured back onstage so that Martin could go stage front to provide harmony vocals, and some delicate flute. That is the great strength of Jadis, loads of contrast and musical ability to carry it all off. They all enjoyed themselves, and John Jowitt ran about like a mad thing. Superb. All in all, a great night. The bands who have released my two favourite albums of the year can cut it live, and this was a gig made in heaven. If you get the opportunity you must see these guys in concert.
#16, Dec 1992

Galahad, Freewill, The Morrigan
Whitchurch Parish Hall 12/12/92

Apparently, the Pendragon/Final Conflict gig the previous night had gone exceptionally well, and the stage was set for another great gig. Pete had hired the same sound crew as before and during the soundchecks it was obvious that this was going to be a very special night indeed. First band on was The Morrigan, a local band, who brought a large contingent to the sell-out gig. Although they were unknown to many of the crowd, they soon gained a load of new fans. They play music strongly influenced by Celtic folk, so I had a great time. Keyboard player Cathy Masson has a lovely clear voice (singing in a style mostly reminiscent of Maddy Prior), and Colin Masson (guitar, vocals), Cliff Eastabrook (hair, bass, vocals), Arch (drums, vocals) and Jon Hayward (guitar, percussion, vocals) know their stuff. Right from the start, "Throwing It All Away" to the closing "Joe Coedyes Reel" everyone enjoyed themselves. There were five-part harmonies, jigs, reels, a great interpretation of "Good King Wenceslas" (with Jon and Cliff taking the vocal leads) and there was even a trombone in sight for one song. All in all, very professional and every person in the hall enjoyed themselves. Apparently, they are based mostly in Hampshire and Wiltshire and rarely make it up to London, but here is a band with real promise and talent.

So, it was up to Freewill to follow on and make an impact. They had been asked back by popular request after their storming set in July, but it was obvious that much of the crowd were there for either a folk-rock act or a prog rock act, and the heavy rock act in the middle was not going to go down too well. Freewill now have an intro tape, lifted from 'Alien', and as the computer counted down from 30 to 1 the band took the stage amid some effective lighting and dry ice. To keep the effect of the taped explosions they have changed the opening number to "Learning To Fly". As the band ripped into it, I was impressed with the sound, as they were strong and powerful. Indeed, talking to Steve later he said that it was the best onstage sound that he had ever had. "Whisper", "Picking Up The Pieces", "Auf" all flew by with the band getting better and better all the time. But the audience were not behind them as they had been before. They finished with "Skin Trade" which proved to those of us prepared to listen that with the right audience here is a band that can go places. It was the best gig they had ever played; it was a shame that the audience were not there to see it.

Stu told me that tonight was going to be a special gig, and it started with all the band wearing Santa hats, playing the old Greg Lake song "I Believe In Father Christmas". Stu joined the merry throng in full Santa costume and the band segued into "Fanfare For The Common Man". Galahad had dropped covers from the set a long time ago, but tonight was going to be something special indeed. "Aqaba" and "The Dentist Song" went down well and this led into "Lady Messiah". This is a song from the 'Moment of Madness' tape which they had performed for the first time in ages the last time they were in Whitchurch. In stark contrast, it was followed by a preview of "Before, After and Beyond" which should be on the new album. "Welcome To Paradise" was another resurrected oldie from the dim and distant past and the Galafans went wild. Galahad could do no wrong, and the songs flowed. A cover version of Steve Hackett's "Clocks" was well received, but possibly the loudest cheer of the night was for the classic "Ghost of Durtal" which they sadly dropped from the set a long time ago. The set closed with "Richelieu's Prayer" and they left the stage with loud cheers ringing in their ears. Of course, there was no way they could leave it at that so as well as the expected "One For The Record" (which is about the Genesis reunion some years ago) they played a storming version of "The Knife" Do you realise that song is twenty years old now? Oh, for the days when Genesis were a proper band. All in all, it was great night.
#17, Mar 1993

Steve Hackett
Whitchurch Parish Hall 20/05/93

Somehow, Steve had been convinced to play Whitchurch Parish Hall as a warm-up for his nationwide tour. I arrived at 5:00, just as Steve was starting his soundcheck. I could not believe the amount of equipment he had decided was necessary for this low-key gig, to say there was overkill was just a minor understatement. As Steve and his band warmed up, I was extremely impressed with his guitar skills as his fingers literally flew up and down the frets with great ease. One number followed another as the band (Julian Colbeck on keyboards plus a drummer and bassist whose names I did not get) played complete songs, instead of just trying to set up levels. My favourite was the new number "Vampyre With A Healthy Appetite" which featured the introduction of the megaphone as a vocal aid as Steve growled into one (held securely around his neck by a Fender strap) and played some devastating guitar in between verses. After nearly two hours Steve was satisfied and I realised that I had already seen one gig, and the night was yet young!

The gig proper started with a version of "Los Endos" which was immediately well received, and Steve was on a roll, when the power failed. It came back up again straight away, but it meant that the computer dumped all the programs, so they were without any keyboards for a while. The band launched into a powerful R 'n' B number just to keep things going, but the computer was soon up and running again and the band continued with "Vampyre". Unfortunately, the megaphone had now died, and the song lost a bit of the effect as Steve had to sing gruffly instead. It was apparent that they have a complete mastery of many different styles, from HR to jazz fusion and everything in-between, but a lot of just washed over me. I found myself thinking back to the recent Jadis gig at the same venue, when for long periods it was alright, but not as brilliant as it should be. Maybe it is the perfection that did not allow any feelings or emotion, such as the use of computers to enhance the backing vocals so that the harmonies were absolutely spot on, or the extended use of guitar synths and effects. Mostly it was the Genesis numbers that got the crowd going, such as the wonderfully jazzed up "In The Quiet Earth" which was one of the highlights of the evening. After the bass solo in "Dark As The Grave", Cliff from The Morrigan told me he was going home to set light to his bass. But, although the solo had tremendously fast and intricate playing, and was of a highly technical nature, it just ended up being boring. The set closer itself was "Everyday", which again featured computer enhanced harmony vocals. They came back with some acoustic songs that became "Spectral Mornings" but this was cut short so that he could play "Firth of Fifth". The night ended with a wonderful rendition of "Clocks". It was nice to see Steve in such a small venue, and I think he enjoyed doing it. However, for the most part the highlights were the old Genesis numbers, and he left them a long time ago. He is an amazing guitarist, but I felt that more emotion and a lesser reliance on computers would have gone down a lot better.
#18, May 1993.

Landmarq, Shadowland, Tracy Hitchings
Walthamstow Standard 28/05/93

I hate The Standard. Well maybe not so much the venue itself, but rather that I get lost going there nearly every time. Consequently, I arrived just as Tracy was launching into the last song of her set, "From Ignorance To Ecstasy". She was accompanied by Garry Lindsay on guitar and Clive Nolan on piano and she was belting it out. Her voice is wonderful, with loads of power, and you should all rush out and buy her album immediately, if not sooner. There was time for a quick chat with Karl Groom, who introduced me to Nick Midson (Threshold), and a longer one with Steve Leigh and Uwe d'Rose of Landmarq, then Shadowland hit the stage. The set was basically the same one they played at The Marquee in December, and indeed it was their first gig since then. The band had all been tied up with other projects and it was felt they needed to get in some valuable gig practice. Kicking off with "The Whistleblower" I was yet again impressed that they are just so heavy live. In fact, although they are patently a prog band, there are many metal bands that cannot cut it like this. "I, Judas" is far more venomous than on the recent SI compilation, "Jigsaw" and "Scared Of The Dark" were blasted through, and then it was time for "The Kruhulick Syndrome". This is a song which proves that instrumentals can be exciting and invigorating without being self-indulgent. Clive plays some beautiful piano, and by the end Karl is into his guitar solo. It was only left for the band to finish with "Hall Of Mirrors" and "Ring of Roses" (with the accompanying Lurve Dance). All in all, a great set, and I am sure that all who were there had become hardened Shadowland fans by the end of the night.

It was my first time seeing Landmarq, and as it transpired, one of their last gigs with Damian Wilson at the vocal helm. Right from the off I was totally impressed with their tightness on stage. Although they hadn't played together for a few weeks it was patently obvious that here was a band who overall had played together a great deal. There was certainly nothing like the number of people at The Standard that night as those who had been seeing them on the recent European tour, but those who were there were in for a real treat. All the band tend to stay back on the edge of the stage and hardly move at all, letting the music speak for them. All that it is apart from Damian. I have spoken in these pages many times about his vocal ability, but this was the first time I had seen him front a band and I was a little pensive. There was no need to worry on that score as he is a consummate showman and can also sing like an angel. "Forever Young", "Tippi Hedren" and "Solitary Witness" soon had the crowd baying for more, while "Gaia's Waltz" in turn led into the epic "Ta Jaing". This came across with loads of emotion and power as the band kicked it along. The closer was "Terracotta Army", one of the heavier numbers, but there was no way that it could be left at that. Landmarq returned to the stage with two extra members, namely Clive and Tracy. They proceeded to perform "Hide and Seek" from Tracy's solo album, with Tracy and Clive taking the vocals and Damian just running around enjoying himself. They closed with "Borders" from the first album, with Clive again on lead vocals – he did write the lyrics after all. A shame that he had to read the words from the CD booklet! All in all, a great night, and fitting that one of Damian's last gigs with Landmarq was a brilliant one.
#19, Aug 1993

Galahad, The Morrigan
Bournemouth King Arthur's Court 18/06/93

What a glorious venue this is. It is an old chapel that has been converted into a medieval banqueting hall complete with banners (and a bar). Tonight, the tables had been removed and a stage built at one end. Fancy dress was an option, but no-one was prepared for super-prog fan Matt Ellis (Matt is well known on the London circuit) turning up resplendent in chain mail and armour! (boy, did he suffer from the heat). This was the official launch party for the 'new' Galahad CD and was the first home gig for some time and was also their eighth birthday, so all the omens were good. No thanks to massive hold ups due to roadworks, I managed to get there early and spent a pleasant twenty minutes sat in Stu's car listening to three new recordings. They've been into the studio and recorded "Aries" (ten minutes), "The Chase" (four minutes) and "Learning Curve" (four minutes) for a radio session CD that will be out in a few months' time. The idea is that these three songs will be sent to stations in Europe and America to get airplay. Just a thousand will be pressed, and some may be sold in the UK. This was my first time seeing The Morrigan as a four-piece, and I was not quite sure what to expect. Due to the medieval feel of the evening they decided to busk it without a set list and played lots of material I hadn't previously heard. Highlights of the set were "Agincourt" (long build up shattered by the bass with some great guitarwork), "The Hunter" (sung by Colin, very tribal feel that eventually rocks out with some soaring guitar) and the menacing "The Morrigan Rides Out". I would have liked to have heard "War In Paradise", but it hadn't been fully rehearsed without Jon. A very enjoyable set was marred only by the fact that they over-ran.

Galahad were on good form again tonight, and I defy anyone (whatever their musical inclination) to go and see them and not come away having enjoyed themselves. Loads of dry ice heralded opener "Sleepers", which is the title cut of the new CD (or will be when they finish it!). The sell-out crowd were with the band right from the off and it was obvious that they were all going to enjoy themselves that night. "Aqaba" was just amazing, with Stu giving his all. "The Dentist Song" gets heavier and better each time I hear it (I do not understand why so many people do not like this, maybe it's the subject matter) and by "Room 801" the hall was approaching meltdown. Old songs, new songs, they were all belted out with gusto. Highlight is still the wonderful "Exorcising Demons", which has some great contrasts within it, and this segued straight into the set closer "Richelieu's Prayer". Stu had handed out loads of party poppers with the instructions to wait for the words "time bomb" during the song. We all duly let them off at the correct moment, and it made a great visual effect. They came back with the extremely heaving instrumental "Dogman" but as they were poised to go into "Face Into The Sun" the hall manager called time. Due to The Morrigan over-running there was no time for this or "One For The Record". Still, even a shortened set could not put a dampener in a great evening. Galahad are a stunning live act and if the new CD is as good as it should be, they could finally make the breakthrough they so richly deserve.
#19, Aug 1993

Legend, Incubus Succubus
Crawley Stocks 07/08/93

For those of you who have never heard of it, Crawley Stocks is a well-known venue on the pub circuit, situated in a very small (virtually un-signposted) village not too far away from Oxford: that I found it was amazing! When I arrived, I was greeted by Debbie, and found Steve slaving away over a hot mixing desk as he set up the sound for Incubus Succubus. It was the first time we had met, although we had spoken frequently on the phone, and we found that we enjoyed each other's company and I felt myself made more welcome that at virtually any other gig you could mention. The 'Inky's' have just signed to Pagan, and Steve was keen to know my opinion on them. I hadn't heard any of their material prior to that night, so I waited to see what was going to happen. They turned out to be a very powerful rock band, with the emphasis on loads of power riffs, yet at the same time extremely melodic. In Candia, they have a vocalist who can really sing, and just oozes sex appeal. Yes, I know that is a sexist comment to make, but I defy any hot-blooded male not to fall in love with her. So, with Candia on vocals, and Tony powering the guitar, the Inky's need a powerful rhythm section to keep it all together and that they have, even down to the point of having a bodhran player on either side of the stage. I'm not too sure what they added to the drum sound, maybe more at the bottom end, but it adds to the overall visual effect. The band are just so full of confidence; I was surprised that I hadn't heard of them before. They started with "Burning Times", which although it had a gentle vocal introduction soon became a belting rock song which even involved some guitar playing by Tony using his teeth. The songs were all short and punchy, and the crowd were really behind them. "Pagan Born" is just anthemic and proved that Candia is not afraid to sing long sustained notes while all hell broke out on stage. Nearly everyone in the audience seemed to be dancing in one form or another, and there was even pogoing as they ripped through the twelve-song set, and by the end I was a convert. They closed with "Church Of Madness", which is incredibly powerful and contains extremely thought-provoking lyrics ("Here comes the Church of Madness, bearing gifts of death and torture"), a song all about the death and horror caused in the name of Christianity. They encored with "Witches", which includes a chant that had all the crowd involved (I presume it is a pagan invocation as I did not understand a word of it). They left the stage and the crowd bayed for more.

So, for Legend it was a case of "follow that!". Still, as they opened with "Pipes of Pan" I needn't have worried as Legend live are a far heavier and harder entity than that on the first album. Paul was throwing the guitar around, and the keyboard/guitar/bass runs had to be seen and heard to be believed. Debbie's vocals were spot on and an initially unenthusiastic crowd were won over. "Legend" showed the keyboards mimicking the guitar (shades of Uriah Heep), and the use of duets instead of solos which in turn led into some intense guitar. Each of Legend's songs has so many mood and style changes that I am amazed that they can keep it all together, but they do, brilliantly! After four songs of differing forms came the instrumental "The Chase". This is a phenomenal animal in the live environment and gained the best crowd reaction of the night with people dancing and having a great time. Of the newer material, the winner had to be the set closer "The Wild Hunt", which started off with unaccompanied folk vocals (heavy Steeleye?) but developed into something altogether more frenetic and intricate. It became a keyboard-driven beast which degenerated into a fast and furious rocker with Paul and Steve trading licks and the crowd going berserk. It was so totally different to the beginning of the song and brought the set to a powerful close with totally controlled mayhem. They returned with "Light In Extension", and the party that had been going on all night just went up another notch. Candia and Tony came up as well, and the song became a storming rousing classic. We were then treated to "Witches" with loads of guest vocalists from the audience, but they still were not allowed to get off the stage so another version of

"Witches" (this time without the audience) was belted out. Legend's drummer was knackered by this time, so the Inky's drummer came up and helped as "Light In Extension" was driven out again. At the end of the night I knew that I had had a great time. Incubus Succubus are more in your face and direct, with Legend having more facets and styles, but they are well-suited to the live scene and I urge any of you who can to go and see them perform. My thanks go to both bands, and to Jon Moreau who did the sound for Legend. What a great guy!
#20, Oct 1993

Freewill, Winter
Brentford Red Lion, 10/09/93

Well, it seemed like I had been waiting for this for ages, then on the Monday prior to the gig I received a phone call from Mark of Grey Lady Down telling me that they had 'lost' their keyboard player and were unable to make the gig. I was disappointed, as I had booked GLD for their first ever London gig, but without a keyboard player it would have been difficult to say the least. So, we were down to just two bands and adjusted the running time accordingly. I hadn't seen Winter for the best part of a year but had arranged for them to support Freewill as I was very impressed with them and loved the CD. To say they let themselves down is an understatement. They have decided to stay as a four-piece, with Richard on bass, bass pedals and keyboards. This meant that he could not move around, and with an extremely static guitarist, all attention had to be focussed on frontman Johnny. Tonight, he again showed himself a great vocalist, but when directly compared with Mark Colton showed that for all the live experience, he still has a long way to go in working the audience. Highlight of the set was still "Toybox", but it just was not as good as I had seen them play before. Winter are going to have to go away and rethink what they are doing, as they have potential, but bands should improve during a year, not get worse.

There was quite a crowd in for Freewill, and even though Winter had not been at their best they had still managed to warm them up a certain extent. Tonight, Freewill were nothing short of phenomenal. I have seen the guys many times, and true the most biased person in the room will be their manager, but tonight they pulled out all the stops and made it a night to remember. Mark's voice was the best I have ever heard him sing, and the guys were just so tight. They were so confident that tonight they even introduced "Tom Sawyer" into the set, and boy was it good! They started with "Off A Shovel" and from that went straight into "Learning To Fly Again". They were cooking and to me it was amazing that here was a band playing their last ever gig together. They played virtually all their repertoire, and even included some one-offs, including "Funk" (which was originally an improvised piece taking the piss out of a James Brown covers band they played with at Fulham Swan) and Mark's solo "My Baby Says" (hopefully the first and last time that Mark will play guitar onstage). Steve even managed to get Mark to perform his infamous 'Rubber Glove' PA check for the first time (Mark normally recites a very crude poem about his rubber sexual fetish for the soundcheck). Highlights were too many to mention, but to hear "Whisper In The Wind" and "Skin Trade" for the last

ever time were certainly sad moments. I mean, these songs are just classics and now there is a good chance that they will never again see the light of day. Mark, Mike, Steve and Louis have all parted on extremely good terms and on a personal level I would like to thank them for all the good times and wish them all the best for the future.
#20, Oct 1993

Legend, Seventh Wave, Albion Abbos
Brighton Concorde 13/12/93

First up were the Albion Abbos, a duo of guitarist and vocalist using backing tapes. I have no doubt that they are the worst act I have ever, ever, seen on stage. In fact, the only interesting thing about their show was that they put feedback onto the tape, and Jon Moreau (sound engineer) had kittens trying to get it out of the sound desk until he realised where it was coming from. Seventh Wave were quite good, with loads of energy, and came across as Levellers/Pogues crossed with a real rock outfit. They certainly got people dancing and I was not surprised to discover that they were a local band. The one thing that let them down was the vocals: they had three lead singers, but none of them were outstanding. The same could not be said of the manic bassist who was just brilliant. Highlight of the set was "Pagan Uprising". So, at long last it was time for… the raffle? Time was getting on by now, and Legend were still to hit the stage. The audience had already started dwindling, but when Legend finally started at 11:45 at least they did it with a bang. "Pipes of Pan" got proceedings off to a rousing start, and the pyros made sure that everyone gave them full attention. During "Dance" the keyboards went down and Jon rushed about like a madman trying to repair a fault that had been caused by one of the previous bands. Legend put on a great show: they are just so tight, and the music is polished, yet raw at the same time. Paul looks every inch a metal god with long hair, tight leathers, and he throws some great shapes. This is in total contrast to Debbie whose pure clear voice provides contrast to the mayhem all around her. Other songs worthy of mention must be "The Chase", which is the most powerful instrumental being played by anyone at present, and "Wild Hunt" which has so many styles and changes within it. By the time they had finished it was 12:45, and there were not many people left for an encore. The band were very critical of their performance, but I had a great time and I know that all of those that waited to see them felt the same. They are touring properly in the next few months, and any lover of good music should get out there see a top band in action.
#21, Jan 1994

Credo
Winchester Railway 28/01/94

This was my first time at a Credo gig, although vocalist Mark Colton has been on at me for ages to see them live. Obviously, I knew Mark from his previous bands Freewill and Casual Affair, but the other band members were all new to me. Tim Birrell (guitar) and Jim Murdoch (bass) played together some eighteen years ago in Armageddon up north.

Meeting up in London they started playing together again and the foundations of Credo were formed with keyboard player Mik Stovold and later drummer Paul Clarke (who has worked with such luminaries as Neil Schon and Ken Hensley). Mark was the final piece of the jigsaw, and after working for a while as Chequered Past they changed the name to Credo after the demise of Freewill. I was looking forward to this, and I was not going to be disappointed A decision was made for Credo to play two forty-five-minute sets, and there were only two cover versions to be found. For a relatively new band I was amazed at this. Especially as I knew that Credo were now dropping material from the set, in favour of newer stronger songs. Right from the opener "Power to the Nth Degree", it was obvious that here is a rock band firing on all cylinders. Credo are more melodic and "proggy" than Freewill were but are still quite a bit heavier than many of the prog bands around. Tim Birrell ("The Rocking Troll") is an outstanding guitarist and has devastating speed on the frets. Jim and Paul have the rhythm section nailed to the floor, and with Mik adding nuances here and there it gives Mark the opportunity to shine. Tonight, he was singing the best I had ever heard him, and I feel that this is because he has finally found a band that is totally right for him. Indeed, talking to some of the audience the feeling was the same throughout.

"Phantom" starts with a strong bass line, but it is transformed into a belter with some stunning guitar and dynamic vocals: the band even used harmonies (something sadly missing from many these days) in numbers such as "Mr Dylan", but for me the highlight of the first set had to be the closing numbers "Whisper In The Wind" and "Auf Wiedersehen". I thought these songs were lost forever after the demise of Freewill, but here they are sounding better than they ever have before. I was afraid that the second set might be an anti-climax after the joy of the first, but I had nothing to worry about. Opener "Just Like A Good Boy" has become a firm favourite of mine, even though that was the first time I had ever heard it. Just stunning, more commercial than others, but who cares? Standout song, however, had to be a brilliant version of "Faith Healer". It was just superb, and my visual memory of the night is Jim stood there banging out the bass line as if his very being was involved. All in all, a great night. Soundman was Rog Patterson, who had requested the opportunity to be able to do it. When the soundman for groups such as Rage Against The Machine, and the owner of a record label to boot, wants to get involved then you get the feeling that they might just be going places. Credo, a name to look out for.
#22, Mar 1994

Galahad
Winchester Railway 05/02/94

Back down to The Railway for the second time in a little over a week, this time to see Galahad. I hadn't seen them play since June and was interested in seeing them in a smaller venue. I arrived in time to hear the soundcheck, which was a new number, "Live and Learn". Although they had been playing a segment of it for some time, this was going to be the first time they had played the whole song live. Very involved and intricate, with long instrumental passages (including great bass from Neil), it certainly

has the makings of a prog classic. Tonight, they opened with "Sleepers", which is going to be the title track of the new album. Karl had problems with the keyboards, and although the song came over well, I had the impression that something was not quite right. "Parade", "Face Into The Sun", "Aqaba" and "Lady Messiah" quickly followed, and although there was positive audience reaction, in places the band just did not seem to be as good as I had seen them before. It is quite possible that they were literally ring rusty having spent so much time in the studio trying to get 'Sleepers' finished. Next up was "Live and Learn", and everything finally clicked into place as Galahad started to take the place by storm. Two other newbies, "Before, After and Beyond" and "Exorcising Demons" followed, and they were tight and kicking. The newer material sounds quite different to the older, and I think Neil has made the biggest single difference in that. He is such an outstanding bassist that he has changed the way they approach songs. As it was the anniversary of Geoff's death, Galahad decided to play "The Ceiling Speaks". It went down well, although I must confess to missing the twin guitarwork of Twelfth Night. Set closer was "Richelieu's Prayer", which seemed to have been rocked up a bit, and they then came back and encored with "Room 801". I got the impression that Galahad are happier playing the newer material, but maybe that was just because that is what they have been working on recently. Not the best gig I have seen them play, but still a lot better than most of the groups around.
#22, Mar 1994

Credo
Walthamstow Royal Standard 04/03/94

Credo's first time at The Royal Standard, on the Monday night new bands slot. I had been asking Cliff if Credo could support Landmarq, as I had their permission, but he wanted to see the boys in action himself first. The deal was that we would get thirty people along and that would guarantee us the place. The opening band were awful, no that's probably unfair – they were worse than that. With just a forty-minute set there was only room for the very strongest songs, and it's just a shame that there were not more people there to see it. The final band were terrible, with the only highlight that I finally got to see a singer who thought that not only was he a peacock but was God's gift to women as well. So, not only were Credo good, they were made to look fantastic and Cliff rewarded us with the support. *#23, May 1994*

Credo, Core
Egham Compasses 26/03/94

Core are a young band still very much in their learning phase. Not my cup of tea, but they did manage to bring in a young crowd. Credo were on form tonight – it was the night before Mark's thirtieth birthday, and even though his drinks were spiked (Barry, ex of Casual Affair being the main culprit), and being quite drunk by the end, they put on a great show. It was good to see both Mike Mishra and Steve Tuckwell in the audience – Freewill really did end on good terms. *#23, May 1994*

Different Trains
Winchester Railway 08/04/94

I was not quite sure what to expect from this gig, as I had heard of the band from Greg Spawton of Big Big Train and hadn't heard of any of the material. On top of that, this was a "showcase" gig, entry by invitation only. I arrived early and chatting to various people was intrigued to discover the history of the band and that the album they were promoting was a concept. I was not expecting the whole album to be played from start to finish, with little or no talking in between. Having not heard the CD at the time, I was a little amazed at this approach. I mean, here was a 'new' band playing a large chunk of music, yet not trying to explain it in anyway whatsoever. After a short time, I was still trying to get my ears around the complexity of what I was hearing, while later I was convinced that I liked it, but had not heard anything quite like it before. By the end I must admit that I was a convert. Different Trains were playing in front of an invited audience, all of whom were very receptive and open to new sounds and ideas, but this will probably not be true if they attempted to play a pub gig. If they can get the right support gigs then they may just reach the audience they so richly deserve.,
#23, May 1994

Landmarq, Credo, GLD
Walthamstow Royal Standard 22/04/94

GLD had the same time length as Credo but decided to go about proceedings in a totally different way. They cut down on the talking between songs and ran many together. It was well done, but I felt that it put a barrier between them and the audience. For me Credo were the best band on the night (yeah, I'm biased). Everyone seemed to appreciate what they were doing, and on talking to Karl Groom later he admitted that while the music they were playing was not his cup of tea, he felt that the band were extremely tight. Tonight, was the first gig Landmarq were playing with their new vocalist, Moon. He has a good voice, although he still has some way to with stagecraft and words. Landmarq overall are an extremely static band, and they rely on the frontman to carry the show. Tonight, he did not, but he is still very much in the learning phase.
#23, May 1994

Credo, Revelation
Guildford Star 27/04/94

Revelation proved themselves to be a fine band, although there were a few too many covers for my liking and there was also the feeling of equipment overkill, but I would like to see them again headlining their own show. This was the worse of the gigs I had seen recently for Credo, for reasons other than musical. Still, they went down well and The Kidney Foundation were pleased (tonight was a charity gig).
#23, May 1994

Credo
Guildford Parrot 30/04/94

Ever been to a gig where the band could reach out and touch the bar? Well, I was at one tonight. This was another gig for The Kidney Foundation and was far better than the one on the Wednesday. After the show was over, contracts were signed with Malcolm Parker of Cyclops who had come down to see the guys in action. So not only did they play a good gig and raise a few hundred pounds for a good cause, but they signed the CD contract into the bargain. All in all, a very good night. The more perceptive of you will have realised that I have been seeing a lot of Credo, which is because I am actively involved with the band. I will try not to let this cloud my judgement but take it from me this is not the last you have heard of Credo.
#23, May 1994

Credo
Egham Compasses 29/08/94

Credo were headlining an all-day charity bash for The Kidney Foundation, with all the bands happily playing for free. A few of us felt that Credo should ask the band who were on immediately before them to play with Credo again. Not that they were any good you understand, but rather that they were so bad that Credo sounded even better than normal! Tonight, was set for a good gig as a new song was being aired for the first time, called "The Letter". It was all about Mark's emotional breakup with his last girlfriend, even more poignant as she was in the audience. Also, tonight they moved "Party" from the end of the set to be the opener and made "Good Boy" second. This meant that they could blast off from the beginning, and so they did. "The Letter" turned out to be a real showstopper and Mark bared his soul. I do not think I have ever heard so much emotion, he was virtually dying on stage, and the reaction at the end was unbelievable. It was obvious that here is the making of a classic as at about ten minutes' length and lots of twists and turns. "Faith Healer" closed the show and Credo had yet again proved that they are one of the best live acts around.
#25, Oct 1994

Credo
Egham Compasses 17/09/94

This was the launch party for the CD, and all was well when Malcolm from Cyclops turned up with a box of the goodies in question. Tonight was party time, and as it went down so well last time they again opened with "Party". Mark was suffering on the vocals front tonight as he could not breathe properly, but as the night went on, he managed to loosen up and by the end was singing better than ever. I should say that the showstopper was the C&W medley of rock classics (which included "Smoke On The Water" and "Twentieth Century Schizoid Man") but I must be honest and say that "The Letter" (tonight renamed "The Bitch") brought the house down. The reaction was so

strong that it brought the song to a halt as they did not play the last section. It is a classic, and this is only the second time it had been played in front of an audience. Credo could do no wrong tonight, being surrounded by friends, but they still pulled out all the stops. A great gig.
#25, Oct 1994

IQ, Threshold, Different Trains
Whitchurch Testbourne 08/05/95

And so, after many moons had passed, it came to be that I returned to Whitchurch. At one time this sleepy town in Hampshire seemed to be the centre of progdom in the UK, but for one reason or another the gigs ceased. Still, we were back again at the local Secondary School sports hall, transformed into a venue for tonight's events. Quite a few of the prog faithful came, and I saw members of Galahad, Credo, Walking On Ice, Primitive Instinct, Sphere, Evolution and Pallas as well as some other fanzines.

Different Trains opened proceedings with most of their superb album 'On The Right Track'. It is very difficult music to appreciate fully if you have not heard and enjoyed the album, as I found when I saw them last time. Still, this time I revelled in it and the band seemed far more relaxed and at ease as well. Damon (vocals, guitar, kitchen sink) has become more of a showman and the whole band seemed tighter and more powerful. The mix of complex prog, jazz and art rock may not be to everybody's liking but I am sure that anyone with an open mind would truly enjoy what they were doing. Melodies and countermelodies rise and fall, daring the ears to fully comprehend the intricacies of what was taking place. Follow that!

I must admit to missing Ken Nicol (I was outside eating fish and chips), but I made sure I was back in the hall for Threshold. I was fortunate enough to witness their soundcheck and it had taken a couple of pints of real ale for my hearing to be fully restored. Threshold crashed onstage with "Sunseeker", the opening cut from the latest album; riffing guitars, extremely heavy, with soaring vocals, who could wish for more? This was heavy rock and prog mixed perfectly into a melodic maelstrom of energy. I was concerned to see/hear if new vocalist Glynn Morgan could possibly match up to previous incumbent Damian Wilson (one of the best frontmen in rock) but I needn't have worried. Although Glynn seemed unsure of himself at the beginning, he was soon wandering around the stage with the best of them. Karl Groom and Nick Midson link well as guitarists and Karl and Jon Jeary (bass) provided visual as well as vocal interplay.

The whole of the audience was totally won over before the first song had finished, and after that there was just no stopping them. Moving between albums with ease the highlight had to be the superb "Sanity's End". This is a storming classic and Glynn managed to make this song his own, not an easy feat. It was worth going all the way there just to hear this! They eventually closed with "Paradox", which certainly cleared my dandruff. They finished and I was left nursing a tender neck – who says that all prog bands are wimps?

After two minutes' silence in respect for the war dead, IQ made their way onstage. A note should be made here that facial hair seems to have made it's, um, mark on the band. They opened with "Wurensh" and it was apparent that Mike was having problems with his amps (like they were not working). In fact, it meant that the start was a little ropey, but after Mike's guitar problems were rectified it was almost as if the band had shifted from neutral into top gear and were up and running. They blasted through "Awake and Nervous" and "Fading Senses" into my favourite from the last album. "Out of Nowhere", This was far heavier than the studio version and was even enjoyed by Sooty who seemed to take part (much to the band's delight) on one side of the stage. After "Nostalgia" we were treated to a newie which starts with a drum machine pattern very like Galahad's "Room 801". This gradually built into a cracking rocker with some great drumming and then segued into "Outer Limits". The piano solo (which included part of "War Heroes", fittingly enough) led into "Nothing At All".

Every song was superb, everyone a highlight. I could tell you that "Darkest Hour" had an extended introduction or that "Common Ground" (about the dead in WWI) was extremely emotional. But all I should say is that by the time they closed with "Widow's Peak" the band and the audience were emotionally and physically drained. However, they were not finished yet and returned for steaming versions of parts of "The Last Human Gateway" and "Headlong". IQ were onstage for the best part of 2 ½ hours, and what with the other bands £6 seemed a very paltry price to pay indeed. IQ have now re-released all their 'official' CDs so there is no excuse at all for not getting to hear one of the top rock bands in the country, prog or otherwise.
#29, Jun 1995

Revelation
Kensington Orange 16/05/95

Off to the Orange Club for the launch of Revelation's debut CD. There was a fair crowd in, but it quickly became apparent that they were not there to see Revelation as there were three bands on the bill that night, the first being a rocky outfit called Cyan (not the Welsh proggers I hasten to add). Some of the songs were not too bad and "World Turned Round" was very good in a Dan Reed Network sort of way. The second band were Josie who did impress me – they impressed some other people as well as they got signed up that night. They had a very '70's feel and reminded me at times of 'Year of the Cat' era Al Stewart: the vocalist played a 12-string and they were very tight indeed. Not a rock outfit, although an electric guitar was used to good effect, but a very song-based outfit.

Most of the people there appeared to have gone to see one of these two bands and by the time Revelation came on stage the audience was already dwindling. This was a shame, as I enjoyed the gig. Elliott is a great pianist, and it is his style of playing keyboards along with Fauzi's stunning guitarwork and Matthew's vocals that make the band what they are. I was glad I had gone as I was not fully aware of just how important Fauzi's guitar playing is to the overall sound. He uses a lot of effects pedals, and this makes him seem quite like Hackett, although it must be said that the ex-Genesis man never belted it out

quite like this. At times Revelation were almost like Jadis as they used controlled emotion and sustained atmosphere, but it was on "Freewheelin'" that they proved their worth. By the time they closed the club it was more than half empty which is a real shame as they put on a good show: so good that it made me realise that they were a heavier and louder band that I previously thought. I look forward to seeing them again.
#29, Jun 1995

Jump, Credo
Brentford Red Lion 28/06/95

It has been a bloody long time since I last ventured over to West London's favourite venue, and boy was I looking forward to it. Due to one reason or another it would be the first time I had seen Credo this year and I had yet to see Jump at all. This is an almighty error on my part that I have been attempting to rectify for some time, and tonight was going to be the night. As a support act tonight, Credo only had limited time to prove the point that they just keep getting better. They blasted through "Party" and "Just Like A Good Boy" before a storming version of "Whisper In The Wind". It is a classic song, and co-writer Mike Mishra (from the days when he and Mark were in Casual Affair) was in the audience to hear it done justice. Highlight of the night had to be the new version of "The Letter". It has recently been recorded for the new Cyclops Sampler CD Volume II, but already that is out of date as there is a whole new section that take the length to about thirteen minutes. From gentle lightness to darkness and vitriol, Mark loves the anguish. All too soon it was time for Credo to depart, having again made more friends.

Jump is a six piece, and although I love the CDs nothing had prepared me for what I was about to receive. The twin guitars of Pete Davies and Steve Hayes are far heavier, Mo adds the bits and pieces on keyboards, Andy Barker provides the powerhouse drumming and then there is Hugh and John! Hugh Gascoyne is a great bassist who is very much the court jester and provides a wonderful visual focal point who would easily upstage most vocalists. However, here the show belongs to John Dexter Jones who takes elements from Alex Harvey, mixes them with a healthy dose of Fish and comes up with a dramatic stage persona all his own. Right from new number "Tower Of Babel", Jump proved that they are one of the tightest outfits around. Gigging all over the country and having recorded four albums without a single line-up change means that they all know exactly what is going on "Share The Shame" was up next and even a keyboard failure did not stop the band from providing a blistering rendition of one of the highlights of the last album. By now I was in heaven as only two numbers in, I was having the time of my life. These guys are brilliant! Highlight of the evening was "A Northern Man" from the second album as Pete and Steve blasted it out in a way that many 'prog' outfits could never imagine. Are Jump a prog band? Possibly in its very truest sense, but overall, they are a melodic rock band with many diverse influences who must be one of the best live bands I have ever seen (and I have seen a lot!).
#30, Aug 1995

Grey Lady Down, Jump
London Marquee 28/07/95

Jump had to go on stage at 7:30 due to the Rave Club later (is this a joke or what?) but proved that no matter what time it is they are the business. Opening with “Blind Birds” from the new album the confidence from the band was obvious, as it has a very low and atmospheric opening. The vocals gave way as the song turned into a powering rock number, and John proved yet again that he is the consummate frontman. “Tower of Babel” segued into “December’s Moon”, a song that is so new that it is not even on the album! Twin guitar a la Ash drove it along and, in my notes, it says, “This is guitar oriented melodic prog hard rock – with attitude!!” “Share The Shame” is fantastic live, but then so is all of it. There is great interplay within the band, they know what they are doing and are out to give a show, not just regurgitate songs so that people will buy the CD. Jump is very much a SAHB for the Nineties, with the same air of drama and unpredictability combined with great musical diversity and skill. John is one of the best frontmen around, fronting one of the best bands.

I had to feel a little sorry for GLD. I mean, how could they follow that? GLD are a totally different outfit to Jump, pursuing a different musical area, prog as presented by Genesis and Marillion. There is no doubt that they are all great musicians but tonight they were upstaged. Although the stage was arranged to give maximum room for Sean (bass), Julian (guitar) and Martin (vocals) they did not utilise it as well as they could. Julian was moving quite a bit by the end, but visually most of the show had to be carried out by Martin, and he is not John Dexter Jones. Musically as well, it all felt too one-dimensional. I enjoyed both CDs but following Jump it seemed very ‘samey’. Maybe it was just me, as the crowd seemed to lap it up. Highlights were the older numbers such as “Circus Of Thieves”, “Thrill Of It All” and the encore “12:02”. They are very, very good at what they do, but tonight the bill was the wrong way around. Maybe if the sound had been better (the guitar was too low in the mix), but the night belonged to Jump.
#30, Aug 1995

Sphere
Dorking Steps, 16/09/95

I’ve been meaning to catch up with these guys for literally years. Seeing as how the new live venue in Dorking had shown great taste in booking them, I felt that it was only right to drive the five minutes down the road to see them (makes a change from trekking all over the country). Being as organised as normal, I now find that all my notes from the night have disappeared, so all I can say for sure is that I enjoyed it. Sphere have been without a vocalist for some time now, but this small matter hasn’t stopped them from playing gigs. Obviously, the songs have taken on new forms, and the set has been shortened, but they are all such great musicians that they have overcome all obstacles. I came away extremely impressed as Neil Durant is one of the new generation of keyboard wizards, but bassist Bill Burnett on six-string bass and guitarist Steve Anderson are no slouches either (it was the drummer’s last gig – more personnel issues). The songs are

very much songs, not meanderings that quickly lose interest: I have never heard an instrumental band play with such power, as they rocked from start to finish. There is probably a higher jazz element than would have been found on the demos, but the overall effect was superb. After the gig, I tried (quite possibly in vain) to convince Neil that Sphere should stay as an instrumental band as it is something quite different within the prog scene. Maybe he will listen, maybe not, but if you get the chance to see Sphere when they gig again with a new drummer then you owe it to yourself to do so.
#31, Oct 1995

IQ, Jadis, Big Big Train
London Astoria 02/02/96

This was the second of a series of progressive rock concerts that started in December with The Enid, and tonight was the turn of the GEP guys and saw the fourteenth gig from Big Big Train in only five years! It was obvious that quite a few people had dared the cold (and that was only inside the venue) and that we were on for a good night.

After a shaky start, Big Big Train proved that in the concert setting they are as good musically as they are on CD. They opened with two new numbers, "Mr Boxgrove Man" and "Picking Cherries" which should be on the new album, and everything was well received. What they are sadly lacking is live practice as when the keyboard player needs sheet music and the vocalist looks out of place when not singing, then the rust shows, but these faults can easily be cured with more live work and I look forward to seeing them again.

This is the first time I had seen Jadis's new line-up and I was not sure what to expect. To say that I was amazed was something of an understatement, and Steve Hunt on bass is a tremendous find: to hear him playing melody lines with Gary was just superb. I could not hear the keyboards very well (I was too close to Gary's amp), but the new guy looked happy enough. Jadis were out to rock tonight and boy did they – it was easily the best I had ever seen them and songs such as "Sleepwalk" and the classic "Wonderful World" were transformed. This is a different band to what they were and tonight they made many converts - I can't wait until they get into the studio.

IQ. I mean, what can you say about them? The masters possibly did not play the best gig of all time (they were suffering with monitor issues), but even on an off night there is virtually no-one who can touch them. All the new material was aired tonight, and the set list was quite different due to time constraints (why do some venues insist on having discos after gigs?), yet there were some real gems in there. "No Love Lost" became a belting rocker and proved that classic songs can be moulded to any occasion (I still remember Martin performing it as a solo/piano ballad) and by the time they got to "Awake and Nervous" the crowd was heaving. IQ are a band that are totally happy on stage (if John smiles any wider his face will crack in half – by the way, isn't he starting to look more and more like Hercule Poirot?) and all bands have a lot to learn from them. They will be recording a new album later this year and undoubtedly it will be a 'must

purchase'. If you have not had the opportunity to see IQ live (and you should) then you will soon be able to get the live boxed set CD and video! Great stuff.
#33, Feb 1996

Credo, World Turtle, Vietgrove
Brentford Red Lion 20/09/96

Well, this was the last time for me at The Red Lion as the threat of it being knocked down was finally being carried out and was due to take place not long after this gig. Yet another well-known London venue bites the dust – there are not many left, but at least it was going out with a proggy bang. This was to be a taster for Credo's gig at the Rotherham Rocks festival the following weekend, and to make it a night to remember World Turtle had come down from Sheffield and Vietgrove from Newcastle. Vietgrove are a keyboard/ guitar instrumental duo and although I had enjoyed the CD, I was not sure as to how it would transfer to the live environment, but I needn't have worried as they were very good indeed. A band for the Tangerine Dream fans, technically very proficient but will probably gain more respect those into the more Electronic Music end of the prog spectrum.

World Turtle are Paul and Chris McMahon, with Paul providing lead vocals and guitar, and Chris bass, keyboards, backing vocals, and he also looks after the computer/drum machine. Paul looks like an accountant, solid as a rock, while Chris is a hippy: not only that, but he is totally manic, moving around the stage like a loon. I do not think anyone enjoys their music more than Chris. So, visually they are an extremely arresting band and add to that great music and you are onto a winner. Dramatic and powerful, songs like "Ember" and "Wolf" are fantastic – the only problem I can see is that they need a 'live' drummer to give them that OTT edge.

That is one thing that you do not have to worry about with Credo, with Paul Clarke firmly on the drum seat. Along with Jim he provides a totally solid platform on which the others can work: Mike is fully integrated into the band now, and his interplay with Tim must be heard to be believed. Tonight was a shorter set, as it was basically a live rehearsal, but there was still room for the first public airing of "Skin Trade". I can remember vividly when I first heard Freewill play "Skin Trade" – I was talking with the manager of Mentaur when this frenetic metallic song started up, and it became one of their highlights. Never one to waste a good lyric, Mark has resurrected it with a new tune and parts of it are dreamlike, although it crashes apart at others and has a blinding finish. "A Kindness" is also taking more of a showstopper role, with Mike and Tim swapping solos, and as always Mark was on fine form, but I wouldn't have expected anything else. It was a sad night for him as he had played The Red Lion more than 100 times, and tonight was the last. Vietgrove were good, World Turtle were better, but Credo are improving exponentially. When 'Rhetoric' (due to be recorded at Thin Ice and produced by Clive Nolan and Karl Groom) hits the streets an awful lot of people within the prog scene are going to sit up and take notice.
#38, Nov 1996

Mr. So & So
Tring Royal Court 16/11/96
So, up to Tring to at long last see the So & So's who were supporting John Wetton. I have been a fan of these guys for quite some time and new recordings I have heard show them going from strength to strength. It was great to finally meet Dave Foster, who I have spoken to many times on the phone, and it was set for a good show. Sean plays a five-string fretless bass, and the bass-led attack gives their sound a totally different dimension to most other bands around. Sean's singing has improved dramatically over the last few years and they have now added to this area by recruiting Charlotte Evans as a backing vocalist. They opened with the new songs, which I had heard on the brilliant demo they had sent me, and "Salamander" is as excellent live as it is in the studio. Musically they can cut it although I felt that Charlotte looked very uncomfortable onstage: give the girl a tambourine or something! She left for the older numbers, and this is where the band relaxed and cranked it up. However, I noticed that while Dave was concentrating on his playing someone was seeking his attention. The result was that Dave knelt on the stage, still playing, while holding a conversation. Apparently, John Wetton had decided to go onstage fifteen minutes earlier than had been thought, which meant that the So & So's had to lose fifteen minutes from their set. This was only decided while they were playing a blinder. Strange, huh? They had to close after the next number (missing "Tick A Box" which I was particularly looking forward to) and stunned all and sundry with an all-powering version of "The Visitor". Still, Steve Rothery saw enough to like it and sign them to Dorian.
#39, Jan 1997

Credo
Mansfield Leisure Centre 17/11/96

The next night saw a trek up to Mansfield, which is rapidly becoming a Northern home from home for Credo. Here they were to play support to Wishbone Ash at the Fan Club Convention. All of Ash's gear was set up early and the band were in the hall playing acoustically in the afternoon, and then holding a question and answer session. Everything went well until it was time for Ash to soundcheck for the night's gig. The hall was cleared, and the punters were asked to return at 6:45. Ash finally deigned to hold their soundcheck, bearing in mind that the equipment was already set up, but it went on and on and on… It started raining, and lots of fans were by the (locked) doors waiting to get into the warm. However, Ash did not clear the stage until 6:40. We have never set up Credo's gear so fast, but with the best will in the world it was not possible to get it onstage, plugged in and checked in less than five minutes. Credo decided to run halfway through one song to check everything was okay, and as they started, the house lights went off! The guy running the desk had decided that this was their set, and it was only by me having a quiet word in his ear that got them turned back on again! So, having had to soundcheck in front of more people than usually see them play a proper gig, the only answer was to play a stunner. I was honoured to be asked to announce them from the stage and then they were on fire, with Tim Birrell under a lot of self-imposed pressure (imagine being a guitarist and having to play in front of Andy Powell). Yet again they

made a load of new fans and proved that with the right breaks they can go a long way.
#39, Jan 1997

Asgard
Zwolle 25/01/97

Those with long memories may just remember a review I wrote about Asgard's wonderful album 'Imago Mundi' a few years ago. My recent search for them in Italy received a response from Germany where the band are now living. Both the singer and drummer left, and they have recently completed a new line-up. Alberto Ambrosi (keyboards) kindly sent me a tape of this gig to see what they sound like and I am pleased to be able to report that they seem to have lost none of their power. It is always difficult to replace a vocalist but Alberto asked me to make allowances for Dietrich Kuhne as he had a cold and fever that night, and if that is what he sounds like when he is ill I look forward to the new album 'Drachenbrut' which should be recorded this month and released in August.
#42, July 1997

Legend
Putney Half Moon 06/03/97

It has been far too long since I last saw Legend live. I realise that their gigs are few and far between, but the last time I saw them I was given a fully autographed copy of their new album 'Second Sight', and many years and countless bass players later they are now promoting the brilliant 'Triple Aspect'. Okay, so my comment on bassists may be a little bit of over-exaggeration, but Legend do appear to be to be to bassists what Spinal Tap are to drummers! The new incumbent is Paul 'Lamby' lamb, whose first gig this was with the band. Each time I have seen them in the past I have bemoaned the lack of instrumental "Toccata" from the set, which I feel has a power and passion all its own; to say that I was as chuffed as nuts to discover that they had rehearsed it specifically for me for tonight was something of an understatement! That song opened proceedings and Legend immediately showed why many people feel that there are few bands that can even approach what Legend achieve on stage. John Macklin must be one of the hardest working drummers around, producing a powerhouse platform on which to build the sound: Lamby, although visually very retiring at present (it was his first gig after all) showed that he is a good bassist but it is the front guys of Steve Paine and Paul Thomson that provide the flair. They have an understanding of each other that goes far beyond virtually every other keyboard/guitar partnership you can think of. I would have to stick my head out and say that they surpass Lord/Blackmore and reach the heady heights of Hensley/Box. I am not saying that Paul is a better guitarist than Ritchie, but rather that he is the perfect foil for Steve and vice versa.

"Toccata" blasted us all into submission, with power, passion and musical vitality. How many bands have the nerve to open with an instrumental? This led straight into "Cunning

Man", the opening cut from 'Triple Aspect', where Legend's other great strength came into play. Debbie Chapman is a vocalist unlike any other in the rock field; often likened to Maddy Prior, her pure clear vocals cut through whatever musical maelstrom is being conjured up by the guys. Are Legend progressive? Yes, in its truest sense as they are mixing hard rock with folk and traditional prog in a way that is totally unique. People were dancing and reeling to the sound, and everyone was having a great time. Steve's keyboards were restrained at times, but cutting loose at others, and I was under the impression that they were more guitar-oriented than before but possibly I was just standing too close to Paul! "Mordred" saw Debbie portraying a different character, singing with a far harsher edge to her voice. She was living the song, providing another visual element. "The Chase", another powering instrumental, followed with Paul and Steve swapping lead roles. "Holly King" was almost madrigal in style, but 400 years ago they never imagined that they could sound like this! "Lyonesse" saw a costumed change for Debbie as the music took on a different feel again, and although this song has quiet balladic passages, when they rock, they rock like bastards and few can touch them!

The announcement of the last number was met with dismay, but "Triple Aspect" clocks in at thirty minutes on the CD so there was still some way to go. If there is one song that sums up all that is there is about Legend, then this is it. Debbie plays three distinct characters in this, the maiden, the mother and the crone, and each needs a different musical and visual portrayal. Commencing life as a rock instrumental, this passage alone was worth the price of admission. By the end of this most demanding of 'songs', Debbie was still hitting the high notes perfectly while John was still powering around the kit, A plea for a fag break from the aforementioned drummer was disregarded as they quickly returned for the demanded encore. "The Wild Hunt" is probably not the most typical Legend song, harkening back to Steeleye Span, but with far more going for it. The "Light In Extension" medley caught John out, who found himself playing the wrong song, but hell it was the end of a long night. All too soon it was over, and I looked at my watch to see that two hours had passed since they started, but it was over way too quickly. Legend are first and foremost a rock band. They do not fit in what most people feel that a prog band should sound like, and do not fit in with what people feel a rock band should sound like either, so they do not get the publicity they deserve. As well as three albums, they also have one of the best live videos available that you can ever see. When I was leaving the Half Moon, Steve was discussing where they could site the pyros the next time. The gig of 97? You had to be there, and you bloody well should have! Next time do not miss out.
#40 March 1997

Galahad
Ferndown 31/05/97

This was not a gig as such, as it was the reception for the wedding of Stu Nicholson to Lin, and as it was his 'do' he wanted to play! A decision was made to only include older material, as virtually none of the guests knew anything about Galahad. There did not seem much point in trying to get the new keyboard player up to scratch on songs that he

may never play again, so Karl seemed the obvious choice to step in. Unfortunately, he was in Australia until the day before the wedding, so they asked Mark Andrews instead. Mark used to be in the band but had left after the release of 'Nothing Is Written'. Old bassist Tim Ashton (who left the band to live in Japan) was also in attendance and was going to play on one song. Karl was going to play just on the one new song, "The Dentist Song" but was roped into playing the whole set. This meant that Galahad hit the stage (well, carpet) with two keyboard players for the first time in many years. Not only that, but Mark was providing backing vocals as well, something I did not realise that he used to do, and it provided another aspect to the band as it gave Stu something to pitch his vocals against. I did not take notes, this was a wedding after all, but it went something like this. They opened with "One For The Record", which has long been a favourite of mine. The story of the reformation of Genesis was great and next up (I think) was "Ghost of Durtal" and "Painted Lady", which also went down well. The surprise of the night had to be "Parade". Why? Because people were up dancing to it and having a great time, that's why! Stu seemed to be lost among a load of people who wanted to be up with the band enjoying themselves. "Room 801" went down well, as always, and the end came all too soon with "The Dentist Song". Everyone, including all the Galavirgins had a great time, which just goes to prove what I have always said, that a great many people would enjoy bands like Galahad if they could be bothered to go out and find them! Apparently, people in the bar next door were asking who the band were and if they had any CDs they could buy! It was a great night, and on behalf of all Feedback members I wish Stu and Lin a long and happy life together.
#42, July 1997

Grey Lady Down, Mastermind, Ars Nova
Kensington Orange 06/06/97

Well, I've managed to lose my notebook (again) and seeing as how it has been a very long time since I went to this gig, I will make it short and sweet. Ars Nova was three Japanese ladies, who played in the style of ELP. The crowd were appreciative and I for one was amazed that anyone as small as their drummer could reach the kit let along play it with such precision and fervour. The set was a nice opener, although I doubt that I would have gone to see them on their own. I was looking forward to Mastermind. I had spoken to Bill (guitar, keyboards, MIDI) and Rich (drums) prior to the gig and these affable Americans made quite an impact on me, I have been enjoying their music much more recently as well, but nothing prepared me for this. Quite simply, Bill is an astonishing guitarist who not only has to remember the notes but how he is supposed to be playing them as he switches from straight guitar to effects with nonchalant ease. However, the revelation was Rich Berends on drums and I can honestly say that it has been a long time since I have been as impressed as I was that night. I have been to hundreds of gigs, and seen countless bands, but have only seen two other drummers who have impressed me as much as he did, Phil Collins and Neal Peart and he might just have the edge on both. The guy was just phenomenal: I just could not believe what I was seeing. Highlight was "Brainstorm" and I wanted them to play all night. GLD were launching their new album 'Fear' and were headlining. Somehow Mark Robotham had

enough nerve to sit at the same drum kit that had been used by Rich, but it was not the same. It was the first time I had seen GLD with two new members, and although they were not bad, the night for me belonged to Mastermind.
#43, Aug 1997

ReGenesis, Martin Orford & Gary Chandler, Grace
Whitchurch Festival 06/08/99

So, it was back down to Whitchurch for the first night of the three-day festival. Unfortunately, I was not going to be able to attend the Saturday or Sunday (which irked me as I wanted to see Haze and you can never get too much of IQ and I quite fancied Gnidrolog as well), but it was nice to meet up with some old friends and faces that I hadn't see for a while. The main reason I was going was that Martin Orford was due to play a solo set between the main bands, but when I arrived I was told that he was currently on his way back from Japan where he had been playing with John Wetton, A car was waiting for him at Heathrow so we were all hoping that he wasn't too delayed.

The first main band of the evening was Grace, a band I have seen many times before. I do not know if tonight was an off night for them, but this was just not the same band that I have seen taking all audiences before them. Mark Price has left the band and has been replaced on keyboards by someone who gave the impression that he did not know what he was doing, while guitarist Dave Edge has been replaced by bassist Dave Rushton's son. I must admit that after opener "The Fool" I was soon very bored. Harry is still as manic as ever but instead of being a focal point tonight I just thought that he was a distraction. Not all numbers were bad, but it was relief for me when they finally finished.

Luckily a very jet lagged Martin arrived to save the evening. I have never seen anyone look so tired. The crowd were pressed up against the stage and when he started with "No Love Lost" everyone joined in. It is one of my favourite IQ numbers, and I prefer this version to the rock treatment the whole band normally give it. He played three numbers, all the time looking as if he was going to fall asleep at any moment and was then joined by Gary Chandler on twelve-string acoustic. A great cheer went up when they kicked off with "This Changing Face" and I realised just how much I have missed seeing Jadis play over the last few years (Gary has been touring Holland as the singer in an orchestra playing versions of rock classics!). They announced a new album, and by the time they played "No Sacrifice" and "More Than Meets The Eye" they had the audience in the palm of their hands. It just proves that two guys with music and good songs just do not need a light show to grip an audience. They closed with an REM cover which had everyone singing along: a good time was had by all!

It was now time for ReGenesis and I decided that I was not going to like them. After all, weren't they just another of these bloody tribute bands that take up places at the few live venues still operating? Where can bands learn their craft if they can't get up on stage? Well, they kicked off with "Watcher of the Skies" and I was transported back in time. 'Peter Gabriel' is a great frontman, and he used most of the costumes throughout the night. The band is spot on musically, as they must be, otherwise they would get crucified, and by the time they had finished the first number I was hooked. On "Return of the Giant Hogweed" he played the flute and prior to "The Musical Box" he even related the story, just as Peter used to. The Old Man mask made an appearance for the final menacing section of the song and the crowd lapped it up. He utilised a crowbar during "The Battle of Epping Forest" and visually the only time they were let down was during "The Cage" where the lighting was not as good as it could have been. "Supper's Ready" was wonderful, worth going for that song alone. As with all the other numbers, everyone joined in with gusto, especially on "A Flower?". They finished with "The Knife" and while my views on tribute bands probably will never change, I must confess that ReGenesis are extremely good at what they do and if I wanted a good night out, I would probably go and see them again.

All in all, a very pleasant evening, just a shame about Grace.
#55, Sept 1999

Llyn Y Morynion
Tilehurst Beethoven's 30/08/99

When I received an e-mail from Lars telling me that the band were playing some UK dates, I was very pleased indeed. I have been singing the praises of this band for some time, and the debut album is still a frequent visitor to my CD player. I ended up catching them on the last night of their tour and was surprised (and pleased) to see the Feedback reviews very prominent in their literature. Apparently, it is the only time they had been reviewed in an English-speaking magazine! I find that desperately hard to believe, as the albums are wonderful. I was treated like an old friend and settled down to the gig. They have had the same line-up since inception, some ten years ago now, so it is not surprising that they know what each other is doing and have a very tight sound. What came across even more in the live environment is just how diverse their sound is, from folk to rock, and even bringing in African rhythms. I had taken a mate, who had heard none of their music, and by the end of opener "If I Was A Painter" he was a fan, with the band moving from hard rock to acoustic within the space of a heartbeat with great vocals. The highlight for me was "Poor Man's Child" which is a modern classic. The guys dedicated it to me as I had been plaguing them beforehand to check when it was on the set list. This was a great night by a wonderful, but unknown, live act. Lars has told me that they are planning to come back here later this year as they manage to impress a lot of people. That would be a tour not to miss.
#56, Jan 2000

Spock's Beard
London LA2 02/10/99

So, what can I remember about what was possibly the best gig I have ever attended? There were five guys on stage, comprising four vocalists, one bassist, three guitarists, two drummers… where to start? The lead singer, Neal Morse, usually plays keyboards or acoustic guitar, although he did find himself behind the drum kit at one point. Alan, his brother, concentrated on lead guitar, acoustic guitar, some keyboards and vocals; Dave Meros played bass (and some keyboards) and providing vocals; drummer Nick D'Virgilio played drums, provided harmony vocals throughout as well as some lead, and played acoustic guitar. It was quite a relief when Ryo Okomuto only played various keyboards.

The crowd were up for Spock's Beard only second ever UK gig (they had played the previous night at Rotherham), and everyone seemed to know all the words and gave the band rapturous reception. From the off, having fun while at the same time providing some of the most complex prog I have ever heard was the order of the day. The fact that the guys can play more than one instrument, while at the same time providing fantastic harmony vocals, give them a tremendous breadth and width to their music.

I know my jaw dropped open at some points because of what they were doing musically, and I was not the only one. Highlights included the three-man acoustic guitar duel, and great versions of songs such as "Day For Night" and "Gibberish" (with some amazing harmony vocals). When they came back for the obligatory encore, last man on stage was Nick who found that Neal was at his drum kit, so he picked up the mike and they powered through "Squonk". That guy has a voice that most front men would die for, and he's the drummer! There were loads of well-known proggers in the audience that night including John Wetton, Steve Hackett, Stu Nicholson et cetera. I met Neil Durant from Sphere outside, and he just asked me why do British bands bother, as they just can't compete with that. I see that Spock's Beard are opening for Dream Theater later this year. I will be there, and so will you if you have any sense.
#56, Jan 2000

Saga
London LA2 26/11/99

It is a long time since I heard 'Careful Where You Step' on the Friday Rock Show, and I never thought I would hear it played live. I knew that Saga were a keyboard-based band, but even I did not expect a semi-circle of keyboards taking up most of the stage (the drummer was behind one of the amp stacks). This was Saga's first UK gig for ten years and the place was packed full of Saga diehards (I got told off by one for talking, bloody music shouldn't have been so quiet), who were determined to sing to every song. This meant that it was a great gig, just because the crowd were so up for it. Every time Mike Sadler stopped singing the crowd sang back to him, it was almost like a hometown gig. They opened with the classic "You're Not Alone" and played many songs from their early days while at the same time playing plenty from the new album. Even though I have not heard much of their material I came away impressed (even if Jim Crichton was wearing an extremely lairy jacket and fancied himself to bits) although it should've been louder. A good gig.
#56, Jan 2000

Spock's Beard
London LA2 28/10/00

There are gigs, and there are also concerts which are so good that the punter is lifted into another plane and transported through time and space into nirvana. The latter also lasts just the length of time for the brain to believe what his eyes and ears are telling him. It probably is not hard for you to work out what category this gig falls into.

For the second consecutive time, thanks to London traffic, I was late to see Spock's Beard, and they were just finishing the opening number. Then they launched straight into "Thoughts", my favourite song from the second album. The harmonies were superb, and I could have gone home after that it was so good. After that it was heads down and have a good time, "All Day & Night", "Skin", "Thoughts Part II", each song was played with finesse – with each band member proving what a complete musician he is. They all sing, most of them play at least two instruments, and they have a mastery of time and composition like no other. Highlight? It is hard to pick them, possibly Ryo's keyboard solo, or Neal and Alan performing an acoustic guitar duet ON THE SAME GUITAR! (you had to be there) or was it the full twenty-eight minutes of "The Great Nothing", or that Nick (the drummer, remember?) sang "Whole Lotta Love" as an encore. This band is truly awesome – and the LA2 crowd responded with enthusiasm. There are few bands in the world that can live with these guys currently. See them in concert, but until then keep playing the albums. *#61, Feb 2001*

Rick Wakeman
Guildford Civic Hall 08/05/03

Before the band came onstage there was the announcement that Damian Wilson would not be performing, but when the crowd heard that Ashley Holt would be returning to stand with Rick once more there was a loud cheer. I am sure that the late change in vocalist was the reason that only two songs were aired from the new album, due partly because it just was not in Ashley's range, but it did give them the chance to reprise some of the material recorded when he was originally in the band. The band were obviously all enjoying themselves and there were lots of smiles, as well as many awful and obviously rehearsed jokes from the tall man in a cape. But it was all about having a good time, and with music such as that from 'Journey To The Centre Of The Earth' and 'No Earthly Connection' being aired it was impossible to do anything but that. "Catherine Parr" was also well received, and the use of back projections and a small camera trained on Rick's hands also more than added to proceedings. New animations from the new DVD were shown and that release looks particularly interesting (due end of July). There were too many highlights to mention, but the way that Rick never fails to take the piss out of himself is endearing. Then he took a keyboard and wandered off into the audience, sat down next to a very surprised woman and talked to her as he continued playing. She was more than surprised when she was dragged onto the stage and became a keyboard stand so that Rick could finish the song. "Starship Trooper" was the perfect end to a great night. What an awesome performer. *#74, Jun 2003*

Spock's Beard, Enchant, California Guitar Trio
Mean Fiddler 23/10/03

So, a triple bill at the Fiddler started with the perfect act. These guys do not need a microphone, and can all plug into the same amp! This is just three guys with acoustic guitars, but boy can they play. The whole crowd was just captivated by what they were doing, it was incredible to watch and hear. And when they played "Bohemian Rhapsody" the crowd joined in and sang as one. Ted Leonard and Nick D'Virgilio joined the band for the rock section, but honestly, we were doing fine without them!

It was a case of 'follow that' and Enchant did so in mighty fine style. For me they were easily the band of the night. This is progressive rock with an AOR edge and cutting guitars that make rock fans sit up and take notice while also providing more than enough of interest to the proghead. Some of the songs had almost a Kansas feel, which can't be a bad thing, but they paced the set so that slower songs were offset by the quicker ones. To my ears they seemed at their happiest when crunching it out, and they proved that the new album more than sits well with their catalogue. Their set ended all too soon, I could have watched them for hours and I hope that they will be back on these shores soon.

So, could the mighty Beard cope with the loss of the main man? Two drum kits were set up, so that Nick could duel with Jimmy Keegan, but also of interest to me was the fact that Ryo had a microphone - surely there had to be some mistake. They kicked off with the hard rocking "A Guy Named Sid" – this is the highlight of the album and by starting with it showed their intention to grab the audience and show that they meant business. This was a great start, with Alan wearing yet another ridiculous jacket and two drummers at the end. Nick also had been playing guitar and throwing himself about the stage. For me it was the next song that started the doubt. "Thoughts" is one of my all-time favourite SB numbers, with great vocal harmonies, but here they let Ryo sing a part. He may be a fine keyboard player, but he can't sing – period. The result was that it felt to me that the band were almost parodying themselves, an SB covers band. This is not what I wanted or expected. I have seen the band three times before and loved them – but this was not SB – it was some guys onstage. "Shining Star" was good and then they announced that they were going to play some songs from "Snow" – an awesome album that I love dearly. I soon found my attention wandering and decided that now would be the right time to catch the train home…I did not stay to watch any more. I have advocated SB in these pages for years, and still like the new album. But the SB of now are very different to the SB that was – let's hope a reunion happens at some point as based on this I am not sure that I would go and see them again. But Enchant were superb…
#77, Dec 2003

Neal Morse
Mean Fiddler 14/11/03

Having been so bitterly disappointed with the Spock's Beard gig, I was hoping that Neal was not going to have the same effect. I needn't have worried. Tonight, Neal was going to perform the whole of his double album, 'Testimony', and to enable him to do this he had put together a very unusual line-up of seven musicians who between them all sing and somehow manage to play violin, cello, saxophone, four keyboards, eight guitars, congas, timbales, bass pedals and a pedal steel! The cellist, John Krovosa, was onstage throughout and apart from drummer Mike Portnoy was the only one who only played the one instrument. Eric Brenton managed to get himself confused at times as to which instrument he was supposed to be playing but as he was switching from keyboards to violin or electric guitar (or even mandolin) then that should be forgiven. It was not unusual for three of the four keyboard players to also all be playing electric guitar within the same song so it certainly meant that that they could cope with whatever musical style they wanted to follow and having to perform 'Testimony' in its entirety it was needed.

The evening started with Neal and the band walking on to Peter Gabriel's "Sledgehammer" and Neal softly saying into the microphone, "This is my story". Then it was into "The Land Of Beginning Again" and the beginning of a gig that was very special indeed. In fact, it was only as the gig went by that realisation dawned that this was a one-off, an event that will probably never be repeated in the UK (please tell me that somewhere on tour that this was filmed for a DVD). The line-up was fluid as musicians swapped instruments, never interrupting the flow as Neal poured out his testimony, his life. He told the story of how hard it was, the successes, the triumphs, and the downsides. When he stopped the gig to tell the story of his daughter and her hole in the heart, he was not the only person there crying.

The show stopped for a short break at the end of the first chapter, which allowed the band time to change and for Neal to rid himself of the troublesome throat mike and move to a more conventional set up, but they were soon back for more. Neal started to relax and talk during the second part, knowing that he was among friends, and the crowd were with him every inch of the way. The relief at the end was obvious, and the whole band appeared to have had a blast (although special mention should be made of Mike Portnoy who enjoyed himself immensely throughout and played like a demon). So, it was back for two encores, "June" (which was sung by everyone there, including yours truly) and Transatlantic's "Stranger In Your Soul". All too soon the three hours had sped by and the most remarkable gig I have ever attended was over. He may have left the Beard, but Neal is driving back the boundaries of prog even more. What a night, what a gig!
#77, Dec 2003

Threshold, Power Quest
Rotherham HLC 04/09/04

So down it was to Rotherham for my first Classic Rock Society gig. Moving up to Yorkshire does have some compensations after all, as the society does put on some good concerts. I was pleasantly surprised to see who the support band was, at least until they started playing. This is a band who are obviously a stadium rock act, at least in their minds if nobody else. They are all 'rock stars', but although the singer is an extremely powerful vocalist the sound was not good enough and I soon found the bar.

Threshold came onstage and although the sound was still initially not as good as it could be, they were soon blasting through it. They hit the ground running and within the first few bars showed why they are the premier prog metal band in the UK, if not Europe. Mac has a great voice, and such a self-deprecating style that you can't help but enjoy what they are doing. Karl and Nick have been playing together for so many years that they have an instinctive feel for what the other is doing, Johanne and Steve play as if they have been in the same band forever instead of just the second tour while Richard is the perfect musical foil providing power chords or sweet melodies as the need arises. I may have come away slightly more deaf than when I went in, as this is a band with stacks of passion and balls that any metalhead into music with more thought than most should be seeking out.
#81, Dec 2004

The Flower Kings
Rotherham Classic Rock Society 09/10/04

This was my third gig of the week, but it was special tonight as it was Amanda's first (aged seven). Next time I will get her some ear plugs. The Flower Kings were a lot louder than I thought they would be, and an awful lot better than I had ever imagined. Roine ought to lose many points for the awful suit he was wearing, but the band he has put around himself more than makes up for it. Daniel Gildenlöw was relishing the part, and by providing percussion and guitar as well as vocals he gave the music an extra dimension. When all three frontmen were on guitar it certainly made an impression, most of it deafening, but there was always a reason and I enjoyed the whole show much more than I had ever imagined I would. Amanda sat on the corner of the stage for the show and her eyes were like saucers, so it is fair to say that she had a good time as well. Numbers new and old worked well, and for me it was one highlight after another and nothing bad! This was the first time that I had seen them and hopefully it will not be the last! Now all I must do is get the T-shirt off Amanda so that we can get it washed……
#81, Dec 2004

IQ
Rotherham Classic Rock Society 27/11/04

I knew that tonight was the CRS Awards Night, but I did not realise that this meant having the support band on at such an unearthly hour of the evening! Arriving long before 8.00 I was most upset to find that I had already missed Magenta and was there just in time to see Martin Hudson get up onstage to announce the first award of the night. I had Amanda with me, and it was a little warm so for the next hour or so we spent as much if not more time outside the hall than inside it, but I was there when IQ were awarded the prize for best album of the year. A huge cheer went up when Peter announced that tonight, they would be playing the whole of 'Dark Matter'.

After that award it was not too long until IQ were back, doing what they do so very well, taking the place by storm. Even in a school hall there is a good lighting show and the use of background videos which enable IQ to put on a real performance. Of course, at the heart of it all is the music and new songs like "Red Dust Shadow" were particularly effective with the stage bathed in red light. There is a strong use of light and shade both in the music and in the projections and this gives the already powerful music a much harder and dynamic edge. Highlights? Too many to mention, but there was a huge cheer for "It All Stops Here" and "Awake and Nervous" always goes down well. This is a band that have been at it for 23 years, and with one of their best-ever albums just released they show no sign of slowing down yet!
#82, Jan 2005

Amanda Rowland, aged seven , at her first ever gig, The Flower Kings

Given how important my family has always been to me, and the incredible amount of support they provide, it feels fitting to end the journey with this photo. In 2006 we left the UK to emigrate to New Zealand, and have discovered a new life here. I didn't write for a few years as I had intended to give it up altogether, but eventually was brought back into the scene and now write more than ever. Perhaps one day there will be a Volume 4 capturing my reviews since I moved to the other side of the world. I sincerely hope people will use these books as a guide to discover some amazing bands and music which is out there for those prepared to look. Progressive rock never died, it just went underground.

Kev Rowland

Kev Rowland is a self-confessed music addict, who has never really been the same since he heard 'Sabbath Bloody Sabbath' in 1975. In the Eighties he spent quite a ridiculous amount of money on all things related to Jethro Tull and was asked by David Rees to write a piece on Carmen (the band including John Glascock, not the opera) for the Tull fanzine 'A New Day'. This simple request was life-changing, although neither realised that at the time.

Following on from that, Kev wrote reviews for the Mensa RockSIG newsletter, before becoming secretary himself in 1990. Over the next 16 years, the newsletter gained a name, and he put out more than 80 issues, many of them doubles, in excess of 11,000 pages. When he moved to New Zealand in 2006, he retired from the music scene, but was pulled back in – initially kicking and screaming until he accepted his fate. These days he can be found contributing to many magazines and websites, is a columnist with the wonderful Gonzo Weekly magazine and is a special collaborator on the most important and comprehensive progressive rock resource on the web, www.progarchives.com. In 2018 he reviewed 850 albums of multiple genres.

When he isn't listening to music, writing about music, or thinking about music, then he can be found on his lifestyle block in Canterbury, New Zealand, with his wonderful and long-suffering wife Sara, and their 8 cats, 5 dogs, chickens, sheep, lambs, calves and cattle. Oh, apparently, he has a day job as well.

Online:
http://www.progarchives.com/Collaborators.asp?id=5626

GONZO
Books

There is still such a
thing as alternative
Publishing

Robert Newton Calvert: Born 9 March 1945, Died 14 August 1988 after suffering a heart attack. Contributed poetry, lyrics and vocals to legendary space rock band Hawkwind intermittently on five of their most critically acclaimed albums, including Space Ritual (1973), Quark, Strangeness & Charm (1977) and Hawklords (1978). He also recorded a number of solo albums in the mid 1970s. CENTIGRADE 232 was Robert Calvert's first collection of poems.

Hype 'And now, for all you speeding street smarties out there, the one you've all been waiting for, the one that'll pierce your laid back ears, decoke your sinuses, cut clean thru the schlock rock, MOR/crossover, techno flash mind mush. It's the new Number One with a bullet … with a bullet … It's Tom, Supernova, Mahler with a pan galactic biggie …' And the Hype goes on. And on. Hype, an amphetamine hit of a story by Hawkwind collaborator Robert Calvert. Who's been there and made it back again. The debriefing session starts here.

Rick Wakeman is the world's most unusual rock star, a genius who has pushed back the barriers of electronic rock. He has had some of the world's top orchestras perform his music, has owned eight Rolls Royces at one time, and has broken all the rules of composing and horrified his tutors at the Royal College of Music. Yet he has delighted his millions of fans. This frank book, authorised by Wakeman himself, tells the moving tale of his larger than life career.

There are nine Henrys, purported to be the world's first cloned cartoon character. They live in a strange lo fi domestic surrealist world peopled by talking rock buns and elephants on wobbly stilts.

They mooch around in their minimalist universe suffering from an existential crisis with some genetically modified humour thrown in.

Marty Wilde on Terry Dene: "Whatever happened to Terry becomes a great deal more comprehensible as you read of the callous way in which he was treated by people who should have known better many of whom, frankly, will never know better of the sad little shadows of the past who eased themselves into Terry's life, took everything they could get and, when it seemed that all was lost, quietly left him ... Dan Wooding's book tells it all."

Rick Wakeman: "There have always been certain 'careers' that have fascinated the public, newspapers, and the media in general. Such include musicians, actors, sportsmen, police, and not surprisingly, the people who give the police their employment: The criminal. For the man in the street, all these careers have one thing in common: they are seemingly beyond both his reach and, in many cases, understanding and as such, his only association can be through the media of newspapers or television. The police, however, will always require the services of the grass, the squealer, the snitch, (call him what you will), in order to assist in their investigations and arrests; and amazingly, this is the area that seldom gets written about."

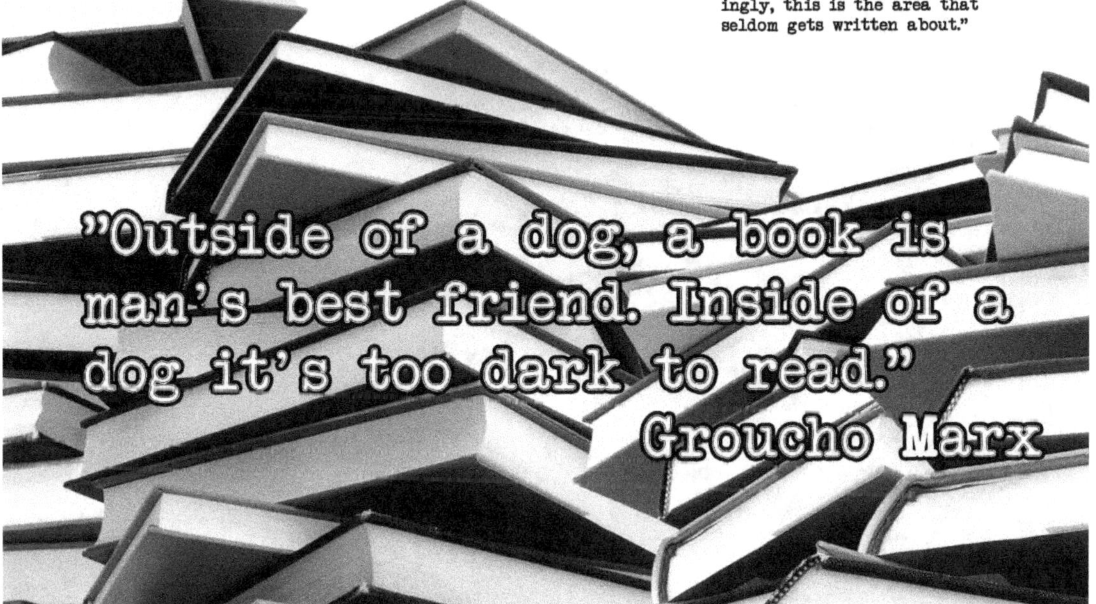

Bill Harkleroad joined Captain Beefheart's Magic Band at a time when they were changing from a straight ahead blues band into something completely different. Through the vision of Don Van Vliet (Captain Beefheart) they created a new form of music which many at the time considered atonal and difficult, but which over the years has continued to exert a powerful influence. Beefheart rechristened Harkleroad as Zoot Horn Rollo, and they embarked on recording one of the classic rock albums of all time Trout Mask Replica - a work of unequalled daring and inventiveness.

Politics, paganism and .... Vlad the Impaler. Selected stories from CJ Stone from 2003 to the present. Meet Ivor Coles, a British Tommy killed in action in September 1915, lost, and then found again. Visit Mothers Club in Erdington, the best psychedelic music club in the UK in the '60s. Celebrate Robin Hood's Day and find out what a huckleduckle is. Travel to Stonehenge at the Summer Solstice and carouse with the hippies. Find out what a Ranter is, and why CJ Stone thinks that he's one. Take LSD with Dr Lilly, the psychedelic scientist. Meet a headless soldier or the ghost of Elvis Presley in Gabalfa, Cardiff. Journey to Whitstable, to New York, to Malta and to Transylvania, and to many other places, real and imagined, political and spiritual, transcendent and mundane. As The Independent says, Chris is "The best guide to the underground since Charon ferried dead souls across the Styx."

This is is the first in the highly acclaimed vampire novels of the late Mick Farren. Victor Renquist, a surprisingly urbane and likable leader of a colony of vampires which has existed for centuries in New York is faced with both administrative and emotional problems. And when you are a vampire, administration is not a thing which one takes lightly.

"The person, be it gentleman or lady, who has not pleasure in a good novel, must be intolerably stupid."

Jane Austen

www.ingramcontent.com/pod-product-compliance
Lightning Source LLC
LaVergne TN
LVHW080308110826
845155LV00023B/93

9781908728906